TEACHER
AND
STUDENT
PERCEPTIONS:

Implications for Learning

Edited by
John M. Levine and Margaret C. Wang
University of Pittsburgh

LEA LAWRENCE ERLBAUM ASSOCIATES, PUBLISHERS
1983 Hillsdale, New Jersey London

Lawrence Erlbaum Associates, Inc., Publishers
365 Broadway
Hillsdale, New Jersey 07642

Library of Congress Cataloging in Publication Data
Main entry under title:

Teacher and student perceptions.

    Based on material originally presented at a research
conference held at the Learning Research and Development Center, University of Pittsburgh.
    Includes bibliographical references and indexes.
    1. Teacher-student relationships—Congresses.
2. Motivation in education—Congresses.   3. Academic
achievement—Congresses.   4. Prediction of scholastic
success—Congresses.   I. Levine, John M.   II. Wang,
Margaret C.
LB1033.T25   1983   371.1'02   82-18299
ISBN 0-89859-206-2

Printed in the United States of America
10 9 8 7 6 5 4 3 2 1

Contents

6. Student and Teacher Perceptions: A Review of Five
    Position Papers
    Thomas L. Good   125

PART II: IMPACT OF PERFORMANCE EXPECTATIONS IN CLASSROOMS

7. Teacher Talk and Student Thought: Socialization
    into the Student Role
    *Phyllis C. Blumenfeld, V. Lee Hamilton, Steven T. Bossert,
    Kathleen Wessels, and Judith Meece*   143

8. Communication of Teacher Expectations to Students
    Harris M. Cooper   193

9. Development and Consequences of Students' Sense
    of Personal Control
    Margaret C. Wang   213

10. Modeling Young Children's Performance Expectations
    Doris R. Entwisle and Leslie Alec Hayduk   249

11. What is an Attribution that Thou Art Mindful of It?
    Donald M. Baer   271

PART III: SOCIAL PERCEPTION AND SCHOOLING: INSTRUCTIONAL DESIGN IMPLICATIONS

12. Extrinsic Reward and Intrinsic Motivation:
    Implications for the Classroom
    Mark R. Lepper   281

13. Intrinsic and Extrinsic Motivational Orientations:
    Limiting Conditions on the Undermining and Enhancing
    Effects of Reward on Intrinsic Motivation
    Thane S. Pittman, Ann K. Boggiano, and Diane N. Ruble   319

Preface

In recent years educational researchers and practitioners have become increasingly aware of the importance of social processes in classrooms. Such processes are crucial for two reasons. First, teacher-student and peer relationships are important mediators of the intellectual outcomes of schooling. Second, the school experience itself may have significant social outcomes. These include students' feelings and beliefs about themselves, as well as their responses toward others inside and outside the school environment. In a very real sense, then, we cannot understand what happens in schools unless we understand the role of social processes as both independent and dependent variables.

In trying to explicate social processes in schools, a number of investigators have focused on how students and teachers perceive their own and one another's performance. This focus is based on the premise that performance perceptions are important determinants of behavior. In the past, investigators interested in performance perceptions tended to adopt one of two general strategies. Educational researchers investigated perceptions in school settings with an eye toward improving educational practice, but generally did not attempt detailed analyses of the perception process itself. In contrast, social psychologists constructed elaborate theories of the perception process, but tested these theories in laboratory settings and paid little attention to their instructional design implications. Recently, however, the line between educational and social psychological research on performance perceptions has begun to blur as investigators from the two disciplines become increasingly aware of one another's work and increasingly interested in exchanging ideas. This desire for dialogue stems from the realization among educational researchers that social-psychological perspectives may be useful in their work and from the motivation among social psychologists to test and refine their theories in "real world" settings.

The purpose of this book is to advance the emerging interdisciplinary dialogue regarding the origin and consequences of performance perceptions in school settings. To this end, we have assembled papers from established investigators in several disciplines who share a common interest in social perception and education. The papers vary in format, ranging from presentations of new empirical findings to integrative reviews. In all cases, however, the chapters treat aspects of performance perception that have practical as well as theoretical implications. In selecting contributions, we sought to reflect the theoretical and methodological diversity of current work. Our goal was to bring together a variety of perspectives on social perception and education in the hope of stimulating discussion and cross-fertilization.

The book is organized into three major sections. Section I deals with students' and teachers' interpretation of achievement-related behaviors. Section II treats the impact of performance expectations in classrooms, and Section III contains work on the instructional design implications of social perception research. Each of these sections is followed by a discussant chapter that highlights important aspects of the preceding contributions and suggests avenues for future research.

In the first of six chapters dealing with students' and teachers' interpretation of achievement-related behaviors, Irene Frieze, William Francis, and Barbara Hanusa point out that attribution theorists have ignored the basic question of how a performance is initially defined as a success or failure. Frieze et al. discuss some of the complexities involved in subjective assessment of success and include this crucial step in an expanded model of the achievement attribution process. In Chapter 2, John Levine discusses social comparison as a means by which students obtain information about their school-related abilities. Levine presents a general model of the social comparison process that integrates previous theoretical and empirical work; an important feature of this model is attention to the intrapersonal and interpersonal consequences of comparison. Chapter 3 by Bernard Weiner concerns the role of affect in the attribution process, with special emphasis on achievement striving in schools. Weiner discusses attribution-affect-behavior linkages from the perspective of both students and teachers. Teachers' responses, interpreted as instances of help giving, are viewed as a crucial element in achievement-change programs. In Chapter 4, Mary Rohrkemper and Jere Brophy present research on how teachers perceive and cope with various types of problem students. Like Weiner, Rohrkemper and Brophy analyze teachers' responses to students as instances of helping behavior. Chapter 5 by Russell Ames focuses on teachers' attributions for their own teaching. Ames discusses linkages between the evaluative feedback that teachers receive, their attributions for this feedback, and their subsequent efforts to alter their behavior. This presentation highlights teachers' value orientations and perceptions of self-worth as determinants of their reactions to evaluative feedback. Finally, in Chapter 6 Thomas Good discusses the degree to which the preceding chapters inform classroom practice and suggests the utility of increased longitudinal and observational research in classrooms.

The five chapters in Section II deal with the impact of performance expectations in classrooms. In Chapter 7, Phyllis Blumenfeld, Lee Hamilton, Steven Bossert, Kathleen Wessels, and Judith Meece report a study of children's socialization into the student role. These investigators assess how teachers communicate expectations regarding various domains of classroom life (teacher talk) and how children perceive and understand these expectations (student thought). Blumenfeld et al. view the management and task structure of the classroom as important determinants of teacher behavior. Chapter 8 by Harris Cooper deals with the enduring question of whether a teacher's expectations for a student's academic performance can actually influence this performance. Cooper offers an attributional model for teacher expectation communication, which assumes that teachers have an overriding concern for classroom management, and presents data relevant to the model. The influence of teacher expectations is also treated by Margaret Wang in Chapter 9. Wang discusses students' sense of personal control as a possible moderator of teacher expectancy effects. She presents evidence regarding how an innovative educational environment, designed to alter sense of personal control, influences teachers' and students' behaviors and students' learning outcomes. In Chapter 10, Doris Entwisle and Leslie Hayduk discuss their longitudinal research on children's academic expectations. Using cyclic structural equation models, Entwisle and Hayduk assess relationships between children's expectations and achievement in middle-class and lower-class schools, taking into account parents' expectations and children's race, sex, and IQ. Donald Baer, in Chapter 11, provides discussant comments from the perspective of a radical behaviorist. He points out interpretive ambiguities in research on attribution and teaching and suggests techniques to strengthen causal inference in future studies.

Although instructional design implications are implicit in many of the preceding chapters, the five chapters in Section III (together with Chapter 9) bear most directly on classroom practice. In Chapter 12, Mark Lepper provides a comprehensive review of research on the detrimental effects of extrinsic reward on intrinsic motivation and immediate task performance. He also explores the relevance of these research findings to classroom practice, addressing questions of engineering, ecological relevance, and values. Intrinsic motivation is also the focus of Chapter 13 by Thane Pittman, Ann Boggiano, and Diane Ruble. These investigators review several experiments designed to clarify factors that enhance and undermine the effect of reward on intrinsic motivation. In discussing classroom implications of their work, Pittman et al. emphasize the nature and context of the reward and the complexity and difficulty of the task. Chapter 14 by Robert Slavin deals with cooperative learning, a recent educational innovation in which students are rewarded for cooperating with classmates on academic tasks. Slavin reviews research concerning the non-cognitive outcomes of cooperative learning, including mutual concern among students, interracial attitudes and friendship, and self-esteem. In Chapter 15, Vernon Allen discusses a much older educational technique: peer tutoring. Allen uses role theory to analyze the impact of peer tutoring on the tutor's cognition, affect, and behavior and discusses implications of this analysis for design of peer tutoring programs in schools. Finally, Richard deCharms in Chapter 16 ties together the four preceding chapters by offering a series of practical maxims based on research concerning intrinsic motivation, peer tutoring, and cooperative learning.

Much of the material in this volume was originally presented at a research conference held at the Learning Research and Development Center, University of Pittsburgh. Appreciation is expressed to the National Institute of Education for providing funds, through the Learning Research and Development Center, that made the conference possible. We are grateful to Professors Robert Glaser and Lauren Resnick, co-directors of the Center, for their encouragement and assistance during all phases of this project. We wish to thank our staff, particularly Rita Catalano, Debbie Connell, and Ellen Cooper, for their help in running the conference, preparing manuscripts, and typing correspondence. Finally, appreciation is expressed to Stephanie Tortu for preparing the subject index.

John M. Levine

Margaret C. Wang

STUDENTS' AND TEACHERS' INTERPRETATION OF ACHIEVEMENT-RELATED BEHAVIORS

1 Defining Success in Classroom Settings

Irene Hanson Frieze
William D. Francis
Barbara Hartman Hanusa
University of Pittsburgh

The question of what individuals mean by success and failure and the implications of deciding whether something is a success or a failure are of particular importance in a success-oriented society such as ours. Casual observations amply document the importance of success. Our bookstores are filled with books that attempt to provide guidance for achieving success in interpersonal relationships, in business, and in school. Courses are offered that provide personalized and detailed guidance for achieving success in one or more of these domains. The commercial "success" of all of these ventures is strong support for the supposition that people in our culture think about and desire success.

In the minds of many people, school is a major training ground for later adult success. Parents and teachers want students to be successful in school and to learn the skills they will need later. Typically, children also want to do well, and they feel good when they are successful. Doing well in school is often a major predictor of positive self concept for children and young adults (Calsyn & Kenny, 1977).

Societal concern over "success," especially academic success, is reflected by the vast educational, sociological, and psychological literature concerned with the determinants of success and failure. Other research has focused on what the student *perceives* to be the determinants of his or her own success or failure. However, little consideration has been given to the epistemotogically prior question of how students decide that a particular performance (e.g., a score on an exam or a grade in a course) is a success or failure. This question seems especially important since performance *labels,* as well as performance *attributions,* may be a major determinant of later *actual* performance. Such labels and attributions may influence variables such as affect, self-esteem, task choice, expectancy, and persistence.

This chapter attempts to extend our understanding of student perceptions of academic performance and the impact of these perceptions on subsequent performance by proposing a new and expanded model of the attribution process. This new model incorporates subjective success definitions and the affect associated with success judgments. The chapter begins by presenting a brief overview of the Weiner model of the attribution process as it has developed to this time. Although originally developed to explain the achievement behaviors of adults, the attribution model has been successfully applied to preschool and older children. Some differences have been reported in the attribution process for children, however, and these will be mentioned where appropriate.

After a brief look at attribution theory as applied to achievement situations, work relating more specifically to the question of how students define success and failure and the consequences of making a success or failure judgment are discussed. Ideas from attribution researchers, as well as other investigators, are used as the basis for the development of an expanded attribution model incorporating the concept of subjectively defined success.

CAUSAL ATTRIBUTIONS FOR SUCCESS AND FAILURE

Given students' success on an exam or some other achievement task, we now know a good deal about how students decide *why* they were successful. The research on this issue is typically discussed under the rubric of "achievement attribution theory." Since this work is central to the proposed subjective success attribution model, the basic findings of achievement attribution research are briefly reviewed.

In 1971, Weiner, Frieze, Kukla, Reed, Rest, and Rosenbaum proposed an attributional theory of achievement motivation. This theory viewed one's affective and cognitive reactions to a success or failure on an achievement task as a function of the causal attributions that one used to explain why a particular outcome had occurred. Causal attributions were hypothesized to relate in systematic ways to feelings of pride and shame, expectancies for the future, and future achievement behavior. The model predicts, for example, that students attributing their failures on a test to lack of ability will feel shame about doing poorly and will be discouraged from trying harder in the future. In contrast, students who feel that their poor performance was due to bad luck (e.g., because those questions on which they were weakest happened to be on the test) will feel less shame and will not be especially discouraged. In such a case students might well assume that their luck would be better next time.

The original Weiner et al. (1971) theory proposed that the four basic causes used to explain achievement successes and failures are the person's ability, effort, luck, and the difficulty of the task. Later research has shown that students also mention other causes, including the teacher, being in a good or bad mood, feeling sick, and help or hindrance provided by other people (Frieze, 1976a; Frieze & Snyder, 1980). It has also been shown that the specific set of causes used to explain success or failure depends heavily upon the specific task being considered (Frieze & Snyder, 1980). For example, classroom exams tend to generate predominantly effort attributions, whereas success or failure in completing an art project is typically attributed to both effort and ability. Other causal factors that have been identified as especially important for school achievement include stable effort (a consistent pattern of diligence or laziness), personality, and the physical appearance of the student (Elig & Frieze, 1975; Frieze, 1980; Weiner, 1979).

Since there are so many possible causes for success or failure, a three-dimensional system for classifying the various causal explanations has been developed (Frieze, 1980; Weiner, 1979). Within this system the three dimensions of internality, controllability, and stability are typically conceptualized as dichotomies, although each is more accurately thought of as a continuum (Frieze, 1981). For example, the first dimension, internality, concerns whether the cause of an event is associated with the primary actor in the situation (typically the student in an academic situation) and is thus internal, or whether the cause relates to something in the environment or to some other person and is thus external. Thus, a student may succeed on an exam because of the internal causes of ability, trying hard, or feeling good. He/she may also succeed because of external factors, such as having an easy test, someone else's help, or a good teacher. These examples represent internal–external extremes. Other causes, such as doing well because of studying with other students, would be intermediate between internal and external causes. Related to the internality dimension, and sometimes confused with it, is the dimension of controllability. Students control their effort, but not their abilities or moods. Thus, effort is categorized as controllable, whereas abilities and moods are viewed as uncontrollable. The final dimension that is important for classifying causal attributions is stability. Ability and certain environmental factors change relatively little over time and therefore are considered stable. Effort, mood, fatigue, and luck are highly changeable and therefore are classified as unstable. Stability involves a relatively unchanging cause during the time period and across the situations to which one is generalizing.[1]

Attribution research assumes that a success or failure is attributed to one of the causes mentioned earlier on the basis of available information about the situation in which the performance occurred and the personal characteristics of the actor.

---

[1]Stability has been a component of recent theorizing by Abramson, Seligman, and Teasdale (1978). However, they limit their definition of "stability" to consistency over time. They use the label of "globality" to discuss generalizability or consistency across situations. Both these conceptions of stability are included in the definition of stability used here.

Empirical research has demonstrated that some of the most important types of information are the past success history of the actor on similar tasks, how well others have performed on the task, the incentives (if any) to do well, and the effort the actor expended in preparing for and actually performing the task (Frieze, 1976b; 1980; Frieze & Weiner, 1971).

The basic attribution model further predicts that causal attributions are important mediators of subsequent performance expectancies and affect. For example, changes in one's expectancy for future success on a particular task have been related to the stability of the causal attribution made to explain the previous performance (e.g., Fontaine, 1974; McMahan, 1973; Valle & Frieze, 1976; Weiner, Nierenberg, & Goldstein, 1976). In addition, an initial expectancy can have an impact upon causal attribution. Thus, expected outcomes are more often attributed to stable causes than are unexpected outcomes (e.g., Feather & Simon, 1971a; 1971b; Valle & Frieze, 1976). In regard to the impact of causal attributions on affective, or emotional, reactions to success and failure, results generally show that a performance attributed to internal and controllable causes produces stronger affective reactions than does a performance attributed to external and uncontrollable factors (e.g., Riemer, 1975; Weiner, 1974). Along with these general affective reactions, attributions also produce specific emotional responses, as is discussed in the following section.

Extension of The Attribution Model to Children

Originally, achievement attribution research was concerned with the causal attributions of college students after they performed some laboratory task which had been defined by the experimenter as relevant to their achievement concerns (see Weiner et al., 1971). In many of these tasks, a hypothetical achievement situation was described, and subjects were asked to imagine how they would feel in that situation. In other experiments, success and failure were manipulated in artificial laboratory situations. Over the last 10 years, as more and more researchers have been investigating achievement attributions, the range of subject populations and situations used to elicit attributions has been greatly expanded. Studies have now been done with individuals from preschool through college age, and research has looked at attributions for achievement in school and in other real-world settings. This work has indicated that people of all ages can make causal attributions for success and failure in a variety of situations (Frieze, 1981).

Most of the attribution research with adults has utilized rating scale techniques for measuring attributions (Elig & Frieze, 1979). Such techniques are not suitable for primary grade children. Most researchers who study the causal attributions of young children use interviews or other open-ended procedures rather than rating scales. For children in the fourth and fifth grades and for older children, the techniques used for adults can be employed. Both rating scale and open-ended techniques have been successfully used with these groups (e.g.,

Frieze & Bar-Tal, 1980; Frieze & Snyder, 1980). Studies indicate that first-grade children use the familiar attributional categories and that age differences in the overall use of attributional categories tend to be relatively minor (e.g., Bar-Tal, 1979a; Frieze & Snyder, 1980; Stipek & Hoffman, 1979).

In contrast to the general similarities between children and adults mentioned earlier, differences have been identified in the specific ways children and adults make causal attributions and implications of their attributions for subsequent cognitions, affect, and behavior. Some age-related changes in the use of the attributional dimensions may be quite substantial (e.g., Bar-Tal, 1979b; Frieze & Snyder, 1980). Very young children may not divide causes into the same internal and external categories as adults and they may not view some attributions on the stability dimension as adults do. For example, children may not see their abilities as stable since their capabilities on many tasks change greatly over the preschool and early school years.

Along with developmental differences in the types of attributions used by children of different ages, there are also developmental effects in the types of information used by children of different ages to form causal attributions and in the ways in which this information is combined (Ruble, 1978). Several studies have been designed to investigate how children of various ages form causal attributions for success and failure involving themselves and other children. The general finding is that when the performance situation is described in simple enough terms, children as young as 4 years use information in much the same way as adults to make an attribution (e.g., Shaklee, 1976). As children get older, they use more types of information and become more systematic in their judgments (Frieze & Bar-Tal, 1980; Nicholls, 1979b; Ruble, & Rholes, 1981; Shaklee, 1976; Weiner, Kun, & Benesh-Weiner, 1980).

In addition to these general developments in information utilization, there is also evidence that children respond differentially to certain types of information. For example, Ruble (Ruble, 1978; Ruble & Rholes, 1981), in a review of the literature, concludes that children do not begin to systematically use information about the performances of other children in evaluating their own performances until the second grade. However, Nicholls (1979b) has found that children as young as 5 years of age *can* use information about the difficulty of the task (which is dependent upon normative data) if it is presented in simple enough form. Thus, it appears that the form of the information presented makes a big difference in how easily children can utilize social comparison and other information (Shaklee, 1976).

CAUSAL ATTRIBUTIONS AND SUCCESS EVALUATIONS

Although the original attributional model (Weiner et al., 1971) has been refined and extended, most of the relevant research has supported the basic model (see reviews by Bar-Tal, 1979a; Frieze, 1980, 1981; Weiner, 1979). Critiques of the basic model have been made (see, for example, Covington & Omelich, 1979a), but most of these critiques are based upon early versions of the model or have failed to take into account the prior success judgment upon which the attributional process depends. Success judgments need to be incorporated into the attribution model to avoid some of these problems.

As has already been described, the basic attribution model ignores the possibility of varying definitions of successful performance. The attribution model starts with an "established" success or failure and describes the consequent processes. However, the manipulations used to establish the success or failure may not be successful. Two common techniques that have been used are: (1) telling subjects that they have succeeded or failed on a task (e.g., Riemer, 1975) and (2) giving subjects norms (which are typically fabricated) about the performance levels of other comparable students and allowing subjects to assess their relative performance level through social comparison (e.g., Bar-Tal & Frieze, 1976). In the latter case, the normative information may simply tell subjects that they performed generally better or worse than other students, or subjects may be artificially placed in some percentile group (such as the top 80% for the success group and the bottom 20% for the failure group). One problem with both of these procedures is that subjects do not always accept the experimenter's definition of success and failure (e.g., Elig & Frieze, 1979).

One of our own studies (Elig & Frieze, 1979) demonstrates the problem with experimenter-defined success and failure. In this study students were assigned to a success or failure group after performing on an anagram task. On the basis of the norms they were given, the success students allegedly solved at least as many anagrams as 75% of other college students. Students who did not solve this many puzzles were assigned to the failure group. Group assignments were done randomly by giving students either very easy or very difficult anagrams to do. Of the original 250 students in the study, about 20% did not place themselves into the "correct" group when asked how successful they had been on the anagram task.

At the very least, these findings demonstrate the necessity for a manipulation check for success/failure assignments. Attribution studies that do not include such manipulation checks may be flawed if a large number of subjects do not consider themselves to be in their assigned group. Other studies that include a success–failure manipulation check often eliminate those subjects who do not assign themselves to the appropriate group. Such a procedure fails to allow for individual differences in success evaluations and limits the generalizability, if not the validity, of the attribution data obtained. As more studies are conducted in classrooms and other natural settings, these problems are likely to become even more important.

It is not too surprising that subjects sometimes reject experimentally defined success criteria. People often have their own standards for what they consider to be a success. A B+ grade will be greeted with joy and a clear feeling of success by one student, while another student will be quite disappointed and have a feeling of failure after receiving this grade.

Our own research has pointed out some of the differences between the objective success definitions used by researchers and the subjective appraisals of success offered by subjects. As part of a larger study of the attribution process as it actually functions in the classroom (Frieze, Snyder, & Fontaine, 1978), we asked fifth graders to evaluate their performance on either a social studies or mathematics exam. Students' subjective success ratings were compared with their actual scores (objective success) on the exam. The correlation between the students' actual scores and their subjective ratings of success was .74. Although this is a relatively high correlation, it is sufficiently below 1.00 to suggest that subjective success ratings are influenced by a variety of factors in addition to objective performance.

In order to better assess the differences in subjective and objective outcomes, Frieze et al. (1978) conducted a series of regression analyses on outcome and self-evaluation variables. Results indicated that subjects who actually performed at high levels saw themselves as trying hard to do well, whereas those who felt more successful saw themselves as having high ability (rather than effort). This corresponds with other data reported by Nicholls (1976) who also found that students gave more positive evaluations of performances (higher subjective success ratings) in situations where the outcome was seen as caused by their ability than in situations where the outcome was attributed to effort. A similar study done with college students taking an exam in a psychology course (Frieze, Snyder, & Fontaine, 1977) again found that subjective and objective outcomes related differently to attribution and affect measures.

Other work within the attribution framework concerns the affective consequences of feeling one is a success or failure. Recent work by Weiner and his associates concerns the affective consequences of attributions for success and failure (Weiner, Russell, & Lerman, 1978, 1979). Originally, based on the work of Atkinson and McClelland with achievement motivation (e.g., Atkinson, 1964; McClelland, Atkinson, Clark, & Lowell, 1953), it was assumed that pride and shame were the primary emotions resulting from achievement success or failure (Weiner et al., 1971). Weiner's work has now shown that pride and shame are not the only, or even necessarily the dominant, emotions associated with academic achievement outcomes. Instead, a wide variety of emotions (such as surprise, frustration, anger, and gratitude) occur as a result of achievement-oriented behavior. Some of these emotions have been found to be stronger for internally attributed outcomes, but others, such as surprise and gratitude, are most associated with external attributions (luck and other people's help, respectively). Weiner (1978a, 1978b, 1980) now suggests two processes: (1) certain emotions are directly associated with the positivity or negativity of the outcome itself (what we would call the success judgment), and (2) other emotions are specifically tied to the attribution that is made for the success or failure outcome.

Weiner's recent work not only supports the importance of the subjective outcome labeling process, but also suggests that this labeling may precede the attributional process. However, other work indicates that attributions affect the success judgment. For example, Maehr (1974) suggests that a person does not feel successful in doing a task unless there is a sense that the outcome of the task was the result of internal, controllable factors. Maehr and Nicholls (in press), extending these ideas, have suggested that the outcomes which are most likely to be experienced as success or failure are those which are attributed to effort and ability. Less perception of success or failure occurs for luck or task difficulty attributions. They go on to state that this association between internal attributions and perceptions of success and failure may depend upon the specific value system of the culture (e.g., our culture values effort).

In a pilot study done last year, we tested some of these ideas by asking college students to rate how successful they would feel if success were associated with one of several attributions. Results indicated that these students saw themselves as most successful if success was due to effort. Other success ratings were solicited for success due to having a good instructor, having an easy exam, being lucky, and cheating. Only the "success" due to cheating was rated as not successful. Moreover, success due to luck was seen as only slightly successful. Thus, it appears that *attribution-like* processing is important during the process of making a success evaluation. However, this does not mean that attributions are made before one decides about his or her degree of success. One of the potential ways to resolve this issue of which comes first, attributions or success evaluations, is to distinguish between two types of attributional statements that are typically seen as similar or identical. The first are questions about prior conditions that might have affected an achievement event, for example: (1) How hard did the student try on the exam?; (2) How smart is the student?; (3) What type of mood was the student in?; and (4) How hard was the exam? These types of questions are often seen as synonymous with making an attribution to effort, ability, mood, or task difficulty. However, the relevant attributional questions really are: (1) How much did the student's effort influence his or her performance on the exam?; (2) How much did the student's ability influence his or her performance on the exam?; and so forth.

We know from prior research that the scales used to assess attributional responses have a large influence upon the response given (Elig & Frieze, 1979). We have also found that responses to the two types of questions outlined above may not be highly correlated (e.g., Frieze, Snyder, & Fontaine, 1977, 1978). A student may state that he tried very hard on the exam, but at the same time he may not rate his effort as a primary determinant of his performance level. In the proposed model, these two types of attributional statements are clearly delineated, with the latter being considered as attributions and the former as information used in forming success evaluations. This distinction can also be applied to other attribution research and may help explain some discrepancies in attributional studies.

Children's Success Criteria

Although there has been very little work done in this area, there is some evidence that children differ from adults in their reactions to success and failure (Ruble, 1978). A number of studies have shown that in the first and second grades, children tend to be optimistic and have high expectancies after both success and failure and to feel that they will do well if they try the task again. They also feel more positive affect after experiencing success on a task than older children do. Starting in the second grade, children begin to show attributional mediation of their affective responses. As they get older, the degree of positive feeling after success and the degree of negative feeling after failure are highly dependent upon the internality of the attribution made to explain the outcome. That is, there is more positive affect for internally caused success and more negative affect for internally caused failure than for externally attributed performances (e.g., Nicholls, 1978, 1979b; Parsons & Ruble, 1972; Ruble & Underkoffler, 1976). This is similar to the adult response. Weiner et al. (1980) further report that, as for adults, children's specific emotional responses to success and failure become more linked to specific attributions as children get older.

The amount of research on children's success evaluations is limited, and a number of important questions remain unanswered. Given the importance of children's perceptions of success for their subsequent cognitions, affective reactions, and behaviors and the centrality of the success concept for attribution research, we need to know more about how children think about success and failure. How do they decide when their performance is a success? Does it matter what type of task they are doing? What effect do other people have upon these judgments?

DEFINITIONS OF SUCCESS IN PRIOR FORMULATIONS

The preceding review has indicated that attribution researchers need to consider more carefully what they mean by success and to integrate success judgments into the achievement attribution process. In a recent attempt to determine how success is conceptualized in studies of the motivational basis of achievement behaviors, it became evident that success is a complex theoretical construct (see Frieze, Shomo, & Francis, 1979). Success has been defined in numerous ways by different researchers. As Maehr and Nicholls (in press) have pointed out, "Success and failure are not concrete events. They are psychological states consequent on perception of reaching or not reaching goals" (p. 9). Perhaps because of this lack of concreteness, there has been little agreement among researchers about what success is (Tresemer, 1977).

Many early researchers depended entirely upon subjective evaluations offered by subjects for their success criteria. In one of the earliest published studies on success and failure, Hoppe (1930) categorized different performances as successes or failures solely on the basis of each subject's level of aspiration. This resulted in success and failure labels that were not bound to a single fixed performance or standard even for a given subject.

Other more recent studies have also used success and failure standards provided by individual subjects. In their massive review of the fear of success literature, Canavan-Gumpert, Garner, & Gumpert (1978) concluded that "A success is any achievement in the personal, interpersonal or academic/occupational domains which a person regards as a success" (p. 26). Highly personalized definitions were also used by Adler (1935), Katz (1964), Knapp and Green (1964), and Schilder (1951).

Somewhat more specific definitions of success were used by some of the early clinical theorists (see Canavan-Gumpert et al., 1978). Freud (1915) and Horney (1937) associated success (and concerns with success) with competition and the defeat of rivals. Growth-oriented clinicians see success in more positive terms. Although Maslow (1954) sees competition as fundamental to success, his ideas stress intellectual and social products that are socially validated. Demonstration of competence and independence is also essential to success according to Sullivan (1953).

Probably the most influential of all achievement and success conceptualizations was offered by McClelland in his work on achievement motivation (e.g., McClelland, 1961). In this formulation, achievement behavior is defined as competition against a personal standard of excellence, and success is equated with achieving that standard. Within this framework, success is usually seen as involving competition with others as well as hard work. It is personal success, not cooperative success. In some of his more recent work, McClelland identifies two types of incentives inherent in any competitive situation: (a) traditional achievement, or doing a good job, and (b) power, or desire to gain prestige or influence. Depending upon one's motives, either or both of these may mean success for the individual (e.g., McClelland & Watson, 1973).

Maehr (1974) has proposed another definition of success. Like McClelland, Maehr suggests that success and failure evaluations are relevant only for behaviors for which there are standards of excellence. He further argues that the individual should be *responsible* for the outcome and that there should be some level of challenge in the task. Similar ideas were proposed in 1930 by Hoppe who found that the experience of success depends upon the person's level of aspiration relative to the task being considered and the person's belief that he or she is *responsible* for the outcome of the performance. Hoppe further specified that for extremely easy tasks there was no perception of success, regardless of the performance level. Thus, McClelland, Hoppe, and Maehr all argue that a person's beliefs about the reasons for his or her performance are important determinants of how successful the performance is perceived to be.

Success criteria are implicit in other work. Positive affect about one's performance and, therefore, presumably greater feelings of subjective success have been shown to be related to several variables. House and Perney (1974) found that doing better than expected led to positive affect in an achievement setting for college students. Doing better than other students or better than one's past performance also increased perceptions of success (e.g., Festinger, 1954; Frieze, 1976b; Frieze, 1980). In work with young children, Crandall (1978) reported that the degree of improvement over one's minimal standards for performance (in whatever way these are determined by the subject) is a major determinant of positive affect (also see Crandall, Katkovsky, & Preston, 1960).

There are a number of common themes that run through these definitions. First, success is individually defined. Second, judgments of success are influenced by societal norms and comparisons with relevant others. Success has also been defined as doing well at a challenging task or a task that requires effort. Other definitions include exceeding one's expectations and defeating rivals. Finally, there were also more concrete definitions, such as doing well in specific situations (such as school). A complete model of success evaluations needs to incorporate all of these types of definitions.

AN EXPANDED MODEL OF THE ATTRIBUTION PROCESS

Overview

As we have seen, achievement attribution research has suffered from its failure to consider adequately the individual definitions people have for success and failure. On the basis of the pilot work described earlier, the thinking of other researchers interested in cognitive and motivational factors in achievement behavior, and our own thinking, we have developed an expanded model of the achievement attribution process. This model explicitly allows for the determination of the subjective level of success before an attribution is made, takes into account the values people have about appropriate areas for achievement strivings, and relates these values to the affective response to the success or failure. This model is outlined in Figure 1.1.

Before presenting a more detailed discussion of the model and the supporting data, a brief overview of the model is presented. As is typical for achievement attribution research, this expanded model of the attribution process focuses on what happens as the person engages in an achievement behavior. In the classic model, once an achievement behavior occurs, information about the performance

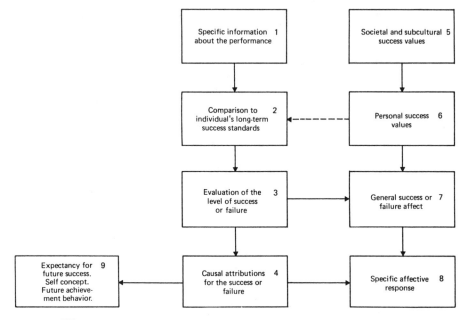

FIG. 1   Short term reactions to achievement event

(Box 1) is used immediately to infer why the outcome occurred (Box 4). In our model, before the determination of the level of success can be made, a more complex sequence of initial information processing is proposed (Boxes 1, 2, and 3). The information included in Box 1, which is believed to be relevant in determining the level of success or failure, includes the objective score or performance level (if such information is available), as well as other information already available to the person, such as how much effort was put into the performance, prior performance expectations, and how challenging the task was.

These bits of information are then assessed against the long-term personal success standards of the individual (Box 2). For example, the objective performance level may be compared to previous performances of the person. The level of effort and mood are also evaluated. These assessments may be made relative to outcomes experienced in the past, or they may be compared to absolute standards. This information processing stage then results in a subjective evaluation of how good (or how successful) the performance was (Box 3). Our model postulates that it is this subjective success evaluation that influences the general positive or negative affect associated with the outcome (Box 7) as well as the causal attribution made (Box 4). Both of these steps then lead to a specific attribution-dependent affective response (Box 8). It is further proposed that both the general affective responses and the attribution dependent affect are moderated by the values of the society (Box 5) and the personal values of the individual (Box 6). Finally, in accord with previous attribution research, the causal attribution is seen as influencing one's expectancies for future success, future achievement behavior (Crittenden & Wiley, 1979; Dweck, 1975), and general self-concept (Bandura, 1971; Dweck, 1975; and Lenney, 1977) (Box 9).

The major feature of the proposed model, then, is that the subjective evaluation of the outcome precedes the formation of the causal attribution but follows the information acquisition stage. Also, the objective and the subjective outcomes are seen as separate variables, with the objective outcome being considered as only one of several determinants of the subjective success appraisal. The affective response is divided into two components, one dependent upon the causal attribution and the other a direct result of the success appraisal. Finally, the model specifically incorporates the influence of values on the affective responses to various levels of outcomes.

Evaluating the Outcome of an Achievement Behavior

Stage 3 of the proposed model is the evaluation of the performance outcome. It is proposed that a variety of sources of information are relevant for this appraisal, including whatever is known about the task being done, the constraints or facilitating factors in the environment, the effort and other inputs of the person into the performance, and the objective performance level. All of these bits of information are filtered through a set of long-term success standards. To clarify how these standards might be used in the evaluation process, they have been separated into three categories in the following discussion, based on previous work by Veroff (1977): task, self, and social standards.

Task Standards.   There are some tasks for which completion by itself signals success. Such tasks tend to be concrete and self-contained and to provide immediate feedback that they are finished. One example of such a task is basic computer programming. Having the computer perform the desired manipulations and calculations provides feedback that the program works. Other examples are the completion of jigsaw puzzles or mazes.

A second kind of task within this domain is one for which there are definite, universally accepted, external standards of performance. For example, nearly everyone would consider winning a city-wide science contest as a success. Successes within this domain of tasks are likely to produce a high degree of consensus that the performance was successful and a great deal of overlap between the individual's objective level of success and subjective assessment of success. In the past this kind of success has been labeled competence (White, 1959) or mastery without an evaluation component (Veroff, 1969).

High degrees of task involvement may elicit similar feelings of success. In an analysis of play behaviors in adults, Csikszentmihalyi (1975) reports that people find great enjoyment and feelings of success in activities that produce total engrossment and feelings of "flow." This is most likely to occur in activities which involve constant challenges, in which there is no time to worry about what might happen next, in which the person can make full use of whatever skills are required, and in which the person receives clear feedback about the results of his or her actions.

Experimental research investigating the impact of tangible rewards for task completion on subsequent interest in the task (e.g., Dollinger & Thelen, 1978; Lepper, this volume; Lepper & Greene, 1975) suggests a related point. In these studies, introduction of an outside evaluation or reward for performing a task decreased subsequent interest in and amount of time spent on the task. This implies that the prior performance was based on intrinsic qualities of the task. For tasks with these intrinsic qualities, "success" may derive from doing the task itself without performance outcomes or tangible rewards.

Personal Standards.   In many instances people have achievement goals that are based on their internal standards. Performance assessments are based on comparing objective levels of performance against these goals. If the goal is met, then the performance is considered a success; if not, then it is considered a failure. Although achievement goals may be quite individual, it is possible to make some empirically supported generalizations about the role of these goals. The goal for any specific performance is based on ability estimates, assessments of the difficulty of the task, expectations based on past experiences, and the relationship of the present performance to longer range goals (e.g., Heckhausen, 1967; McClelland, 1961).

Most research on goal setting behavior has focused on the effect of goals on performance rather than the effect of goals on *assessments* of performance. However, work in several areas points to the importance of including individual goals and aspirations in understanding how people make success–failure judgments. Most interesting is the work on the relationship between self-esteem and performance assessments. People with high self-esteem (or self-regard, self-evaluation, etc.) evaluate their performance more highly than those with low self-esteem, even when objective levels of performance are equivalent (Diggory, 1966; Shrauger & Terbovic, 1976; Warren, 1975). It is unlikely that this difference is due to greater discrepancies between expected level of performance and objective performance for low self-esteem people, since high self-esteem people tend to have higher expectancies than do low self-esteem people (Diggory, 1966). One possibility is that low self-esteem individuals' *desired* level of performance is much higher than their expected level. We know that the discrepancy between desired and obtained performance is critical for subjective assessment of success (Jucknat, 1937, reported in Heckhausen, 1967; Warren, 1975).

Social Standards.   Many success standards are set by others' performances or expectations. For example, for many exams only the overall distribution of exam scores and the relative placement of scores gives meaning to any individual score. Those who are near the top are generally seen as succeeding, while those near the bottom are viewed as failing. However, the self-assessment of any individual is dependent not only on where the individual is in the overall distribution, but also on how the person's current performance compares to his or her past achievements (Albert, 1977). A person doing more poorly than usual may interpret current performance as failing even if the score is high in the overall ranking.

Even with tasks for which clear criteria of objective success or failure exist, social comparison information may be essential to subjective assessments of success or failure (see Levine, this volume). People may want to find out how many other people can do the task as a way of assessing their general ability or their specific abilities for that task. It is probably general ability assessments that are most relevant to feelings of success, not the ability to perform a specific task.

Teachers, parents, and other adults often provide additional information about how well one is doing in school. In addition to comparing themselves with peers, students may also judge how successful they are by the amount of praise they receive from their teachers and parents. This praise may in turn be compared to amounts of praise received in the past or the amount given other students. Past research indicates that children who are high in achievement motivation have parents who are supportive of their accomplishments and who expect them to do well in achievement tasks (e.g., Hoffman, 1972). In addition, teachers often know about the student's past performance and have prior expectations about how the student will do on any particular task. Data indicate that teacher expectations influence students even though teachers spend very little time communicating attributions and expectations directly to students (Blumenfeld, Hamilton, Bossert, Wessels, & Meece, this volume; Cooper, 1977, 1979, this volume; Rosenthal & Jacobson, 1968).

The Process of Making a Success Appraisal.   While students are taking an exam, they may subjectively evaluate its difficulty, how much effort is being expended, and their performance. At this time, students may experience feelings of being very involved in taking the exam—the flow discussed by Csikszentmihalyi (1975). At the end of the exam, they may feel that the project is complete and in that sense a success. Then a comparison process may begin based on discussions of the difficulty of the exam with others who took the same exam. The return of the exam scores lets students compare their performances with how well they wanted and expected to do. If there is a discrepancy between the expected and obtained scores, they may ask how others did. Even in cases in which expected levels are reached, a student might consider whether the test seemed easy. A combination of the assessments made in both the past history comparisons and social comparisons, plus the original information about how one felt when taking the exam, will then yield a success judgment.

As can be seen, the process of making a success appraisal involves several types of information. Some data about their uses were collected in a pilot study of 54 college students who rated how successful they would feel under various conditions. The conditions included a number of personal criteria for success (doing better than in the past, doing better than expected, feeling that you did a good job, etc.) and several social criteria (social comparison, performance in relation to others' expectations, etc). One item, doing well in spite of being sick, might be considered a task standard. Results are shown in Table 1.1. All the success criteria were heavily used by these older students.

The process of evaluating a performance as a success or failure appears, at least from indirect evidence, to depend upon the age of the student. Starting with preschool and the early primary grades, students appear to rely primarily upon task standards in determining whether they were successful or not. Simple task completion leads to a good deal of positive affect (Bialer, 1961). As discussed earlier, these young children do not appear to utilize social comparison information in evaluating their performance until about the second grade (Nicholls, 1979b; Ruble, Feldman, & Boggiano, 1976). These beginning students may also rely heavily upon teacher and parent praise as a determinant of their level of success, but this has not been systematically studied.

In a study that indirectly assessed children's success judgments, Stipek and Tannatt (1980) asked 4- to 8-year-old children how they would determine (a) how smart they were and how smart another student was, (b) who was the best and the worst thinker in their class, and (c) who was best and worst at doing specific tasks. Although these judgments are not identical to a success judgment, it would appear that similar processes might operate in making these determina-

TABLE 1.1
Comparison of "Success" Ratings for
Different Types of Success

Types of Success Standards	Mean	Standard Deviation
Task		
Doing well in spite of being sick	7.6*	1.4
Personal		
Doing better than you've ever done	8.3	1.0
Doing as well as you've ever done	7.2	1.5
Doing better than you thought you would	8.0	1.1
Feeling you did a really good job	8.0	1.2
Social		
Doing better than everyone	8.5	1.1
Doing better than everyone else thought you would	8.0	1.1
Knowing everyone felt you did well	7.6	1.5
Doing better than most students	7.3	1.0
Doing better than average student	6.0	1.7

*1 = Not at all successful to 9 = extremely successful

tions, especially for the ratings of smartness. The reasons the children gave were coded into several categories, including information about specific performance on a task (such as finishing a task or doing a task correctly), statements about the effort exerted, and feedback from the teacher. These categories correspond roughly to the three types of information discussed earlier: task, personal, and social. Task information was most heavily used by the students, followed by personal information. Teacher feedback was rarely cited.

In another study, Minton (1979) asked third through sixth graders how they would judge how good they were at their schoolwork. Students checked one of ten reasons, including task responses of not having much homework and doing the work fast; personal standards, such as feeling that one is learning something, working hard, listening to the teacher, and studying; and social responses of feedback from other children, teachers, parents and grades (which are really a form of teacher feedback). Although mean responses to these items were not reported, other analyses suggested that personal standards were most important for children in the older elementary grades. Since social comparison information was not included in this study, its relative importance could not be determined.

These studies of children's success appraisals are only indirectly related to the issue of how children determine their level of success on school tasks. However, they do imply that for first and second graders, specific information about the task performance is weighted most heavily, whereas older elementary school children rely more upon personal standards and social information, as do college students.

Success Appraisals and Causal Attributions

As discussed earlier, our model proposes that once students have decided how successful their performance is, then a causal attribution is made. Much of the research dealing with attributions for success and failure has dealt with this process, and we know fairly clearly what attributions will be made given varying situations (see Frieze & Weiner, 1971; Frieze, 1980). Thus, the step from Box 3 to Box 4 in our model has been well documented and is not a focus of our discussion here. However, there is some question about how "attributions," such as amount of studying, ability level, or task difficulty, affect the success appraisal. As noted earlier, these are sources of information about the performance and enter into the expanded model in Box 1. They are not attributions in the sense that this term is used here and hence need to be clearly separated from them.

Affective Responses to Success

The model described in Figure 1.1 includes two affect boxes, Box 7 and Box 8. As we see it, there is an initial affect directly associated with the success appraisal and a later attribution-dependent affect. This distinction is similar to one recently proposed by Weiner (1979; 1980). Weiner sees three major linkages between performance outcomes and affective reactions. First, Weiner has found that there are a number of outcome-dependent affective responses which appear to represent broad positive or negative reactions to success and failure. This type of affective response is represented by Box 7 in our model. Typical affects that might be placed here include (1) happiness, confidence and satisfaction for success and (2) upset, depression, disappointment, and frustration for failure. Weiner mentions that these feelings, although independent of the attribution made for the performance, are based on a prior cognitive process through which the level of success or failure is determined (Weiner, 1980). We equate this process with boxes 1, 2, and 3 of our model. A second type of affective response discussed by Weiner is directly linked to both the success/failure affect and to the causal attribution made for the outcome. This corresponds to Box 8 in our model.

Finally, in accord with his earlier theorizing, Weiner proposed a third type of affective response that links the underlying dimensional analysis of the causal attribution to the affective response. Causes attributed to internal factors are associated with self-esteem related emotions, such as pride, confidence in oneself, feelings of competence, and self-satisfaction. For failure, internal attributions lead to feelings of guilt. External attributions lead to other-directed emotions, such as gratitude or thankfulness for success and anger or surprise for failure. The other dimensions of stability and controllability are also seen as influencing the emotional response. For purposes of our model, both types of attribution-emotion associations are grouped together in Box 8 and the general affective response is shown in Box 7.

General and attribution-mediated affect are both seen in young children. Before the age of 6 or 7, the child responds to any goal attainment or task completion with pleasure (Bialer, 1961). Perhaps because the success feeling is directly associated with task completion and does not involve a complex process of comparison to personal standards or to the performances of others, the young child tends to prefer to do easy tasks where such completion is highly likely or tasks that have already been successfully solved (Halperin, 1977; Veroff, 1969). By the second or third grade, children appear to be able to combine information about task difficulty, their own ability level and effort, and the objective outcome and to use this information to formulate a causal attribution for their success or failure (see Nicholls, 1978). At this point, it is likely that children begin to have attributionally mediated affective responses to their performance.

Values in the Achievement-Attribution Process

As suggested by the model in Figure 1.1, there are also societal (Box 5) and personal (Box 6) values that influence success affect. As Weiner et al. (1979) have suggested, subjective success evaluations are mediated by a number of factors such as the importance of the outcome, the level of ego-involvement, and the long-term implications of the performance. They call these factors intensity moderators. Our model suggests that societal, subcultural, and personal values play a major role in the determination of affect intensity.

Societal Values. As discussed earlier, people in our society define success in various ways. However, our society also has some agreed upon definitions of success that most people would subscribe to. Thus, a person earning a good deal of money or having a high status job would generally be seen as successful. We also tend to associate success with accomplishing things through effort and with having special skills (e.g., Weiner, 1974).

By looking at other cultures, some of our own societal conceptions of success become more clear. Such analyses have indicated that other cultures have quite different perceptions of the means to achieve success (Maehr, 1980). Mexican and Mexican-American cultures stress high performances achieved through group cooperation rather than through individual competition as the basis of feeling successful. In Japan there is also am emphasis upon group accomplishment rather than individual achievement (Maehr & Nicholls, in press), and the general concept of "success" in Japan is associated with courage, cooperation, and the future. In Iran, courage, love, work, progress, the future, power, education, and competition are associated with success. Other cultures show yet other definitions of success (Fyans, 1980; Maehr, 1980). McClintock (1978) also reports cross-cultural and age differences in cooperation-competition with competitive success being maximally valued for second through fourth graders in the United States, Japan, and Greece and for fourth through sixth graders in Belgium. He interprets these inter-cultural variations as resulting from the type of values that children of different ages are taught in school.

There do seem to be some common themes, however, in definitions of success across cultures. In many cases, being successful is seen as indicative of having high ability. Data based on an analysis of semantic differential responses of adolescent males from 30 language communities indicate a general association between the ideas of achievement and success, power, work, effort, knowledge, freedom, father, and masculinity (Fyans, 1980).

There are also specific ideas in our culture about what constitutes success in school. Typically, success in school is associated with hard work and having high ability (Covington & Omelich, 1979b; 1979c). Success is also typically seen in competitive terms as doing better than other students (Cohen, 1979; McClintock, 1978). Although other success goals, such as making money or having lots of friends, are also found, schools tend to emphasize academic values. Several researchers have discussed the important role that schools play in socializing competitive success values in children (e.g., Cohen, 1979; McClintock, 1978; Nicholls, 1979a). It has also been suggested that the value placed on competition may make it impossible for the students with lower ability levels to be successful in school and that this may be the reason for their "underachievement" (Cohen, 1979).

Given the role of schools in socializing the success values of the dominant culture, it is not unreasonable to hypothesize that students who do not subscribe to these values may not be performing at high levels in school. Maehr (1980) suggests that blacks do not achieve at their potential in school because they value other domains, such as athletics, more. Of course, black students' focus on nonschool achievements as a means of achieving success may reflect realistic evaluations of their chances for being rewarded in traditional schools. For other children as well, the schools may not reflect their own value systems or they may find that they are not able to succeed in school and then turn to other areas in which they might be more successful. Both Blumenfeld, Hamilton, Wessels, and Falkner (1977) and Nicholls (1979a) have discussed problems that can arise if children do not see school as relating to their own values.

The proposed model assumes that societal success values act on affective responses to performances by creating more positive feelings for good performances and more negative feelings for poor performances in valued areas. Societal values have their effect by influencing personal success values (Boxes 5 and 6).

Personal Values. The proposed model assumes that individuals form their own personal values about what types of success are most meaningful for them. These individual success values are partially determined by the values of the culture in which the person lives (Box 5 and Box 6), but there is also a good deal of variation across individuals in what types of success are most important for them. These personal values are assumed to act as multipliers of affect. Success (failure) on more valued tasks causes a greater degree of positive (negative) affect than the same level of performance on less valued tasks (Boxes 6 and 7). In addition, we suspect that these individual success values partially determine the personal success standards of the individual (Box 2).

There is a good deal of empirical support for the idea that individuals within a given culture may have quite different success values. For example, Jenkins (1979) asked students to define the things that a successful life would contain for them. The most often mentioned success criteria fell into four main categories: goals dealing with people, such as getting married, having people like you, having children, and contributing to humanity; goals relating to money; goals stressing personal satisfaction; and goals concerning having a good or a pleasurable job. Parsons and Goff (1978) also asked college-age subjects to state in their own words what would have to happen in their lives for them to feel their lives were successful. They found similar categories of responses.

Although there are many ways of conceptualizing these success domains, one of the most interesting has been developed by Parsons and Goff (1980). They have elaborated two general types of success orientations, which are based on

Bakan's (1966) model of agency and communion as orientations toward life. Agency success values are concerned with self-expansion, self-assertion, self-protection, isolation, and the need for power or impact on others. Communion values are more concerned with how the task is done and with doing something interesting, helping others, and having close interpersonal relationships. Within each of these domains, there are specific criteria (related to task accomplishment, personal standards, or social standards) that are used to determine the level of success. All of these success values are proposed as multipliers of the affective response associated with success. If the area is a valued one, there will be more affect, given the same level of success evaluation.

Sex Differences in Individual Success Values.   Much of the research on how societal success values influence personal values concerns sex differences in success values. It appears that girls are socialized to be more communal in their success values, whereas boys are more agentic. For many females, achievement at the expense of friends does not give a sense of achievement. Females tend to be more satisfied when working with others to accomplish a goal (Parsons & Goff, 1980). In terms of long-term success goals, those with an agentic orientation feel that making a lot of money and gaining fame are indicative of having a successful life. Communally-oriented people see helping others as central to life success. These differences correspond to conventional sex role stereotypes.

CONCLUSIONS

Although empirical support for the proposed model has been cited where appropriate, the model has not yet been tested in its entirety. We are now beginning a program of research to do this. However, even this review of the literature has suggested that there are a number of factors that attribution researchers need to consider more carefully. First is the basic question of what do we mean by success. This question has not been systematically answered in previous research, either for the experimenter or for the subjects. Second, we need to clearly separate factors such as how hard someone tries or how bright someone is from attributions regarding the causes of a specific performance (How much did the person's effort or ability effect the outcome?). A third major consideration is the individual success values of the people being studied. How many students in our schools have communal rather than agentic success orientations? And, do these orientations differentially affect school performance and learning? Educators as well as attribution researchers need to be more sensitive to these individual differences in student success values.

Although not a major focus of this chapter, we have also seen that the age of the child affects the attribution process at several points. More systematic research is needed to develop models appropriate to elementary school students, middle-school children, and older students. We may find that general models which attempt to analyze the attribution process for students of all ages are not feasible.

Finally, although this chapter deals only indirectly with failure, we suspect that failure judgments are quite different from success evaluations. Not being successful does not necessarily imply that one is a failure. A student may feel that he needs an A to be successful, but only a D or an F would be considered a failure. Thus, the questions remain of how a student decides that he or she is a failure and what the consequences of such a judgment are. We hope to develop a model for failure evaluations in the near future.

ACKNOWLEDGMENT

Preparation of this chapter was supported by funds from the National Institute of Education to the Learning Research and Development Center at the University of Pittsburgh.

REFERENCES

Abramson, L. Y., Seligman, M. E. P., & Teasdale, J. D. Learned helplessness in humans: Critique and reformulation. *Journal of Abnormal Psychology*, 1978, *87*, 49–74.

Adler, A. Introduction: The fundamental views of individual psychology. *International Journal of Individual Psychology*, 1935, *1*, 5–8.

Albert, S. Temporal comparison theory. *Psychological Review*, 1977, *84*, 485–503.

Atkinson, J. W. *An introduction to motivation*. Princeton, N.J.: Nostrand, 1964.

Bakan, D. *The quality of human existence*. Chicago, ILL: Rand McNally, 1966.

Bandura, A. Vicarious and self-reinforcement process. In R. Glaser (Ed.), *The nature of reinforcement*. New York: Academic Press, 1971.

Bar-Tal, D. Interactions of teachers and pupils. In I. H. Frieze, D. Bar-Tal, & J. S. Carroll (Eds.), *New approaches to social problems: Applications of attribution-theory*. San Francisco: Jossey-Bass, 1979. (a)

Bar-Tal, D. *Development of causal perception of success and failure*. Unpublished manuscript, School of Education, Tel-Aviv University, 1979. (b)

Bar-Tal, D., & Frieze, I. H. Attributions of success and failure for actors and observers. *Journal of Research in Personality*, 1976, *10*, 256–265.

Bialer, I. Conceptualization of success and failure in mentally retarded and normal children. *Journal of Personality*, 1961, *29*, 303–320.

Blumenfeld, P. C., Hamilton, V. L., Wessels, K., & Falkner, D. *"You can," "You should," and "You'd better": Teacher attributions regarding achievement and social behaviors*. Paper presented at the annual meeting of the American Psychological Association, San Francisco, 1977.

Calsyn, R. J., & Kenny, D. A. Self-concept of ability and perceived evaluation of others: Cause or effect of academic achievement. *Journal of Educational Psychology*, 1977, *69*, 136–145.

Canavan-Gumpert, D., Garner, K., & Gumpert, P. *The success-fearing personality*. Lexington, MASS: Lexington Books, D. C. Heath & Co., 1978.

Cohen, M. *Recent advances in our understanding of school effects research*. Paper presented at the annual meeting of the American Association of Colleges of Teacher Education, Chicago, Illinois, March 1979.

Cooper, H. M. Controlling personal rewards: Professional teachers' differential use of feedback and the effects of feedback on the students' motivation to perform. *Journal of Educational Psychology,* 1977, *69,* 419-427.

Cooper, H. M. Pygmalion grows up: A model for teacher expectation communication and performance influence. *Review of Educational Research,* 1979, *49,* 389-410.

Covington, M. V., & Omelich, C. L. Are causal attributions causal? A path analysis of the cognitive model of achievement motivation. *Journal of Personality and Social Psychology,* 1979, *37,* 1487-1504. (a)

Covington, M. V., & Omelich, C. L. Effort: The double-edged sword in school achievement. *Journal of Educational Psychology,* 1979, *71,* 169-182. (b)

Covington, M. V., & Omelich, C. L. It's best to be able and virtuous too: Student and teacher evaluative responses to successful effort. *Journal of Educational Psychology,* 1979, *71,* 688-700. (c)

Crandall, V. C. *Toward a cognitive-learning model of achievement behavior and development.* Paper presented at the annual meeting of the Motivation and Education Group, Ann Arbor, 1978.

Crandall, V. J., Katkovsky, W., & Preston, A. Conceptual formulation for some research on children's achievement development. *Child Development,* 1960, *31,* 787-797.

Crittenden, K. S., & Wiley, M. G. *Causal attribution and behavioral response to failure.* Paper presented at the annual meeting of the American Psychological Association, Boston, 1979.

Csikszentmihalyi, M. *Beyond boredom and anxiety.* San Francisco, Calif.: Jossey-Bass, 1975.

Diggory, J. C. *Self-evaluation: Concepts and studies.* New York: John Wiley & Sons, 1966.

Dollinger, S., & Thelen, M. Overjustification and children's intrinsic motivation: Comparative effects of four rewards. *Journal of Personality and Social Psychology,* 1978, *36,* 1259-1269.

Dweck, C. S. The role of expectations and attributions in the alleviation of learned helplessness. *Journal of Personality and Social Psychology,* 1975, *31,* 647-685.

Elig, T., & Frieze, I. H. A multi-dimensional scheme for coding and interpreting perceived causality for success and failure events: The coding scheme of perceived causality (CSPC). JSAS *Catalog of Selected Documents in Psychology,* 1975, *5,* 313.

Elig, T., & Frieze, I. H. Measuring causal attributions for success and failure. *Journal of Personality and Social Psychology,* 1979, *37,* 621-634.

Feather, N. T., & Simon, J. G. Attribution of responsibility and valence of outcome in relation to initial confidence and success and failure of self and other. *Journal of Personality and Social Psychology,* 1971, *18,* 173-188. (a)

Feather, N. T., & Simon, J. G. Causal attributions for success and failure in relation to expectations of success based upon selective or manipulative control. *Journal of Personality,* 1971, *37,* 527-541. (b)

Festinger, L. A theory of social comparison processes. *Human Relations,* 1954, *7,* 117-140.

Fontaine, G. Social comparison and some determinants of expected personal control and expected performance in a novel task situation. *Journal of Personality and Social Psychology,* 1974, *29,* 487-496.

Freud, S. Some character-types met within psychoanalytic work, 1915. In E. Jones (Ed.), *Sigmund Freud: Collected Papers* (Vol. IV). New York: Basic Books, 1959.

Frieze, I. H. Children's attributions for success and failure. In S. S. Brehm, S. M. Kassin, & F. X. Gibbons (Eds.), *Developmental social psychology.* New York: Oxford University Press, 1981.

Frieze, I. H. Causal attribution and information seeking to explain success and failure. *Journal of Research in Personality,* 1976, *10,* 298-305. (a)

Frieze, I. H. The role of information processing in making causal attributions for success and failure. In J. S. Carroll & J. W. Payne (Eds.), *Cognition and social behavior.* Hillsdale, N.J.: Lawrence Erlbaum Associates, 1976. (b)

Frieze, I. H. Beliefs about success and failure in the classroom. In J. H. MacMillan (Ed.), *The social psychology of school learning.* New York: Academic Press, 1980.

Frieze, I. H., & Bar-Tal, D. Developmental trends in cue utilization for attributional judgments. *Journal of Applied Developmental Psychology*, 1980, *1*, 83-94.

Frieze, I. H., Shomo, K. H., & Francis, W. D. *Determinants of subjective feelings of success*. Paper presented at the LRDC Conference, Teacher and Student Perceptions of Success and Failure: Implications for Learning, Pittsburgh, 1979.

Frieze, I. H., & Snyder, H. N. Children's beliefs about the causes of success and failure in school settings. *Journal of Educational Psychology*, 1980, *72*, 186-196.

Frieze, I. H., Snyder, H. N., & Fontaine, C. M. *Student attributions and the attribution process during an actual examination*. Paper presented at the annual meeting of the American Psychological Association, San Francisco, 1977.

Frieze, I. H., Snyder, H. N., & Fontaine, C. M. *Fifth graders' attributions and the attribution model during an actual examination*. Unpublished manuscript, Learning Research and Development Center, University of Pittsburgh, 1978.

Frieze, I. H., & Weiner, B. Cue utilization and attributional judgments for success and failure. *Journal of Personality*, 1971, *39*, 591-606.

Fyans, L. J. *Cultural variation in the meaning of achievement*. Paper presented at the annual meeting of the American Educational Research Association, Boston, April 1980.

Halperin, M. S. Sex differences in children's response to adult pressures for achievement. *Journal of Educational Psychology*, 1977, *69*, 96-100.

Heckhausen, H. *The anatomy of achievement motivation*. New York: Academic Press, 1967.

Hoffman, L. W. Early childhood experiences and women's achievement motives. *Journal of Social Issues*, 1972, *28*, 129-155.

Hoppe, F. Erfolg and Misserfolg. *Psychologische Forschung*, 1930, *14*, 1-62.

Horney, K. *The neurotic personality of our time*. New York: W. W. Norton, 1937.

House, W. C., & Perney, V. Valence of expected and unexpected outcomes as a focus of locus of goal and type of expectancy. *Journal of Personality and Social Psychology*, 1974, *29*, 454-463.

Jenkins, S. R. *"And what do you mean by success?": Fear of success and personal success goals*. Paper presented at the annual meeting of the Eastern Psychological Association, Philadelphia, 1979.

Katz, F. M. The meaning of success: Some differences in value systems of social classes. *Journal of Social Psychology*, 1964, *62*, 141-148.

Knapp, R. H., & Green, H. B. Personality correlates of success imagery. *Journal of Social Psychology*, 1964, *62*, 93-99.

Lenney, E. Women's self-confidence in achievement settings. *Psychological Bulletin*, 1977, *84*, 1-13.

Lepper, M., & Greene, D. Turning play into work: Effects of adult surveillance and extrinsic rewards on children's intrinsic motivation. *Journal of Personality and Social Psychology*, 1975, *31*, 479-486.

Maehr, M. L. Culture and achievement motivation. *The American Psychologist*, 1974, *29*, 887-896.

Maehr, M. L. *Culture and achievement motivation: Beyond Weber and McClelland*. Paper presented at the annual meeting of the American Educational Research Association, Boston, April 1980.

Maehr, M. L., & Nicholls, J. G. Culture and achievement motivation: A second look. In N. Warren (Ed.), *Studies in cross-cultural psychology*, (Vol. 3). New York: Academic Press, in press.

Maslow, A. *Motivation and personality*. New York: Harper & Row, 1954.

McClelland, D. C. *The achieving society*. New York: The Free Press, 1961.

McClelland, D. C., Atkinson, J. W., Clark, R. A., & Lowell, E. L. *The achieving motive*. New York: Appleton-Century-Crofts, 1953.

McClelland, D. C., & Watson, R. I., Jr. Power motivation and risk-taking behavior. *Journal of Personality*, 1973, *41*, 121-139.

McClintock, C. G. Social values: Their definition, measurement and development. *Journal of Research and Development in Education,* 1978, *12,* 121–136.

McMahan, I. D. Relationships between causal attributions and expectancy of success. *Journal of Personality and Social Psychology,* 1973, *28,* 108–114.

Minton, B. A. *Dimensions of information underlying children's judgments of their competence.* Paper presented at the Society for Research in Child Development, San Francisco, 1979.

Nicholls, J. G. Effort is virtuous, but it's better to have ability: Evaluative responses to perceptions of effort and ability. *Journal of Research in Personality,* 1976, *10,* 306–315.

Nicholls, J. G. The development of the concepts of effort and ability, perception of academic attainment, and the understanding that difficult tasks require more ability. *Child Development,* 1978, *49,* 800–814.

Nicholls, J. G. Quality and equality in intellectual development: The role of motivation in education. *American Psychologist,* 1979a, *34,* 1071–1084.

Nicholls, J. G. *The development of cognitive mediation of difficulty level performances with different difficulty cues.* Paper presented at the SRCD Meeting, San Francisco, 1979b.

Parsons, J. E., & Ruble, D. N. *Attributional processes related to the development of achievement-related affect and expectancy.* Paper presented at the annual meeting of the American Psychological Association, Hawaii, 1972.

Parsons, J. E., & Goff, S. B. *Sex differences in achievement motivation: The influences of values, goals, and orientation.* Paper presented at the annual meeting of the Motivation and Education Group, Ann Arbor, Mich., 1978.

Parsons, J. E., & Goff, S. B. Achievement motivation and values: An alternative perspective. In L. J. Fyans (Ed.), *Achievement motivation: Recent trends in theory and research.* New York: Plenum, 1980.

Riemer, B. S. The influence of causal beliefs on affect and expectancy. *Journal of Personality and Social Psychology,* 1975, *31,* 1163–1167.

Rosenthal, R., & Jacobson, L. *Pygamalion in the classroom.* New York: Rinehart & Winston, 1968.

Ruble, D. N. *A developmental perspective of theories of achievement motivation.* Paper presented at the Conference on Motivation and Education, University of Michigan, Ann Arbor, October 1978.

Ruble, D. N., Feldman, N., & Boggiano, A. Social comparison between young children in achievement situations. *Developmental Psychology,* 1976, *12,* 192–197.

Ruble, D. N., & Rholes, W. S. The development of children's perceptions and attributions about their social world. In J. Harvey, W. J. Ickes, & R. F. Kidd (Eds.), *New directions in attribution research,* (Vol. 3). Hillsdale, N.J.: Lawrence Erlbaum Associates, 1981.

Ruble, D. N., & Underkoffler, D. *Attributional processes mediating affective responses to success and failure: A developmental study.* Paper presented at the annual meeting of the Eastern Psychological Association, New York, 1976.

Schilder, P. *Psychoanalysis, man, and society.* New York: Norton, 1951.

Shaklee, H. Development in inferences of ability and task difficulty. *Child Development,* 1976, *47,* 1051–1057.

Shrauger, J. S., & Terbovic, M. L. Self-evaluation and assessments of performance by self and others. *Journal of Consulting and Clinical Psychology,* 1976, *44,* 564–572.

Stipek, D. J., & Tannatt, L. M. *Children's judgments of academic competence.* Manuscript submitted for publication, 1980.

Stipek, D. J., & Hoffman, J. M. *Children's perceptions of the causes of failure.* Unpublished manuscript, University of California, Los Angeles, 1979.

Sullivan, H. S. *The interpersonal theory of psychiatry.* New York: W. W. Norton, 1953.

Tresemer, D. W. *Fear of success.* New York: Plenum Press, 1977.

Valle, V. A., & Frieze, I. H. The stability of causal attributions as a mediator in changing expectations for success. *Journal of Personality and Social Psychology,* 1976, *33,* 579–587.

Veroff, J. Social comparison and the development of achievement motivation. In C. P. Smith (Ed.), *Achievement-related motives in children*. New York: Russell Sage Foundation, 1969.

Veroff, J. Process vs. impact in men's and women's achievement motivation. *Psychology of Women Quarterly*, 1977, *1*, 283–293.

Warren, N. T. *Self-esteem and cognitive bias in the evaluation of past performance*. Paper presented at the annual meeting of the American Psychological Association, 1975.

Weiner, B. Achievement motivation as conceptualized by an attribution theorist. In B. Weiner (Ed.), *Achievement motivation and attribution theory*. Morristown, N.J.: General Learning Press, 1974.

Weiner, B. A theory of motivation for some classroom experiences. *Journal of Educational Psychology*, 1979, *71*, 3–25.

Weiner, B. *The role of affect in rational (attributional) approaches to human motivation*. Paper presented at the annual meeting of the American Educational Research Association, Boston, April 1980.

Weiner, B., Frieze, I., Kukla, A., Reed, L., Rest, S., & Rosenbaum, R. M. *Perceiving the causes of success and failure*. New York: Generaal Learning Press, 1971.

Weiner, B., Kun, A., & Benesh-Weiner, M. The development of mastery, emotions, and morality from an attributional perspective. In W. A. Collins (Ed.), *Development of cognition, affect, and social relations*. The Minnesota Symposia on Child Psychology (Vol. 13). Hillsdale, N.J.: Lawrence Erlbaum Associates, 1980.

Weiner, B., Nierenberg, R., & Goldstein, M. Social learning (locus of control) versus attributional (causal stability) interpretations of expectancy of success. *Journal of Personality*, 1976, *44*, 52–68.

Weiner, B., Russell, D., & Lerman, D. Affective consequences of causal ascriptions. In J. H. Harvey, W. J. Ickes, & R. F. Kidd (Eds.), *New directions in attribution research* (Vol. 2). Hillsdale, N.J.: Lawrence Erlbaum Associates, 1978a.

Weiner, B., Russell, D., & Lerman, D. The cognitive-emotion process in achievement-related contexts. *Journal of Personality and Social Psychology*, 1978b, *37*, 1211–1220.

White, R. W. Motivation reconsidered: The concept of competence. *Psychological Review*, 1959, *66*, 297–333.

2 Social Comparison and Education

John M. Levine
University of Pittsburgh

The typical classroom setting is pervaded by evaluation. It seems probable, therefore, that one of the major outcomes of schooling is sensitization to the quality of one's own and others' intellectual performance. Although evaluative processes in the classroom are widely recognized in discussions of educational theory and practice, most commentary focuses on the teacher as the source of such evaluation. The teacher's role in assigning formal grades has been discussed for some time. More recently, attention has been paid to subtle verbal and nonverbal messages that convey teachers' evaluations to students. Although it is no doubt true that teachers influence students' perceptions of their performance, research on the reward system of the classroom often implies that the teacher is the *only* source of evaluative information and that students are passive recipients, rather than active seekers, of such information. The major premise of this chapter is that another source of evaluative information is available in the classroom and that students actively utilize this source to evaluate their own performance. The alternative information source is peers' performance. The active process by which students obtain and use this information is social comparison.

It has been argued (Pepitone, 1972) that the classroom environment is ideally suited to elicit social comparison behavior. One reason for this is that the classroom generates cognitive uncertainty in students. This uncertainty is produced by new instructional materials, alterations in the normal routine of classroom activities, and other novel or ambiguous aspects of classroom life. In order to reduce uncertainty, students need information about how to adapt to their changing environment. Moreover, the typical classroom has a strongly evaluative atmosphere because of a reward system based on academic performance, perceived teacher concern with achievement, and parental pressure to perform well. This evaluative atmosphere produces a need in students to evaluate their own performance. Finally, because of the accessibility of relatively similar peers, students can reduce their cognitive and evaluative uncertainty by engaging in social comparison.

Other investigators share Pepitone's conviction that social comparison is a pervasive aspect of classroom life. For example, Veroff (1969, 1978), in his analysis of autonomous and social achievement motivation, cites classroom experience as a crucial facilitator of social comparison interest in young children. Suls and Sanders (1979) also suggest that participation in the educational system encourages children to compare themselves with their peers. In fact, social comparison interest seems to be so ubiquitous in schools that a good deal of comparison occurs even in educational environments explicitly designed to minimize ability ranking and grade competition (Crockenberg & Bryant, 1978). A poignant example of the pervasiveness of social comparison, even among very young children in a school setting that actively discourages such comparison, is contained in an anecdotal report by Hechinger and Hechinger (1974):

> When still in kindergarten, our sons were zealously protected from any knowledge about their relative standing in the class; yet they regularly came home with detailed information about who was where in the workbooks. When the teachers, in disapproval of such rampant competitiveness, cut the page numbers off the workbooks, the children simply started to count the pages and continued to issue their own communiques. (pp. 86 and 92)

Finally, it is important to note that desire for comparison information is not restricted to young children: older children and even college students display strong motivation to compare their performance with that of their peers (e.g., Brickman & Berman, 1971; Schofield & Sagar, 1979; Suls & Tesch, 1978).

The foregoing discussion suggests that acquisition of social comparison information for self-assessment purposes is a pervasive phenomenon in schools. But what are the consequences of this acquisition for students' responses (affective, cognitive, and behavioral) to themselves and others? One context in which this question has been addressed is the "mainstreamed" classroom—a classroom in which academically handicapped students join regular students for all or part of the school day. Advocates of mainstreaming have tended to assume that regular class participation would reduce the stigma associated with special class placement (cf. Kaufman, Gottlieb, Agard, & Kukic, 1975). That is, through increased contact and social comparison, "normal" students would learn that handicapped students are reasonably competent and hence would not reject them. Similarly, handicapped students would perceive that they could succeed in a regular classroom and hence would feel better about themselves than they would in a special classroom. Unfortunately, in contrast to these optimistic assumptions, recent evidence suggests that handicapped students in mainstreamed classrooms sometimes suffer more social rejection from peers and have lower self-concepts than similar children who remain in special classrooms (Bryan & Bryan, in press; Gottlieb & Leyser, 1981; Smith, 1980; Strang, Smith, & Rogers, 1978). The impact of social comparison information on students' interpersonal and intrapersonal responses has also been revealed in other contexts. For example, research on classroom goal structures indicates that cooperative learning techniques, which give students a sense of relative competence vis-a-vis their peers, can positively influence such diverse school outcomes as self-esteem, peer relations, and academic achievement (see Aronson & Osherow, 1980; Johnson & Johnson, 1978; Slavin, 1980, this volume). As the above examples indicate, social comparison research that seeks to clarify the schooling process must focus on the consequences as well as the causes of comparison.

Although a number of investigators have recognized the importance of social comparison in educational settings, a systematic analysis of the causes and consequences of comparison in such settings has not been offered. This is no doubt partially attributable to the absence of a general framework for organizing the extensive social comparison literature. Although Leon Festinger was not the first theorist to be interested in comparison processes (see Hyman & Singer, 1968, for a historical review of early comparison theories), his seminal 1954 paper stimulated the bulk of subsequent research on the topic. In the quarter century since Festinger's paper was published, social comparison theory has been elaborated and refined (for reviews, see Latane, 1966; Pettigrew, 1967; Suls & Miller, 1977), and many of the central tenets of the theory have been incorporated in other formulations (e.g., Albert, 1977; Carver, 1979). Surprisingly, in spite of the large volume of theoretical and empirical work on social comparison, little effort has been made to conceptualize various aspects of the comparison process as parts of a unified whole.

In order to provide an integrated picture of the social comparison process and to clarify the relevance of this process to classroom phenomena, a general model of the social comparison process has been developed. This model, which views social comparison in terms of four sequential phases, is useful not only in organizing past work conducted under the social comparison rubric, but also in integrating related work that clarifies the comparison process.

A MODEL OF THE SOCIAL COMPARISON PROCESS

Several aspects of the following presentation should be mentioned. First, the model focuses on ability comparison; opinion and emotion comparison are not explicitly treated (see Suls & Miller, 1977, for reviews of relevant research). Second, rather than presenting an exhaustive review of research dealing with social comparison of ability, selected studies are cited to illustrate particular aspects of the model. Finally, the model is more appropriately viewed as a

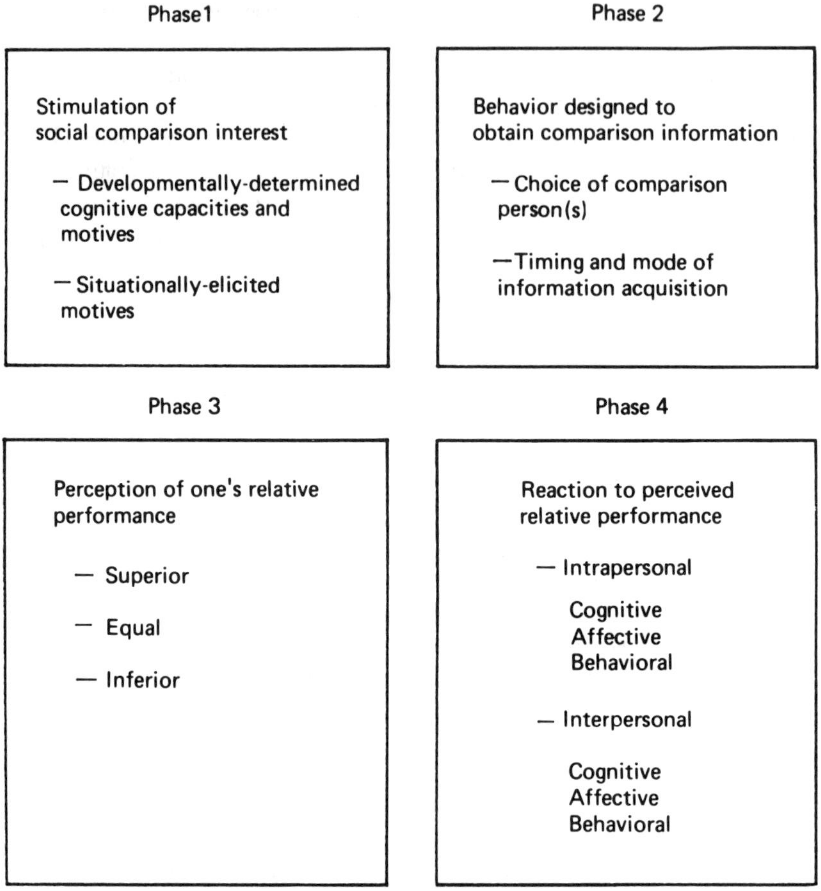

Phase 1

Stimulation of
social comparison interest

— Developmentally-determined
cognitive capacities and
motives

— Situationally-elicited
motives

Phase 2

Behavior designed to
obtain comparison information

— Choice of comparison
person(s)

— Timing and mode of
information acquisition

Phase 3

Perception of one's relative
performance

— Superior

— Equal

— Inferior

Phase 4

Reaction to perceived
relative performance

— Intrapersonal

Cognitive
Affective
Behavioral

— Interpersonal

Cognitive
Affective
Behavioral

FIG. 2.1.   Model of the social comparison process.

heuristic device for summarizing past work and suggesting future research, rather than as a formal theory.

The model can be briefly summarized as follows (see Figure 2.1). Social comparison interest is stimulated by developmentally-determined cognitive capacities and motives and by situationally-elicited motives (Phase 1). This interest produces behavior designed to obtain social comparison information (Phase 2). Such behavior can be analyzed in terms of the person(s) chosen for comparison and the timing and mode of information acquisition. Social comparison behavior, in turn, provides relative performance information indicating that one is superior, equal, or inferior to the comparison person(s) (Phase 3). Finally, this relative performance information elicits intrapersonal and interpersonal reactions that are cognitive, affective, and behavioral in nature (Phase 4). Each phase of the model is discussed in greater detail below.

Stimulation of Social Comparison Interest (Phase 1)

As Figure 2.1 indicates, two major determinants of social comparison interest have been identified: (a) developmentally-determined cognitive capacities and motives (including personality traits) and (b) situationally-elicited motives. With regard to the former, it is assumed that developmental changes reflect the interaction of age-related structural shifts in cognitive processing abilities and the cumulative impact of social and nonsocial experiences. Developmental changes have been observed in several perceptual-cognitive phenomena that seem likely to affect social comparison interest. These include a child's conception of ability, feeling of responsibility for goal-oriented outcomes, awareness of the challenge value of tasks, and ability to integrate achievement-related information (Ruble, 1980; Ruble & Boggiano, 1980). Even more relevant to our present interest is evidence indicating developmental changes in the degree to which social comparison information is sought and used. Thus, although some social comparison behavior is exhibited by preschool children (Mosatche & Bragonier, 1981), interest in social comparison information increases during the early school years (e.g., Ruble, Feldman, & Boggiano, 1976). Moreover, there is evidence that social comparison information is not used for self-evaluation until at least the second grade (e.g., Ruble, Boggiano, Feldman, & Loebl, 1980; Ruble, Parsons, & Ross, 1976) and does not influence behavior based on competence judgments for children younger than 7–8 years (e.g., Boggiano & Ruble, 1979; Spear & Armstrong, 1978). Finally, consistent with the notion that use of social comparison information is influenced by developmental factors, research suggests that children's ability to assess accurately their own academic performance increases rather dramatically with age (Nicholls, 1978, 1979), as does their tendency to behave competitively (McClintock, 1978).

A developmental analysis of social comparison in children has been offered by Ruble et al. (1980). These investigators argue that social comparison is a multilevel process, with different levels developing at different times. More specifically, they suggest the following developmental sequence: (a) motivation to seek information about others' performance, (b) information-seeking strategies, (c) use of comparison information for tangible rewards (e.g., equalizing rewards between self and other), and (d) use of comparison information for abstract assessment (e.g., self-evaluation) and behavior based on such assessment. In speculating about why young children do not use comparison information for abstract assessment and related behavior, Ruble and her colleagues suggest that young children assign low weight to comparison information when evaluating themselves. This low weight, in turn, may be due to children focusing on their direct experience with the task, teachers' lack of emphasis on social comparison, and children's perception that their abilities are changing so quickly that relative performance information is meaningless.

In a more recent paper, Ruble (in press) elaborated the above ideas by citing evidence that 6-year-old children have the basic cognitive capacities (i.e., awareness of individual differences, recognition of relative standing), motivation, and information-acquisition strategies necessary for social comparison. However, these children lack certain inferential capabilities (e.g., ability to shift from surface to depth application of comparison information and to make self-reflective inferences) that are essential to the use of comparison information for abstract assessment of one's abilities and behavior based on such assessment. These inferential capabilities are needed in part because, as discussed later, abilities are invisible entities that must be inferred from overt performance and performance can be influenced by both ability and nonability factors (Darley & Goethals, 1980; Goethals & Darley, 1977).

Finally, Suls and Mullen (1982) have recently offered an ambitious life-span developmental model of self-evaluation of ability. These authors suggest that temporal comparisons (i.e., comparisons between one's present and past performances) predominate in both early childhood (ages 3–4) and old age (ages 65 and over). In contrast, social comparisons (i.e., comparisons between one's own and others' present performances) are dominant in (a) middle childhood (ages 4–8), (b) late childhood, adolescence, and young adulthood (ages 8–40), and (c) middle age (ages 40–65). Suls and Mullen argue that young children use temporal comparison because of their cognitive inability to make social comparisons (e.g., failure to understand the discounting principle), whereas elderly people use temporal comparison primarily because of social factors (e.g., unavailability of similar comparison others). In addition, as will be discussed in the following section, these authors contend that preferred targets of social comparison change systematically over the life span.

Turning now to situationally-elicited motives as determinants of social comparison interest, it is appropriate to mention briefly Festinger's (1954) position, since it is the basis of subsequent developments in this area. Festinger suggested that individuals are motivated to evaluate their abilities and opinions (i.e., to obtain accurate information about themselves, regardless of its hedonic value), because accurate self-evaluation is essential to behavioral adaptation and hence survival. He went on to argue that when objective nonsocial standards for self-evaluation are absent, individuals compare their abilities and opinions with those of similar others.

Subsequent analyses have suggested that, in addition to desire for *accurate* self-evaluation, other motives can also produce social comparison interest. One of these is desire for *flattering* self-evaluation, or self-enhancement (e.g., Goethals & Darley, 1977; Gruder, 1977; Israel, 1956; Thornton & Arrowood, 1966). Also, social comparison interest can be stimulated by desire to (a) cope with environmental ambiguity (e.g., Pepitone, 1972); (b) optimize effort on a task (e.g., Halisch & Heckhausen, 1977); and (c) select potential partners for cooperative tasks and potential opponents for competitive tasks (Harvey & Smith, 1977).

Finally, some investigators have taken issue with the basic notion that people actively strive to obtain comparison information. They argue that social comparison is inherently aversive and therefore is often avoided. Thus, Brickman and Bulman (1977) present evidence that, regardless of whether one is superior, equal, or inferior to another, social comparison will produce unpleasant feelings, which in turn will cause one to avoid comparison. While not denying that people sometimes seek comparison information, Brickman and Bulman point out substantial costs that may sometimes cancel the rewards of comparison.

In addition to attempts to differentiate general motive states that facilitate or inhibit social comparison, efforts have been made to identify specific situational variables that affect desire for comparison. (In most cases, the resulting comparison behavior is assumed to be motivated by desire for self-evaluation.) These variables include presence versus absence of competition (e.g., Feldman & Ruble, 1977; Mithaug, 1973; Wilson & Benner, 1971); attraction to the comparison other (e.g., Miller, 1977); relevance of comparison information to anticipated action (e.g., Jones & Regan, 1974); degree of uncertainty about one's own ability (e.g., Schwartz & Smith, 1976); and degree of self-focused attention (Pallak, 1978).

Unresolved Issues Regarding Comparison Interest in Classrooms.   Although, as the above discussion suggests, determinants of social comparison interest have received a good deal of theoretical and empirical attention, we still have much to learn about comparison interest in classrooms. A major problem is that our knowledge of comparison interest is derived primarily from laboratory experiments. To redress this methodological imbalance and increase the ecological validity of our findings, observational and interview studies of children's comparison interest in school settings must be conducted.

In subsequent work on the determinants of social comparison interest, attention should be given to both developmental and situational factors. Regarding the former, it is interesting that most of the research with children has assumed that social comparison interest is based on desire for accurate self-evaluation. However, as mentioned before, work with adults has suggested that desire for flattering self-evaluation is at least as important. It would seem useful, therefore, to attempt to specify the various motives that facilitate and inhibit social comparison interest in children of different ages.

With regard to situational determinants of comparison interest, classroom variables would seem to warrant investigation. One such variable is the degree to which instruction is individualized. Although it might seem plausible that comparison interest would be lower in individualized than in nonindividualized instructional settings, this may not be true for several reasons. First, because individualized classrooms allow children to move at their own pace and to work at tasks within their level of competence, children's frequency of task completion and concomitant desire for self-evaluation may be relatively high in such classrooms. This in turn may lead to increased comparison interest. Second, because more talking and freedom of movement are allowed in individualized classrooms, children in these settings may be more inclined to compare their performance with that of their peers. Finally, to the extent that parents can influence the type of classroom in which their children are placed, parents who choose individualized classrooms may be particularly concerned about academic achievement and may communicate this concern to their children. If so, students in these classrooms may be relatively anxious about their performance and therefore eager to evaluate themselves through social comparison.

Another classroom variable that may influence social comparison interest is ability grouping, or tracking. According to Richer (1976), low-ability students only adopt high-ability students as a reference group when the high-ability students are both *visible* (i.e., available for observation) and *meaningful* (i.e., important as a source of comparison or reward). Visibility is assumed to vary positively with the degree of subgroup differentiation and negatively with the size of the total group and the number of subgroups. Meaningfulness is assumed to vary positively with the similarity of subgroups and degree to which rewards are based on subgroup membership. Thus, in Richer's view, comparison between ability groups is not automatic, but rather depends on specific characteristics of the groups involved.

An important aspect of social comparison interest that presumably is influenced by both developmental and situational factors is the dimension on which comparison information is sought. Preschool children, for example, may be more aware of and concerned about physical than intellectual performance (cf. Darley & Goethals, 1980). If so, to the extent that they seek comparison information, they will be more likely to compare themselves on physical than on intellectual dimensions. When children enter school, efforts will be made to teach them to value specific types of intellectual performance. To the extent that these efforts are successful, children will alter the kinds of comparison information that they seek. As children mature, they will come to value new performance dimensions and will strive to obtain comparison information concerning these dimensions. To understand the social comparison process, then, we must understand how dimensions of comparison are selected. Although the above line of reasoning implies that selection of a dimension precedes and causes comparison interest, this relationship might be reversed in some cases. For example, a new child in school who wishes to compare his or her abilities to those of classmates will have to choose performance dimensions that are salient and acceptable to classmates. In addition, it is important to note that valuing a given performance dimension does not necessarily lead one to seek social comparison information regarding it. If an individual believes that comparison information is not relevant to self-evaluation, that no appropriate comparison agents are available, or that embarrassment may result from comparison, he or she probably will not seek comparison even on a valued dimension (cf. Brickman & Bulman, 1977).

Finally, it is interesting to consider cases in which individuals compare relative performances on apparently different dimensions. For example, a child may compare his math grade to a peer's spelling grade, or the win/loss record of his baseball team to the win/loss record of a peer's football team. At a high school reunion, a lawyer and an artist may assess their relative "success" by comparing how well each has done in his/her respective occupation. This type of social comparison raises a number of interesting questions. For example, does the degree of perceived dissimilarity between performance dimensions influence the "meaningfulness" of the comparison? And are there developmental changes in children's ability to compare on the same versus different dimensions?

Behavior Designed to Obtain Comparison Information (Phase 2)

Once social comparison interest is elicited, the individual emits behavior designed to obtain comparison information (see Figure 2.1). Two major components of this information acquisition behavior can be identified: (a) choice of comparison person(s) and (b) timing and mode of information acquisition.

As will be recalled, Festinger (1954), who viewed accurate self-evaluation as the goal of social comparison, suggested that individuals seek to compare with *similar* others, because these others provide the most accurate and reliable self-evaluative information. Most subsequent investigators have interpreted this similarity hypothesis literally, assuming that an individual who performs at level X on a task seeks to compare with others who also perform at level X. Recently, however, it has been suggested that similarity is sought, not on the specific performance dimension under consideration (e.g., tennis skill), but rather on dimensions related to and presumably predictive of the performance (e.g., age, sex, years of practice) (Goethals & Darley, 1977; Suls, Gaes, & Gastorf, 1979; Suls, Gastorf, & Lawhon, 1978). Thus, this "related attributes" interpretation, although still predicting that individuals desire similar others for comparison, expands the range of dimensions on which similarity is sought.

Festinger's similarity hypothesis has been altered even more radically by the suggestion that under certain circumstances *dissimilar,* rather than similar, others will be preferred for comparison (e.g., Brickman & Bulman, 1977; Mettee & Smith, 1977). Evidence indicates that individuals sometimes do choose dissimilar comparison others and that the relationship between the target's similarity and probability of being chosen for comparison depends on the specific motive underlying the comparison (Fazio, 1979; Goethals & Darley, 1977; Gruder, 1977). Thus, Goethals and Darley suggest that when an ability is being considered, individuals motivated to obtain accurate self-evaluation will compare with similar others, while those seeking self-enhancement will compare with inferior others and will cognitively distort upward the others' standing on nonability factors presumably related to performance. Other investigators have found that, rather than comparing with similar or inferior others, individuals sometimes compare with superior others (see Feldman & Ruble, 1981; Gruder, 1977; Pepitone, 1980, Chapter 7; Suls & Tesch, 1978). It appears, then, that in order to predict choice of a comparison other one must know, first, the specific motive underlying social comparison interest and, second, the degree to which comparison with a particular other is likely to satisfy this motive.

A developmental analysis of preferences for similar and dissimilar others recently has been offered by Suls and Mullen (1982), who suggest that preferred targets of social comparison change over the life span. During the earliest phase in which social comparison is sought (middle childhood), children lack the cognitive capacity to distinguish between ability and nonability causes of performance and hence do not appreciate the unique advantages of comparing with similar others. Therefore, children in this phase manifest indiscriminate comparisons with both similar and dissimilar others. During the next phase in which social comparison predominates (late childhood, adolescence, and young adulthood), increased cognitive sophistication, social pressures, and availability of peers cause individuals to prefer similar comparison others. Finally, during the last social comparison phase (middle age), people shift to a preference for mixed (i.e., both similar and dissimilar) comparison others. This relative increase in preference for dissimilar others occurs for two reasons. First, middle-aged people seek comparison with dissimilar others in order to feel unique. Second, dissimilar comparisons are forced on middle-aged people by their social environment (e.g., through competition with younger workers).

In the above discussion it has been implicitly assumed that social comparison is basically an interpersonal phenomenon that takes place at a single point in time and is directed toward assessing a single dimension of ability. It is also possible, of course, for individuals to undertake sequential comparisons and to assess several ability dimensions. Sequential comparisons might involve tracking performance on a single dimension over time or assessing performance on different dimensions at different times. Both types of comparisons could vary in frequency and could involve the same or different comparison others. Such complex forms of comparison may be particularly likely in the classroom, where students perform many times on several ability dimensions (e.g., math, reading, athletics) and have available a range of potential comparison others on each dimension. Like the assumptions that comparison occurs only once and involves only one ability dimension, the assumption that comparison is an exclusively interpersonal phenomenon also may impose unnecessary constraints on our understanding of comparison processes and on our ability to apply this understanding to the classroom. Intrapersonal comparison (i.e., comparison with one's own past performance) no doubt is also important. Although the remaining discussion will focus on interpersonal comparison, it is clear that we must begin to build a comprehensive theoretical framework that integrates intrapersonal and interpersonal comparison. Albert's (1977) temporal comparison theory and Suls and Mullen's (1982) life-span model of self-evaluation provide a beginning for the kind of integration advocated.

Given that a particular other (or group of others) is selected for social comparison, the individual desiring comparison must then decide on the timing and mode of information acquisition. Relatively little attention has been devoted to these important aspects of the social comparison process. In most previous studies, subjects were given a list of potential comparison others differing in performance and were simply asked to select the individuals whose performance they wished to see. In the few studies that have examined active efforts to obtain social comparison information, a relatively small subset of possible comparison behaviors was measured: frequency of glances at another's work (Halisch & Heckhausen, 1977; Pepitone, 1972), frequency of button-pushing that allows visual monitoring of another's performance (Hake, Vukelich, & Kaplan, 1973; Mithaug, 1973; Ruble, Feldman, & Boggiano, 1976; Vukelich & Hake, 1974), and competitive behavior (Conolley, Gerard, & Kline, 1978; Hoffman, Festinger, & Lawrence, 1954; Pepitone, 1972).

Unresolved Issues Regarding Acquisition of Comparison Information in Classrooms. As in the case of the determinants of social comparison interest, we know very little about either choice of comparison persons or timing and mode of information acquisition in classrooms. These aspects of social comparison are likely to be influenced by several factors, including: (a) the motive(s) underlying comparison interest (e.g., desire for self-evaluation, desire for self-enhancement, desire to optimize task effort), (b) the availability of potential comparison persons, (c) one's relationship to potential comparison persons, (d) the dominant task structure of the classroom (cooperative, competitive, individualistic), and (e) one's own and the comparison person's anticipated reaction to the probable outcome of comparison (Pepitone, 1980, Chapter 7). Not only do we lack information concerning how each of these variables independently affects social comparison behavior in classrooms, we have not even begun to assess their interactive effects.

Several interesting questions can be raised regarding the impact of the above variables: At what age do children begin to select comparison persons of different performance levels to satisfy different comparison motives? Under what circumstances are group membership, friendship, and physical proximity as important as (or more important than) performance level in determining comparison choice? How does an individual's familiarity with and past performance on a task influence his or her choice of a comparison person? What preferences do children of different ages have for reciprocal versus nonreciprocal disclosure of performance information (cf. Brickman & Kessler, cited in Brickman & Bulman, 1977)? And, how do people build "deniability" into the comparison process to avoid their own and/or the other person's discomfort following comparison? These represent only a sample of the questions that need to be investigated if we are to understand comparison behavior in classrooms and other natural settings.

Perception of One's Relative Performance (Phase 3)

Behavior designed to obtain social comparison information yields a perception of one's relative performance (see Figure 2.1). This process would appear to be straightforward, producing one of three outcomes: perception that one's performance is superior, equal, or inferior to that of the comparison person(s). However, reflection reveals several complexities. For example, how does an individual integrate conflicting social comparison information (e.g., better performance than Person A and worse performance than Person B) in arriving at a general assessment of his or her relative performance? Is all the conflicting information weighted equally, or is each piece weighted differentially as a function of such factors as source, valence, and time of acquisition (Anderson, 1974)? Moreover, how does the motivation underlying social comparison interest affect information weighting? Finally, how do age-related changes in cognitive processing abilities influence the weighting process (cf. Ruble, in press; Ruble & Boggiano, 1980)?

Even when comparison information is consistent (because there is only one piece of information or because two or more pieces have the same implications for one's performance), the question of how much weight to assign to the information remains. This is because people compare *performances,* but often are really interested in assessing *abilities* (Darley & Goethals, 1980). In order to infer confidently that one's own or another's performance reflects ability, one must rule out other potential determinants of performance (e.g., effort, luck). As Harvey and Smith (1977) suggest, the probability that performance reflects ability is increased when the incentive value of good performance is high and performance is consistent over time. Thus, the weights assigned to one's own and the comparison person's performances depend on knowledge (or assumptions) about the context in which the performances occurred and the history of prior performances. Performance weighting may be further complicated by affective and cognitive consequences of comparison. It seems likely, as Darley and Goethals (1980) suggest, that individuals who are distressed because their performance was lower than that of a comparison person might reduce this distress by attributing their own performance to inhibiting nonability factors (e.g., fatigue) and the other's performance to facilitating nonability factors (e.g., high motivation). In contrast, individuals who are pleased because they outperformed a comparison person might increase this pleasure by attributing *both* their own and the other's performance to ability.

In the above discussion, it has been assumed that individuals are motivated to obtain relative performance information and emit behaviors designed to acquire such information. However, it is important to recognize that relative performance information also can be acquired when an individual is indifferent to such information or even desires to avoid it. Here I am referring to "forced social comparison," that is, comparison information that intrudes upon individuals and compels them to evaluate their performance even though they are not initially motivated to do so (cf. Allen & Wilder, 1977; Mettee & Smith, 1977). Forced social comparison may be particularly prevalent in classrooms, where peer performance on valued achievement dimensions is highly salient. It might be argued that in many classrooms a conspiracy exists against students who wish to ignore or avoid relative performance information. No matter how hard students try to attend only to their own performance, they are bombarded with information about peers' performances. Thus, to the self-initiated social comparison that occurs in the classroom, we must add the forced social comparison that often characterizes this environment.

Reaction to Perceived Relative Performance (Phase 4)

The final phase of the social comparison process concerns responses that follow acquisition of relative performance information (see Figure 2.1). These responses can be conceptualized along two dimensions: (1) response direction (intrapersonal, interpersonal) and (2) response type (cognitive, affective, behavioral). These two dimensions can be combined to yield a 2 × 3 classification scheme that is useful in organizing past work concerning how people respond to comparison information. It should be noted that much of the research reviewed below was not originally conceptualized in terms of social comparison. Thus, the notion of reaction to comparison information is useful in organizing a rather disparate set of studies.

Intrapersonal Responses

Intrapersonal responses are those responses that have consequences only, or primarily, for oneself. These responses include (a) cognitions about oneself; (b) affect, or feelings, about oneself; and (c) overt behaviors involving task performance and self-reward.

Cognitive Intrapersonal Responses. Several studies have investigated the impact of social comparison information on expectancies for future performance. Early research was conceptualized in terms of level of aspiration (e.g., Anderson & Brandt, 1939; Chapman & Volkman, 1939; Dreyer, 1954). More recent work was stimulated by interest in a variety of topics, including normative-informational influence (Gerard, 1961), cognitive dissonance (Fishbein, Raven, & Hunter, 1963), attributional processes (Fontaine, 1974; Nicholls, 1975), learned helplessness (Brown & Inouye, 1978), and selection of achievement tasks (Trope, 1979; Zuckerman, Brown, Fischler, Fox, Lathin, & Minasian, 1979).

Explicit attention has been given to how social comparison information affects performance expectancies in school settings. For example, after reviewing research on the impact of desegregation, Pettigrew (1967) concluded that "*many of the consequences of interracial classrooms for both Negro and white children are a direct function of the opportunities such classrooms provide for cross-racial self-evaluation"* (p. 287). Pettigrew argued further that black children's performance expectancies can be affected both positively and negatively by the relatively high peer performance standards that often characterize interracial classrooms. The impact of social comparison information on performance expectancies is also suggested by Rosenbaum's (1980) data on the consequences of high school tracking. Rosenbaum found that (a) students often misperceive what track they are in and (b) students' track perceptions are as good a predictor of their college plans as are actual track placements. Finally, Davis (1966), in a large-scale study entitled "The Campus as a Frog Pond," found that male college graduates' career aspirations were more strongly associated with college grades than with college quality. Davis interpreted his data as suggesting that students evaluate their academic abilities by comparing with peers on their own campus.

In addition to performance expectancies, performance attributions also have received attention from investigators interested in cognitive intrapersonal responses to social comparison information. Attributions refer to explanations of past outcomes, rather than to predictions of future outcomes (expectancies). (According to Weiner, 1979, attributions determine expectancies, but recent evidence obtained by Covington and Omelich, 1979, casts doubt on the strength of this causal relationship.) Although the question of how social comparison information affects self-attributions can be subsumed under the more general question of how consensus information affects attributions, this is typically not done. Thus, in a recent review of consensus information research, Kassin (1979) failed to mention several studies that investigated how social comparison information influences self-attributions of ability. Nonetheless, a number of studies have yielded data indicating that social comparison information is an important determinant of self-attribution (e.g., Ames, 1978; Ames, Ames, & Felker, 1977; Harvey, Cacioppo, & Yasuna, 1977; Levine, Snyder, & Mendez-Caratini, in press; Nicholls, 1975; Sanders, Gastorf, & Mullen, 1979; Stephan, Kennedy, & Aronson, 1977; Wortman, Costanzo, & Witt, 1973).[1]

Affective Intrapersonal Responses.   Affective intrapersonal responses to social comparison information involve feelings (e.g., happiness-sadness) that result from perception of one's relative performance. Relevant research indicates that social comparison information is a potent determinant of feelings about oneself (e.g., Ames et al., 1977; Brickman & Bulman, 1977; Drury, 1980; Gastorf & Suls, 1978; Mettee & Smith, 1977; Rogers, Smith, & Coleman, 1978; Smith, 1980; Tesser, 1980). Moreover, as suggested earlier, anticipation of these affec-

---

[1]Some evidence suggests that social comparison information, in addition to influencing expectancies and attributions, can also affect recall of past performance (e.g., Vreven & Nuttin, 1976).

tive responses to social comparison importantly influences the amount and kind of comparison information sought. It is important to point out that affective intrapersonal responses can be long-lasting (e.g., increased self-esteem) as well as transitory (e.g., momentary happiness) and are complexly related to attributional dimensions, such as causal locus and stability of performance (Covington & Omelich, 1979; Weiner, 1979).

Behavioral Intrapersonal Responses. The final category of intrapersonal responses involves overt behavior. Two major subcategories of such behavior have been studied: task performance and self-reward. Regarding the former, evidence indicates that social comparison information affects several dimensions of task performance, including attention to the task (e.g., Santrock & Ross, 1975), monitoring of one's own performance (e.g., Hake, Vukelich, & Kaplan, 1973), time spent on the task (e.g., Nicholls, 1975), task persistence in the face of failure (e.g., Brown & Inouye, 1978), reaction time (e.g., Rijsman, 1974), performance speed (e.g., Halisch & Heckhausen, 1977), and performance quality (e.g., McClintock & Van Avermaet, 1975).[2] Regarding the second subcategory of intrapersonal behavioral responses, several studies have demonstrated that social comparison information affects the degree to which individuals reward themselves following task performance (e.g., Ames, 1978; Ames et al., 1977; Crockenberg, Bryant, & Wilce, 1976; Hook & Cook, 1979; Masters, 1971, 1973). Taken as a whole, then, research on task performance and self-reward indicates that social comparison information has a substantial effect on "nonsocial" behavior.

Interpersonal Responses

Let us turn next to an examination of interpersonal responses to social comparison information. Interpersonal responses are responses that are directed toward or involve other persons. As with intrapersonal responses, interpersonal responses can be placed into three categories: cognitive, affective, and behavioral.

Cognitive Interpersonal Responses. Relevant research has dealt primarily with performance attributions, rather than performance expectancies. Again, as with attributions for one's own performance, the question of how social comparison information affects attributions for others' performance is related to the more general question of how consensus information affects attributions. Although the impact of consensus information on attributions is not fully understood, several experimental studies indicate that, when individuals receive information about their own and another's performance, this comparison information affects at-

---

[2]Recent research also indicates that social comparison information can influence task preference (Boggiano & Ruble, 1979; Tesser & Campbell, 1980).

tributions about the comparison agent (e.g., Ames, 1978; Ames et al., 1977; Snyder, Stephan, & Rosenfield, 1976; Stephan, Burnam, & Aronson, 1979). In addition to experimental research on performance attributions, several studies conducted in classrooms indicate that students form perceptions of their peers' academic competence (e.g., Fisher, 1978; Rosenholtz & Wilson, 1980; Simpson, 1981; Stipek, 1981). Presumably these perceptions are based at least in part on social comparison information.

Affective Interpersonal Responses.   A number of experimental studies have assessed the impact of social comparison information on interpersonal affective responses (i.e., liking). Early work on this topic was reviewed by Lott and Lott (1965), who listed several determinants of attraction that involve explicit or implicit ability comparison. These include (a) sharing success or failure with another person, (b) learning that another person is responsible for one's success or failure, (c) succeeding or failing in the presence of another person, and (d) observing (or learning about) a person who succeeds or fails. More recent experiments dealing with relative performance and liking have been conducted by Harvey and Kelley (1973), Lerner (1965), and Senn (1971). (Also see reviews by Byrne, 1971, and Mettee & Smith, 1977.)

In several experiments, attraction was operationalized as choice of a coworker for a subsequent cooperative, competitive, or individualistic task (e.g., Levine et al., in press; Martens & White, 1975; Miller & Suls, 1977; Swingle, 1969; Wilson & Benner, 1971). Although the implications of such choice have not been investigated in school settings, they may be quite important. For example, it seems likely that the coworker selected for an academic task will substantially affect students' access to information regarding how to complete the task. In addition, such choice will determine the relative performance information that students receive, thereby influencing their feelings about their own performance, their aspirations for future performance, and their task-related behavior. Work choices, when unreciprocated, may cause a student to feel rejected and socially isolated. When such choices are reciprocated consistently, the student may be seen by others as part of a clique, which in turn may reduce his or her opportunities for wider social comparison.

In addition to the experimental studies mentioned above, numerous attempts have been made to assess the relationship between relative performance and popularity in classrooms. Early work on this topic was reviewed by Hartup (1970), and more recent studies have been conducted by Carter, DeTine, Spero, and Benson (1975), Gottlieb, Semmel, and Veldman (1978), MacMillan and Morrison (1980), and McMichael (1980). It has been suggested that the relationship between academic performance and popularity may be influenced by the task structure of the classroom (Hallinan, 1981). Consistent with this hypothesis, Bossert (1979) recently found that performance is a stronger determinant of friendship choice in "recitation" classrooms (where all students work on the same task and their performance is public and comparable) than in "multitask" classrooms (where students work on different tasks and their performance is nonpublic and noncomparable).

Behavioral Interpersonal Responses. The last category of reaction to social comparison information involves interpersonal behavior. It has been found, for example, that comparison information affects the magnitude of reward given to the comparison agent (e.g., Ames, 1978; Crockenberg et al., 1976; Hook & Cook, 1979; Kennedy & Stephan, 1977; Masters, 1971). In addition, research indicates that social comparison can produce a number of other interpersonal behaviors. These include increased competitiveness in a game situation (e.g., Toda, Shinotsuka, McClintock, & Stech, 1978), aggression toward the comparison agent (e.g., Santrock, Smith, & Bourbeau, 1976), efforts to disrupt the agent's performance (e.g., Pepitone, 1972), and forcible acquisition of the agent's rewards (Santrock, Readdick, & Pollard, 1980).

Reaction to Comparison Information in the Classroom

As the foregoing discussion suggests, social comparison can have a number of intrapersonal and interpersonal consequences. On a priori grounds, it seems likely that some of these consequences might be beneficial to children in classroom settings, whereas others might be detrimental. It is interesting, therefore, that discussions of social comparison have tended to dwell on its hazards. It has generally been assumed that social comparison is more bad than good and that its harmful effects are particularly obvious for children whose performance is lower than that of their peers. Among the alleged negative consequences of comparison are feelings of intellectual inferiority, low aspiration level, lack of task motivation, interpersonal hostility, and competitiveness.

In an effort to avoid these undesirable outcomes, educational environments that reduce the potential for "maladaptive" social comparison have been created. For example, educators have attempted to build individualized learning environments in which the salience of peers' performance is so low that children must evaluate themselves solely in terms of their own past performance. As mentioned earlier, there is reason to question the effectiveness of such environments in eliminating social comparison interest. In addition, cooperative learning techniques have been devised, in which children of all ability levels receive relative performance information that allows them to feel academically competent (Aronson & Osherow, 1980; Johnson & Johnson, 1978; Slavin, 1980, this volume).

It still seems reasonable, however, to ask, "Is social comparison generally detrimental in classroom settings?" In attempting to answer this question, one must consider the validity of the assumption that comparison is particularly detrimental to low-performing children. Of the several negative consequences of comparison mentioned earlier, the first two (i.e., feelings of intellectual inferiority and low aspiration level) presumably occur only when one's performance is lower than that of others. In contrast, the last three consequences (i.e., lack of task motivation, interpersonal hostility, and competitiveness) may be related to relative performance in a more complex fashion. For example, it seems possible that a child who feels superior to his or her classmates may have as little motivation to work hard as a child who feels inferior. In addition, perceived superiority may produce as much hostility to classmates as perceived inferiority. Finally, competitiveness may be most probable, not when a child performs markedly better or worse than peers, but rather when he or she performs at approximately the same level. Thus, it is difficult to argue on a priori grounds that one particular type of relative performance information (superiority, equality, inferiority) is inherently better or worse than another (cf. Brickman & Bulman, 1977). Moreover, in the case of superiority and inferiority, it seems likely that the size, as well as the direction, of the performance difference will mediate the beneficial/harmful consequences of social comparison.

Even when we consider inferiority feelings produced by negative comparison information, the issue is more complex than it may seem at first glance. It is a cultural truism that low self-esteem, or negative self-concept, is detrimental to academic achievement. If this is true, and if social comparison produces low self-esteem in low-performing children, then it follows that social comparison is harmful. However, are we really sure that self-esteem is an important determinant of academic achievement? The somewhat surprising answer is "no." As Scheirer and Kraut (1979) conclude in their recent review of educational intervention programs designed to alter self-concept, "the overwhelmingly negative evidence reviewed here for a causal connection between self concept and academic achievement should create caution among both educators and theorists who have heretofore assumed that enhancing a person's feelings about himself would lead to academic achievement" (p. 145). Recent research by Maruyama, Rubin, and Kingsbury (1981) points to the same conclusion.

It would seem that a more sophisticated conceptualization of the relationship between self-esteem and academic performance is needed. First, it must be recognized that the causal arrow between self-esteem and performance might run in both directions (cf. Bachman & O'Malley, 1977; Scheirer & Kraut, 1979). In the case in which performance causes self-esteem, a linear relationship between these variables is plausible (i.e., increased performance produces increased self-esteem). However, in the case in which self-esteem causes performance, a curvilinear relationship may exist. That is, both very low and very high self-esteem may inhibit performance. People with low self-esteem may avoid challenging tasks because they expect to fail, whereas people with high self-esteem may avoid the same tasks because they expect to succeed and do not feel the need to "prove" their competence. This line of reasoning suggests that the need to convince oneself and others of one's competence may be a major determinant of effortful striving in school and work settings. If so, it would be interesting to investigate the amount of self-esteem that produces optimal effort in different academic domains and in children of different ages. Perhaps more self-esteem is needed to produce a unit of effort in young children than in older children and adults. If so, educators might seek to design learning environments in which evaluative feedback is calibrated to the developmental level of the student, so that "optimal" self-esteem is produced in children of all ages. Finally, as Bachman and O'Malley (1977) suggest, a correlation between self-esteem and performance might be attributable to a third factor (e.g., SES, academic ability) that influences both variables. If this is the case, efforts to alter self-esteem are likely to have little effect on academic achievement. (See Shavelson & Stuart, 1981, for a discussion of how causal modeling techniques can be used to clarify the relationship between self-concept and achievement.)

A major source of difficulty in assessing the relationship between self-esteem and academic performance is confusion regarding the conceptual and operational definition of self-esteem (see Gergen, 1971; Scheirer & Kraut, 1979; Wells & Marwell, 1976; Wylie, 1974, 1979). One important definitional issue involves the centrality, or salience, of various performance dimensions to a person's self-esteem. This issue is addressed by Tesser (1980; Tesser & Campbell, 1980) in a recent model of self-esteem maintenance. Tesser argues that the impact of social comparison information on a person's self-esteem is mediated by the "relevance" of the underlying performance dimension to the person's self-definition. Thus, performing better or worse than another on a high-relevance dimension has greater impact on self-esteem than the same performance on a low-relevance dimension. Although not dealing explicitly with social comparison, Darley and Goethals (1980) also stress the need to clarify the dimensions underlying self-esteem. They assert that most people typically have high self-esteem, but differ in regard to the specific abilities or characteristics they feel they possess. This variability in "claimed abilities" means that persons who believe they have the specific abilities assessed by standard self-esteem scales receive high self-esteem scores, whereas others whose self-perceived abilities are not measured by the scales receive low scores. From these assumptions, Darley and Goethals conclude that "it would be more important to map the scope of a person's ability claims rather than to measure some generalized notion of self-esteem" (p. 34). Such a strategy would seem useful in investigating the potentially complex relationships between self-esteem and achievement in school settings.

Another question related to the issue of how comparison information influences achievement striving concerns the circumstances under which low-performing students (a) become discouraged about their ability and "give up" or (b) seek to emulate their higher-performing peers and learn from them. This question underlies much of the controversy regarding the advantages and disadvantages of desegregation and ability grouping for black and low-ability students, respectively. According to Richer (1976), giving up occurs when higher performing peers are taken as a "comparative" reference group, whereas emulation occurs when these peers are taken as a "normative" reference group. Richer goes on to argue that, when higher performing peers are visible and meaningful, "the greater the perceived possibility of upward mobility, the more likely positive normative reference-group behavior, and the less likely comparative selection resulting in relative deprivation" (p. 69). Thus, Richer suggests that students' perceived inferiority can have either positive or negative consequences for their achievement striving, depending on the degree to which students perceive that status mobility (presumably mediated by academic achievement) is possible (cf. Tajfel, 1979).

Finally, the relationship between relative performance and aspiration level might be mentioned. Although negative performance information may sometimes reduce aspiration to such a low level that challenging tasks are avoided and learning is retarded, it is not clear that a relatively low aspiration level is always harmful. For example, do we really want all children, regardless of ability, to have a high aspiration level for academic performance? How long will low-ability children be able to sustain these aspirations, and how will they react when performance and aspiration diverge? Is the increased effort really worth the dashed hopes? If we decide that low aspiration is only *sometimes* detrimental, a good deal of thought must be given to defining "appropriate" aspiration levels for children of varying ages and abilities. (See Janoff-Bulman and Brickman, 1982, for a thoughtful discussion of the costs of task persistence when performance expectations are unrealistically high.)

On the positive side, social comparison would seem to have two major potential benefits. First, to the extent that self-evaluation is desired, comparison can provide information that is not obtainable in any other manner. This information may be valuable, not only for assessing current performance, but perhaps even more importantly for allowing selection of future tasks that are within one's level of competence. Thus, obtaining self-evaluation of an ability that is known to be predictive of success in a particular domain can be helpful in deciding whether to invest time and effort in that domain. In addition, observing the performance of a similar peer on a novel task can provide information regarding whether one should attempt the task. Second, comparison information may be useful in sustaining motivation. No matter what one's level of performance, higher-performing comparison agents can usually be identified and, through explicit or implicit competition, can increase one's effort (Suls & Sanders, 1979). (It should be noted that Festinger, 1954, viewed competition as an outgrowth of self-evaluation motivation, based on the interaction of desire for a similar comparison agent and desire for continually increasing performance.)

In summary, it would seem that social comparison can be both beneficial and detrimental in school settings. As with many other social behaviors (e.g., conformity, aggression, competition), commentators often forget the adaptive significance of the behavior and decry it as evil because one or more of its manifestations is offensive. Clearly, value judgments cannot be avoided when one is making prescriptive statements about how schools should be organized and the kinds of intellectual and social behaviors that schools should encourage. Because of the potentially important consequences of such prescriptive statements, educators must examine carefully their ultimate educational goals and the risks as well as benefits of various means to achieve these goals. If this is done in an open-minded fashion, it seems likely that social comparison will emerge as a useful means for promoting certain educational goals.

ACKNOWLEDGMENT

Preparation of this chapter was supported by funds from the National Institute of Education to the Learning Research and Development Center at the University of Pittsburgh. Thanks are extended to Phil Brickman, Bill Francis, Diane Ruble, and Jerry Suls for their helpful comments on an earlier draft of this paper.

REFERENCES

Albert, S. Temporal comparison theory. *Psychological Review,* 1977, *84,* 485–503.
Allen, V. L., & Wilder, D. A. Social comparison, self-evaluation, and conformity to the group. In J. M. Suls & R. L. Miller (Eds.), *Social comparison processes: Theoretical and empirical perspectives.* Washington, D.C.: Hemisphere, 1977.
Ames, C. Children's achievement attributions and self-reinforcement: Effects of self-concept and competitive reward structure. *Journal of Educational Psychology,* 1978, *70,* 345–355.
Ames, C., Ames, R., & Felker, D. W. Effects of competitive reward structure and valence of outcome on children's achievement attributions. *Journal of Educational Psychology,* 1977, *69,* 1–8.
Anderson, H. H., & Brandt, H. F. A study of motivation involving self-announced goals of fifth-grade children and the concept of level of aspiration. *Journal of Social Psychology,* 1939, *10,* 209–232.
Anderson, N. H. Cognitive algebra: Integration theory applied to social attribution. In L. Berkowitz (Ed.), *Advances in experimental social psychology* (Vol. 7). New York: Academic Press, 1974.
Aronson, E., & Osherow, N. Cooperation, prosocial behavior, and academic performance: Experiments in the desegregated classroom. In L. Bickman (Ed.), *Applied social psychology annual* (Vol. 1). Beverly Hills, Calif.: Sage, 1980.
Bachman, J. G., & O'Malley, P. M. Self-esteem in young men: A longitudinal analysis of the impact of educational and occupational attainment. *Journal of Personality and Social Psychology,* 1977, *35,* 365–380.
Boggiano, A. K., & Ruble, D. N. Competence and the overjustification effect: A developmental study. *Journal of Personality and Social Psychology,* 1979, *37,* 1462–1468.
Bossert, S. T. *Tasks and social relationships in classrooms: A study of instructional organization and its consequences.* ASA Arnold and Caroline Rose Monograph Series. Cambridge: Cambridge University Press, 1979.
Brickman, P., & Berman, J. J. Effects of performance expectancy and outcome certainty on interest in social comparison. *Journal of Experimental Social Psychology,* 1971, *7,* 600–609.

Brickman, P., & Bulman, R. J. Pleasure and pain in social comparison. In J. M. Suls & R. L. Miller (Eds.), *Social comparison processes: Theoretical and empirical perspectives.* Washington, D.C.: Hemisphere, 1977.

Brown, I., & Inouye, D. K. Learned helplessness through modeling: The role of perceived similarity in competence. *Journal of Personality and Social Psychology,* 1978, *36,* 900-908.

Bryan, T. H., & Bryan, J. H. Some personal and social experiences of learning disabled children. In B. Keogh (Ed.), *Advances in special education* (Vol. 3). Greenwich, Conn.: JAI Press, in press.

Byrne, D. *The attraction paradigm.* New York: Academic Press, 1971.

Carter, D. E., DeTine, S. L., Spero, J., & Benson, F. W. Peer acceptance and school-related variables in an integrated junior high school. *Journal of Educational Psychology,* 1975, *67,* 267-273.

Carver, C. S. A cybernetic model of self-attention processes. *Journal of Personality and Social Psychology,* 1979, *37,* 1251-1281.

Chapman, D. W., & Volkman, J. A. A social determinant of the level of aspiration. *Journal of Abnormal and Social Psychology,* 1939, *34,* 225-238.

Conolley, E. S., Gerard, H. B., & Kline, T. Competitive behavior: A manifestation of motivation for ability comparison. *Journal of Experimental Social Psychology,* 1978, *14,* 123-131.

Covington, M. V., & Omelich, C. L. Are causal attributions causal? A path analysis of the cognitive model of achievement motivation. *Journal of Personality and Social Psychology,* 1979, *37,* 1487-1504.

Crockenberg, S., & Bryant, B. Socialization: The "implicit curriculum" of learning environments. *Journal of Research and Development in Education,* 1978, *12,* 69-78.

Crockenberg, S. B., Bryant, B. K., & Wilce, L. S. The effects of cooperatively and competitively structured learning environments on inter- and intrapersonal behavior. *Child Development,* 1976, *47,* 386-396.

Darley, J. M., & Goethals, G. R. People's analyses of the causes of ability-linked performances. In L. Berkowitz (Ed.), *Advances in experimental social psychology,* (Vol. 13). New York: Academic Press, 1980.

Davis, J. A. The campus as a frog pond: An application of the theory of relative deprivation to career decisions of college men. *American Journal of Sociology,* 1966, *72,* 17-31.

Dreyer, A. Aspiration behavior as influenced by expectation and group comparison. *Human Relations,* 1954, *7,* 175-190.

Drury, D. W. Black self-esteem and desegregated schools. *Sociology of Education,* 1980, *53,* 88-103.

Fazio, R. Motives for social comparison: The construction-validation distinction. *Journal of Personality and Social Psychology,* 1979, *37,* 1683-1698.

Feldman, N. S., & Ruble, D. N. Awareness of social comparison interest and motivations: A developmental study. *Journal of Educational Psychology,* 1977, *69,* 579-585.

Feldman, N. S., & Ruble, D. N. Social comparison strategies: Dimensions offered and options taken. *Personality and Social Psychology Bulletin,* 1981, *7,* 11-16.

Festinger, L. A theory of social comparison processes. *Human Relations,* 1954, *7,* 117-140.

Fishbein, M., Raven, B. H., & Hunter, R. Social comparison and dissonance reduction in self-evaluation. *Journal of Abnormal and Social Psychology,* 1963, *67,* 491-501.

Fisher, L. Peer judgment of competence in junior high school classrooms. *Developmental Psychology,* 1978, *14,* 187-188.

Fontaine, G. Social comparison and some determinants of expected personal control and expected performance in a novel task situation. *Journal of Personality and Social Psychology,* 1974, *29,* 487-496.

Gastorf, J. W., & Suls, J. Performance evaluation via social comparison: Performance similarity versus related-attribute similarity. *Social Psychology,* 1978, *41,* 297-305.

Gerard, H. B. Some determinants of self-evaluation. *Journal of Abnormal and Social Psychology,* 1961, *62,* 288-293.

Gergen, K. J. *The concept of self.* New York: Holt, Rinehart, & Winston, 1971.

Goethals, G. R., & Darley, J. M. Social comparison theory: An attributional approach. In J. M. Suls & R. L. Miller (Eds.), *Social comparison processes: Theoretical and empirical perspectives.* Washington, D.C.: Hemisphere, 1977.

Gottlieb, J., & Leyser, Y. Friendship between mentally retarded and nonretarded children. In S. R. Asher & J. M. Gottman (Eds.), *The development of children's friendships.* Cambridge: Cambridge University Press, 1981.

Gottlieb, J., Semmel, M. I., & Veldman, D. J. Correlates of social status among mainstreamed mentally retarded children. *Journal of Educational Psychology,* 1978, *70,* 396-405.

Gruder, C. L. Choice of comparison persons in evaluating oneself. In J. M. Suls & R. L. Miller (Eds.), *Social comparison processes: Theoretical and empirical perspectives.* Washington, D.C.: Hemisphere, 1977.

Hake, D. F., Vukelich, R., & Kaplan, S. J. Audit responses: Responses maintained by access to existing self or coactor scores during non-social, parallel work, and cooperation procedures. *Journal of the Experimental Analysis of Behavior,* 1973, *19,* 409-423.

Halisch, F., & Heckhausen, H. Search for feedback information and effort regulation during task performance. *Journal of Personality and Social Psychology,* 1977, *35,* 724-733.

Hallinan, M. T. Recent advances in sociometry. In S. R. Asher & J. M. Gottman (Eds.), *The development of children's friendships.* Cambridge: Cambridge University Press, 1981.

Hartup, W. W. Peer interaction and social organization. In P. Mussen (Ed.), *Carmichael's manual of child psychology* (3rd ed., Vol. 2). New York: Wiley, 1970.

Harvey, J. H., Cacioppo, J. T., & Yasuna, A. Temporal pattern of social information and self-attribution of ability. *Journal of Personality,* 1977, *45,* 281-296.

Harvey, J. H., & Kelley, D. R. Effects of attitude-similarity and success–failure upon attitude toward other persons. *Journal of Social Psychology,* 1973, *90,* 105-114.

Harvey, J. H., & Smith, W. P. *Social psychology: An attributional approach.* St. Louis: C. V. Mosby, 1977.

Hechinger, G., & Hechinger, F. M. Remember when they gave A's and D's? *New York Times Magazine,* May 5, 1974, pp. 84, 86, 92.

Hoffman, P. J., Festinger, L., & Lawrence, D. H. Tendencies toward group comparability in competitive bargaining. *Human Relations,* 1954, *7,* 141-159.

Hook, J. G., & Cook, T. D. Equity theory and the cognitive ability of children. *Psychological Bulletin,* 1979, *86,* 429-445.

Hyman, H. H., & Singer, E. (Eds.). *Readings in reference group theory and research.* New York: Free Press, 1968.

Israel, J. *Self evaluation and rejection in groups: Three experimental studies and a conceptual outline.* Stockholm: Almqvist and Wiksell, 1956.

Janoff-Bulman, R., & Brickman, P. Expectations and what people learn from failure. In N. T. Feather (Ed.), *Expectancy, incentive, and action.* Hillsdale, N.J.: Lawrence Erlbaum Associates, 1982.

Johnson, D. W., & Johnson, R. T. Cooperative, competitive, and individualistic learning. *Journal of Research and Development in Education,* 1978, *12,* 3-15.

Jones, S. C., & Regan, D. T. Ability evaluation through social comparison. *Journal of Experimental Social Psychology,* 1974, *10,* 133-146.

Kassin, S. Consensus information, prediction, and causal attributions: A review of the literature and issues. *Journal of Personality and Social Psychology,* 1979, *37,* 1966-1981.

Kaufman, M. J., Gottlieb, J., Agard, J. A., & Kukic, M. B. Mainstreaming: Toward an explication of the construct. In E. Meyen, G. Vergason, & R. Whelan (Eds.), *Alternatives for teaching exceptional children: Essays from Focus on Exceptional Children.* Denver: Love, 1975.

Kennedy, J., & Stephan, W. G. The effect of cooperation and competition on ingroup-outgroup bias. *Journal of Applied Social Psychology*, 1977, *7*, 115-130.

Latane, B. (Ed.). Studies in social comparison. *Journal of Experimental Social Psychology*, 1966, Supplement 1.

Lerner, M. J. The effect of responsibility and choice on a partner's attractiveness following failure. *Journal of Personality*, 1965, *33*, 178-187.

Levine, J. M., Snyder, H. N., & Mendez-Caratini, G. Task performance and interpersonal attraction in children. *Child Development*, 1982, *53*, 359-371.

Lott, A. J., & Lott, B. E. Group cohesiveness as interpersonal attraction: A review of relationships with antecedent and consequent variables. *Psychological Bulletin*, 1965, *64*, 259-309.

MacMillan, D. L., & Morrison, G. M. Correlates of social status among mildly handicapped learners in self-contained special classes. *Journal of Educational Psychology*, 1980, *72*, 437-444.

Martens, R., & White, V. Influence of win-loss ratio on performance, satisfaction and preference for opponents. *Journal of Experimental Social Psychology*, 1975, *11*, 343-362.

Maruyama, G., Rubin, R. A., & Kingsbury, G. G. Self-esteem and educational achievement: Independent constructs with a common cause? *Journal of Personality and Social Psychology*, 1981, *40*, 962-975.

Masters, J. C. Effects of social comparison upon children's self-reinforcement and altruism toward competitors and friends. *Developmental Psychology*, 1971, *5*, 64-72.

Masters, J. C. Effects of age and social comparison upon children's noncontingent self-reinforcement and the value of a reinforcer. *Child Development*, 1973, *44*, 111-116.

McClintock, C. G. Social values: Their definition, measurement, and development. *Journal of Research and Development in Education*, 1978, *12*, 121-137.

McClintock, C. G., & Van Avermaet, E. V. The effects of manipulating feedback upon children's motives and performance: A propositional statement and empirical evaluation. *Behavioral Science*, 1975, *20*, 101-116.

McMichael, P. Reading difficulties, behavior, and social status. *Journal of Educational Psychology*, 1980, *72*, 76-86.

Mettee, D. R., & Smith, G. Social comparison and interpersonal attraction: The case for dissimilarity. In J. M. Suls & R. L. Miller (Eds.), *Social comparison processes: Theoretical and empirical perspectives*. Washington, D.C.: Hemisphere, 1977.

Miller, R. L. Preferences for social vs. nonsocial comparison as a means of self-evaluation. *Journal of Personality*, 1977, *45*, 343-355.

Miller, R. L., & Suls, J. M. Affiliation preferences as a function of attitude and ability similarity. In J. M. Suls & R. L. Miller (Eds.), *Social comparison processes: Theoretical and empirical perspectives*. Washington, D.C.: Hemisphere, 1977.

Mithaug, D. E. The development of procedures for identifying competitive behavior in children. *Journal of Experimental Child Psychology*, 1973, *16*, 76-90.

Mosatche, H. S., & Bragonier, P. An observational study of social comparison in preschoolers. *Child Development*, 1981, *52*, 376-378.

Nicholls, J. Causal attributions and other achievement-related cognitions: Effects of task outcome, attainment value, and sex. *Journal of Personality and Social Psychology*, 1975, *31*, 379-389.

Nicholls, J. G. The development of the concepts of effort and ability, perception of academic attainment, and the understanding that difficult tasks require more ability. *Child Development*, 1978, *49*, 800-814.

Nicholls, J. G. Development of perception of own attainment and causal attributions for success and failure in reading. *Journal of Educational Psychology*, 1979, *71*, 94-99.

Pallak, S. S. *Attentional antecedents of social comparison processes.* Paper presented at the meeting of the American Psychological Association, Toronto, August 1978.

Pepitone, E. A. Comparison behavior in elementary school children. *American Educational Research Journal*, 1972, *9*, 45-63.

Pepitone, E. A. *Children in cooperation and competition: Toward a developmental social psychology.* Lexington, Mass.: Heath, 1980.

Pettigrew, T. F. Social evaluation theory: Convergences and applications. In D. Levine (Ed.), *Nebraska Symposium on Motivation* (Vol. 15). Lincoln: University of Nebraska Press, 1967.

Richer, S. Reference-group theory and ability grouping: A convergence of sociological theory and educational research. *Sociology of Education,* 1976, *49,* 65-71.

Rijsman, J. B. Factors in social comparison of performance influencing actual performance. *European Journal of Social Psychology,* 1974, *4,* 279-311.

Rogers, C. M., Smith, M. D., & Coleman, J. M. Social comparison in the classroom: The relationship between academic achievement and self-concept. *Journal of Educational Psychology,* 1978, *70,* 50-57.

Rosenbaum, J. E. Track misperceptions and frustrated college plans: An analysis of the effects of tracks and track perceptions in the national longitudinal survey. *Sociology of Education,* 1980, *53,* 74-88.

Rosenholtz, S. J., & Wilson, B. The effect of classroom structure on shared perceptions of ability. *American Educational Research Journal,* 1980, *17,* 75-82.

Ruble, D. N. A developmental perspective on theories of achievement motivation. In L. J. Fyans (Ed.), *Achievement motivation: Recent trends in theory and research.* New York: Plenum, 1980.

Ruble, D. N. The development of social comparison processes and their role in achievement-related self-socialization. In E. T. Higgins, D. N. Ruble, & W. W. Hartup (Eds.), *Developmental social cognition: A socio-cultural perspective.* Cambridge: Cambridge University Press, in press.

Ruble, D. N., & Boggiano, A. K. Optimizing motivation in an achievement context. In B. Keogh (Ed.), *Advances in special education: Basic constructs and theoretical orientations* (Vol. 1). Greenwich, Conn.: JAI Press, 1980.

Ruble, D. N., Boggiano, A. K., Feldman, N. S., & Loebl, J. H. Developmental analysis of the role of social comparison in self-evaluation. *Developmental Psychology,* 1980, *16,* 105-115.

Ruble, D. N., Feldman, N. S., & Boggiano, A. K. Social comparison between young children in achievement situations. *Developmental Psychology,* 1976, *12,* 192-197.

Ruble, D. N., Parsons, J. E., & Ross, J. Self-evaluative responses of children in an achievement setting. *Child Development,* 1976, *47,* 990-997.

Sanders, G. S., Gastorf, J. W., & Mullen, B. Selectivity in the use of social comparison information. *Personality and Social Psychology Bulletin,* 1979, *5,* 377-380.

Santrock, J. W., Readdick, C. A., & Pollard, L. Social comparison processes in sibling and peer relations. *The Journal of Genetic Psychology,* 1980, *137,* 91-107.

Santrock, J. W., & Ross, M. Effects of social comparison on facilitative self-control in young children. *Journal of Educational Psychology,* 1975, *67,* 193-197.

Santrock, J. W., Smith, P. C., & Bourbeau, P. E. Effects of social comparison on aggression and regression in groups of young children. *Child Development,* 1976, *47,* 831-837.

Scheirer, M. A., & Kraut, R. E. Increasing educational achievement via self-concept change. *Review of Educational Research,* 1979, *49,* 131-150.

Schofield, J. W., & Sagar, H. A. The social context of learning in an interracial school. In R. Rist (Ed.), *Desegregated schools: Appraisals of an American experiment.* New York: Academic Press, 1979.

Schwartz, J. M., & Smith, W. P. Social comparison and the influence of ability difference. *Journal of Personality and Social Psychology,* 1976, *34,* 1268-1275.

Senn, D. J. Attraction as a function of similarity–dissimilarity in task performance. *Journal of Personality and Social Psychology,* 1971, *18,* 120-123.

Shavelson, R. J., & Stuart, K. R. Application of causal modeling methods to the validation of self-concept interpretations of test scores. In M. D. Lynch, A. A. Norem-Hebeisen, & K. J. Gergen (Eds.), *Self-concept: Advances in theory and research.* Cambridge, Mass.: Ballinger, 1981.

Simpson, C. Classroom structure and the organization of ability. *Sociology of Education*, 1981, *54*, 120–132.

Slavin, R. E. Cooperative learning. *Review of Educational Research*, 1980, *50*, 315–342.

Smith, M. D. *Affective reactions to academic outcomes: A social comparison perspective*. Paper presented at the annual meeting of the American Psychological Association, Montreal, September 1980.

Snyder, M. L., Stephan, W. G., & Rosenfield, D. Egotism and attribution. *Journal of Personality and Social Psychology*, 1976, *33*, 435–441.

Spear, P. S., & Armstrong, S. Effects of performance expectancies created by peer comparison as related to social reinforcement, task difficulty, and age of child. *Journal of Experimental Child Psychology*, 1978, *25*, 254–266.

Stephan, C., Burnam, M. A., & Aronson, E. Attributions for success and failure after cooperation, competition, or team competition. *European Journal of Social Psychology*, 1979, *9*, 109–114.

Stephan, C., Kennedy, J. C., & Aronson, E. The effects of friendship and outcome on task attribution. *Sociometry*, 1977, *40*, 107–112.

Stipek, D. J. Children's perceptions of their own and their classmates' ability. *Journal of Educational Psychology*, 1981, *73*, 404–410.

Strang, L., Smith, M. D., & Rogers, C. M. Social comparison, multiple reference groups, and the self-concepts of academically handicapped children before and after mainstreaming. *Journal of Educational Psychology*, 1978, *70*, 487–497.

Suls, J., Gaes, G., & Gastorf, J. Evaluating a sex-related ability: Comparison with same-, opposite-, and combined-sex norms. *Journal of Research in Personality*, 1979, *13*, 294–304.

Suls, J., Gastorf, J., & Lawhon, J. Social comparison choices for evaluating a sex- and age-related ability. *Personality and Social Psychology Bulletin*, 1978, *4*, 102–105.

Suls, J. M., & Miller, R. L. (Eds.). *Social comparison processes: Theoretical and empirical perspectives*. Washington, D.C.: Hemisphere, 1977.

Suls, J. M., & Mullen, B. From the cradle to the grave: Comparison and self-evaluation across the life-span. In J. M. Suls (Ed.), *Social psychological perspectives on the self*. Hillsdale, N.J.: Lawrence Erlbaum Associates, 1982.

Suls, J., & Sanders, G. S. Social comparison processes in the young child. *Journal of Research and Development in Education*, 1979, *13*, 79–89.

Suls, J. M., & Tesch, F. Students' preferences for information about their test performance: A social comparison study. *Journal of Applied Social Psychology*, 1978, *8*, 189–197.

Swingle, P. G. Effects of the win-loss ratio and challenge on speed in a two-person lever-pressing race. *Journal of Experimental Psychology*, 1969, *80*, 542–547.

Tajfel, H. (Ed.). *Differentiation between social groups: Studies in the social psychology of intergroup relations*. London: Academic Press, 1979.

Tesser, A. Self-esteem maintenance in family dynamics. *Journal of Personality and Social Psychology*, 1980, *39*, 77–91.

Tesser, A., & Campbell, J. Self-definition: The impact of the relative performance and similarity of others. *Social Psychology Quarterly*, 1980, *43*, 341–347.

Thornton, D. A., & Arrowood, A. J. Self-evaluation, self-enhancement, and the locus of social comparison. *Journal of Experimental Social Psychology*, 1966, Supplement 1, 40–48.

Toda, M., Shinotsuka, H., McClintock, C. G., & Stech, F. J. Development of competitive behavior as a function of culture, age, and social comparison. *Journal of Personality and Social Psychology*, 1978, *36*, 825–829.

Trope, Y. Uncertainty-reducing properties of achievement tasks. *Journal of Personality and Social Psychology*, 1979, *37*, 1505–1518.

Veroff, J. Social comparison and the development of achievement motivation. In C. P. Smith (Ed.), *Achievement-related motives in children*. New York: Sage, 1969.

Veroff, J. Social motivation. *American Behavioral Scientist*, 1978, *21*, 709–730.

Vreven, R., & Nuttin, J. R. Frequency perception of successes as a function of results previously obtained by others and by oneself. *Journal of Personality and Social Psychology,* 1976, *34,* 734-745.

Vukelich, R., & Hake, D. F. Effects of the difference between self and coactor scores upon the audit responses that allow access to these scores. *Journal of the Experimental Analysis of Behavior,* 1974, *22,* 61-71.

Weiner, B. A theory of motivation for some classroom experiences. *Journal of Educational Psychology,* 1979, *71,* 3-25.

Wells, L. E., & Marwell, G. *Self esteem: Its conceptualization and measurement.* Beverly Hills, Calif.: Sage, 1976.

Wilson, S. R., & Benner, L. A. The effects of self-esteem and situation upon comparison choices during ability evaluation. *Sociometry,* 1971, *34,* 381-397.

Wortman, C. B., Costanzo, P. R., & Witt, T. R. Effect of anticipated performance on the attributions of causality to self and others. *Journal of Personality and Social Psychology,* 1973, *27,* 372-381.

Wylie, R. C. *The self-concept: A review of methodological considerations and measuring instruments* (Vol. 1, Rev. ed.). Lincoln: University of Nebraska Press, 1974.

Wylie, R. C. *The self-concept: Theory and research on selected topics* (Vol. 2, Rev. ed.). Lincoln: University of Nebraska Press, 1979.

Zuckerman, M., Brown, R. H., Fischler, G. L., Fox, G. A., Lathin, D. R., & Minasian, A. J. Determinants of information-seeking behavior. *Journal of Research in Personality,* 1979, *13,* 161-174.

3 Speculations Regarding the Role of Affect in Achievement-Change Programs Guided by Attributional Principles

Bernard Weiner
University of California, Los Angeles

There is a growing interest in the creation of achievement-change programs based on attributional principles (e.g., Andrews & Debus, 1978; Chapin & Dyck, 1976; Dweck, 1975; Sparta, 1978; Zoeller, 1979). An attributional approach to achievement change begins with the assumption that the perception of why an event has occurred is an important determinant of subsequent action. If this assumption is correct, then it logically follows that a modification in causal perceptions should produce a change in action. Attribution change attempts in the achievement domain have been implicitly guided by this reasoning. There is a focus on altering the perceived causes of failure in the expectation that this also will change (enhance) achievement strivings. At times there also is expressed consideration about the causal ascription for success (e.g., Andrews & Debus, 1978; Chapin & Dyck, 1976), but this is relatively rare and is ignored in the following discussion.

The question then raised concerns "*from* what *to* what," that is, what attribution(s) is impairing achievement striving and what attribution(s) will be beneficial. Identification of the debilitating ascription is not settled: It is believed to be either any external attribution for failure, such as bad luck or powerful others, or an ascription of failure to low ability. On the other hand, there is general consensus that lack of sufficient effort expenditure is the most adaptive attribution for failure. Hence, achievement-change programs based on attributional principles attempt to change external and/or low ability attributions for failure to a lack of effort ascription. For economy of space and conceptual clarity the following discussion is confined to lack of ability as the ascription to be altered, although the analysis would not essentially differ if the ascription to be changed were an external factor.

TABLE 3.1
Ability and Effort Ascriptions Related to
Causal Dimensions

Causal Dimensions	Causes	
	Ability	Effort
Locus	Internal	Internal
Stability	Stable	Unstable
Controllability	Uncontrollable	Controllable

To distinguish functional from dysfunctional qualities of an attribution requires a specification of the underlying properties of causes, or what has been
called "causal dimensions" (Weiner, 1979). Three such dimensions have been
identified: locus (whether the cause resides within, or is external to, the actor);
stability (whether the cause is relatively constant or varies over time); and controllability (the degree to which the cause is subject to personal influence). Table
3.1 compares the ability and effort attributions on these three dimensions of
causality. Concerning locus, the table indicates that both ability and effort are
conceived as internal to the actor. However, ability (aptitude) is relatively stable
and is not under volitional control, whereas effort is perceived as unstable and
controllable. The ability versus effort ascriptions therefore differ on two dimensions of causality.

Relative placement on these two dimensions of causality has far-reaching
psychological consequences. Perceived stability of a cause relates to the expectancy of future success and failure. If failure is ascribed to a stable cause, such as
lack of ability, then failure again will be anticipated. Conversely, effort is unstable and can fluctuate from one achievement episode to the next. Thus, ascription of failure to a lack of effort need not imply that future failures will follow,
for effort expenditure can be augmented (see review in Weiner, 1979).

The perceived controllability of a cause also influences expectancy of success
and failure (Chapin & Dyck, 1976; Seligman, 1975). If failure is ascribed to
controllable factors, then an experienced negative outcome might be subject to
future change. Although investigators with a learned helplessness perspective
have not been clear on this matter, it appears that ascription to an uncontrollable
cause may or may not lower future expectancies of success, depending on the
stability of the cause (e.g., both luck and ability are uncontrollable, but luck is
perceived as unstable whereas ability is viewed as stable). Perceptions of a lack
of control additionally are thought to give rise to a state labeled "helplessness"
(Seligman, 1975). Hence, attributions to an uncontrollable cause such as lack of
ability are not only associated with a low expectancy of success, but also relate to
the subsequent effects of a helpless belief system. On the other hand, attributions
to a lack of effort intimate that there is response-outcome covariation. One
succeeds when one has tried and fails when one has not tried. Feelings of

helplessness therefore are not anticipated given lack of effort attributions for failure (Dweck, 1975; Seligman, 1975).

In sum, achievement-change programs are designed to alter attributions for failure from low ability to a lack of effort. In so doing, expectancy of success is more likely to be maintained at a relatively high level and feelings of helplessness are not evoked. Low expectancy of success and helplessness, which are associated with lack of ability ascriptions, are hypothesized to retard achievement strivings, whereas high expectations of success and feelings of control are believed to aid performance. These attribution-consequent linkages are schematically shown in Diagram 3.1.

Diagram 3.1
Assumed attribution-consequent linkages in achievement-change programs

FROM

failure→ lack of ability ⟋ stable→ low expectancy ⟍ performance
⟍ uncontrollable→ helplessness ⟋ decrement

TO

failure→ insufficient ⟋ unstable→ high expectancy ⟍ performance
effort ⟍ controllable→ no helplessness ⟋ enhancement

A CONCEPTUAL PROBLEM

These analyses, which have implicitly governed much of the pertinent achievement-change research, and the confirmatory data, can be considered as supporting the attributional approach that my colleagues and I have advocated (Weiner, 1979). However, I now believe that the change analysis is inadequate. There is a complete disregard of any consideration of affect (although helplessness might be considered an affective state). This neglect is especially significant because attributions have been definitively shown to relate to affect (Weiner, Russell, & Lerman, 1978, 1979), and emotions are motivators of behavior (see Tomkins, 1963; Weiner, 1980a).

Let us consider the findings regarding attribution-affect linkages and then examine their implications for achievement-change attempts. In our initial study in the emotion area (Weiner et al., 1978), a dictionary list of approximately 250 potential affective reactions to success and failure was compiled. The dominant causal attributions for achievement performance also were identified. Then a cause for success or failure was given within a brief story format, the success- or failure-related affects that had been identified were listed, and the subjects reported the intensity of the affective reactions that they thought would be experienced in this situation. Responses were made on simple rating scales. A typical story was:

> Francis studied intensely for a test he took. It was very important for Francis to record a high score on this exam. Francis received an extremely high score on the test. Francis felt that he received this high score because he studied so intensely [his ability in this subject; he was lucky in which questions were selected; etc.]. How do you think Francis felt upon receiving this score? (Weiner et al., 1978, p. 10)

To overcome some of the shortcomings of this simulational and respondent experimental procedure, in a follow-up investigation (Weiner et al., 1979) the subjects reported a "critical incident" in which they actually succeeded or failed on an exam for a particular reason, such as help from others or lack of effort. They then recounted three affects that were experienced.

Both investigations yielded systematic and remarkably similar attribution-affect unions. Only the failure data given ability versus effort attributions are relevant to the present discussion. These data revealed that following failure ascribed to a lack of ability, subjects reported experiencing a feeling they labeled as *incompetence*. On the other hand, lack of effort attributions gave rise to feelings of *guilt* and *shame*.

It might be contended that feelings of incompetence impede achievement strivings, whereas feelings of guilt and shame generate renewed efforts. Hence, the observed prior effects of achievement-change procedures, which have been ascribed primarily to changes in the expectancy of success, could be explained as due to alterations in the affective state of the performer. This sequence is depicted in Diagram 3.2.

Diagram 3.2
Postulated attribution-affect-behavior sequence
in achievement-change programs

FROM
failure → lack of ability → feelings of incompetence → performance
decrement
TO
failure → lack of effort → guilt and shame → performance enhancement

A FAILURE AT RESOLUTION

It has been argued that interpretations of the effects of attributional change on achievement strivings are confounded. Two potential determinants of behavior, namely, expectancy and affect, both can be influenced by the attributional manipulation that has been employed. Hence, it is not possible to determine which of these factors is responsible (or, undoubtedly, *more* responsible) for the observation of relative increments in behavior when low ability ascriptions are altered to lack of effort attributions.

One way to aid in the resolution of this issue is to find related evidence that might support or contradict one or the other of the interpretations. Unfortunately, this search has not proven effective. Consider first the relation between affect and performance. There has been little concern with this issue in the achievement literature when excluding the emotion of anxiety. In opposition to my speculation that guilt and shame might augment effort, Atkinson (1964) has argued that anticipated shame impedes achievement strivings. Conversely, the proposed incompetence feelings-performance decrement linkage is consistent with the general belief that low self-esteem interferes with effective functioning. Yet the experimental literature separating the affective component of low self-esteem from the "cold" cognition of "I cannot" is nonexistent. As indicated previously, the only emotion research in the achievement domain related to task performance has involved anxiety. And the possible effects of anxiety are interactive with factors such as task difficulty, optimal level of motivation, specificity of the anxiety, and so forth.

Somewhat surprisingly, the effects of expectancy on performance are also unclear. Diagram 3.1 implies a linear and positive relation between expectancy and performance intensity. But Atkinson (1964) has contended that the relation between expectancy of success and aroused motivation is curvilinear, with intermediate expectancies maximizing performance for one sub-group of the population and minimizing performance for another sub-group. And Locke (1968) has provided evidence that the higher one's level of aspiration and the more difficult the task (that is, the lower the expectancy of success), the more intense is the performance. In sum, the simple hypothesis of "If high expectancy, then high performance intensity" has not been supported (also see Kukla, 1972).

To provide data that might be useful in disentangling the unresolved achievement-change issues, I would like to present some research findings from the domain of helping and altruism. Data from the helping domain are germane to this issue because one can test the cognition-affect-behavior model from the point of view of an observer (helper) just as readily as from the perspective of an actor (person striving to achieve success). In educational settings the "observer" is the teacher, the individual who helps students. To explain the teacher's helping behavior, it is essential to understand the teacher's perceptions of why the student is in need of aid and the teacher's affective reactions generated by the causal attributions. That is, the causal cognition-affect-behavior model that conceivably underlies achievement behavior also is assumed to be the foundation of helping behavior.

THE MOTIVATIONAL SEQUENCE

To answer the question of whether cognitions or affects function as motivators of action requires an understanding of the sequence in a motivational episode. Many behavioral sequences appear to be initiated following a causal ascription for an event. For example, in an achievement-related context, an individual may succeed at an exam. The success is then attributed to help from others, such as a classmate who lent him or her the class notes. Attribution of success to others gives rise to gratitude (Weiner et al., 1978, 1979) and seems likely to promote actions instrumental to the maintenance of the relationship, such as the purchase of a gift. In a similar manner, in an affiliative context, assume that an individual attempting to establish a dating relationship is rejected. This rebuff could be attributed to an aspect of the self, such as an aversive personality characteristic or an unbecoming physical appearance. A self-ascription for rejection engenders a number of negative esteem-related affects and "hurt feelings" (Folkes, in press) which, in turn, may initiate actions anticipated to be instrumental to the avoidance of these affects, such as not appearing at a party.

In the above scenarios, following the perception of an event a cognition (attribution)-emotion-action temporal sequence is suggested in which causal ascriptions produce affect (although there are other sources of affect; see Weiner et al., 1978, 1979), and this emotion, in turn, provides the motor and direction for behavior (Tomkins, 1963). Thus, a sequential organization between the tripartite division within psychology of thought, feeling, and action is proposed. Note that expectancy of success is ignored in this analysis, although the argument still is that affects are the motivators of action.

The postulated motivational ordering is examined here by analyzing a situation of help-giving first investigated by Piliavin, Rodin, and Piliavin (1969). In the study conducted by Piliavin et al., an individual (a confederate) falls in a subway. In one condition the confederate appears to be drunk (carrying a bottle and smelling of alcohol), while in a second condition he seems disabled (carrying a black cane). Piliavin et al. related bystander help to the perceived cause of falling and a number of other variables. For the present purposes, the two experimental conditions described above are the only ones of importance.

Guided by the proposed attribution-affect-action model of motivated behavior that I am advocating, it is presumed that the perception of an event (falling) gives rise to a search for causation (although this may be a secondary appraisal, following reflexive approach or avoidance reactions and a primary emotional reaction such as fear or startle; see Lazarus, 1966). The reasons for falling, in this case, are made evident by the experimental manipulations of drunkenness and illness (just as the experimenter directly manipulates effort feedback in the change-program studies). These attributions are then subject to further causal analysis, with the ascriptions placed within the causal dimensions shown in Table 3.1 that describe the basic properties of causes. In the present context, the controllability dimension seems to be of greatest importance. It is reasoned that illness is perceived as not subject to personal control, whereas the individual is believed to be personally responsible for being drunk. These opposing construals are hypothesized to give rise to differential affects, labeled here pity and sympathy (toward the ill person) and disgust and/or anger (toward the drunk). These affects, in turn, respectively beget approach versus avoidance behavior, or help versus neglect. Hence, the hypothesized sequence of motivated behavior is depicted as:

(observation from Piliavin et al.)

falling →   help (or neglect)

↘causal analysis → affect↗

(inference)

Other motivational sequences also may be hypothesized. For example, it might be presumed that a causal attribution gives rise to both affect and behavior so that thought (in other contexts, expectancy), rather than affect, is the immediate cause of action:

affect

falling → causal analysis ─⟨ behavior

Given this model, falling might be perceived, for example, as caused by an internally controllable cause, and this attribution generates both anger and neglect.

I have recently completed a series of six experiments investigating the motivational sequence in the Piliavin et al. setting (Weiner, 1980a). Presenting two of these studies will be sufficient to illustrate the point I want to make here.

Experiment I

In the initial study to be discussed, the situations created by Piliavin et al. were described and subjects merely reported what their feelings would be in those situations and judged the causal properties of drunkenness and illness. More specifically, the following scenarios were presented:

> At about 1:00 in the afternoon you are riding a subway car. There are a number of other individuals in the car and one person is standing, holding on to the center pole. Suddenly, this person staggers forward and collapses. The person is carrying a black cane and apparently is ill [or, the person apparently is drunk. He is carrying a liquor bottle in a brown paper bag and smells of liquor].

Subjects then read: "Try to assume that you actually are on the subway and try to imagine this scene. Describe your feelings in this situation." Three spaces were provided for affective descriptions.

The subjects then rated the causes of falling on the three dimensions of locus, stability, and controllability. The meaning of each dimension was elaborated with specific examples. The rating scales were anchored at the extremes with the poles of the dimensions (internal–external; permanent–temporary; controllable–uncontrollable) and were responded to immediately following each scenario and the emotional reports. For scoring purposes the scales were divided into nine equal intervals. The subjects were 40 male and female students at the University of California, Los Angeles, enrolled in introductory psychology classes.

Results and Discussion.   The 240 affects listed by the subjects (40 Ss × 2 causes × 3 affects) were classified into 13 categories, with a 94% inter-rater agreement. Table 3.2 shows the categories, the percentage of responses in each category, and the number of subjects giving a category response as their first reaction. The categories are labeled sympathy (e.g., pity, sorry), concern (concern and worry), negative affect toward the person (e.g., anger, disgust), general discomfort (e.g., embarrassed, upset), fear, caution, surprise, positive action (e.g., seek help), apathy, personal shortcomings (e.g., helpless, inadequate), information seeking (e.g., curious), description (e.g., a wino), and unclassified.

The largest difference between the drunk and the ill conditions involves negative affects toward the person. Twenty-seven percent of the responses elicited by the description of the drunk person were negative affects directed toward him, while such negativity characterized only 3% of the responses toward the ill individual. In addition, nearly one-third (13/40) of the subjects listed a negative emotion toward the drunk as their initial feeling, while this was not true in any instance given the ill person. Concerning the more positive outward-directed affective categories of sympathy and concern, there was a trend in the reverse direction, with 46% of the responses toward the sick individual being positive emotions (19 Ss indicated this as their initial feeling), while 30% of the emotional responses toward the drunk were positive emotions (14 persons stated this would be their first reaction). The difference between the positive and the negative affective reactions in the two causal conditions is highly significant. In addition, some of the responses were action-oriented rather than what is usually meant by feelings and emotions. Ten percent of the responses toward the ill person were help-related (positive action), while 1% implied apathy. Conversely, 2% of the responses toward the drunk were help-related, whereas 7% conveyed a lack of concern. Furthermore, the ratings of the three causal dimensions revealed that drunkenness was perceived as more controllable than illness.

In sum, the results of this experiment encouraged further pursuit of the belief that affects, as well as attributions, mediate judgments of help-giving. As anticipated, there was evidence that negative emotions such as disgust and anger were more likely to be experienced when exposed to the drunk individual, while positive emotions such as pity and sympathy were more likely to be experienced given the ill person. These other-directed emotions were stated as the initial

TABLE 3.2

Emotional Responses, Including All Reactions and Only the First Reaction for Each Subject

Affective Category

Cause	Sympathy	Concern	Negative Affect	Discomfort	Fear	Caution	Surprise
Ill	33% (14)[1]	13% (5)	3% (0)	6% (0)	10% (4)	6% (3)	7% (7)
Drunk	25% (13)	5% (1)	27% (13)	9% (3)	3% (0)	3% (2)	4% (3)

	Positive Action	Apathy	Personal Shortcomings	Information Seeking	Description	Unclass.
Ill	10% (2)	1% (1)	5% (0)	5% (3)	1% (1)	0% (0)
Drunk	2% (0)	7% (1)	1% (0)	4% (2)	6% (1)	4% (1)

[1]Written in parentheses are the numbers of subjects giving an emotion in the category as their initial response.

65

feeling by nearly 60% of the subjects. Furthermore, the causes differed in their degree of perceived controllability, or how responsible the person was perceived for the cause of falling: One is judged as personally responsible for being drunk, but not for being ill.

Experiment II

The experiment just reported suggested that drunkenness-controllability-anger-neglect and illness-no control-sympathy-help are linked. But it did not provide evidence concerning a motivational sequence. The second study to be reported addresses the sequence issue. The subjects were 28 male and female students enrolled in introductory psychology classes at the University of California, Los Angeles. They again were given the drunk and the ill scenarios in counterbalanced order. Following each scenario, the subjects rated the degree to which the cause was perceived as personally controllable (under personal control-not under personal control), their feelings of pity and sympathy (a great deal–none), their feelings of disgust and distaste (a great deal–none), and their likelihood of helping (definitely would aid–definitely would not aid). The order of the attribution and affect scales was counterbalanced so that one would not always immediately precede the helping judgments. For scoring purposes the scales were divided into nine equal intervals. It was thus possible to determine the relations between personal control, affect, and ratings of help in both the drunk and the ill conditions.

Results and Discussion.   Table 3.3 shows the correlations across both the drunk and the ill scenarios between perceptions of personal control, positive and negative outward-directed affects, the resultant of the positive minus the negative emotions, and judgments of help-giving. Because each subject made ratings in both the drunk and the ill conditions, Table 3.3 includes only the responses in the drunk condition of the 14 Ss judging the drunk individual first and the responses in the ill condition of the remaining 14 Ss judging the ill person first. When the

TABLE 3.3
Correlations between the Judgments of Control, Affect, and Help,
Including Both the Drunk and Ill Conditions

	Variables				
	Control	Sympathy (S)	Disgust (D)	S-D	Help
Control		-.77***	.55**	-.73***	-.37*
Sympathy (S)			-.64***	.90	.46**
Disgust (D)				-.91	-.71***
S-D					.65***

***p < .001
**p < .01
*p < .05

TABLE 3.4
Correlation of Variables With Judgments of Helping, Including Both
the Drunk and III Conditions, With Individual Variables
Statistically Partialled from the Analysis

Partialled Variable	Variables			
	Control	Sympathy (S)	Disgust (D)	S-D
None	-.37*	.46**	-.71***	.65***
Control		.30	-.66***	.60***
Sympathy (S)	-.02[1]		-.61***	
Disgust (D)	.04	.01		
S-D	.20			

***p < .001
**p < 01
*p < .05

[1]Indicates the correlation between perceptions of control and helping ratings, with sympathy ratings partialled out.

other one-half of the data for the 28 Ss are used in a separate (albeit not independent) analysis, there is a clear replication of the findings reported in Table 3.3.

Examination of Table 3.3 reveals that perceptions of personal control were negatively related to feelings of sympathy, positively related to feelings of disgust, and negatively related to judgments of help. That is, personal responsibility for falling was accompanied by the absence of positive affect, the presence of negative affect, and neglect. Furthermore, sympathy was positively related to judged help-giving, whereas disgust was negatively associated with judgments of help. In sum, Table 3.3 strongly supports the hypothesized linkages between (a) perceived lack of personal control, sympathy, and help and (b) perceived personal control, disgust, and neglect.

Further analyses were conducted in which attributions of personal control were related to ratings of help-giving with affects statistically held constant, and affects were related to helping judgments with personal control partialled out (see Table 3.4). This analysis will permit some inferences to be made about the sequence issue. Column 1 of Table 3.4 reveals that when sympathy and/or disgust are held constant, the correlation between personal control and judgments of help is no longer significant. On the otherhand, Row 2 of Table 3.4 shows that the correlations between disgust and help ratings, and between resultant affect (sympathy minus disgust) and help, are scarcely reduced with personal control statistically held constant. These findings are further elaborated with step-wise multiple regression analyses. These analyses indicate that resultant affect, by itself, contributes 42% to R^2, while the addition of personal control contributes only an additional 2% to the variance accounted for in the helping judgments. When personal control is entered as the first predictor, then it contributes 13% to R^2, while the addition of resultant affect accounts for another 31% of the variance. In sum, the affect variable independently contributes 31%, and attribution independently contributes 2%, to R^2, with 11% of the variance accounted for jointly by these two variables.

Table 3.4 also suggests that disgust is the more influential of the two affective ratings. However, this was the only effect not replicated using the second half of the data set, where sympathy and disgust emerged as equally strong correlates of the helping judgments. Thus, this finding is not considered further.

Correlations were then computed within the drunk and the ill conditions. Because of severe restrictions in range, it was anticipated that the correlations reported in Tables 3.3 and 3.4 would be reduced in magnitude. The upper half of Table 3.5 shows the correlations within the drunk condition, while the lower half of Table 3.5 reports the data within the ill condition. Examination of the judgments within the drunk condition reveals the identical pattern to that shown in Table 3.3, without the anticipated reduction in the magnitudes of the correlations. Personal control relates negatively with sympathy, positively to disgust, and negatively with helping judgments. In addition, sympathy relates positively, and disgust negatively, with helping ratings.

The partial correlations within the drunk condition also are consistent with the overall analyses and do not differ in magnitude from the data in Table 3.4 (see Table 3.6). With affective ratings held constant, causal attributions are only marginally related to judgments of help (see Column 1, Table 3.6). On the other hand, with personal control statistically held constant (Row 2, Table 3.6) the correlations between the affects and the helping ratings are only slightly reduced. Step-wise multiple regression analyses reveal that resultant affect, by itself, contributes 48% to R^2, while the addition of personal control accounts for no further variance. When control is entered as the first predictor, then it contributes 13% to R^2, while the addition of affect accounts for another 35% of the rating variance. In sum, affect independently contributes 35%, and personal control independently contributes nothing, to R^2, while these two variables share 13% of the variance in the helping ratings.

The lower half of Table 3.5 shows the correlations within the ill condition. It

TABLE 3.5
Correlations between Judgments of Control, Affect, and Help
Within the Drunk (Upper Half) and Illness (Lower Half) Conditions

	Variables				
	Control	Sympathy (S)	Disgust (D)	S-D	Help
Control		-.55**	.46*	-.55**	-.36
Sympathy (S)	-.53**		-.68***	.92	.61***
Disgust (D)	.15	-.17		-.91	-.67***
S-D	-.42*	.83	-.69		.69***
Help	-.12	.17	-.34	.32	

***p < .001
**p < .01
*p < .05

TABLE 3.6
Correlations of Variables With Judgments of Helping, In Only
the Drunk Condition, With Individual Variables
Statistically Partialled from the Analysis

Partialled Variable	Variables			
	Control	Sympathy (S)	Disgust (D)	S-D
None	-.36	.61***	-.67***	.69***
Control		.52**	-.60***	.63***
Sympathy (S)	-.04[1]		-.44**	
Disgust (D)	-.08	.27		
S-D	.03			

***p <.001
**p <.01
*p <.05

[1]Indicates the correlation between perceptions of control and helping ratings, with sympathy ratings partialled out.

is evident that these correlations are greatly reduced compared to those in Table 3.3, although the directions of the findings are consistent with what already has been reported. That is, helping judgments related negatively to personal control, positively with sympathy, and negatively to disgust. Furthermore, resultant affect uniquely contributes 9% to R^2, whereas personal control independently accounts for no additional variance, and the two variables jointly share 1% of the variance.

Analyses of the ratings over both conditions also revealed highly significant differences between the drunk and the ill individuals, with drunkenness perceived as more personally controllable, less provoking of sympathy, more evocative of disgust, and less likely to lead to help than illness (all p's < .0001). Hence, further evidence is provided that drunkenness is associated with personal control, disgust, and neglect, while illness is associated with lack of responsibility, sympathy, and help.

In sum, although the experiment presented was correlational, it lends strong support to the contention that there is a causal sequence of events in a motivational episode. Attributions tell us what to feel, and feelings tell us what to do.

BACK TO CHANGE PROGRAMS: THE SOCIAL PSYCHOLOGY OF EMOTION

Recall that this quest started with the contention that affects are ignored in achievement-change research. It has been clearly demonstrated that attributions do influence affect, so that if causal ascriptions for failure are altered from ability to effort, then the feelings that accompany failure also will be altered. Furthermore, in the helping domain, feelings rather than causal perceptions guide action. Perhaps this also is true in the achievement domain—feelings rather than cognitions, such as attributions and expectancies, could determine behavior.

Now I wish to pursue one further relation between help-giving, affect, and attributions. In the discussion of change programs, I conveyed how individuals might feel toward *themselves* given differential causal ascriptions. But the explanation of help-giving centered around how individuals feel toward *others* given differential attributions. It therefore might appear that two distinct areas of emotion have been merged, or confounded. These might be called the psychology of emotion and the social psychology of feelings. By the psychology of emotion I mean individuals' feelings toward themselves, while by social psychology of emotion I mean affect conveyed by one person toward another.

In change programs these branches of emotion make contact. Change programs do not occur in a social vacuum. The agents of change are people and their communications. What other individuals feel toward the actor, and what interpersonal affects are communicated and exhibited in action, are likely to influence the achievement strivings of the actor.

Consider, for example, the effects on a teacher given an ascription of a pupil's failure to a lack of effort. There is ample evidence that failure ascribed to a perceived lack of effort is especially punished. Indeed, in one of the very first experiments I conducted from an attributional perspective, in one condition students were described as failing at an academic task because of low effort and/or low ability (Weiner & Kukla, 1970). The data clearly revealed that failure due to insufficient effort was evaluated much more negatively than failure due to lack of ability.

The helping experiments just described also demonstrated that "failure" because of a controllable cause (drinking) results in anger and neglect. We have additionally found, with little surprise, that when a student requests to borrow the class notes because "he went to the beach," other students react with anger and refusal (Weiner, 1980b).

In sum, when failure is perceived as due to a controllable cause such as insufficient effort expenditure, anger and punishment from others are likely consequences. In addition, help will tend to be withheld. Individuals are well aware of these contingencies and realize the consequences that follow from a lack of effort ascriptions.

On the other hand, the helping investigations also indicated that "failure" due to a lack of "ability" elicits sympathy and help. In a similar manner, we have found that students are willing to lend their class notes and tend to convey sympathy when the notes are needed because the student had eye problems (Weiner, 1980b). Hence, when failure is due to an uncontrollable cause such as low ability, there is likely to be pity and sympathy and aid is given.

Table 3.7 summarizes the affective and behavioral consequences of ability and effort ascriptions for failure from the perspective of the actor (pupil, trainee) and the observer (teacher, trainer). When low ability is the causal ascription, the

TABLE 3.7
Affective and Behavioral Consequences Given Ability vs. Effort
Attributions from the Perspective of the Actor and the Observer

	Ability		Effort	
	Actor	Observer	Actor	Observer
Affect	incompetence	sympathy	guilt	anger
Behavior	low achievement strivings	help	high achievement strivings	neglect

student is thought to feel incompetent and receives sympathy; low achievement strivings are believed to be a consequence of feelings of incompetence, and help is given. This sounds very symbiotic. But paradoxically, communication of sympathy and help-giving might function as attributional cues to strengthen the actor's low ability self perception. In a recent television program the teacher of Helen Keller commanded to her parents: "The worst thing we can show her is pity." That is, she will use this affect to infer the absence of ability and give up self-responsibility.

Now consider lack of effort as the causal attribution. The actor is thought to feel guilty, anger is communicated from others, and there is neglect. Again paradoxically, these negative feelings and actions might have positive consequences for achievement behavior. The conveyance of anger and neglect might function as cues that the person has not tried, rather than that he or she is unable. Hence, a high-ability self-perception is maintained and the actor retains self-responsibility. In addition, there might be an increment in effort expenditure to avoid punishment from others.

Do I mean that personal guilt and anger from others will always enhance achievement strivings? Of course not—this depends on many factors, including the general affective climate in which these affects are embedded, whether help or neglect is instrumental to self-help, whether anger is reciprocated or leads to a focus on the task, and so on. What I primarily want to suggest is that the psychology of emotions and the social psychology of emotions have points of contact, and that self and other affective sources are likely to influence achievement-oriented behavior and play a hidden role in the effectiveness of achievement-change attempts.

We have recently initiated a program of research to examine the hypothesis that emotions from others function as attributional cues and that affects influence achievement behavior. Some of the investigations have been completed (see Weiner, Graham, Stern, & Lawson, in press), whereas others are still in progress. In one study, we asked our college subjects to pretend that they were observing a situation in which a child failed and a teacher displayed one of five affects: anger, pity, guilt, surprise, and sadness. We then asked a question of meta-inference: The subjects had to infer the teacher's inference about the cause of failure. Four attributional inferences were rated: ability, effort, teacher, and luck.

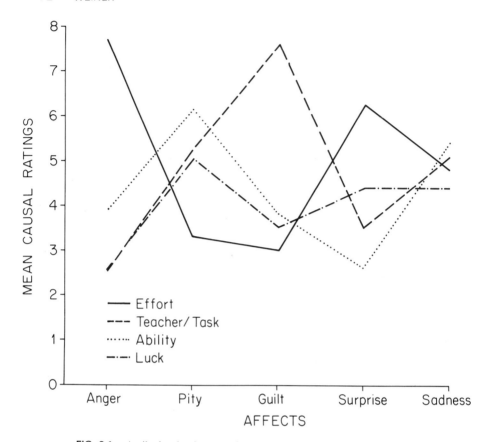

FIG. 3.1. Attributional ratings as a function of the displayed teacher affect.

The results were quite clear and are shown in Figure 3.1. The figure indicates that when the teacher feels anger, the teacher's inferred cause of failure is lack of effort; pity is related to lack of ability as the cause; guilt gives rise to the inference that the teacher was responsible for the failure; surprise relates to effort attributions; and sadness is weakly related to low ability ascriptions. In sum, it does appear that there are clear affective-attribution linkages. The questions we now want to pursue are: (1) are these affective displays processed and correctly labeled by the students? and (2) do the communicated affects influence the self-perceptions of the pupils, their self-directed affects, and, in turn, achievement-related behavior?

ACKNOWLEDGMENT

The research detailed in this chapter was supported by a grant from the Spencer Foundation.

REFERENCES

Andrews, G. R., & Debus, R. L. Persistence and causal perception of failure: Modifying cognitive attributions. *Journal of Educational Psychology,* 1978, *70,* 154-166.

Atkinson, J. W. *An introduction to motivation.* Princeton, N.J.: Van Nostrand, 1964.

Chapin, M., & Dyck, D. G. Persistence in children's reading behavior as a function of N length and attribution retraining. *Journal of Abnormal Psychology,* 1976, *85,* 511-515.

Dweck, C.S. The role of expectations and attributions in the alleviation of learned helplessness. *Journal of Personality and Social Psychology,* 1975, *31,* 674-685.

Folkes, V. S. Communicating the reasons for social rejection. *Journal of Experimental Social Psychology* (in press).

Kukla, A. Foundations of an attributional theory of performance. *Psychological Review,* 1972, *21,* 166-174.

Lazarus, R. S. *Psychological stress and the coping process.* New York: McGraw-Hill, 1966.

Locke, E. A. Toward a theory of task motivation and incentives. *Organizational Behavior and Human Performance,* 1968, *3,* 157-189.

Piliavin, I. M., Rodin, J., & Piliavin, J. A. Good Samaritanism: An underground phenomenon? *Journal of Personality and Social Psychology,* 1969, *13,* 289-299.

Seligman, M. E. P. *Helplessness.* San Francisco: Freeman, 1975.

Sparta, S. N. *Treatment of "helpless" children through cognitive interpretations of failure: An examination of some therapeutic influences.* Unpublished doctoral dissertation, University of California, Los Angeles, 1978.

Tomkins, S. S. *Affect imagery, consciousness* (Vol. II). *The negative affects.* New York: Springer, 1963.

Weiner, B. A theory of motivation for some classroom experiences. *Journal of Educational Psychology,* 1979, *71,* 3-25.

Weiner, B. A cognitive (attributional)-emotion-action model of motivated behavior: An analysis of judgments of help-giving. *Journal of Personality and Social Psychology,* 1980, *39,* 186-200. (a)

Weiner, B. May I borrow your class notes? An attributional analysis of judgments of help giving in an achievement-related context. *Journal of Educational Psychology,* 1980, *72,* 676-681. (b)

Weiner, B., Graham, S., Stern, P., & Lawson, M. E. Using affective cues to infer causal thoughts. *Developmental Psychology* (in press).

Weiner, B., & Kukla, A. An attributional analysis of achievement motivation. *Journal of Personality and Social Psychology,* 1970, *15,* 1-20.

Weiner, B., Russell, D., & Lerman, D. Affective consequences of causal ascriptions. In J. H. Harvey, W. J. Ickes, & R. F. Kidd (Eds.), *New directions in attribution research* (Vol. 2). Hillsdale, N.J.: Lawrence Erlbaum Associates, 1978.

Weiner, B., Russell, D., & Lerman, D. The cognition-emotion process in achievement-related contexts. *Journal of Personality and Social Psychology,* 1979, *37,* 1211-1220.

Zoeller, C. J. *An attribution training program with mentally retarded adults in a workshop setting.* Unpublished doctoral dissertation, University of California, Los Angeles, Calif., 1979.

4 Teachers' Thinking About Problem Students

Mary M. Rohrkemper
University of Maryland
Jere E. Brophy
Michigan State University

The data presented in this chapter came from a larger investigation, the Classroom Strategy Study (CSS), which is focused on teachers' thinking about, and strategies for coping with, 12 types of "problem" students (see Figure 4.1). These 12 types of "problem" or "difficult" students all concern, frustrate, or worry their teachers in some way. The 12 types are defined so as to be mutually exclusive, although the possibility that more than one problem type could coexist within a student is recognized. When dealing with such students who present multiple difficulties, however, teachers are able to discern separate behavior patterns and discuss them without difficulty. Thus, the CSS is focused on the following 12 types of problem students: instructional problems (failure syndrome, perfectionist, underachieving, and low-achieving students); aggression problems (hostile aggressive, passive aggressive, and defiant students); classroom adjustment problems (hyperactive, short attention span, and immature students); and peer relation difficulties (students who are rejected by their peers and shy/withdrawn students). (See Figure 4.1.)

The CSS is not an experiment, but rather a large scale, systematic gathering of self-report data from 98 experienced (i.e., at least 3 years of classroom teaching) elementary school teachers who are distributed roughly evenly across grades K through 6 and who teach in either the Lansing (N = 54) or the innercity Detroit (N = 44) schools. All teachers involved in the study (approximately 75% of those originally contacted) were nominated by their principals as either outstanding or average in their ability to deal with difficult students.

Data collection procedures were constant across all teachers and occurred in three phases: (1) two half-day observations; (2) a vignette interview which captured teachers' immediate responses to 24 descriptions of student problem be-

1. *Failure Syndrome.* These children are convinced that they cannot do the work. They often avoid starting or give up easily. They expect to fail, even after succeeding. Signs: easily frustrated; gives up easily; says "I can't do it."

2. *Perfectionist.* These children are unduly anxious about making mistakes. Their self-imposed standards are unrealistically high, so that they are never satisfied with their work (when they should be). Signs: too much of a "perfectionist"; often anxious/fearful/frustrated about quality of work; holds back from class participation unless sure of self.

3. *Underachiever.* These children do a minimum to just "get by." They do not value schoolwork. Signs: indifferent to schoolwork; minimum work output; not challenged by schoolwork; poorly motivated.

4. *Low Achiever.* These children have difficulty, even though they may be willing to work. Their problem is low potential or lack of readiness rather than poor motivation. Signs: difficulty following directions; difficulty completing work; poor retention; progresses slowly.

5. *Hostile Aggressive.* These children express hostility through direct, intense behaviors. They are not easily controlled. Signs: intimidates and threatens; hits and pushes; damages property; antagonizes; hostile; easily angered.

6. *Passive Aggressive.* These children express opposition and resistance to the teacher, but indirectly. It often is hard to tell whether they are resisting deliberately or not. Signs: subtly oppositional and stubborn; tries to control; borderline compliance with rules; mars property rather than damages; disrupts surreptitiously; drags feet.

7. *Defiant.* These children resist authority and carry on a power struggle with the teacher. They want to have their way and not be told what to do. Signs: (1) resists verbally; (a) "You can't make me..."; (b) "You can't tell me what to do..."; (c) makes derogatory statements about teacher to others; (2) resists nonverbally; (a) frowns, grimaces, mimics teacher; (b) arms folded, hands on hips, foot stomping; (c) looks away when being spoken to; (d) laughs at inappropriate times; (e) may be physically violent toward teacher; (f) deliberately does what teacher says not to do.

8. *Hyperactive.* These children show excessive and almost constant movement, even when sitting. Often their movements appear to be without purpose. Signs: squirms, wiggles, jiggles, scratches; easily excitable; blurts out answers and comments; often out of seat; bothers other children with noises, movements; energetic but poorly directed; excessively touches objects or people.

FIG. 4.1.   The 12 problem student types investigated in the Classroom Strategy Study.

9. *Short Attention Span/Distractible.* These children have short attention spans. They seem unable to sustain attention and concentration. Easily distracted by sounds, sights, or speech. Signs: has difficulty adjusting to changes; rarely completes tasks; easily distracted.

10. *Immature.* These children are immature. They have poorly developed emotional stability, self control, self care abilities, social skills, and/or responsibility. Signs: often exhibits behavior normal for younger children; may cry easily; loses belongings; frequently appears helpless, incompetent, and/or dependent.

11. *Rejected by Peers.* These children seek peer interaction but are rejected, ignored, or excluded. Signs: forced to work and play alone; lacks social skills; often picked on or teased.

12. *Shy/Withdrawn.* These children avoid personal interaction, are quiet and unobtrusive, and do not respond well to others. Signs: quiet and sober; does not initiate or volunteer; does not call attention to self.

continued

havior (two descriptions for each of the 12 types of problem students); and (3) a more reflective problem type interview in which teachers elaborated their general philosophies about and strategies for coping with each of the 12 types of problem students.

The second phase of the study, the vignette interview, is the source of the data discussed here. This involved presenting the teachers with a series of 24 vignettes, two for each of the 12 types of problem students previously mentioned (see Figure 4.2). The vignettes depicted classroom incidents in which students' actions (or failure to act) produced outcomes that teachers view as undesirable and that most teachers will try to alter by instructing or socializing the students involved. In addition, the incident depicted in each vignette is presented as only the latest in a series of similar incidents involving the same student. Thus, in each vignette a student presents the teacher with some problem that calls for teacher response, and the student is one who has presented similar problems many times before. The specific incident, then, is presented within the context of a chronic behavior problem involving the student in question.

Beyond this, however, the students depicted in the vignettes are identified only by sex (we felt this was necessary for realism). There is no direct mention of age, race, ethnicity, or social class, and no clues (direct quotes or other language data, pictures or drawings, etc.) that might suggest these status characteristics. This was done to allow teachers from various geographical locations and grade levels to imagine the depicted events as occurring in their own classrooms and as involving the kinds of students with whom they were most familiar. Also, this method allowed us to avoid confounding the behavioral characteristics of the

1. (Failure syndrome student, shared problem)
Joe could be a capable student, but his self-concept is so poor that he actually describes himself as stupid. He makes no serious effort to learn, shrugging off responsibility by saying that "that stuff" is too hard for him. Right now he is dawdling instead of getting started on an assignment that you know he can do. You know that if you approach him he will begin to complain that the assignment is too hard and that he can't do it.

2. (Hostile aggressive student, teacher-owned problem)
This morning, several students excitedly tell you that on the way to school they saw Tom beating up Sam and taking his lunch money. Tom is the class bully and has done things like this many times.

3. (Hyperactive student, shared problem)
Bill is an extremely active child. He seems to burst with energy, and today he is barely "keeping the lid on." This morning, the class is working on their art projects and Bill has been in and out of his seat frequently. Suddenly, Roger lets out a yell and you look up to see that Bill has knocked Roger's sculpture off his desk. Bill says he didn't mean to do it, he was just returning to his seat.

4. (Student rejected by peers, student-owned problem)
Mark is not well accepted by his classmates. Today he has been trying to get some of the other boys to play a particular game with him. After much pleading the boys decide to play the game, but exclude Mark. Mark argues, saying that he should get to play because it was his idea in the first place, but the boys start without him. Finally, Mark gives up and slinks off, rejected again.

5. (Perfectionist student, student-owned problem)
Beth has average ability for school work, but she is so anxious about the quality of her work that she seldom finishes an assignment because of all her "start overs." This morning you have asked the children to make pictures to decorate the room. The time allocated to art has almost run out and Beth is far from finished with her picture. You ask her about it and find out she has "made mistakes" on the other ones and this is her third attempt at a "good picture."

6. (Passive aggressive student, teacher-owned problem)
The class is about to begin a test. The room is quiet. Just as you are about to begin speaking, Audrey opens her desk. Her notebook slides off the desk, spilling loose papers on the floor. Audrey begins gathering up the papers, slowly and deliberately. All eyes are upon her. Audrey stops, grins, and then slowly resumes gathering papers. Someone laughs. Others start talking.

7. (Distractible student, shared problem)
George's attention wanders easily. Today it has been divided between the discussion and various distractions. You ask him a question, but he is distracted and doesn't hear you.

FIG. 4.2. Vignette instrument.

8. (Shy/withdrawn student, shared problem)
Linda is bright enough, but she is shy and withdrawn. She doesn't volunteer to participate in class, and when you call on her directly, she often does not respond. When she does, she usually whispers. Today, you are checking seatwork progress. When you question her, Linda keeps her eyes lowered and says nothing.

9. (Underachieving student, teacher-owned problem)
Carl can do good work, but he seldom does. He will try to get out of work. When you speak to him about this, he makes a show of looking serious and pledging reform, but his behavior doesn't change. Just now, you see a typical scene: Carl is making paper airplanes when he is supposed to be working.

10. (Defiant student, teacher-owned problem)
Roger has been fooling around instead of working on his seatwork for several days now. Finally, you tell him that he has to finish or stay in during recess and work on it then. He says, "I won't stay in!" and spends the rest of the period sulking. As the class begins to line up for recess, he quickly jumps up and heads for the door. You tell him that he has to stay inside and finish his assignment, but he just says "No, I don't!" and continues out the door to recess.

11. (Immature student, shared problem)
Betty seems younger than the other students in your class. She has difficulty getting along with them and is quick to tattle. She has just told you that she heard some of the boys use "bad words" during recess today.

12. (Low-achieving student, student-owned problem)
Jeff tries hard but is the lowest achiever in the class. This week you taught an important sequence of lessons. You spent a lot of extra time with Jeff and thought he understood the material. Today you are reviewing. All the other students answer your questions with ease, but when you call on Jeff he is obviously lost.

13. (Failure syndrome student, shared problem)
Mary has the intelligence to succeed, if she applied herself, but she is convinced that she can't handle it. She gets frustrated and disgusted very easily, and then she gives up. Instead of trying to solve the problem another way, or coming to you for help, she skips the problem and moves on. Today she brings you her assignment, claiming to be finished, but you see that she has skipped many items.

14. (Hostile aggressive student, teacher owned problem)
Class is disrupted by a scuffle. You look up to see that Ron has left his seat and gone to Phil's desk, where he is punching and shouting at Phil. Phil is not so much fighting back as trying to protect himself. You don't know how this started, but you do know that Phil gets along well with the other students but Ron often starts fights and arguments without provocation.

15. (Hyperactive student, shared problem)
Paul can't seem to keep his hands off the things and people in the room. He also

continued

seems to want to inspect or play with whatever is at hand. When he is not physically manipulating someone or something else, he hums, whistles, grimaces, drums his fingers, taps his feet, or makes other noises through physical activity. Just now he has discovered that one of the screws holding the back of his chair to its frame is loose, and he is pushing and pulling at the loose piece. In the process, he is further loosening the connection and at the same time distracting the class with the noise he is making.

16. (Student rejected by peers, student-owned problem)
Kathy is a loner in the classroom and an onlooker on the playground. No one willingly sits with her or plays with her. You divided the class into groups to work on projects, and those in Kathy's group are making unkind remarks about her, loud enough for all to hear.

17. (Perfectionist student, student-owned problem)
Chris is a capable student who is exceptionally anxious about making mistakes. He doesn't contribute to class discussions or recitation unless he is absolutely sure he is right. You recognize his anxiety and try to call on him only when you are reasonably sure he can handle it. When you do this today, he blanches and stumbles through an incorrect answer. He is clearly upset.

18. (Passive aggressive student, teacher-owned problem)
The class has just been given instructions to line up quickly. The students comply, with the exception of Jack, who is always the last to follow directions. Jack remains at his desk, working on a drawing. He looks up, in the direction of the line, then resumes work on his drawing.

19. (Distractible student, shared problem)
Sarah never seems to finish an assignment. She is easily distracted, and then isn't able to recapture what she had been thinking about before the interruption. You distribute a work sheet to the class, and the students, including Sarah, begin their work. After a couple of minutes you see that Sarah is looking out the window, distracted again.

20. (Shy/withdrawn student, shared problem)
John often seems to be off in his own world, but today he is watching you as you lead a discussion. Pleased to see him attentive, you ask him what he thinks. However, you have repeated his name and he looks startled when he realizes that you have called on him. Meanwhile, you realize that he has been immersed in daydreams and only appeared to be paying attention.

21. (Underachieving student, teacher-owned problem)
Nancy is oriented toward peers and social relationships, not school work. She could be doing top grade work, but instead she does just enough to get by. She is often chatting or writing notes when she is supposed to be paying attention or working. During today's lesson, she has repeatedly turned to students on each side of her to make remarks, and now she has a conversation going with several friends.

continued

22. (Defiant student, teacher-owned problem)

Squirt guns are not permitted in school. Scott has been squirting other students with his squirt gun. You tell him to bring the squirt gun to you. He refuses, saying that it is his and you have no right to it. You insist, but he remains defiant and starts to become upset. Judging from his past and present behavior, he is not going to surrender the squirt gun voluntarily.

23. (Immature student, student-owned problem)

Greg often loses his belongings, becomes upset, whines, and badgers you to help him. Now he has misplaced his hat, and he is pestering you again. Other students smirk and make remarks about this, and Greg becomes upset.

24. (Low-achieving student, student-owned problem)

Tim is a poor student. He has a low potential for school work and also lacks the basic experiences that help a child function in the classroom. You have just presented a new lesson to the class and have assigned related seatwork. You look over the class and see that Tim is upset. When you ask him if something is wrong, he tells you that he can't do it—it's too hard.

continued

depicted students with various status characteristics (other than sex) that might affect teachers' attributions or response strategies.

In the vignette interview, the teachers were asked to read each vignette and respond to the situation as if it had occurred in their classroom. Specifically, they were asked to state what they would say and do if this happened, tell why they would say and do this, and describe the student involved in their own words. These data presumably reflect teachers' responses to classroom incidents in which there are real consequences for themselves, for the student engaging in the problem behavior, and for the class as a whole, which both witnesses the event and vicariously experiences its effects. It follows that teachers' attributions about the depicted students should affect their sense of their own role as the teacher, which in turn should affect their response to the student, a response which has important implications for all concerned. This causal sequence apparently orders the data meaningfully, but it should be noted that the sequence is only assumed here, and not actually tested.

Also, although the teachers responded in their own words (no psycho-educational terms or jargon were introduced by the materials) and for as long as they desired to vignettes which had been pretested and revised several times to enhance realism and familiarity, the data are from self-report and not from actual classroom observation. We *assume*, then, that the teachers' attributions about self and student obtained from these vignettes reflect the same attributions that would be obtained in real life situations (c.f. Bar-Tal & Frieze, 1976; Fontaine, 1975; Frieze & LaVoie, 1972). This assumption is currently being examined directly through an examination of teacher vignette responses as they relate to observed classroom behavior.

CONCEPTUAL FRAMEWORK

In this chapter, linkages from teachers' attributions about the student to teachers' attributions about self to teachers' strategies and goals for the student are examined within the context of problem ownership and viewed as instances of helping behavior.

Problem Ownership

The notion of problem ownership has its origins in the parenting literature. Gordon (1970) posited that conflicts between parents and children can be subdivided into categories which reflect different types of need frustration. These categories, or levels, of "problem ownership" have been investigated in parenting research and have been shown to be associated with unique patterns in parents' responses to their children (Kallman, 1974; Stollak, Scholom, Kallman, & Saturansky, 1973).

Gordon (1974) has suggested that these levels of problem ownership are also profitably examined in the classroom context. Specifically, he suggests that problems in teacher-student interaction can be divided into three types: (1) teacher-owned problems, which occur when student behavior interferes with the teacher's meeting his/her own needs or causes the teacher to feel frustrated, upset, irritated, or angry; (2) (teacher-student) shared problems, which occur when the teacher and student interfere with each other's need satisfaction; and (3) student-owned problems, which exist separately from the teacher and do not tangibly and concretely affect him/her.

While the teacher is ultimately responsible for the events which occur in the classroom and therefore has some "ownership" in all that occurs there, we maintain, and the data support, that student problem behavior can be examined on a continuum ranging from primarily teacher-owned problems to primarily student-owned problems. With this in mind, the 24 vignettes have been grouped into three levels which reflect the degree of problem ownership (see Figure 4.2). Primarily teacher-owned problems include vignettes 2, 6, 9, 10, 14, 18, 21, and 22. In each of these vignettes, the student does *not* suffer feelings of inadequacy or selfdevaluation, and the student's actions present an immediate threat to the teacher's needs for authority and control.

The second category includes those situations in which the teacher and student *share* the problem. Included are vignettes 1, 3, 7, 8, 11, 13, 15, 19, and 20. In each of these vignettes, the student has difficulty living up to the demands of the student role. These difficulties pose no *intentional* or direct threat to the teacher's authority, but they do arouse the teacher's management/control needs. Finally, the primarily student-owned problems include vignettes 4, 5, 12, 16, 17, 23, and 24. In these vignettes, the students have general feelings of inadequacy or self-devaluation. Their internal conflicts and actions frustrate progress toward their *own* goals, but they do not directly thwart the needs of the teacher.

These three levels of problem ownership comprised the "independent variable" employed in this analysis. Differential patterns of teachers' attributions concerning both self and student and teachers' reported strategies for dealing with problem behavior comprised the "dependent variables."

Helping Behavior

The second premise of this investigation is the interpretation of teacher responses to student problem behavior as instances of helping behavior. Within this framework, the teacher is seen as the individual upon whom requests for assistance are made.

Previous research on helping behavior indicates that attributions regarding (1) the locus of causality of the victim's problem and (2) the control the victim has over his or her plight have important implications for helping behavior (Piliavin, Rodin, & Piliavin, 1969; Weiner, 1980). Also important are the personal risk factors involved in helping another and the degree of ambiguity within the situation (Crano, 1978).

We expected to find similar effects in the teachers' responses to the behavior described in the vignettes. Specifically, we expected that the teachers' understanding of the problem and its intensity, as well as their attributions about the students' self-control capacity and underlying intentions, would (1) differ as a function of problem ownership and (2) be associated with the teachers' perceptions of their role (if any) in the onset of the problem, their perceived ability to effect remediation of the problem, and their subsequent strategies for that remediation.

METHOD

Teachers' responses to vignettes were analyzed using three separate coding systems and then grouped by level of problem ownership (teacher-owned, shared, and student-owned) for analyses. The Attribution Inference coding system is addressed to teachers' attributions about the students and about their own role in causing or remediating the problem. The Rewards and Punishments coding system examines the types of reward, punishment, supportive behavior, and threatening or pressuring behavior which teachers report using when dealing with difficult students. Finally, the Universal coding system addresses qualitative aspects of the teachers' responses, including the instructive versus imperative content of the teachers' language to the students, the goal of the teachers' intervention, and others. The emphasis of this discussion is on the attributional inferences which teachers make about the student and about their own involvement in solving the problem. Findings concerning intervention strategies will be discussed less thoroughly, as these data are available in greater detail elsewhere (Rohrkemper and Brophy, 1980a).

Coding Attributions

The Attribution Inference coding system employed five attributional dimensions: the locus of causality, stability, and controllability dimensions identified by Weiner (1979); the intentionality dimension identified by Rosenbaum (1972); and the globality dimension identified by Abramson, Seligman, and Teasdale (1978). As indicated in Figure 4.3, all five of these dimensions are applied to the teachers' perceptions of the student portrayed in each vignette.

For example, a teacher's response to vignette 2, where Tom has beaten up Sam and taken his lunch money, would be considered as follows. In assessing the locus of causality attributed by the teacher to Tom's problem, raters distinguished between responses indicating that the problem was the result of factors internal to Tom ("He is hostile and aggressive"), the result of factors external to Tom ("Sam was probably teasing, waving his money in Tom's face"), or the result of an interaction between internal and external factors ("Tom's quick to anger and all he needed was the aggravation Sam apparently provided"). Teachers who mentioned more than one of these possibilities were coded for "multiple possibilities" (this was done in coding the remaining dimensions as well).

The teacher's response was then analyzed for controllability attributions. Does the teacher indicate that Tom is capable of self-control, but is not exercising it and is therefore responsible for the problem ("Tom knows better than to fight and take money"); or is Tom perceived as incapable of self-control, the "victim" of his impulses ("He has this anger inside that just seems to explode")? Similarly, the response was rated for intentionality: Tom's behavior could be interpreted as intentional and goal-oriented ("Tom wanted attention, so he picked on Sam"), or perceived as a mistake, perhaps careless and thoughtless, but not purposeful in a planned sense ("Tom was probably broke and worried about lunch and there was Sam, throwing his money around").

Stability attribution codes concerned whether Tom's problem was seen as persistent ("That boy fights all the time") or sporadic ("Some days are just bad days for him"). Finally, globality attribution codes concerned whether Tom's problem was viewed as generalized ("This kid fights with anyone, anywhere, anytime—even his parents") versus more situationally specific ("Tom fights only when he's provoked"). It should be noted that both stability and globality of the problem behavior were "built into" the vignettes, in that the depicted inci-

Perception of Specific Case (Vignette)	→	Attributions	→	Cognitive and Affective Reactions to Attributions	→	Cost/Decision Analysis	→	Decisions re Strategies
Initial perception determined by general beliefs about teaching and children, and by knowledge about type of problem depicted.		I. Attributions about student A. Locus of causality B. Controllability C. Intentionality D. Stability E. Globality II. Attributions about self A. Locus of causality (*re* student's problem) B. Controllability (over student's behavior) C. Stability (of change in student) D. Globality (of change in student)		Assessment of guilt, affective reaction to student Judgment *re* probable recurrence, need for action Affect *re* self-esteem, efficacy Expectancy for success Judgments *re* breadth of actions to take		Cost to teacher: social, personal demands Cost to student: present, future growth Cost to class: loss of teaching time; unintended ripple effects Cost to other parties: family, administration		goals, general approach, methods, language, rewards, punishments, unique strategies, preventive systems, etc.

FIG. 4.3. Process model of teacher strategy construction.

dents were portrayed as just the latest episodes in a continuing pattern of chronic problem behavior.

Besides coding these five dimensions of teachers' attributions about the *students* in the vignettes, we coded four of the same dimensions in the teachers' attributions about *themselves* in relation to the depicted students. The intentionality dimension was not applied to the teachers' self-attributions, because we took as given that teachers' reported attempts to change the students would be intentional.

In coding the teachers' self-attributions, the locus of causality dimension referred to the teacher's sense of his/her own role in causing the students' problem behavior. Responses were rated as indicating that the problem was caused by factors internal to the teacher, so that the problem resulted from the teacher's actions ("I could have prevented this by allowing students to 'charge' their lunch"); caused by factors external to and independent of the teacher ("This kid is a real extortionist"); or caused by an interaction between factors internal and external to the teacher ("Tom is angry all the time. He needs to be taught other, better ways to express that anger. I obviously haven't taught him that").

Controllability codes assessed the teachers' beliefs about whether or not the problem behavior could be changed. Teachers could be coded for perceiving that meaningful change in the student could be accomplished through their own (the teachers') strategies ("I would let Tom know that this is inappropriate and will not be tolerated. I would work with him to plan alternatives . . ."); or through someone else's efforts ("Tom's learning this at home. We need mom and dad in on this. I'd get the social worker talking to the parents"). Or they could be coded for believing that meaningful change was not possible ("This kid is a bully. Always was. Always will be. A real problem in the classroom").

Stability codes for teachers' self attributions refer to the teachers' assessments of the endurance of any improvements in the student's behavior. Such changes could be seen as stable ("Once Tom thinks in terms of alternatives to anger, you're on your way") or as unstable and fleeting ("After this big blow up, Tom'll cool it for a while . . ."). Globality codes in the teachers' self-attributions refer to the generalization of any changes in the student's behavior. Teachers were rated as expecting either generalized change ("Looking at the whole child . . . how he's doing at home, in the neighborhood and so on . . .") or specific, situational change ("You want to get him to school with no fights"). As in the codes for the teachers' attributions about the student, teachers' self-attribution codes also included a "multiple possibilities" category to indicate the consideration of more than one of the options available within each dimension.

Other Coding

Teachers' reported strategies for dealing with the vignette situations were coded with other systems. These systems included the Rewards and Punishments system, which catalogued the types of rewards, punishments, supportive and threatening/pressuring behaviors which teachers reported using, and the Universal system, which addressed qualitative aspects of the teachers' responses, using variables found important in parenting research. These variables included the nature and extent of the language used with the student (a scaled variable ranging from terse commands to highly instructive rationales for teacher requests and behavior) and the nature of the goals the teacher pursued with the student. Goals were defined as either short-term or long-range. Short-term goals included control/desist strategies confined to immediate, situational responses and teacher avoidance of the problem (not to be confused with systematic extinction procedures). Long-range goals included "getting to the bottom of it" attempts by the teacher to promote mental hygiene/student coping and systematic efforts to substitute undesirable behavior with behavior which is more appropriate. Details about coding and analyses involving these and other systems can be found in Rohrkemper and Brophy (1980a, 1980b) and Brophy and Rohrkemper (1980).

Coder Reliability

All teachers' responses to each vignette were coded twice, by separate coders, with each of the three systems. Coders were unaware of the identities of the teachers, the grouping of vignettes, and the hypotheses of this analysis. Disagreements were resolved by each coding pair, with involvement of the authors where necessary. Coding reliabilities were computed as percent exact agreement before resolution (percent agreement = number of codes made and agreed upon by both coders divided by itself plus number of disagreements plus number of codes made by the first coder but not the second plus number of codes made by the second coder but not the first). These agreement percentages were: Attribution Inference System: 76%; Rewards and Punishments System: 72%; Universal System: 68%. The coding systems, and breakdowns of the percent exact agreement analysis by individual variables, are available upon request.

Data Analysis

Each category within each variable in each of the three systems (nine variables in the Attribution System, four in the Rewards and Punishments System, and six in the Universal System), except three variables in the Universal System which were treated as scales, was treated as a 0 (not used) or 1 (used) possibility and aggregated across the vignettes within each of the three levels of problem ownership. Averaging the codes in each of these three levels of problem ownership yielded mean proportion scores indicating the likelihood that the teacher would use each category in responding to any particular vignette within that level of problem ownership. In addition, sum scores were computed which reflected multiple use of categories within a given variable. This was especially useful in the Rewards and Punishments Coding system for which teachers often reported using more than a single category (i.e., "type" or "level") within the reward, punishment, supportive, and threatening/pressuring variables.

RESULTS

As indicated in Table 4.1, teachers' attributions about the *students* portrayed in the vignettes differed across the three levels of problem ownership, as did teachers' *self*-attributions regarding their ability to influence those students. In addition, examination of Tables 4.2 and 4.3 reveals that teachers' reported *strategies* for dealing with these students also differed by levels of problem ownership.

Teachers' Attributions About the Students

Data from the teachers' attributions about the students depicted in the vignettes are shown in the first half of Table 4.1. As with teachers' self-attribution data, we have included for each variable: (1) data on the category within each variable which was used most frequently; (2) data on teachers' consideration of multiple possibilities (where appropriate); and (3) data for the category indicating an interaction between the factors listed in separate categories within the variable.

As Table 4.1 indicates, teachers generally perceived the students' problem behavior (across all levels of problem ownership) as caused by factors internal to the student. In addition, teachers perceived the students' problem behavior as stable and global, two factors which were built into the vignettes. Within these general trends, however, teachers were slightly more likely to perceive the student as the source of the problem ($.77_T$, $.76_{SH}$, $.70_S$) and slightly less likely to see the behavior as stable ($.85_T$, $.87_{SH}$, $.93_S$) and global ($.80_T$, $.83_{SH}$, $.88_S$) in teacher-owned problem situations. (Data from Tukey post hoc tests of the statistical significance of paired comparisons of group means are given in the last three columns of the table.) The effects of problem ownership on teachers' attributional inferences concerning student behavior are more evident in the remaining variables, controllability and intentionality.

Controllability.   Teachers' attributions of the students' ability to control their behavior, and thereby assume responsibility for their actions, showed a main effect for problem ownership. The group means were $.79_T$, $.36_{SH}$, $.16_S$. Behavior depicted in the vignettes grouped as primarily teacher-owned problems was seen as controllable by the student. Behavior in student-owned problems was seen as *un*controllable by the student. That is, rather than being responsible for their problems, these students were seen as victims. Finally, although the finding is not as strong as in student-owned problems, students in teacher-student shared problems also were likely to be seen as victims of uncontrollable forces.

For example, in the underachievers' vignette #9, a teacher-owned problem, Carl is seen as able to control his behavior. Teachers believe that Carl is not working because he is *choosing* not to, not because he doesn't understand directions or doesn't know how to do the assignment. In contrast, Jeff, the low achiever in vignette #12 (a student-owned problem), is *not* seen as in control of his behavior. His not knowing the answer is not attributed to poor motivation that he would be expected to control (as Carl's is). Instead, his behavior is attributed to low ability, over which he has no control. Finally, Betty, the immature student in vignette #11, which represents a teacher-student shared problem, elicits more mixed responses. Some teachers see her as driven to tattle by an immature and overly rigid conscience, but other teachers believe that Betty knows better than to tattle such things (she knows what is important for the teacher to know about and what is not) and hold her responsible for her actions.

Intentionality. The intentionality data also indicate a main effect for problem ownership. Intentionality is very likely to be attributed when the teacher owns the problem but unlikely when the student owns the problem ($.70_T$, $.19_{SH}$, $.05_S$). Intentionality attributions are also infrequent in shared problem situations. The main difference between controllability and intentionality data is that teacher-owned problems are usually seen as both controllable and intentional, but teacher-student shared problems and student-owned problems are likely to be seen as unintentional, even if the student is seen as capable of control. That is, even when students may "know better than that," their behavior is seen as a mistake, a slip-up with no underlying motivations.

For example, in a teacher-owned problem, as in the case of Carl, the underachiever (vignette 9), the teachers not only expect Carl to be able to control his behavior (i.e., to get to work), but also believe that he is intentionally making paper airplanes (as an act of defiance, to get their attention, or to show off to his classmates). In vignette #12, the low-achieving vignette, Jeff exhibits a student-owned problem. He is not seen as in control of his behavior, nor is his lack of achievement seen as intentional. Jeff is not trying to get out of class recitation, to play to the class, or to get the teacher's goat. His behavior is a legitimate mistake with no hidden agendas.

Representing the third level, teacher-student shared problems, the hyperactive student, Bill (vignette #3), is typically seen as able to control his behavior. Teachers often temper this, however, by recognizing that it is difficult for Bill to control his movements, so that when incidents such as that described in vignette #3 do occur, they are seen as unfortunate accidents. So while Bill is held responsible for self-control, his failures to meet these control standards are judged *un*intentional by the teacher.

TABLE 4.1
Means, Standard Deviations, and Probability Data from Analyses of Variance On
Teachers' Attributional Inferences Classified by Problem Ownership (N = 98)

Category	Proportional Use of Category						Main Effects for Problem Ownership		Tukey Post-Hoc Comparisons[1]		
	Teacher-owned Problems (T)		Shared Problems (SH)		Student-owned Problems (S)						
	X	SD	X	SD	X	SD	F	P	T - S	T - SH	SH - S
Teachers' Perceptions About the Students											
Locus of causality: internal to student	.77	.19	.76	.20	.70	.20	3.83	.0229	.07*	.01	.06
Locus of causality: internal-external interaction	.03	.06	.02	.06	.03	.07	.12	.8861	.00	.01	-.01
Locus of causality: multiple possibilities	.06	.07	.13	.13	.13	.17	6.71	.0014	-.06*	-.07*	.00
Controllability: student responsible	.79	.16	.36	.21	.16	.14	342.75	<.0001	.63*	.43*	.20*
Controllability: both possibilities	.06	.08	.08	.09	.06	.08	1.57	.2206	.00	-.02	.02
Intentionality: student acts intentionally	.70	.16	.19	.12	.05	.09	742.70	<.0001	.65*	.51*	.14*
Intentionality: both possibilities	.08	.11	.07	.09	.05	.09	2.58	.0776	.03	.01	.01
Stability: problem is stable over time	.85	.15	.87	.14	.93	.12	7.38	.0008	-.08*	-.02	-.06*
Stability: both possibilities	.06	.09	.06	.09	.03	.07	4.02	.0191	.03	-.01	.03*
Globality: problem is generalized	.80	.16	.83	.14	.88	.14	7.33	.0008	-.08*	-.04	-.05
Globality: both possibilities	.09	.10	.09	.09	.07	.10	2.66	.0718	.02	.00	.03

Teachers' Perceptions about Themselves

Locus of causality: problem is external to the teacher	.92	.12	.93	.11	.90	.13	1.59	.2067	.02	-.01	.03
Locus of causality: teacher-student interaction	.01	.03	.01	.04	.03	.06	5.25	.0058	-.02*	-.01	-.01
Locus of causality: multiple possibilities	.07	.11	.05	.08	.06	.08	1.01	.3640	.01	.02	.01
Controllability: teacher can effect change	.61	.23	.78	.20	.66	.19	17.45	<.0001	-.05	-.17*	.12*
Controllability: meaningful change not possible	.02	.05	.04	.07	.05	.10	6.48	.0018	-.04*	-.02	-.02
Controllability: multiple possibilities	.32	.22	.16	.17	.26	.19	16.82	<.0001	.06	.16*	-.10*
Stability: expects stable improvements	.55	.23	.57	.20	.64	.22	4.33	.0140	-.09*	-.03	-.07
Stability: both possibilities	.04	.08	.04	.08	.04	.07	.05	.9472	.00	-.00	.00
Globality: expects generalized improvements	.32	.22	.41	.23	.54	.26	21.22	<.0001	-.22*	-.09*	-.13*
Globality: both possibilities	.01	.04	.02	.05	.01	.05	.96	.3836	.00	-.01	.01

[1]Discrepancies between the differences implied by the group means and the group differences given in these columns are due to rounding errors. The group differences given are correct to two decimal places.

*p < .05

In summary, the teachers typically looked to factors within the student to understand student problem behavior. In addition, teachers generally perceived the depicted student behavior as chronic (i.e., as stable and global), as was intended. Dramatic differences as a function of problem ownership, however, did occur in teachers' notions of the students' control over their behavior and intentions with respect to that behavior.

Teachers' Self Attributions

With the exception of their perceived role in causing the students' problem behavior, teachers' perceptions of their own ability to influence this behavior also revealed different patterns across the levels of problem ownership. As indicated in the second half of Table 4.1, teachers typically attributed all the students' problem behaviors to factors which were independent of and external to themselves. The remaining variables, however, reflect differences in teachers' self attributions, which, when viewed within the context of their attributions concerning the student, yield three distinct profiles.

Controllability. Means for the teachers' perceptions of their own control over the problem students were moderately high ($.61_T$, $.78_{SH}$, $.66_S$), with teachers perceiving the least sense of control in teacher-owned problem situations and the most control in teacher-student shared problem situations. This variable, more than any other, reflected teachers' considerations of more than a single possibility in making sense of their own (or the students') role with regard to the problem behavior. Thus, while teachers were somewhat optimistic about their *own* ability to change the students, they also recognized that others might also be needed to bring about change. Mention of an outside resource to work in combination with the teachers themselves was especially evident in teacher-owned problem situations ($.32_T$, $.16_{SH}$, $.26_S$). These support services typically included the principal, counselor, and/or parent for hostile/aggressive and defiant students, and special aides and tutors for low achievers. Teachers were most likely to handle teacher-student shared problems by themselves. Statements of inability to influence change were rare, but when they did occur, they appeared most frequently with regard to hyperactivity.

Stability. The perceived stability of expected changes also varied by problem ownership. Overall, teachers were cautious but were more likely than not to see themselves as able to produce stable change ($.55_T$, $.57_{SH}$, $.64_S$). Within this, however, teachers felt more able to effect stable change in student-owned problems than in either teacher-owned or shared problems.

Globality. As compared to teachers' expectations for inducing stable change in students, the means for teacher confidence in being able to induce global changes likely to generalize across situations were lower and more variable ($.32_T$, $.41_{SH}$, $.54_S$). Overall, teachers did not expect to effect generalized change. Within this trend, they were most confident that change induced in the student would generalize in student-owned problems. This is in contrast to both teacher-owned and teacher-student shared problems, for which changes in student behavior were seldom seen as generalizing to other contexts.

In summary, teachers' perceptions of their own efficacy when dealing with difficult students varied according to the "ownership" of the problem. In teacher-owned problem situations teachers were least likely to believe that they could effect change by themselves and most likely to involve outside help. Any improvements that were expected were viewed skeptically. Thus, when a student presented a teacher-owned problem behavior, the teachers were least likely to see any "improvement" as stable and most likely to view any changes as situation specific, unlikely to generalize beyond the immediate context.

Shared problems yielded a different profile. In these problem situations, where students had difficulty with student role adjustments, teachers indicated the most optimism about influencing the student and were most likely to rely on their own strategies to bring about change. Teachers generally perceived these improvements as cautiously as those in teacher-owned situations, although they were more likely to believe that changes would endure and generalize.

Finally, when dealing with student-owned problems, teachers' beliefs that meaningful change could be realized were bolstered by additional sources of support. Of the three types of problems, teachers were most likely to expect that changes effected in student-owned problem situations would result in lasting and generalized improvement.

These separate profiles of teachers' self-attributions are especially revealing when examined in combination with teachers' attributions concerning the student. Recall that in teacher-owned problem situations, teachers perceived the students both as capable of self-control and as intentionally choosing to act as they did. These attributions about students were associated with teachers' relative pessimism about their own ability to successfully influence these students in any long-term sense.

Teachers were mixed in their assessments of students' capacity to control themselves in shared problem situations. Regardless of how these students' controllability was perceived, teachers did not believe that they were acting intentionally. Thus, while perhaps the students should have known better, they were seen as acting thoughtlessly, not purposefully. These attributions about students were related to teachers' high optimism about successfully coping with the problems within their own classrooms. Despite this confidence, however, the teachers did not expect any behavior changes within the classroom to generalize to other settings.

In contrast to both of the above, student-owned problem situations were characterized by teachers' attributions of *un*controllability and *un*intentionality to the students. This perception of the student as "victim," as one whose behavior is beyond his/her control, results in teachers combining their own and others' efforts to bring about changes. Furthermore, these changes were expected to be more enduring and global than the changes expected in students presenting teacher-owned or shared problems.

Problem-Solving Strategies

The three levels of problem ownership, then, clearly differentiate teachers' attributions about students and, given these, teachers' attributions concerning their own ability to influence those students. These distinct attributional profiles are in turn related to contrasting patterns in the strategies teachers reported using when dealing with problem students.

These differences due to level of problem ownership are readily apparent in teachers' use of reward, punishment, supportive, and threatening/pressuring behavior (see Sum Scores in Table 4.2). Rewards were mentioned most often in strategies designed for students presenting shared problems ($.03_T$, $.14_{SH}$, $.05_S$), and punishments were mentioned most often in teacher-owned problem situations ($.65_T$, $.27_{SH}$, $.04_S$). Supportive behavior, the most typical teacher behavior overall (see Rohrkemper & Brophy, 1980b) was especially prevalent in student-owned problem situations ($.50_T$, 1.37_{SH}, 1.98_S). Finally, the use of threatening/pressuring techniques to coerce students to change their behavior was most characteristic of teacher-owned problem situations ($.35_T$, $.20_{SH}$, $.06_S$).

Differential teacher behavior across the levels of problem ownership was also evidenced in teachers' language with and goals for students. Teachers' language with the students was examined for its richness of meaning, independent of teacher action, using a scale which ranged from teacher provision of rationales for requests and extensive instructive content that would provide the student with information as to the reason his/her behavior was inappropriate (code = 1); to the provision of minimal instruction (i.e., "padded commands"); to terse demands for behavior change (code = 3). Thus, for the language scale, the higher the mean value, the more restricted the language.

The character of teacher language differed as would be expected across the different levels of problem ownership. Teacher-owned problem strategies were likely to involve language that was restricted in content. As compared with both the shared and student-owned problem situations, language in teacher-owned problem situations was more terse and often confined to mere commands for behavior change (1.51_T, 1.21_{SH}, 1.08_S). In contrast, language in student-owned problem situations provided more contextual information for the student. The language used with shared problem situations was between these two extremes, although closer to that involved in responding to student-owned problems.

A final aspect of teacher problem-solving strategies to be considered here is the teacher's goal in responding to the problem behavior. This analysis involved

TABLE 4.2

Means, Standard Deviations, and Probability Data from Analyses of Variance on Teachers' Use of Rewards, Punishments, Supportive Behaviors, and Threatening/Pressuring Behaviors Classified by Problem Ownership (N = 98)

| | Proportional Use of Category | | | | | | Main Effects for Problem Ownership | | Tukey Post-Hoc Comparisons[1] | | |
| | Teacher-owned Problems (T) | | Shared Problems (SH) | | Student-owned Problems (S) | | | | | | |
Category	$\overline{X}$	SD	$\overline{X}$	SD	$\overline{X}$	SD	F	P	T - S	T - SH	SH - S
Rewards											
No rewards	.72	.07	.94	.11	.89	.13	189.52	.0001	-.22*	-.17*	-.06*
Symbolic	.01	.03	.02	.05	.03	.07	7.79	.0006	-.01	-.03*	.01
Material	.00	.02	.01	.03	.02	.04	5.65	.0041	.00	-.01*	.01*
Special privileges	.02	.04	.02	.05	.05	.07	15.37	.0001	.00	-.04*	.03*
Teacher reward	.00	.01	.01	.03	.02	.04	6.06	.0028	.00	-.01*	.01*
Contracts	.00	.01	.00	.01	.01	.04	6.36	.0021	.00	-.01*	.01*
Punishments											
No punishments	.30	.17	.96	.09	.80	.15	703.92	.0001	-.65*	-.49*	-.16*
Loss of privileges	.05	.08	.01	.04	.04	.07	9.24	.0001	.04*	.01	.03*
Punitive isolation	.14	.14	.00	.02	.06	.08	54.00	.0001	.14*	.08*	.06*
Extra time	.03	.07	.00	.01	.02	.05	8.91	.0002	.03*	.01	.02*
Extra requirements	.02	.05	.00	.01	.01	.04	5.23	.0061	.02*	.00	.01*
Restitution	.04	.06	.01	.03	.06	.06	33.94	.0001	.03*	-.03*	.06*
Physical punishment	.03	.07	.00	.01	.01	.02	11.78	.0001	-.03*	.02*	.00
Other adult	.22	.15	.00	.02	.04	.08	164.59	.0001	.22*	.19*	.03*
Other	.13	.13	.01	.04	.03	.06	58.99	.0001	.12*	.10*	.02

(continued)

TABLE 4.2 (Continued)

Category	Proportional Use of Category						Main Effects for Problem Ownership		Tukey Post-Hoc Comparisons[1]		
	Teacher-owned Problems (T)		Shared Problems (SH)		Student-owned Problems (S)						
	X̄	SD	X̄	SD	X̄	SD	F	P	T - S	T - SH	SH - S
Supportive											
No support	.39	.20	.21	.18	.05	.09	148.76	.0001	.35*	.19*	.16*
Specific behavioral praise	.02	.05	.08	.11	.08	.11	16.44	.0001	-.06*	-.06*	.01
Global personal praise	.00	.01	.02	.06	.02	.05	7.72	.0006	-.02*	-.02*	.01
Encouragement	.01	.02	.14	.12	.14	.13	68.07	.0001	-.13*	-.14*	.00
Comfort	.00	.01	.01	.04	.15	.13	119.83	.0001	-.15*	-.01	-.14*
Kid gloves	.11	.13	.22	.17	.19	.16	17.90	.0001	-.08*	-.11*	.03
Supportive isolation	.04	.08	.07	.09	.01	.03	15.79	.0001	.03*	-.03*	.06*
Involve peers	.04	.07	.09	.11	.38	.19	227.43	.0001	-.34*	-.05*	-.29*
Involves other adults	.03	.07	.07	.11	.09	.12	10.88	.0001	-.05*	-.04*	-.01
Instruction	.14	.15	.37	.19	.55	.22	170.83	.0001	-.41*	-.23*	-.18*
Other	.07	.09	.21	.16	.17	.16	30.54	.0001	-.10*	-.14*	.04
Threatening/Pressuring											
No threats	.51	.20	.82	.18	.94	.10	295.21	.0001	-.44*	-.32*	-.12*
Specific behavioral criticism	.09	.12	.10	.12	.03	.07	16.74	.0001	.07*	.00	.07*
Global personal criticism	.06	.10	.03	.08	.01	.03	13.57	.0001	.05*	.03*	.02*
Sarcasm/ridicule	.03	.06	.03	.07	.01	.03	5.09	.0070	.02	-.01	.02*
Diagnosing	.02	.08	.00	.01	.00	.02	8.21	.0004	.02*	.02*	.00
Third degree	.01	.04	.01	.03	.00	.02	3.57	.0300	.01*	.01	.01
Other	.07	.11	.02	.05	.01	.03	27.00	.0001	.07*	.05*	.01

(continued)

Sum Scores

Total Rewards	.03	.08	.14	.16	.05	.11	26.98	.0001	-.02	-.11*	.08*
Total Punishments	.65	.35	.27	.22	.04	.08	188.39	.0001	.62*	.39*	.23*
Total Supportive Behaviors	.50	.34	1.37	.47	1.98	.53	401.76	.0001	-1.48*	-.87*	-.61*
Total Threatening/ Pressuring Behavior	.35	.39	.20	.25	.06	.10	45.33	.0001	.29*	.15*	.14*
R/R + P	.04	.11	.31	.33	.24	.42	22.36	.0001	-.19*	-.27*	.08
S/S + T	.61	.31	.87	.15	.97	.05	112.26	.0001	-.37*	-.26*	-.10*
R + P/R + P + S + T	.46	.20	.27	.17	.07	.12	151.80	.0001	.39*	.19*	.19*
Specific Praise/Specific + Global Praise	.14	.34	.45	.48	.40	.48	18.07	.0001	-.26*	-.31*	.05
Praise/Total Supportive	.02	.05	.10	.11	.08	.11	21.62	.0001	-.06*	-.08*	.01
Specific/Specific + Global Criticism	.37	.44	.45	.46	.15	.35	13.26	.0001	.23*	-.07*	.30*

[1] Discrepancies between the differences implied by the group means and the group differences given in these columns are due to rounding errors. The group differences given are correct to two decimal places.

$*p < .05$

examining the teacher's strategies to determine what student behaviors would indicate that the strategy had been successful. Four types of teacher goals were thus identified: long-term mental hygiene/coping goals and rewards/shaping goals, and short-term control goals and avoidance of the problem (distinguished from systematic extinction techniques).

Long-term goals were characteristic of both shared and student-owned problem situations. Within this, however, mental hygiene/coping goals, which reflect a concern for dealing with the underlying problem rather than the surface, symptomatic behavior, were most likely to occur in response to student-owned problems ($.19_T$, $.39_{SH}$, $.65_S$).

Although some concern for "getting to the bottom of it" is also seen in shared problems, teachers' goals when dealing with students who exhibited role adjustment difficulties were most likely to involve rewards/shaping goals ($.16_T$, $.47_{SH}$, $.28_S$). These also were long-term goals, focused on the substitution of the present undesirable behavior with more appropriate behavior rather than addressing the cause of the problem behavior, as in mental hygiene goals.

Short-term control/desist goals characterize teachers' objectives with students presenting teacher-owned problems ($.85_T$, $.38_{SH}$, $.20_S$). With these students, teachers confined their strategies to techniques which would stop the troublesome behavior in the immediate situation. These strategies did not include more long-term pervasive goals involving both acting on the immediate situation and trying to prevent such problems from occurring in the future.

It is evident, then, that teachers' attributions about students and their perceived ability to influence those students differed significantly as a function of problem ownership. Differential patterns also emerged in teachers' reported strategies for coping with students' problem behavior. In teacher-owned problem situations, teachers perceived the students as capable of self-control but intentionally choosing to act as they did. Given these attributions, the teachers were pessimistic about their own efficacy in successfully influencing student behavior in any long-term sense. These negative expectations were reflected in the restricted language shown in their responses to vignettes depicting teacher-owned problems. Instructions and rationales were infrequent in these responses, which often were confined to terse demands for behavior change. Goals were typically limited to short-term control of the symptomatic behavior and did not include more preventive strategies involving addressing possible causes of the problem (mental health goals) or substituting desirable behaviors (rewards/shaping goals). These restricted goals were reflected in the relative absence of rewards and teacher-supportive behavior in these responses and the frequent use of punishments and threatening/pressuring behavior.

Teacher-student shared problems also yielded a distinctive pattern of teachers' attributions and response strategies. Teachers' goals for students in these shared problem situations were more varied, but they were primarily long-term, with an emphasis on replacement of the current problem behavior with behavior more appropriate for the classroom. This is in contrast to both the short-term desist techniques employed in teacher-owned problem situations and the more generalized long-term mental health goals characteristic of student-owned problem situations. Recall that in teacher-student shared problems, in which students had difficulty adjusting to the student role, students were perceived as acting unintentionally, but perhaps carelessly. Even if these students were seen as not in control of themselves at present, they were seen as able to learn such control. However, teachers expected these changes to be limited to specific contexts and perhaps limited in stability over time as well.

Students in these shared problem situations were typically exposed to behavior modification programs, with high teacher involvement. These strategies involved some use of language for instruction or socialization, but also included methods that did not rely on language as the major treatment (i.e., environmental engineering, modeling, or shaping the students' actions without explanation). Students in shared problem situations received the most rewards, as well as their share of punishments. In addition they were often praised by their teachers, primarily with praise that was tied to specific behavior (i.e., praise that was part of a behavior modification strategy rather than part of an attempt to encourage or build a close personal relationship).

These strategies, based heavily on teacher controlled rewards, punishment, supports, and praise, are consistent with teachers' perceptions of the students' problems and with teachers' beliefs that any changes in the student would likely be specific and unstable. Thus, teachers, when dealing with student role behavior problems, expected that the students would cooperate but also believed that constant ongoing environmental manipulations would be necessary to maintain appropriate behavior. The teachers apparently were concerned about maintaining smooth-running classrooms. In any case, they generally were willing to continually engineer events to maximize the fit between the student and the classroom expectations.

Finally, the third level of problem ownership, student-owned problems, revealed a third unique profile of teacher attributions and behavior. Recall that in student-owned problem situations, students were perceived as unable (as opposed to unwilling) to control their behavior. Further, any problems the student did cause were believed to be unintentional. These students were apparently viewed as victims of their own behavior. This attributed lack of self-control was seen as causing serious problems for the student. Effecting change was seen as difficult, but as likely to have a meaningful effect on students' lives (if accomplished).

These attributions appeared to translate into teacher commitment to help these students. In student-owned problem situations, teachers were nurturant and supportive. They talked extensively to these students, providing encouragement and comfort (without an emphasis on rewards), and they worked on long-term goals involving improving the students' mental health through improving their self-evaluations or teaching them coping techniques.

DISCUSSION

The three levels of problem ownership (teacher-owned, student-owned, and teacher-student shared) produced different patterns in teachers' perceptions of and attributions about students, and in turn, in teachers' beliefs about the effects that they could have on these students. These patterns indicate that the dimensions of locus of causality, controllability, intentionality, stability, and globality are important in distinguishing teachers' attributions about differing student behaviors from their attributions about their own involvement in the onset and remediation of those student behaviors.

These patterns of self versus other attributions which emerge across the levels of problem ownership are related to the strategies and goals teachers report using with students. The three strategy profiles which emerged in this research echo the findings of the helping behavior investigations.

Research examining the likelihood of helping behavior has established that bystanders' withholding of aid is associated with situations in which victims are perceived as responsible for their plights—i.e., the observer attributes the victims' problems to internal causes and sees the problem behaviors as controllable (Weiner, 1980). Similar patterns are seen in the Carroll & Payne (1977) analysis of parole decisions: Punishment is most harsh and parole least likely when the offender is seen as the source of the problem, as having acted intentionally, and as likely to persist in criminal behavior. Conversely, crimes that are judged the result of external, unintentional, and unstable causes are punished less severely, and the offender has a good chance of parole. Our analysis of teachers' behavior toward problem students, given their attributions regarding the students' behavior, parallels these results.

We suspect that these attributional patterns are key factors in the self-fulfilling prophecy phenomena, where teachers' unexamined attributions about self and student result in expectations that influence teacher behavior. It also seems likely that these patterns of attribution are important elements in the process of strategy construction. Thus, we believe that teachers' examination of their attributions about students and themselves would yield information useful in helping them to construct new, successful strategies (or to change current, unsuccessful strategies) for coping with problem students. Figure 4.3 presents a model which illustrates this process of teacher strategy construction.

The model, influenced by Carroll and Payne's model of parole decisions, appears useful for understanding the interplay between teachers' cognition and subsequent behavior. It begins with the teacher's perception of a specific event interpreted against a background of previous beliefs and experiences with this type of behavior. This leads to an attributional analysis of the student and of the teacher' own involvement. These attributional inferences are hypothesized to be associated with certain cognitive and affective reactions. These three elements—generalized experience and knowledge, attributional inference in the immediate situation, and affective reactions and expectations—are the mediational factors which the teacher imposes on interactions with difficult students. The degree of conscious awareness of these processes is likely to differ across individuals and situations. The processes probably remain unexamined in most routine dealings with students, but they can become conscious and deliberate when teachers practice self-examination. The final components in the model are constraints within which teachers must work. These impose cost factors that must be taken into account in selecting actual strategies from among recognized options.

The cost decision analysis involves an examination and weighing of these real world constraints and trade-offs. These costs encompass: (1) the teacher, with the social demands of the teacher role and personal expectations involved in decisions of time, energy, and emotional investment; (2) the problem student, with concerns for present and future growth given any action or nonaction; (3) the cost to the class in terms of lost teaching time, vicarious learning, and unintended ripple effects; and (4) other cost factors that need to be examined: family values, administration policies, and so on.

These cost factors appear to be key elements in determining the strategies teachers ultimately use to influence student behavior. The CSS data support this point. For example, in teacher-owned problems, risk factors to the teacher's role status are high and are compounded by the presence of the class and by administrators' expectations. Recall that teachers attributed controllability and intentionality to students presenting teacher-owned problems and indicated low expectations for promoting stable and global changes. In these situations, we found teacher strategies characterized by higher frequency of punishment, restricted language, and minimizing of long-term mental health goals in favor of more short-term, control-desist attempts.

In teacher-student shared problems, the risk involves primarily a threat to a smooth-running classroom (and therefore to teacher role demands) and, secondly, a threat to the student's learning and self-evaluation. Recall that the teachers' controllability attributions were mixed with these students, but teachers did not attribute intentionality to them. Teachers also believed they were capable of effecting stable, specific change in these students. Here we found a second distinctive strategy profile. Teachers used relatively less punishment and more rewards and praise in pursuing long-term behavior modification goals with specific objectives through use of contracts, behavior charting, and so on.

Finally, in student-owned problems, the risk factors are less immediate and more focused on the student. Teachers attributed uncontrollability and unintentionality to these students and indicated a hopeful prognosis for change. We found this level of problem ownership associated with teacher encouragement and support, extended language, and long-term mental health goals involving development of coping techniques and self-approval.

This model of the process involved in teachers' development of strategies for dealing with difficult students appears useful for examining events that occur in classrooms. In addition to its usefulness for explication, the model facilitates the generation of research questions that examine the reciprocal nature of classroom events and, as such, should enhance our understanding of classroom life.

CONCLUSION

This investigation has focused on teachers' attributions about student behavior and, given these "other" attributions, on teachers' self-attributions about their own involvement in the behaviors' onset and change and their subsequent strategies for implementing such change. Attributions about others' behavior appear to be part of the natural process of making sense of one's social environment. Within the teaching profession, however, this process needs to be examined and professionalized. Although attributional inferences are clearly essential for accurate diagnosis of students' behavior, they can be self-defeating and perhaps self-fulfilling as they apply to teachers' perceptions of their own roles in the onset and remediation of problem behavior.

We suggest that this attribution process, when allowed to follow its natural course (which may be appropriate for accurate and reliable parole decisions), is counterproductive for decision making in the classroom. Teachers need to be made aware of the effects that various attributions about students can have on their self-assessments and subsequent behavior. This is particularly so for teacher-owned problem situations. Disrupting the naturally occurring other attribution → self attribution → behavior process would help teachers to construct strategies that extend beyond the mere control and desist techniques which currently dominate teachers' thinking.

Although the data presented here are based on teacher self-report, they suggest the desirability of training programs using the process model depicted in Figure 4.3 to help teachers examine their attributional inferences about their students and themselves, and their consequent behavior. Such insight should help teachers to take a more proactive, problem-solving, mental health oriented stance toward problem students.

ACKNOWLEDGMENTS

This work is sponsored in part by the Institute for Research on Teaching, College of Education, Michigan State University. The Institute for Research on Teaching is funded primarily by the Program for Teaching and Instruction of the National Institute of Education, United States Department of Education. The opinions expressed in this publication do not necessarily reflect the position, policy, or endorsement of the National Institute of Education. (Contract No. 400-76-0073)

Portions of this chapter were presented at the annual meeting of the American Educational Research Association in Boston, April, 1980. The authors wish to acknowledge and thank Jane Smith, Carolyn Rettke, Janis Elmore, Jean Medick, Lonnie McIntyre, Susan Rubenstein, Stephan Katz, and JoAnn Hite, who assisted in the project planning and data collection; Jane Smith, Lynn Scott, Patricia Linton, Caroline Wainright, Linda Ripley, and Sheba Dunlap, who coded the data; Suwatana Sookpokakit, who assisted with data preparation and analysis; and June Smith, who assisted in manuscript preparation.

REFERENCES

Abramson, L. V., Seligman, M. E. P., & Teasdale, J. D. Learned helplessness in humans: Critique and reformation. *Journal of Abnormal Psychology*, 1978, *87*, 49–74.

Bar-Tal, D., & Frieze, I. Attributions of success and failure for actors and observers. *Journal of Research in Personality*, 1976, *10*, 256–265.

Brophy, J. E., & Rohrkemper, M. M. *Teachers' specific strategies for dealing with hostile aggressive students*. Paper presented at the annual meeting of the American Educational Research Association, Boston, April, 1980.

Carroll, J. S., & Payne, J. W. Judgments about crime and the criminal: A model and a method for investigating parole decisions. In B. D. Sales (Ed.), *Perspectives in law and psychology* (Vol. 1): *The criminal justice system*. New York: Plenum Press, 1977.

Crano, W. D. Personal communication, 1978.

Fontaine, G. Causal attribution in simulated versus real situations: When are people logical and when are they not? *Journal of Personality and Social Psychology*, 1975, *32*, 1021–1029.

Frieze, I., & LaVoie, A. *A comparison of causal attributions for success and failure in a real and in a simulated situation*. Unpublished manuscript, University of California at Los Angeles, 1972.

Gordon, T. *Parent effectiveness training*. New York: Wyden, Inc., 1970.

Gordon, T. *Teacher effectiveness training*. New York: Wyden, Inc., 1974.

Kallman, J. R. *A developmental study of children's perceptions and fantasies of maternal discipline procedures*. Unpublished dissertation, Michigan State University, 1974.

Piliavin, I. M., Rodin, J., & Piliavin, J. A. Good samaritanism: An underground phenomenon? *Journal of Personality and Social Psychology*, 1969, *13*, 289–299.

Rohrkemper, M. M., & Brophy, J. E. *The influence of problem ownership on teachers' perceptions of and strategies for coping with problem students*. Paper presented at the annual meeting of the American Educational Research Association, Boston, April, 1980. (a)

Rohrkemper, M. M., & Brophy, J. E. *Teachers' general strategies for dealing with problem students*. Paper presented at the annual meeting of the American Educational Research Association, Boston, April, 1980. (b)

Rosenbaum, R. M. *A dimensional analysis of the perceived causes of success and failure*. Unpublished doctoral dissertation, University of California at Los Angeles, 1972.

Stollak, G. E., Scholom, A., Kallman, J., & Saturansky, C. Insensitivity to children: Responses of undergraduates to children in problem situations. *Journal of Abnormal Child Psychology*, 1973, *1*, 169–180.

Weiner, B. A theory of motivation for some classroom experiences. *Journal of Educational Psychology*, 1979, *71*, 3–25.

Weiner, B. A cognitive (attribution)—emotion—action model of motivated behavior: An analysis of judgments of help-giving. *Journal of Personality and Social Psychology*, 1980, *39*, 186–200.

5 Teachers' Attributions for Their Own Teaching

Russell Ames
University of Maryland

After attempting to teach something to students, teachers receive feedback about the effectiveness of their behavior in the form of the student's actual performance, their own self-assessment, and/or formal and informal evaluation from students. The basic tenet of this chapter is that a teacher's response to positive or negative feedback is a function of his or her explanations for the causes of that feedback. These explanations can be characterized as causal attributions that teachers make about why their behavior is effective or ineffective. This chapter presents an analysis of the attributional beliefs which may be associated with teachers' responses to positive and negative feedback about their teaching. The analysis is deemed important because it is theorized that teachers' attributions affect whether or not they modify or change their teaching actions, particularly in response to negative feedback. For example, it seems reasonable to expect that teachers who blame the cause of negative feedback on students' lack of ability would not modify their own teaching behavior as much as would teachers who blame the feedback on something about their own teaching. These latter teachers might be much more likely to try alternate teaching strategies. The major purpose of this chapter is to examine the link between the feedback teachers receive and their attributions for the feedback. The subsequent link relating teacher attributions to teacher behavior is beyond the scope of this report, but some theory and speculation are proffered.

Teacher attribution research has typically investigated the problem of how teachers make attributions for student success and failure (Ames, 1975a; Beckman 1970, 1973; Johnson, Fiegenbaum, & Weiby, 1964; Ross, Bierbrauer, & Polly, 1974). Within this line of research, the most important question has been whether teachers credit themselves or the pupils for success and whether they blame themselves or the students for failure. The research, however, on teachers' attributions for success and failure has shown mixed results. That is, some studies provide evidence for an ego-enhancing/defensive pattern in which teachers credit themselves for success and blame the student for failure, and others provide evidence for a nondefensive pattern in which teachers credit the student for success and blame themselves for failure.

In the typical study which has found evidence for the ego-enhancing/defensive pattern (Beckman, 1970; Beckman, 1973; Brandt, Hayden, & Brophy, 1975; Johnson et al. 1964), teachers teach one or more fictitious students over a series of learning trials. The teachers in these studies never see the students in person and have only one-way communication with them. Teachers receive feedback about student performance after each trial, and they are asked to make attributions for patterns of success and failure including constant success or failure and increasing success over trials. Teachers have tended to credit themselves for ascending performance and to blame the student for constant failure. This attribution pattern has been taken as evidence for self-serving biases of ego-enhancement and ego-defensiveness.

A number of authors, including Kelley (1972) and Miller and Ross (1975), have shown that these apparent self-serving teacher attribution data can be explained within an information processing rather than a motivational framework. Namely, an ascending pattern gives the illusion of covariation between teacher behavior and student performance, while constant failure gives the illusion of negative or no covariation from which the teacher reasonably draws an inference or little or no control. Additionally, Ames (1975a) has argued that the experimental factors including a one-way mirror and lack of face-to-face communication could have been perceived as inhibitory factors (see also Kelley, 1972) increasing the illusion of teacher causation for success and, at the same time, giving the teacher a reasonable excuse for failure.

Studies which have found the contrasting pattern in which teachers assume responsibility for failure are typical of those conducted by Ames (1975a) and Ross et al. (1974) in which the teacher had face-to-face interaction with students over a meaningful period of time. Ames argued that instructional situations involving face-to-face encounters allow for the establishment of an interpersonal relationship, with the physical presence of the child increasing the teacher's sense of responsibility for the welfare of the pupil. This physical presence may have elicited what Schwartz (1968) termed "awareness of consequences for others" which he indicated was a necessary condition for a situation to be defined as a moral encounter involving ascriptions of responsibility.

The present author has argued that responsibility attribution characterized within such a moral framework invokes a value dimension not endemic to causal attributions. Thus, teachers can have beliefs about the importance of worthwhileness of trying hard or caring about the welfare of students and they can have beliefs about the causes of student performance. For example, it may make perfectly good sense for teachers, as they appeared to do in the Ames (1975a) study, to say that students failed because they did not try hard enough while ultimately viewing themselves as responsible for arousing student interest.

Nevertheless, the debate between self-serving bias versus information processing interpretations of teacher attributions remains unresolved, and the issues have been argued in a recent exchange of papers between Bradley (1978) and Miller (1978). Bradley cogently argues that self-serving attributions can be used to protect oneself from one's own negative self-evaluations or from the negative evaluations of others. In this context, a teacher might publicly accept responsibility for student failure in order to remain in the good graces of the experimenter, principal, or colleagues while privately denying responsibility and blaming the student. Miller argues that while the public versus private distinction has merit, there is little evidence for the alteration of perceptions of causality so as to protect or enhance self-esteem. In Miller's view, the weight of the evidence on the subject favors informational processing interpretations associated with covariation data or prior expectancies.

This chapter takes an entirely different tack regarding the self-esteem maintenance debate represented in the opposing views of Bradley and Miller. It builds upon Ames' (1975 a & b) moral or value framework for responsibility attribution and upon the work of Covington (see Covington and Beery 1976; Covington and Omelich, 1979a,b, and c) on a self-worth theory of achievement. Recently, Covington and Omelich (1979a), Nicholls (1975), and Maehr and Nicholls (1978) have characterized achievement strivings within the context of a valuing of ability in relation to one's self-worth. Within this framework achievement strivings are directly coordinated to attempts to maintain a self-concept of high ability. Nicholls (1975) has noted that when a task is thought to measure skills important to the self-image, there is more reason for defensive or self-enhancing interpretations than when the task is thought relatively unimportant. Maehr and Nicholls (1978) have broadened the self-worth, achievement paradigm to a general characterization of goal attainment in which persons seek goals because goal attainment implies something desirable about themselves (such as that they are friendly, capable, or obedient). This characterization of goal attainment suggests that a study of a person's value hierarchy (see Rokeach, 1973) may indicate which goals are relatively more important to attain than others. Further, it is theorized that causal attributions for the attainment or nonattainment of a particular goal are related to the degree to which attainment of that particular goal is valued.

An integrative framework for understanding teacher attributions is presented in terms of a value-belief framework for attributions. It is shown that this value-belief framework provides a theoretical resolution for the teacher attribution studies showing conflicting evidence for ego-enhancing/defensive attributions. Further, this value-belief framework is shown to account for a broader spectrum of teacher attributions including both causal and responsibility ascriptions, and it explains how teachers deal with a number of sources of information available to them in an instructional setting, including knowledge about their own behavior as well as student performance data and characteristics of the instructional setting. New data are presented which support some key hypotheses related to this value-belief model.

VALUE-BELIEF MODEL FOR TEACHER ATTRIBUTIONS

Teachers are viewed as processing information about their own behavior and the performance of students in the context of a value orientation which assigns a level of importance to various goals related to teaching. These importance ratings are closely tied to one's sense of self-worth. Within this framework, persons are thought to select and pursue goals because attainment of these particular goals implies something desirable about themselves such as that they are competent, caring, or effective task or discussion leaders. Teachers are viewed as making attributions in response to information about their own behavior as well as student performance. Teacher and student performance outcomes are classified as types of feedback which teachers use in judging their teaching effectiveness. It is asserted that teachers process this informational feedback through a belief system centrally organized around certain values (see Rokeach, 1973), and that they attribute positive and negative feedback in terms of centrally important values which serve as purposes or reasons for behavior (see Buss, 1978; Kruglanski, 1975, 1980).

A reanalysis of the previous literature on teacher attribution for success and failure suggests that in some cases the teacher's sense of self-worth is best maintained by crediting himself or herself for student success and blaming the student for failure. In other cases, the teacher's sense of worth is best protected by maintaining a belief that he or she is a responsible person who cares about the welfare of students.

The particular attribution pattern that is elicited depends on the situational context, the consistency of information about teacher and student behavior, and the value priorities of the individual teacher. The value that is perceived as relevant to the attributional judgment is hypothesized to be a function of both the teacher's personal value hierarchy and the situational context. In the Ames (1975a) study, it was reasoned that the nondefensive attribution pattern was obtained because the face-to-face interaction elicited a strong concern for the welfare of the pupil. In fact, as Brandt et al. (1975) noted, face-to-face interaction may be one of the key factors separating the studies that found a nondefensive teacher attribution pattern from those that found a defensive pattern. And it is argued here that this face-to-face interaction elicited a value to be concerned for the welfare of the pupil (see also Ames, 1975b).

FIG. 5.1   Value-belief attribution model

The value-belief attribution model depicted in Figure 5.1 shows that both person and situational factors contribute to determining what value is relevant to a specific attributional judgment. The final attributional judgment is shown to be a function of the combination of the elicited value and positive or negative performance information. Student performance data are seen as informational feedback to the teacher which are filtered through a belief and value system and interpreted so as to maintain the teacher's sense of self-worth. For example, if it is important for the teacher to maintain a high self-concept of teaching ability, then attributions will be made in support of that value. Or, if it is important for the teacher to maintain a high self-concept of caring and concern for others, then the teacher will make causal attributions in support of that value. Various factors including personality predispositions to be concerned about the welfare of others or situational factors such as face-to-face communication would make a particular value orientation salient in a given setting. This value analysis is consistent with Heider's (1958, pp. 120–121) view that attributions are affected by "what ought to be" (value belief), "what one would like to be" (self-worth belief), as well as "what is" (perception of situation).

In the perception of an instructional situation, teachers can make use of two general classes of information: performance data (e.g., student success) and situational aids or constraints (e.g., audio-visual equipment; large class size). There are actually two types of performance data. The first, student success or failure, is the typical outcome data investigated in teacher attribution studies. But the second type, positive or negative evaluation of the teacher's own teaching acts, has received less attention. Nevertheless, an analysis of attributions for teaching acts appears important because teaching is viewed as an intentional act to bring about learning, (i.e., student success). Thus, teaching acts can be considered manifestations of an effort-related strategy to produce a desired result. In this sense the teaching act is inexorably tied to the student outcome. As an example of this linkage a teacher might say, "I want the students to learn historical facts about the Civil War; therefore, I will prepare an interesting lecture on this topic." Suppose, however, that the lecture on the Civil War turned out to be very boring, but nevertheless, the students, when examined, performed well. Even though the act and the outcome are so linked, the teacher could be asked for independent explanations for his or her lecture performance and for the results of the student examination. In giving such explanation, the teacher might say, regarding the lecture, that this was the first time the lecture had been given, or

Exemplary Teacher Outcomes   **Exemplary Attributions**

Poor Lecture

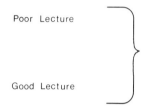

Lack of teaching ability, teacher lack
of effort, biased or "dull" students,
difficult material, lack of adequate
audiovisual resources to give a lecture.

Good Lecture

Strong teaching ability, tried hard,
"bright" students, easy material,
attended workshops to improve teaching
skill.

Exemplary Student Outcomes   **Exemplary Attributions**

Student Failure

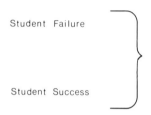

Lack of teaching ability, little
effort by teacher to help students,
lack of student effort and/or ability,
difficult material.

Student Success

Strong teaching ability, teacher tried
hard, "bright" students, motivated
students, easy material.

FIG. 5.2   Summary of causal attributions for teacher and student performance
outcomes.

that there had been little time to practice the delivery. And, regarding the successful students' performance, the teacher might say that the students found the
topic of the Civil War very interesting and thus studied a great deal on their own.

Examination of Figure 5.2 shows exemplary attributions which teachers can
use in explaining their own or student performance. For each teacher and student
outcome there is a corresponding teacher action which can be independently and
subjectively given a positive or negative evaluation. From the teacher's perspective, he or she can make separate attributional judgments for each of the teacher
and student outcomes. And, as indicated in Figure 5.2, those attributional judgments can be made to the ability or effort of the teacher or student and to factors
in the situation which can be seen as a help or a hindrance both to the teacher's
effective action and to the student's performance (see Weiner, 1979).

It seems reasonable to assume that some teachers perceive their teaching acts
to be more strongly related to student outcome than do other teachers. This belief
about the relationship of one's teaching acts to student performance is characterized as a general a priori belief about the relationship of teacher behavior to
student performance. In essence, it is a belief that one's effort, as connoted in
one's intentional acts, causes outcomes and that, in general, success results from
trying hard and failure results from not trying. It is asserted in this chapter that a
teacher's a priori belief in an effort-outcome covariation is in fact derived from a

more general value orientation that teachers are "responsible" for their students. Such a value for responsibility involves three key beliefs—that teaching is an important activity, that teachers engage in intentional acts to produce positive outcomes, and that student success is generally feasible given the situational aids and constraints (see Ames, 1975a). Of the three, the overriding belief is "importance" because it is hypothesized that this belief determines the strength of the effort-outcome covariation belief (intentional beliefs, e.g., "The more important the outcome the more I should try to accomplish it") and leads to perceptions that student success is feasible in most situations (feasibility beliefs, e.g., "If I persist and try different teaching strategies, I'm sure I can succeed even in these difficult circumstances"). Conversely, such strong intentionality and feasibility beliefs do not follow when the importance belief is not held.

It is predicted that teachers who have a strong belief in the importance of teaching and its associated outcomes (i.e., value competence and effort in teaching) attribute the evaluation of their own teaching acts and associated student outcomes differently than do teachers who do not hold strongly to this value. Table 5.1 shows the expected teacher, student, and situational attributions for teachers placing high and low value on the importance of being competent and effortful teachers. High and low value teachers are shown to make attributions for both their own teaching performance and the corresponding student performance. Since the teaching act is so closely linked to the student outcome, teachers are shown to consider information about the success or failure of the student in attributing the teaching evaluation and to consider information about

TABLE 5.1
Hypothesized Attributions of Teachers Placing a
High and Low Value on Teaching

Attribution for	Student Performance	Value			
		High		Low	
		Teacher Performance Evaluation			
		Positive	Negative	Positive	Negative
Teacher Performance	Success	Teacher	Teacher	Student/ Situation	Student/ Situation
	Failure	Teacher	Teacher	Teacher	Student/ Situation
Student Performance	Success	Student	Student	Student	Student
	Failure	Teacher	Teacher	Student/ Situation	Student/ Situation

the positive or negative teacher performance evaluation in attributing the student's performance. Thus, attributions for all possible combinations of positive and negative teaching evaluations and successful and failing student performances are shown for high and low value teachers, respectively.

Most significantly, examination of Table 5.1 shows some key differences in the way high and low value teachers make attributions. In general, high value teachers are shown to take responsibility for their actions and consequent student outcomes (i.e., attribute their own and student performance to something about themselves or their teaching). One exception is noted; when high value teachers attribute a successful student performance they credit the student. Such credit is, of course, logically consistent with the "importance" belief—"Good teachers reinforce their students for success in order to encourage them to work hard." In contrast, since low value teachers do not place much value on the importance of being effortful and competent teachers, they would not be expected to see a relationship between their intentions and the student outcome. Thus, teacher acts cannot, logically, be attributed to something about the teacher (with one exception noted below), but must be attributed more to situational or student factors that made the task easy or difficult.

Some of the most interesting differences between high and low value teachers occur with student failure. Because high value teachers hold to an effort-outcome covariation belief they are predicted to take more responsibility for student failure, particularly when their own teaching performance was evaluated negatively. For a high value teacher, a poor teaching performance is viewed as the major cause of the student failure. Thus, when attributing their own performance, they blame themselves, primarily focusing on effort. Since low value teachers do not see themselves as responsible for either their success or their failure, a poor teaching evaluation is easily blamed on biased or difficult students and an inhibiting situation. For them, intentional teaching acts are not seen as strongly related to student outcomes, and hence an ineffective performance is not necessarily related to failure. Further, whereas high value teachers blame themselves for the student performance, the low value teachers do not see themselves as part of the causal chain and hence attribute the student's poor performance to the student or situation. The only exception to this psycho-logic for the low value teacher is in making an attribution for a positively evaluated teacher performance when the student failed. Here, the low value teacher can say, "If my teaching performance was evaluated positively by a failing student, I must have been doing something right."

In summary, because the high value teachers place importance on being competent and effortful instructors, they view themselves as trying hard to accomplish student success even in the face of situational obstacles. Hence, when the student fails, it is the teacher's efforts as connoted in his or her teaching acts which have been ineffective. In contrast, low value teachers are shown to shift responsibility onto the student. Since low value teachers do not hold that teaching is important, student outcomes are not viewed as consequences of intentional teacher actions. Thus, low value teachers are less likely to see themselves as accountable for their actions and associated outcomes, and thus attributions are externalized to the student or situation. For the low value teachers, even a positively evaluated teacher action is usually perceived as the result of external rather than internal teacher factors.

EMPIRICAL EVIDENCE FOR THE VALUE-BELIEF MODEL

Two experimental studies were conducted in order to test some of the key components of the value-belief model presented in Table 5.1. Both studies tested the general assumption that teachers' values affect how they attribute evaluative information about their teaching. A general value for teaching effectiveness was examined in the first study, while a specific value for teaching acts (i.e., lecture versus discussion) was used in the second study. In the first study, teachers were provided with information about whether a teacher received positive or negative evaluation and about the student performance. In the second, only information about the teacher's performance evaluation was given. The first study looked at relatively global tendencies to make attributions internally to the teacher or externally to the student or situation, whereas the second examined more differentiated attributional categories (e.g., ability, effort, task difficulty, unusual help from others). The studies were designed to establish whether or not teacher beliefs about the importance of teaching and its associated acts resulted in teacher or student blame given information about the student's level of performance (Study 1) and whether or not these importance beliefs were related to a general effort-outcome covariation belief (Study 2).

In order to test the theoretical assumptions posited in Table 5.1, the first experimental study examined how teachers placing a high or low value on effective teaching attribute positive and negative feedback from high and low performing students. The feedback to teachers was characterized as student ratings of instruction, and student performance data were in the form of high or low course grades. College instructors received detailed descriptions of hypothetical good and poor ratings from students described as high or low performers. The ratings summaries were designed to simulate a commonly used instruction rating and feedback format.

A questionnaire was mailed to 100 college instructors at a large university who were asked to respond anonymously. The instructors represented a wide variety of subject matter fields including science, mathematics, social science, humanities and education. Thirty-nine instructors returned the questionnaire. In accordance with recent research in value theory (Rokeach, 1973), attainment value of teaching was defined as involving a cognitive, affective, and attitudinal component with the cognitive component as most important. A five-item scale was constructed. Three items assessed instructors' beliefs about the importance of teaching (i.e., believing that one is competent, that one tries hard, and that teaching is an important work activity) to the instructor's self-image (cognitive component). The importance ratings were made on a 5-point Likert type scale ranging from "Extremely Important" to "Of Little Importance." The affective item asked teachers to rate how much they "enjoy teaching" on a 5-point scale ranging from "always" to "never." The attitudinal item asked teachers to rate how much they like to spend time with and work closely with students on a 5-point scale ranging from "always" to "never." An attainment value of teaching score was derived for each instructor by summing across the five items. The instructors scoring in the lower third of the sample were defined as the Low Attainment Value group and those scoring in the upper third were defined as the High Attainment Value group.

As part of the questionnaire package, the instructors received four sets of hypothetical ratings summaries each presented on a separate legal-size sheet with the caption, "Summary Profile for Teaching Skills," at the top of the page. The summary included a graphical presentation of an excellent or poor instructor rating. The profile stated that 30 students had been sampled, and the teaching factors summarized in the profile included planning, presentation, subject knowledge, organization, and discussion. To the right of the graph summary, the overall rating was verbally summarized as excellent or poor, and a statement about student performance in the course was provided which read, "student grades: well above average, or well below average." This summary format was designed to be similar to that reported by the Endeavor Instructional Rating System (1979; see also Frey, 1973), a widely used instructor rating and feedback system. The teacher respondents were instructed to imagine that they had taught a class which was asked to evaluate their teaching.

After reviewing the ratings and grade summaries, the respondents were asked to select a probable cause from each of ten pairs of statements representing possible reasons for the student ratings of the teachers. The teachers were asked to assume they had received the ratings summarized at the top of each page of the questionnaire and instructed to indicate why they believed the students in the course rated them the way they did by selecting the most plausible reason from a pair of statements. An exemplary pair of statements was:

      _____A. You were quite good (poor) at making clear explanations to students. (Teacher ability)

      _____B. The students in this course were very (not very) bright and grasped (did not grasp) concepts easily. (Student ability)

Each of the causal attribution items contained in the paired statements was designed to represent one of the three major attribution dimensions defined by Weiner (1979): locus, control, and stability, and these dimensions corresponded to three scales. One additional scale, student blame, was derived. A given causal attribution statement included one of the following specific attribution factors: teacher ability, teacher effort, student ability, student effort, luck, and task ease/difficulty. Two different attribution statements were paired to form each item on the questionnaire, and subjects were instructed to select one statement within each pair. Scores were derived for each scale by counting the number of causal choices subjects made along each of the four attribution dimensions.

A 2(high versus low value) × 2(good versus poor ratings) × 2(above versus below average grades) factorial design with repeated measures on the last two factors was used to examine hypotheses related to how high versus low attainment value teachers attributed good and poor feedback from high and low performing students. Main effects for attainment value indicated that instructors who placed a high value on teaching attributed the causes of their ratings to internal, $F(1,24) = 13.95$, $p < .001$, and controllable, $F(1,24) = 7.45$, $p < .05$, factors more than did instructors who placed a low value on teaching. High value teachers also blamed the student less than did low value teachers, $F(1,24) = 20.35$, $p < .01$ (see Table 5.2 for means on these scales).

A significant three-way interaction was obtained on the locus, control, and student blame scales, $F(1,24) = 14.24$; 10.80; 12.70, $p < .01$, respectively. Further analyses yielded a rather consistent set of findings across these scales. That is, negative ratings from low-performing students were more likely to be attributed to internal, controllable, teacher factors (blaming the student less) by teachers who placed a high value on teaching than by teachers who placed a low value on teaching ($p < .01$ for all simple, simple main effects tests). Thus, high value teachers were much more likely to blame themselves rather than the student for negative ratings from low-performing students than were low value teachers. Also as predicted, low value teachers viewed themselves as responsible for positive performance evaluations from low-performing students.

The data from this study provide rather strong support for the value-belief model presented in Table 5.1. High value teachers, in general, took significantly

TABLE 5.2
Means for Values x Grades x Ratings Analysis (Study #1)

| Grades | | High Value | | | | Low Value | | | |
| | | High | | Low | | High | | Low | |
Causal attribution	Ratings	Good	Poor	Good	Poor	Good	Poor	Good	Poor
Locus		1.00[a]	0.62	0.77	1.38	3.31	1.85	0.46	4.15
Stability		3.08	2.38	2.92	3.15	3.00	3.31	2.38	4.00
Control		1.15	1.00	1.06	1.30	2.15	1.31	0.77	2.38
Student blame		2.08	1.08	1.46	2.31	4.61	1.31	0.77	4.77

[a]The higher the mean the more the attribution was to external, unstable, uncontrollable, and student factors.

more responsibility (i.e., made internal teacher attributions) than did low value teachers. Further, when the student's performance was successful, high value teachers took credit for positive teaching evaluations and blamed themselves for negative evaluations. In contrast, low value teachers did not take credit for positive teaching evaluations and blamed the student and situation for negative evaluations. More interestingly, when the student failed, high value teachers blamed a negative teaching evaluation on themselves whereas low value teachers assigned blame to the student and situation. Attributions were reversed when teachers attributed positive teaching evaluations from a failing student. These attributional assignments support the hypothesis that high value more than low value teachers perceive a connection between their performance and student outcomes.

The value-belief model proposed here states that attributions are made in reference to purposes, and as such it is a teleological view. Kruglanski (1979) and Buss (1978) have advanced this teleological view, and Kruglanski's recent work suggests that all attributions are purposive. In the present context, a centrally important value serves as the purpose or reason for behavior. For example, if a teacher values the welfare of the pupil, he or she may be willing to spend time with and help that student more than a teacher who does not value the welfare of the pupil. If asked to explain their behavior, teachers placing a high value on student welfare would say that it is important for them to put forth the effort to work with the student in this way; their value for helping students suggests that such helping is an endogenous rather than exogenous act for them (see Kruglanski, 1979, and Nicholls, 1979). Further, if they receive feedback that their helping behavior was ineffective, they would be expected to attribute the cause to something about their own teaching indicating they should try harder in the future because endogenous activities, according to Kruglanski, should be closely associated with attributions to intentional factors. In this sense, the value construct can be generalized to include a variety of important goals in teaching beyond the goal or value of competence investigated in the study just reported. Further, Kruglanski's work has extended explanations for outcomes or occurrences to an examination of how persons use concepts of purpose to attribute action or behavior. Thus, it was of interest to examine the power of the value-belief model to encompass teachers' attributions for both their behavioral actions as well as performance outcomes made within the context of a variety of educationally relevant values.

A second study was conducted in which college instructors were first asked to rate values associated with instructional actions, that is, presentation-planning skills versus discussion skills. The investigation of attributions related to endogenous versus exogenous actions requires that actions be identified which can be viewed as endogenous (i.e., ends in themselves) and as exogenous (i.e., means to an end). In fact, teaching actions lend themselves rather easily to being defined as both means and ends. For example, teaching students facts and concepts is an action (i.e., presentation of facts and concepts) and an outcome (i.e., learning of facts and concepts). The characterization of teacher actions in this manner allowed for the rating of the action as a valued end in and of itself, for example, "I value teaching students to learn facts and concepts as an important educational outcome." Further, since this action involves the act of presenting facts and concepts, it can be evaluated, allowing for the investigation of attributions for positive and negative feedback about the action. Following the work of Nicholls (1979), the endogenous-exogenous distinction was drawn in terms of the individual value priorities of the instructors. An instructor placing a high value on "teaching students to learn facts and concepts" as an important educational outcome has stated in effect that this action is important as an end in itself (i.e., is an endogenous action). Thus, in this study the endogenous-exogenous distinction was made in terms of the individual value priorities of the subjects. A person placing high value on certain teaching actions sees that action set as endogenous whereas a person placing low value on the action set sees the action as exogenous. Although teaching actions can be considered endogenous or exogenous relevant to a particular value priority, the actions can also be given a positive or negative evaluation, and hence attributions can be made for the evaluation of these actions.

It was hypothesized that teachers who placed a high value on presentation-planning actions would respond to positive and negative feedback about their presentation skills differently than teachers who placed a high value on discussion actions. Similarly it was expected that these two types of teachers would respond differently to positive and negative feedback about discussion skills. Specifically, teachers placing a high value on presentation actions ought to perceive the effective use of presentation skills as related to intentional, controllable factors such as effort (Weiner's 1979 framework) because the value-belief model predicts that persons try hard to achieve what they value. A similar relationship between effort attributions and discussion skills was expected for teachers placing a high value on these skills. When attributing positive and negative feedback about their presentation and discussion skills, teachers were expected to perceive controllable factors as covarying with positive and negative feedback relative to their valued skills. That is, effort should be seen as the cause of positive feedback on valued skills and a lack of effort as the cause of negative feedback. This perceived effort-outcome covariation was not expected for feedback on skills unrelated to achieving the valued outcome, for example, discussion value teachers' attributions for feedback about their presentation skill.

In order to test the hypotheses outlined above, a questionnaire was mailed to 120 college instructors. Thirty-seven of them returned completed questionnaires. The methodology used in this second study was similar to that used in the first, described earlier. That is, instructors were asked to complete a questionnaire containing, in this case, four sets of hypothetical rating profiles including an excellent and poor rating for presentation skills and an excellent and poor rating for discussion skills. Since the focus of this study was teacher attributions for how teacher actions were evaluated, information regarding student performance outcomes was not provided. To assess attributions, instructors were asked to rate the importance of eight different causes as determinants of these ratings which corresponded to Weiner's (1979) analysis of attributional factors into locus, control, and stability dimensions. Specifically, instructors were asked to rate the following eight attributional factors: ability, stable effort, unstable effort, mood, task difficulty, luck, unusual help from others, and bias. A sample item related to a poor discussion skill rating was: "You (the teacher) were *not very able* at leading discussions," and a sample item related to a positive presentation-skill rating was, "You put forth an *unusual amount of effort* in planning and presenting lectures *this* semester." These causal attribution items were rated on a 5-point scale ranging from, "Very Important as a Cause" to "Little Importance as a Cause."

Prior to receiving the ratings summaries and completing the attribution questionnaire, instructors indicated their value priorities for lecture versus discussion actions. The instructors completed a questionnaire asking them to check one statement among each of ten pairs of statements according to the following instructions: "... check the item (A or B) which most closely represents what you think is *most important* and *valuable* in a student's education." In response to the question, "Which is more important to students?" teachers selected between a presentation-planning action and a discussion action statement. A sample pair of statements was:

A. Teaching students to work cooperatively with each other (discussion action)
B. Teaching students how to work towards specific goals and complete them on schedule (presentation planning action)

Instructors were then classified as either high discussion or high lecture value teachers based on their responses to this instrument. Instructors scoring in the upper and lower thirds of the sample were used in the analysis, yielding 12 subjects per group.

In general, the results of the study supported the major hypotheses derived from the value-belief model (see Table 5.3). In order to examine how teachers made attributions for their actions (i.e., use of presentation or discussion skills), an overall 2(presentation versus discussion values) × 2(presentation versus discussion skills) × 2(positive versus negative feedback) design was used with repeated measures on the last two factors. Recall that the major hypothesis was that instructors placing high value on a certain set of skills would attribute positive and negative feedback on those skills to intentional (controllable) factors. And, according to Weiner (1979) those attributional factors over which persons have the most volitional control are the internal factors of unstable effort, "You (didn't) put forth an unusual amount of effort in conducting lectures

TABLE 5.3
Means for Value X Skill X Evaluation Analysis (Study #2)

Attribution Factor	Presentation				Discussion			
	Presentation		Discussion		Presentation		Discussion	
	Pos	Neg	Pos	Neg	Pos	Neg	Pos	Neg
Controllable-Variable Index	6.58[a]	6.00	6.50	5.67	5.58	5.67	6.17	6.50
Unstable Effort	4.17	3.92	4.17	3.75	3.50	3.50	3.83	4.00
Unusual Help	2.42	2.08	2.33	1.92	2.08	2.17	2.33	2.33

[a]The higher the mean the more important the perceived cause.

(discussions) this semester,'' and the external factor of unusual help from others, "You made use of special workshops on lecture (discussion) techniques which the University offered this semester." In the first analysis of the data these two factors were combined into a single controllable-variable index, and, as expected, a skill by value interaction was obtained, $F(1,22) = 6.54$, p < .02. The major contributing factor appeared to be unstable effort in that when the factors were analyzed individually, a significant skill by value interaction for unstable effort was found, $F(1,22) = 6.19$, p < .03, but was not obtained for unusual help from others. Further analysis of the data indicated (simple effects tests, p < .05) that presentation value instructors attributed evaluations for presentation skill to this internal-controllable factor significantly more than did discussion value instructors. The strongest support for the model came from the comparison of presentation and discussion value teachers' attributions for presentation skill evaluations. Although the data on the controllable-variable index were in the predicted direction, these two types of instructors did not show a significant difference in their attributions for discussion skill evaluations.

Toward an Integrated Theory of Teacher Attribution

The data from the two studies reported here provide clear support for the hypothesis that teachers' causal attributions were closely related to their values. This value-attribution relationship held for both outcome and action attributions. In both studies, college instructors who differed in value priorities were presented with a vignette in which they were described as having received positive or negative teaching evaluations. Hence, they were asked to make causal ascriptions for the effectiveness or ineffectiveness of their actions. The results of both studies indicated that high value teachers tended to take more personal responsibility for their teaching actions. In the first study, high more than low value teachers blamed factors in their own teaching for poor ratings even when it would have been easy to blame the students (e.g., when they performed poorly). Further, in the second study, teachers who placed value on certain teaching acts viewed effort as the major factor in determining whether or not they received good or poor ratings, whereas teachers who placed a low value on these actions did not perceive such an effort-outcome covariation.

Taking the two studies together, high more than low value teachers took personal responsibility for their teaching actions by crediting and blaming themselves for positive and negative evaluations, respectively, and at the same time focusing on effort as the cause of the good or poor teaching performance. From a practical standpoint, the perception of such an effort-outcome covariation suggests that teachers will continue to try to achieve the valued outcome. That is, they believe that making use of help from any available source will contribute to continued success, and thus they indicate a willingness to attend teaching workshops or take advantage of other aspects of "unusual help from others." In this manner, it is assumed that high value teachers will continue to seek to improve their instructional attempts with the low achieving student. This type of teacher not only appears to believe in an effort-outcome covariation, but also in the modifiability of the situation (i.e., the manipulation of external controllable factors) to increase the chance of success. In contrast, it appears that low value instructors, ones who do not seem to believe in this effort-outcome covariation, focus on other causal factors such as student ability and situational constraints over which they have little control. It would be expected that those instructors would be less persistent with the low-achieving student and that they would put forth little effort to try and improve their instructional activities. While the two studies reported here did not directly investigate teacher attributions for student outcomes (see Table 5.1), the first study did find that high and low value teachers differed in their tendencies to assign blame to themselves versus the student. Thus, indirect evidence for predictions about attributions for student outcomes in the value-belief model was obtained.

The diagram in Figure 5.3 presents in more formal terms examples of and expected relationships between three types of beliefs. Values are depicted as the superordinate belief structure within which causal attributions and instrumental beliefs are embedded. Instrumental beliefs are shown to be activated only when the goal is considered to be important, and thus success or failure at the goal is perceived to be a function of effort. When the goal is not important, then teachers are considered to be less inclined to intend to accomplish the goal. Without intention, actions cannot follow from effort, and hence outcomes are perceived as a function of more uncontrollable factors. Since a specific instrumental action requires an intention belief, low value teachers would not be expected to consider

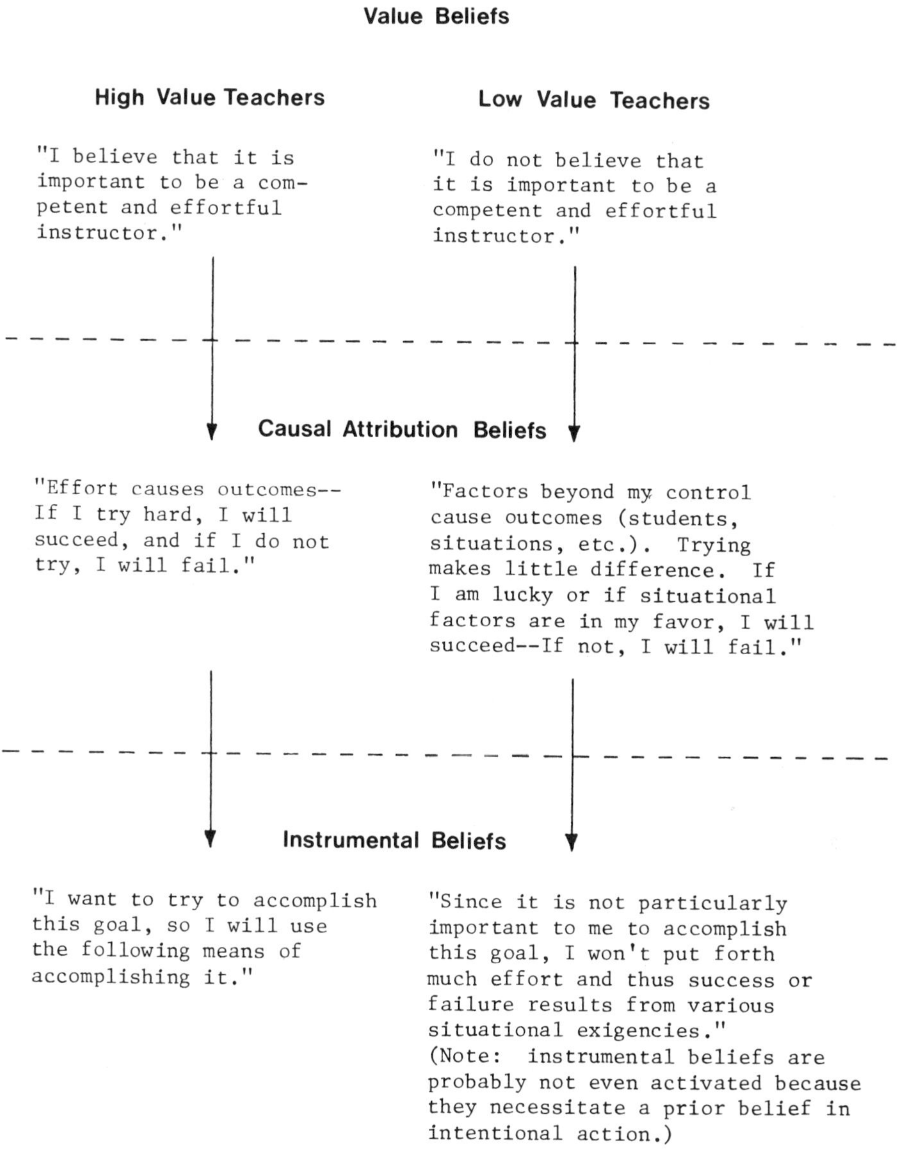

Value Beliefs

High Value Teachers

"I believe that it is
important to be a com-
petent and effortful
instructor."

Low Value Teachers

"I do not believe that
it is important to be a
competent and effortful
instructor."

Causal Attribution Beliefs

"Effort causes outcomes--
If I try hard, I will
succeed, and if I do not
try, I will fail."

"Factors beyond my control
cause outcomes (students,
situations, etc.). Trying
makes little difference. If
I am lucky or if situational
factors are in my favor, I will
succeed--If not, I will fail."

Instrumental Beliefs

"I want to try to accomplish
this goal, so I will use
the following means of
accomplishing it."

"Since it is not particularly
important to me to accomplish
this goal, I won't put forth
much effort and thus success or
failure results from various
situational exigencies."
(Note: instrumental beliefs are
probably not even activated because
they necessitate a prior belief in
intentional action.)

FIG. 5.3   Hierarchical relation of values, causal attributions, and instrumental beliefs

even the available instrumentalities in which they might engage to accomplish a
particular goal. It is hypothesized, then, that the behavior of high value teachers
should reflect greater persistent action relative to the valued goal and thus they

should be likely to continue trying a variety of instructional strategies until they have achieved success with a student.

Finally, it should be noted that the two issues that have been plaguing teacher attribution research since its inception (i.e., responsibility versus causal attribution and the defensive versus non-defensive debate) may be resolved by viewing teacher attributions within this more general value-belief model. Prior confusion in use of the terms "responsibility" and "causal attribution" is clarified by the value-belief model, which suggests that causal attributions are made within a value framework and to believe that one is responsible for an outcome entails that one believes that that outcome is valuable and can be achieved through effort given one's level of ability and the situational constraints. The resolution of the defensive versus non-defensive attribution debate is perhaps even more significant. Within the value-belief model defensive attributions are defined as coordinated to protecting one's sense of self-worth. For a teacher who places a high value on being seen as a competent and effortful teacher, lecturer, or discussion leader, the sense of self-worth is defined, in part, by these value priorities. In general, teachers with this high value orientation have been shown to believe in the covariation of effort and their teaching effectiveness. Further, student failure or negative teaching evaluations will not be a threat to their sense of teaching ability because a negative outcome can be changed to a positive one through effort. For low value teachers, the sense of self-worth is not maintained through effort, because one does not intentionally try to accomplish what one does not value. And, since effort is not part of the perceived causal chain for these teachers, a negative evaluation must reflect either on one's ability or on some external factors. It is generally easier to blame the student or the situation.

The empirical studies reported in this chapter operationally defined value in terms of a person's a priori "importance" beliefs. As noted in the earlier analysis of the teacher responsibility literature, certain situational factors could elicit a certain value priority for making attributional judgments in a given setting (i.e., as when face-to-face communication elicits concern for the welfare of the student). It is interesting to speculate on other situational factors that might elicit values for an effort-outcome covariation belief versus an ability-outcome covariation. For example, the work of Ames, Ames, and Felker (1976) and Ames and Ames (1981) has shown that competitive settings focus a person's attention on his or her ability, whereas non-competitive settings focus attention on a person's intention or effort. It is interesting to speculate as to whether or not such a competitive environment would override a teacher's value for competence and effort in teaching. If high value teachers became concerned about their lack of teaching ability, they, like the low value teachers, might blame the student or situation for negative outcomes. Such speculations, of course, need testing in further research. It is hoped, however, that the global concept of defensive versus non-defensive attributions can be put to rest in favor of the more specific value-related attribution analysis profferred in this paper.

ACKNOWLEDGMENTS

This work was supported in part by the Office of Graduate Studies, University of Maryland University College.

The author wishes to thank Janet Lee Jones for her assistance in data collection and analysis, and Carole Ames and John Nicholls for their review and comments on earlier drafts of this chapter.

REFERENCES

Ames, C., & Ames, R. Competitive versus individualistic goal structures: The salience of past performance information for causal attributions and affect. *Journal of Educational Psychology,* 1981, *73,* 411–418.

Ames, C., Ames, R., & Felker, D. W. Effects of competitive reward structure and value of outcome on children's achievement attributions. *Journal of Educational Psychology,* 1977, *69,* 1–8.

Ames, R. Teachers' attributions of responsibility: Some unexpected non-defensive effects. *Journal of Educational Psychology,* 1975, *67,* 668–676. (a)

Ames, R. A methodology of inquiry for self-concept. *Educational Theory,* 1975, *25,* 314–322. (b)

Beckman, L. J. Effects of students' performance on teachers' and observers' attributions of causality. *Journal of Educational Psychology,* 1970, *61,* 76–82.

Beckman, L. Teachers' and observers' perceptions of causality for a child's performance. *Journal of Educational Psychology,* 1973, *65,* 198–204.

Bradley, G. W. Self-serving biases in the attribution process: A reexamination of the fact or fiction question. *Journal of Personality and Social Psychology,* 1978, *36,* 56–71.

Brandt, L., Hayden, M. E., & Brophy, J. Teachers' attitudes and descriptions of causation. *Journal of Educational Psychology,* 1975, *67,* 677–682.

Buss, A. R. Causes and reasons in attribution theory: A conceptual critique. *Journal of Personality and Social Psychology,* 1978, *36,* 1311–1321.

Covington, M. V., & Beery, R. *Self-worth and school learning.* New York: Holt, Rinehart, & Winston, 1976.

Covington, M. V., & Omelich, C. L. Effort: The double-edged sword in school achievement. *Journal of Educational Psychology,* 1979, *71,* 169–182. (a)

Covington, M. V., & Omelich, C. L. It's best to be able and virtuoso too: Student and teacher evaluative responses to successful effort. *Journal of Educational Psychology,* 1979, *71,* 688–700. (b)

Covington, M. V., & Omelich, C. L. Are causal attributions causal? A path analysis of the cognitive model of achievement motivation. *Journal of Personality and Social Psychology,* 1979, *37,* 1487–1504. (c)

The Endeavor Instructional Rating System: User's Handbook. Evanston, Illinois: Endeavor Information Systems Inc., 1979.

Frey, P. W. Student ratings of teaching: Validity of several rating factors. *Science,* 1973, *182,* 83–85.

Heider, F. *The psychology of interpersonal relations.* New York: Wiley, 1958.

Johnson, T. J., Feigenbaum, R., & Weiby, M. Some determinants and consequences of the teacher's perception of causation. *Journal of Educational Psychology,* 1964, *55,* 237–246.

Kelley, H. H. *Attribution in social interaction.* New York: General Learning Press, 1972.

Kruglanski, A. W. The endogenous-exogenous partition in attribution theory. *Psychological Review,* 1975, *82,* 387–406.

Kruglanski, A. W. Causal explanation, teleological explanation: On radical particularism in attribution theory. *Journal of Personality and Social Psychology,* 1979, *37,* 1447–1457.

Kruglanski, A. W. Lay epistemo-logic-process and contents: Another look at attribution theory. *Psychological Review,* 1980, *87,* 70–87.

Maehr, M. L., & Nicholls, J. G. Culture and achievement motivation: A second look. In Warren, N. (Ed.), *Studies in cross-cultural psychology* (Vol. 3). New York: Academic Press, 1978.

Miller, D. T. What constitutes a self-serving attributional bias? A reply to Bradley. *Journal of Personality and Social Psychology,* 1978, *36,* 1221–1223.

Miller, D. T., & Ross, M. Self-serving biases in the attribution of causality: Fact or fiction? *Psychological Bulletin,* 1975, *82,* 213–225.

Nicholls, J. Causal attributions and other achievement-related cognitions: Effects of task outcome, attainment value, and sex. *Journal of Personality and Social Psychology,* 1975, *31,* 379–398.

Nicholls, J. G. Motivation for intellectual development: The role of motivation in education. *American Psychologist,* 1979, *34,* 1071–1084.

Rokeach, M. *The nature of human values.* New York: Free Press, 1973.

Ross, L., Bierbrauer, G., & Polly, S. Attribution of educational outcomes by professional and nonprofessional teachers. *Journal of Personality and Social Psychology,* 1974, *29,* 609–619.

Schwartz, S. H. Words, deeds, and the perception of consequences and responsibility in action situations. *Journal of Personality and Social Psychology,* 1968, *10,* 232–242.

Weiner, B. A theory of motivation for some classroom experiences. *Journal of Educational Psychology,* 1979, *71,* 379–398.

6

Student and Teacher Perceptions: A Review of Five Position Papers

Thomas L. Good
University of Missouri—Columbia

Overview

It was a distinct pleasure to read the five chapters and to have the opportunity to comment upon them. All of the chapters were contributed to by major investigators who have extensive backgrounds in research and in explicating and analyzing the topics about which they have written. These chapters collectively provide an important opportunity to combine and synthesize much of what is known about research on teacher and student motivational processes. They also provide a significant base upon which future research studies in this area can be designed. In my opinion, the works do not lead to concrete statements or suggestions for classroom practice, but they do present important concepts that should encourage classroom teachers to think more extensively about their behavior and its potential effects upon students. In particular, the chapters may lead practitioners to consider more fully their own behavior and beliefs as potential determinants of student performance. Future research should integrate these individual positions into broader and more comprehensive frameworks for understanding motivational process in the classroom.

It is pointless to reproduce all the arguments which the individual authors have raised in each chapter; however, it will be useful to briefly describe the major points of each one in order to raise a few issues concerning individual chapters. I have also tried to assess briefly each topic's potential for classroom application. After discussing each of the chapters individually, I point out a few weaknesses which are common to all areas and argue that future researchers and theorists will have to deal with these issues if their work is to become more meaningful for classroom practitioners. Again, in my opinion, each of the chapters presents a significant statement that is worthy of serious study and reflection.

Frieze, Francis, and Hanusa

The authors argue that how a student decides whether a particular performance is a successful one has been a neglected area of inquiry. They note that there may be major differences between how individual students and/or subjects define success and how researchers define success. Frieze, Francis and Hanusa provide a reasonably systematic discussion of the concepts that have most often been used to define success and suggest areas where more research is needed.

These authors believe that more attention needs to be paid to students' individual, subjective definitions of success. They also suggest that more differentiation should be made between objective *information* that students possess about their performance and the *attributions* that students make about the causes of their performance. For example, they note that a student may report that he/she tried hard on an exam (information) but still not rate effort as the major influence (attribution) on performance. These authors thus argue for clearer distinction between objective information, subjective reaction, and attributions that are made about performance. They argue that the subjective evaluation of an outcome *precedes* the formation of a causal attribution but follows the information acquisition stage. Hence, objective and subjective outcomes are seen as separate phenomena, with the objective outcome as only one of several influences on students' and/or subjects' subjective definitions of success.

The authors have combined the foregoing distinctions (and several other important ones) to form a comprehensive model which theorizes about how a student decides that a particular performance is successful or is inadequate. Considering available research information, the model appears to be an excellent and comprehensive statement. At a minimum, it should help to improve our hypotheses and help investigators to frame better questions as they attempt to study students' reactions to particular performances.

Another important aspect of this work is the careful analysis of the proposition that in American culture, being successful implies having high ability, and that success in schoolwork requires hard work plus ability. The authors point out that an overemphasis upon competition may make it impossible for low-ability students to view themselves as successful in school environments. Students have both communal and agentic views, but American classrooms favor agentic views and neglect communal values.

I basically agree with most of the major arguments that have been presented in this chapter. To me the most important omission is the lack of any data to illustrate that the model can be used to analyze ongoing classroom events. It would be very instructive to see how the model can be applied in a classroom situation (interviewing students before and after an exam and noting how various definitions of success could be used in order to understand future predictions about student performance on upcoming tests, etc.) and how student definitions of success are influenced by classroom factors (Bossert, 1979; Doyle, 1980) and by teacher beliefs (see for example the chapters by Ames, and Rohrkemper and Brophy in this volume).

I believe that the authors are correct in arguing that the basic attributional model ignores variation in students' and/or subjects' definitions of success. Although their model addresses this important omission, it does not clearly provide an operational framework for identifying and using the idiosyncratic definitions of success which individual students may possess. What norms do students naturally use? Although students at all ages are capable of making causal attributions, do they do so routinely or only under special circumstances? At a certain age, do students stop seeking causal explanations for their school performance? How stable are students' individual perceptions of success and under what conditions are they likely to vary? These are some of the questions this paradigm must attend to in the future.

If one begins to examine classroom process to explain and to understand the antecedents of and effects of specific attributions (why do students use a different set of "causes" for explaining performance on an art project versus an exam?), or to explore students' *criteria* for "success " a number of new issues will appear. For example, the authors suggest that one mechanism through which students may define success is teacher praise. However, the criteria that students use for defining teacher praise may vary widely from student to student, and, as Weinstein et al. (1981) suggest, students and researchers may define praise in different ways. Furthermore, teachers' attempts to praise present interpretative problems for both researchers and students (Brophy, 1981). Teachers, students, and researchers have been found to have only minimal agreement concerning the amount of praise that individual students receive (Cooper and Good, in press). Although the call for more attention to individual definitions of success is important, it will be very difficult to study. In time, research on both "objective" classroom events and teachers' and students' subjective reactions may yield firmer intervention points. At present, however, the chapter leaves us with a clear picture of the problem but with no solutions.

As I noted in my introductory remarks, I do not believe that any of the chapters presents information so compelling that it suggests concrete changes which are universally necessary in ongoing classroom situations. However, I think a number of important issues that practitioners need to consider are raised in this chapter. One especially important point is that different students define success in varied ways. Through conversations with students, teachers should attempt to increase their understanding of these differences and perhaps broaden the range of success possible in the classroom in order to accommodate these individual definitions. Teachers also need to consider whether their emphasis on competition may inadvertently make it impossible for low-ability students to define their performance as successful and whether they systematically deny the expression of communal values and processes in the classroom. Finally, the authors' distinction between general statements of ability and/or effort and beliefs about the relative influence of these factors on specific outcomes is an important one. Teachers might attempt to understand this aspect of classroom life more fully by routinely collecting from students anonymous information describing the amount of time they spend preparing for an exam, how successful they believe their performance has been, etc.

Weiner

Weiner begins his chapter by describing the growing interest in achievement-change programs and emphasizing their basic intent to alter attributions for failure from low ability to lack of effort. He argues that these past efforts at change analysis are incomplete and he calls for more attention to affect. In particular, he notes that the effects of achievement-change programs which have been ascribed to changes in expectations of success could be explained as due to alterations in the affective state of the performer.

To evaluate these competing conceptualizations he reviews existing literature and notes that extant data can be used to support both positions. He then reviews two recent experiments of his own and although cautioning the reader that his results are based upon correlational evidence, he contends that attributions tell us what to feel and feelings tell us what to do.

In addition to advocating increased study of the use of affect, Weiner also argues for the need to integrate "help giver" and "help receiver" perspectives if we are to understand reciprocal influences, because change programs do not occur in a vacuum. For example, he notes that there is ample evidence that when failure is ascribed to a perceived lack of effort, there is a tendency to punish the receiver. In contrast, when failure is believed to be due to inability, the giver tends to provide help to the individual who has failed. Paradoxically, then, communication of sympathy from the "help giver" to the "help receiver" may function as an attributional cue which strengthens the "help receiver's" belief that low ability is an accurate self-perception. In contrast, Weiner notes that anger under certain circumstances might indicate to the receiver that he/she has *not* tried rather than that he/she is unable.

I, too, have had some reservations about the easy assumption that "help givers" need to shift their focus from ability to effort attributions. One of my major concerns relates to the incredibly difficult task that a teacher has to perform when deciding whether a failure is due to lack of effort. For example, when a student provides a wrong answer to a teacher's question about material that the student was to have read the night before, is the student's inability to perform due to effort (e.g., not reading the assigned passage) or due to lack of comprehension? Making these distinctions is a very difficult task, and, under some circumstances, perhaps is impossible. Weiner's new conceptualization even adds to the complexity of the teacher's (or any other "help giver's") task. That is, under certain circumstances teacher expression of negative affect following student failure may be appropriate, but under other circumstances it may be inappropriate.

In order to assess the effects of teacher affect on student perceptions and behavior, research needs to take place in ongoing classrooms. In order to conduct classroom research, many practical problems will have to be solved, and their successful resolution may provide implications for practitioners in the future. Among the many issues that Weiner and colleagues will have to confront are: How do teachers' role definitions influence their expression of affect? Do students and researchers differ in their definitions of affect and do different students ascribe various affective interpretations to the *same* teacher behavior? How does the ratio of high to low-ability students present in a classroom influence the teacher's expression of affect and the interpretation of those affective expressions by individual students (see for example Beckerman and Good, in press)? For example, if a student is one of several students who occasionally receive expressions of teacher anger, it may have beneficial effects upon the student's performance. In contrast, if the student is the only one towards whom the teacher expresses anger, such teacher behavior would probably have detrimental effects upon that student's performance. Furthermore, it would seem that various types of students might react differently to teacher affect, regardless of the teacher's behavior toward other students in the class. For example, a student who is distrustful of adults and teachers might not react to anger "positively" even if other students also received teacher anger occasionally.

Much work needs to be done before the recent conceptualization of Weiner will have practical implications in the classroom. However, the perspective from which his chapter is written is a helpful and refreshing one that should encourage teachers to think much more extensively about their behavior toward individual students in the classroom. I think his warning that an emphasis upon changing failure attributions from ability to effort without concomitant attention to affect may do as much harm as good is an important statement (concern about the effects of teacher effort attributions have been expressed elsewhere as well, see Schunk, 1981). I have recently been impressed with the possibility that teachers may show much more variation in their behavior and expectations for low-achieving students than they do for high-achieving students (Good, 1981). Specifically, I have argued that variations in teacher behavior and expectations may make it difficult for students to define their roles as they move from classroom to classroom. It will be important to see if teachers show variation in the degree of affect that they express following low-achieving students' failures. If these cues vary widely from one classroom to another, it may be very difficult for low-achieving students to understand when and how to approach their teachers for help.

It will also be interesting to see if students have a generalized view of how a teacher regards them and if this opinion is relied upon consistently to interpret ambiguous cues from that teacher. I suspect that many statements in the classroom which appear to be affect-free from the observer's or researcher's point of view provide a basis for students to interpret teacher affect. Whether students' affective reactions to teacher statements are rather general or whether they depend upon particular classroom events (e.g., a poor exam) will be exciting and important research topics. Making these distinctions and many others will require clever, if not ingenious, interview strategies and I wait with interest to see how Weiner and others resolve these complex methodological problems.

Levine

Levine notes that the destructive effects of social comparison have been argued in many position papers. He also notes that a major problem is that our knowledge of social comparison is derived primarily from lab experiments, and he advocates observational studies in classrooms, along with detailed interviews, to understand the process as it actually occurs.

He also argues that social comparison effects are very complex and often do not operate in the way in which some researchers and/or theorists have conceptualized. For example, he notes that many handicapped youngsters have been mainstreamed into regular classrooms, on the assumption that day-to-day contact with regular students would improve handicapped students' concepts of their own efficacy. As Levine notes, some results from recent mainstreaming literature suggest that improvement does not occur automatically, and that in some instances students find themselves in pejorative environments that may very well lead to destruction of their motivation rather than to its enhancement.

He further notes that individualized instruction may increase rather than decrease the need for social comparison. He argues that many researchers and theorists have contended that individualized environments may decrease the number of invidious comparisons that individual students make with other students. However, as Levine points out, some individualized classrooms may lead to more social comparisons because students move at their own pace. Also, because of their high rate of task completion, students' needs for self-evaluation may be even higher in individualized classrooms. In some individualized classrooms students have more freedom to move about the room and talk with other students, and they may thus receive more social comparison information and some of this information may be pejorative.

Although social comparison is generally assumed to do more harm than good, especially for low-achieving students or for students with low self-concepts, Levine questions this assumption and hypothetically argues that both low and high self-concepts may inhibit performance. Specifically, he argues that low self-esteem may lead students to avoid certain situations because they expect to fail, and that high self-esteem may erode the need to prove oneself or to demonstrate competence. In essence, he points out that the need to convince oneself and others of one's competence may be a major determinant of effortful striving in school and work and hence may have desirable effects. To deny students access to social comparison information may thus be detrimental in some situations.

Levine argues that there are no compelling data to illustrate that self-esteem is an important determinant of achievement. Hence, it is hard to estimate how different types of self-comparison function and under what circumstances a comparison will lead to increased or decreased motivation or effort. Among several possible determinants, he notes that the size as well as the direction of differences between one's own performance and another's may well mediate the benefits and/or harmful consequences of social comparison. I suspect that comparisons of whether or not one is making progress are also relevant. That is, one might compare oneself with another individual and see that there is a large negative discrepancy in performance. However, if such a comparison yields a sense of becoming better or "closing the gap," then the social comparison may still be beneficial.

Levine presents a very useful and comprehensive model for thinking about social comparison and advocates that research on social comparison questions occur in actual classrooms. The model which he presents raises a number of questions about why social comparison information is sought and how such information can be obtained. His model will be very helpful in organizing information that is relevant to social comparison processes as well as in identifying unresolved issues.

One limitation on his work is the failure to list priorities for needed research. The reader is left with a number of potential questions but there is no explicit suggestion of how these questions might be addressed programmatically. Surely some of the questions are more important than others, but Levine is unwilling to provide this information for the reader. Also, related to the conceptualization of Weiner, it seems important to consider social comparison processes, both from the standpoint of the *help giver* and the *help receiver*. That is, it would be very instructive to determine whether students' needs and interests for social comparison are related to the needs that their teachers have for social comparison information. Teachers who are more concerned about their own skills (in comparison to other teachers) may well create environments which cause their students to be much more interested in obtaining social comparison information.

Levine provides a very comprehensive review of the literature related to social comparison processes. As he notes, much more research and conceptualization will have to occur before practical guidelines (even in the form of probability statements) are forthcoming. The chapter is very valuable for promoting a full consideration of possible relationships between social comparison and performance. Practitioners are challenged to think more about some of the positive consequences of social comparison effects, as well as the negative ones upon which most emphasis is now placed. Clearly, information about the performance of others relative to a student's own performance appears to have problematic effects. Teachers will thus have to monitor from time to time how students feel and react to their performances in class relative to the performances of other students. Through informal conversations, some teachers may be able to detect and to correct erroneous assumptions which students have made about themselves.

Ames

In Ames' opinion, teachers make attributions about their own performances in response to their own behavior and beliefs as well as to student performance. He contends that teachers arrive at attributions about their teaching effectiveness through a belief system organized around certain values of personal interest to themselves. The central argument is that teachers' attributions for the feedback they receive (e.g., self-assessment, student performance) affect whether or not they modify or change their teaching behavior.

One area of concern in attribution research has been teacher behavior following student failure. In some studies teachers appear to engage in defensive (ego-enhancing) behavior which indicates that essentially they blame the failure on students. However, in other studies teachers have been willing to assume partial responsibility for student failure. Ames argues that there has been little evaluation of the values that teachers hold for certain teaching acts and that such research may be helpful in trying to understand whether or not teachers will engage in ego-enhancing behavior. For example, he notes that depending upon whether a person is concerned about the adequacy of his/her teaching ability or about his/her concern for others, the explanations for student failure may be quite different.

He assumes that some teachers perceive their teaching acts to be more strongly related to student outcomes than do other teachers. This belief that their positive efforts can lead to positive outcomes from students is derived from these teachers' more general value orientation that they are responsible for students. More explicitly, Ames organizes the chain of beliefs in the following way: (1) teaching is important; (2) teachers engage in intentional acts to produce positive outcomes; (3) students' success is generally feasible, given situational aids and constraints. He presents results from an empirical study to support this conceptualization. He found that teachers who placed importance upon being competent and who believed that teaching was an important activity were more likely to consider their own behavior as a possible source of influence than were teachers who did not believe that teachers were responsible for student learning. In general, the study found empirical support for many of the hypothesized relationships between teachers' beliefs in their ability to produce positive outcomes and teachers' explanations for student success and/or failure.

In another study Ames examined teacher attributions for behavioral action (rather than performance outcomes). To do this, he stratified teachers on the basis of whether they valued discussion or lecture techniques. The major hypothesis tested was that if teachers valued a particular teaching activity, they would more likely consider their role as a possible determinant of student behavior during that activity if students did poorly. Essentially, the results that Ames obtained are consistent with the argument that teachers are more likely to avoid defensive explanations when they are engaging in high-value activities.

Frieze et al. discussed the need to include students' subjective definitions of success in the attribution framework. Implicitly, Ames makes the same argument at the teacher level. According to different values they hold, teachers may look for different cues and feedback in order to derive feelings of efficacy in the classroom. Teachers think and interpret classroom behavior and ultimately make attributions. If, as Ames argues, teachers' values mediate their interpretations and responses to classroom events, then the same level of child behavior and performance may elicit different attributions and responses from different teachers. The fact that teachers may make attribution statements on the basis of their value frameworks is thus an important perspective.

Conceptually, the framework which Ames presents is somewhat similar to the position of Cooper (1979), who contended that teachers under certain circumstances may react differently to equivalent student behaviors, depending upon whether they have relatively high or low control needs. Teachers with greater control needs were hypothesized as being more likely to discourage students (especially low-achieving students) from initiating contacts with them in public classroom situations (because these situations were much more problematic and threatened teachers' classroom control). The work of Ames, like that of Cooper, suggests that teachers interpret and value student responses in terms of their own frameworks, as well as by examining student performances.

Perhaps the chief weakness of Ames' chapter is that the data presented are in questionnaire form. Whether these relationships would exist in ongoing classrooms is unknown. The form in which the data were collected may have caused teachers to respond much more systematically than they would have under real classroom conditions. Furthermore, in actual classroom situations teachers have many competing goals. Some teachers may feel that teaching is important and value discussion highly. Others may feel that teaching is important but not value discussion activities. Because of these competing value orientations (and many others which are operating simultaneously, as well as the ways in which individual students present themselves to teachers) the relationship between belief systems that teachers hold and their subsequent analyses and responses may not be as direct as illustrated in the set of empirical studies Ames presents.

Similar questions and/or concerns can be raised about the antecedents of various teacher beliefs. For example, where does the belief that teaching is an important and manageable activity originate from? Or, where does the belief that discussion is an important activity come from? Does the belief in the importance of discussion skills and student expression during discussion develop because some teachers believe that this is an important instructional activity, or does it come from social comparison with other teachers? That is, perhaps teachers select instructional activities according to their perceived skill at conducting particular activities. Information about the antecedents of beliefs and the tenacity with which they are held may ultimately help us to understand more fully which values are more likely to be reflected in actual classrooms. In its present form the chapter should at least encourage teachers to think about their beliefs generally and to consider how certain views (e.g., teachers aren't responsible) may have "negative effects" on their own behavior and subsequently that of students as well.

Rohrkemper and Brophy

Rohrkemper and Brophy have theorized that teachers' attributions about student performance affect their ideas concerning their teaching roles which in turn affect their responses to students. Teachers who had been identified as good or average teachers by their principals were asked to read vignettes depicting various student problems and to assume that the problems had actually occurred in their classrooms. Teachers were then asked to describe what they would say and do when this happened in their own classrooms.

Based upon distinctions made by Gordon (1974), these researchers included in the vignettes problems that reflected teacher-owned problems (student behavior interferes with the teacher's meeting his/her own needs); teacher-student shared problems (when the teacher and student interfere with each other's need for satisfaction); and student-owned problems (problems which exist independent of the teacher).

Their results indicate that teachers' attributions about students, as well as teachers' beliefs about their potential impact on students, varied across the three levels of problem ownership. Their results for teacher-owned problems are particularly thought-provoking. Teachers' descriptions of their intentions in such situations were characterized by a higher frequency of punishment, restricted language, and emphasis upon short-term control attempts. Such teacher actions would appear to be self-defeating and would simply maintain inappropriate behavior of students. Presumably, because teachers' prognoses for long-term change were poor, they chose to respond to specific problems without attempting to eradicate or to change basic problems in role assumptions which the students presented.

Rohrkemper and Brophy have provided a useful strategy for relating teacher attributions to potential sequences of classroom behavior. More specifically, they have illustrated how an attributional framework can be utilized for describing and understanding teachers' reactions to particular problem situations. Like Weiner, they have stressed the close connection between *help giver* and *help receiver*; and like Ames, they have emphasized the potential role of teachers' attributions. The methodology presented here may encourage subsequent application of attributional concepts to other aspects of classroom behavior.

In addition to providing a research strategy of considerable heuristic value, this work illustrates that attributional inferences are necessary but potentially harmful (particularly in the case of teacher-owned problems). The chapter provides some important distinctions that teachers could use to think about their behavior when they interact with problem students in the classroom. Although the particular teacher behaviors which would be important for use with individual students remain problematic, teachers at least need to be aware of possible self-defeating sequences of behavior when they are responding to problem behavior in the classroom. Distinctions between teacher-owned, student-owned, and shared problems should cause teachers to consider potential negative responses that they may make when dealing with these three types of problems and provide a framework for thinking about alternative responses that might be of greater long-term value.

Rohrkemper and Brophy carefully point out that their causal sequence is assumed and not tested. That teacher attributions about students affect their sense of their roles as teachers, which in turn affects their responses to students probably is a causal sequence that operates with some frequency in the classroom. However, many other patterns probably can be found in classrooms. For example, according to Ames, teachers' values may sometimes influence attributions about students. Teachers' responses to students may lead them to reevaluate their roles as teachers and the attributions that they have been making about a particular student (Why did I respond so angrily to that student?).

Teacher responses to vignettes cannot be equated to classroom behavior, as the authors note. However, this point needs to be stressed because it is relatively easy to assume that beliefs and preferences translate into behavior. Such a correspondence does not necessarily exist, and it will be important to see if actual classroom behavior can be associated with teachers' thoughts about the three types of hypothesized problem situations. In assessing such relationships in actual classroom situations, *style* issues as well as particular behaviors should be examined. The general manner in which a teacher intervenes and the intensity of such teacher behavior may be as important as the presence or absence of certain actions.

The authors have chosen to study teacher reactions to problem students in a generalized context. This approach has many advantages but it also has some disadvantages. For example, the way in which a teacher reacts to a problem situation during reading could be quite unlike his/her reaction to a similar problem during social studies. Subsequent research needs to examine the impact of context and particular students upon teachers' attributions and responses. Future studies on teacher attributions should also integrate the framework presented by Ames with the model articulated by Rohrkemper and Brophy. Teachers who are more serious about teaching and who believe that they can have an effect upon students would probably show some qualitative differences in attributional thinking and in overt responding to students in the classroom.

A Few Suggestions

All five chapters which I have revieweu have raised some new and important questions which illustrate how rapidly changing the area of attributions and student motivation is. Issues addressed by these authors generally were not being discussed 2 to 3 years ago. As I have pointed out, distinctions, concepts, and general ideas presented in these chapters will be helpful for practitioners who want to study their behavior and its potential effects upon students. It is encouraging to see that models for explaining possible motivational sequences are becoming much more complex and comprehensive.

Perhaps the greatest deficiency of these chapters (from my perspective) is that the research reported does not include systematic observation. To be more useful for practitioners, research must move into the classroom. One wonders to what extent teachers express affect in the classroom, how aware students are of such affect, and how they interpret this teacher behavior when they do perceive it. The conceptualizations presented in the various chapters are intriguing, but they provide no evidence that student and teacher attributions can be related to classroom behavior and performance. Because of numerous competing needs and demands that both teachers and students have, it is difficult to assume that any single motivation will translate into behavior. Current motivational research should include intensive observational measures along with assessments of students' affective responses and their performance on selected academic tasks.

Such observation should be reasonably comprehensive because teachers often vary their behavior toward individual students according to whether an interaction is public or private. The *context* of interaction should be studied in an attempt to relate interactions to distinct theoretical positions. For example, in the work of Weiner, it is important to determine how teacher affect (e.g., expressed in private feedback) influences student behavior (e.g., after the teacher leaves, is the rate and/or quality of the seatwork affected?). In the case of Rohrkemper and Brophy, it will be important to determine if in fact teachers do behave differently when they encounter teacher-owned problems than they do in other problem situations, to determine if students are aware of such differential teacher behavior, and to assess students' perceptions of problem interactions (Do they feel that their behavior is appropriate/controllable? Do students feel that teachers approve of them? etc.).

Although classroom observational research has shown distinct differences in the ways in which teachers interact with individual students and the ways in which they vary their behavior in different contexts, it may be that students are largely unaware of such variations in teacher behavior. We need much more research which employs interview techniques in order to determine how students interpret teacher behavior. For example, are students aware of the fact that teachers behave differently toward them in private and public situations, and if so, what significance does a particular student attach to this differential behavior? In addition, more interpretive information should be collected from both students and teachers about the meaning and importance of individual classroom events (e.g., teachers and students could be asked to discuss videotaped classroom proceedings and to explain the importance of various events). Some students may conclude that they are not good in mathematics and thus pay little attention during mathematics instruction. They may not perceive desirable teacher behaviors even when objective observers do. Other students may hear pejorative teacher comments but choose to ignore them for a variety of reasons (e.g., a neighbor says, "There goes Mr. X again"). There are countless mediating factors in the classroom and it will be important to test motivational research there if one's goal is to generalize about classroom practice.

Although there are some rich conceptualizations of how motivational processes influence student and teacher performance, there are virtually no data to illustrate this dynamic influence. Actual demonstrations of how teacher behaviors are interpreted and acted upon by students and how student behaviors may influence teacher attributions and subsequent behaviors are needed. It seems important to demonstrate such motivational sequences if we are to begin to understand how to intervene in teaching and learning situations.

For instance, we now have general notions about how attributions may affect a person's own behavior and behavior toward others; however, we have comparatively little validity data that is drawn from actual classroom settings. The few data that do exist are typically pen and paper measures (e.g., an IAR measure) that are taken at one time and related to student achievement at another time. The IAR data do not describe how students develop internality beliefs, the ways in which classroom environments maintain such beliefs (or alter them), and why such beliefs relate to achievement. It is now widely known that under various conditions, people (even very young children) often make different attributions for their success or failure (when requested to do so). However, we do not know whether students of any age commonly make attributions about their performance. It might be instructive to tape students who are spontaneously talking with one or two peers after receiving an important paper or test. Similarly, it would seem interesting to determine whether students' study habits are affected by such information and by their own attributions. For example, do students actually spend more time studying for the next exam if they conclude that lack of effort was a cause for a poor performance? Gathering case information which documents this possibility would be useful research. Do students who have different beliefs about the extent to which they can learn in different classes adjust their study time accordingly? Do they actually spend more time preparing for tests and/or assignments in classrooms where they believe that effort is important than they do in classrooms where they believe that ability is of chief importance?

The authors have discussed and argued a number of important viewpoints. Their individual and collective conceptualizations are impressive, but I think that the ultimate test of these ideas will be made by classroom research. Because of the vast number of potential sources of influence on individual perception and performance, it may be particularly important to collect observational, perceptual, and performance data on teachers and students using a longitudinal design. Such a methodology allows observation of the same subject over a number of "equivalent trials," while simultaneously allowing for a degree of fortuitous variation (for example, seeing how a student reacts differently to two teachers who use different levels of affect). Also, I think subsequent classroom research will have more value if observation and participant measures are collected in specific contexts (e.g., observing in the same class for a week rather than five days spread out over the entire year). This is especially the case if teacher and student perception data and observational findings are related to immediate outcomes (e.g., student work habits following specific teacher behaviors or exam performance that comes at the end of the week's observation).

It is time for motivational research to move beyond a "two-variable" framework and to explore the simultaneous and reciprocal effects of several variables. The authors have done a commendable job of identifying specific variables worthy of attention in theory and practice. It will be important for future researchers to synthesize these perspectives and to look for interaction effects among them (e.g., "How do social comparison effects moderate effects of teacher affect?"). Such integrative research may ultimately generate more specific classroom strategies than is possible at present.

ACKNOWLEDGMENT

The author would like to acknowledge the typing support provided by the Center for Research in Social Behavior, University of Missouri—Columbia and to thank Gail Hinkel for her comments on this manuscript.

REFERENCES

Beckerman, T., & Good, T. A classroom ratio of high- and low-aptitude students and its effect on achievement. *American Educational Research Journal,* in press.

Bossert, S. Task and social relationships in classrooms: A study of classroom organization and its consequences. *American Psychological Association,* Arnold & Caroline Rose, Monograph Series. New York: Cambridge University Press, 1979.

Brophy, J. On praising effectively. *Elementary School Journal,* 1981.

Cooper, H. Pygmalion grows up: A model for teacher expectation communication and performance influence. *Review of Educational Research,* 1979, *49,* 389–410.

Cooper, H., & Good, T. *Pgymalion grows up: Studies in the expectation communication process.* New York: Academic Press, in press.

Doyle, W. *Student mediating responses in teacher effectiveness.* N.I.E. Final Report (NIE-G-76-0099), North Texas State University, Denton, Texas, 1980.

Good, T. Teacher expectations and student perceptions: A decade of research. *Educational Leadership,* 1981 (February), *38,* 415–422.

Gordon, T. *Teacher effectiveness training.* New York: Wyden, Inc., 1974.

Schunk, D. Modeling and attributional effects on children's achievement: A self-efficacy analysis. *Journal of Educational Psychology,* 1981, *73,* 93–105.

Weinstein, R., et al. *Student perceptions of differential teacher treatment.* N.I.E. Final Report (NIE-G-79-0078), University of California, Berkeley, Calif., 1981.

IMPACT OF PERFORMANCE EXPECTATIONS IN CLASSROOMS

7

Teacher Talk and Student Thought: Socialization into the Student Role

Phyllis C. Blumenfeld
V. Lee Hamilton
Steven T. Bossert
Kathleen Wessels
Judith Meece
The University of Michigan

In modern societies systems of formal schooling are charged with the dual responsibilities of providing academic training and citizenship training. Some of the socialization of scholars and citizens is expected to occur in the home; but a large, and probably increasing, proportion of the burden of this socialization falls on our teachers. Researchers probing the effectiveness of our schools have tended to focus on one or the other of these dual concerns. For example, those concerned with academic achievement generally examine the effects of particular curricular content or instructional methods (e.g., Doyle, 1978; Posner, 1974; Walker & Schaffarzick, 1974). Others whose concerns are social tend to investigate outcomes resulting from participation in student government, exposure to moral training programs, or use of techniques for modifying disruptive classroom behaviors (e.g., Bar-Tal & Saxe, 1978; Kounin, 1970; Rest, 1974; Simon & Kirschenbaum, 1973). What remains to be done is a simultaneous examination of socialization for both scholarship and citizenship from the point of view of both the agent and the target of this effort: teacher and child.

Researchers agree that somehow teachers influence the development of scholarship and citizenship through day-to-day communication of expectations in the classroom (cf. Brophy & Good, 1974). In this day-to-day interaction lies a thread unifying the two concerns and two functions of education. To impart academic knowledge, teachers must also get children to attend to tasks, to persevere when requirements seem difficult, and to complete assignments. To create

143

citizens, they must foster adherence to both procedural norms governing orderly life in the classroom and general social/moral norms embodying concern for the rights and welfare of others. The underlying common process is successful socialization of the child into the role of student. Yet relatively little is known about the daily accretions that turn children into students.

The present chapter reports on an interdisciplinary study of this socialization process. It is a preliminary report in that we cover only the first two years of longitudinal data gathering and discuss only two types of data out of an overall total of eight.[1] We are focusing on the effect of teachers' socializing communication on children's views of norms for classroom life: on teacher talk, student thought, and the link between the two.

The overall model within which we are working can be summarized briefly. Everyone agrees that roles are learned. Yet the vocabulary of the "role theory" literature is metaphorically rich and scientifically sloppy (cf. Biddle, 1979; Biddle & Thomas, 1966). The central scientific meaning of role appears to be action within a prescribed social position or status. Roles are socially determined, in that groups have expectations for how role occupants *ought* to behave and *will* behave. Roles are socially understood, in that group members give common descriptions of action within role. Roles are socially learned, in that people learn appropriateness of behavior through direct or vicarious rewards and punishments. Thus there are three logically exhaustive components of a role to be observed: prescriptions for action (what *should* you do?); descriptions of action (what *did* you do?); and evaluations after action (what did the others think of it?) (cf. Thomas & Biddle, 1966, p. 28).

These components are also isomorphic with a recent model of human responsibility judgments (Hamilton, 1978; Hamilton & Sanders, 1981). The model argues that judgments of responsibility—i.e., accountability or liability for sanctions—involve normative or role *expectations* and *deeds* performed or omitted as determinants of *sanctions*. The data indicate that one is indeed liable both for what one did and for what one should have done, as the model predicts. This model deals with adults and already-socialized members of a group. But to learn a role in the first place is to learn its boundaries—what things garner praise, what things evoke blame. Thus the elements of a model of responsibility judgments for the already-socialized can also be seen as the crucial elements for the learning of a role.

---

[1]In addition to the data reported here, data gathering included extensive ethnographic field notes on teacher and student activities in 12 of the classrooms; sociometric choices of friendship for classmates; interviews with students concerning reasons why various norms were important to follow; questionnaires to students embedding experimental variations of norms previously investigated, with children asked to judge responsibility and sanctions; targeted observations of children selected from teachers' evaluations as particularly good or disruptive students; and questionnaires to teachers that included the responsibility experiments presented to their students plus teacher assessments of math and verbal achievement for each child.

Given a traditional psychological approach to the components of this model, two theoretical literatures would appear relevant: the social psychological area of attribution theory, where decisions about how to describe an event, assign causality for it, and determine responsibility have been studied; and of course, social learning theory, where basic psychological findings regarding learning processes are applied and modified to accommodate human learning in social contexts. But two further concerns of great relevance to the theoretical model and the present research design are sometimes slighted in educational applications of attribution or social learning. The first concern, represented in recent educational literature on classroom management and in traditional sociological work on organizations, is the structural question of how the teacher's managerial role and the task structure she implements determine the effectiveness of her socialization practices.[2] The second concern, often appearing under the rubric of "individual differences" in psychological treatments, is the issue of how the teacher's impact may differ depending on certain key characteristics of the pupils. (In the present study we chose to focus on age, social class, and sex as potentially crucial differentiators of children's student role socialization.) We briefly summarize salient findings and predictions from these relevant literatures before turning to a description of the study itself.

Attribution Theory: Teacher Descriptions and Evaluations

"Attribution theory" is by now a generic label for an array of theories of how humans judge causality or responsibility and a large number of empirical applications of such theories (see, e.g., Harvey, Ickes, & Kidd, 1976, 1978). Although a substantial body of the empirical work in this area has been focused on children or teachers, actual observation of attribution processes in the classroom context has been relatively rare (e.g., Blumenfeld, Hamilton, Wessels & Falkner, 1979; Cooper, 1979; Dweck, Davidson, Nelson, & Enna, 1978). Thus we must draw on general predictions from the literature, with some information from prior studies concerning the likely results in a classroom setting.

If the teacher is to socialize children about student role expectations, one of the things she must do is discuss or describe classroom behaviors: the deeds, or "what happened," part of the role/responsibility model. Although such descriptions are in general potentially important as socializing information, descriptions also typically either embed an implicit judgment about causality or involve some follow-up judgment. And attribution theories provide evidence that causal judgments are not evaluatively neutral (e.g., Heider, 1958; Jones & Davis, 1965; Kelley, 1967, 1973). First, causal judgments are typically made or sought when

---

[2]The teacher is referred to as "her" ("she") throughout for convenience, as all but one of the teachers involved are female.

the event in question was one calling for evaluation or sanctioning. In addition, in the allocation of causality itself, the perceiver indicates what was seen as controlling or producing the event. Attribution of outcomes to internal causes leads people to see themselves as personally responsible for outcomes, which can be psychologically satisfying—especially when the outcome in question was a positive one (e.g., deCharms, 1968; Weiner, 1972). Thus attributions may be positive or negative in their direct evaluative implications as well as internal or external in their control implications, with potential positive connotations to internality. In sum, attributions represent potentially key—if non-neutral— aspects of teacher descriptions of events. Their power as influence tools is suggested by the recent finding that making appropriate attributional statements to a child can be more effective in changing that child's behavior than more conventional persuasion strategies (Miller, Brickman & Bolen, 1975).

The very few studies of attributions in classrooms indicate that both the overall preponderance of focus on positive versus negative classroom events and the type of events focused on—academic versus other more procedural concerns—may alter the effectiveness of a teacher's communication (e.g., Blumenfeld et al., 1979; Dweck et al., 1978). Thus the importance of attributions may include their channeling of student definitions of the role itself, as well as their communication to the student about control and their contribution to self-concept. We have therefore selected causal attributions as an important locus of further information in teacher talk of a descriptive sort. In doing so we of course accept the inevitable interweaving of expectation and evaluation that occurs in description itself, despite the logical separation of these components suggested in the role/responsibility model.

Social Learning: Teacher Sanctions and Expectations

Certain basic social learning principles suggest a strategy for producing behavioral conformity in the classroom. Frequency, consistency, and intensity of praise and criticism should influence the degree of children's conformity to teacher desires (e.g., Bandura, 1969; Cartledge & Milburn, 1978; Clarizio, 1971). In general, consistent use of social evaluations coupled with appropriate behavioral sanctions, delivered in a manner that focuses children's attention on the behavior in question, should result in high conformity to that particular expectation. However, overall frequency of sanctioning need not be a good predictor of conformity, as its effects may be attenuated by inconsistency of response or by failure to draw appropriate attention to the behavior (Bandura, 1969, 1977; Mischel & Mischel, 1976; Parke, 1969, 1970). Blame or punishment that appears noncontingent on the child's behavior can even have severely negative effects (Seligman, 1975). Thus it need not be surprising that low correlations between sheer use of sanctions and children's level of misbehavior have been reported (Kounin, 1970).

But overt conformity is not the usual goal—or certainly not the only goal—proposed for socialization in the schools. Long-term stability of behavior rests on internalization of the socializer's goals by the socializee, and the use of explicit rewards and punishments may even act to retard that internalization process. Overreliance on threats or sanctions appears to create busy learners, but not necessarily motivated or interested ones (Covington & Beery, 1976). Even the provision of external rewards or incentives as a justification for children's behavior can decrease their intrinsic interest in a task (Lepper, this volume; Lepper & Green, 1975; Pittman et al., this volume). Thus the teacher who socializes by carrying "carrots" and wielding "sticks" would appear to be endangering the long-term enterprise of socialization itself.

The use of rewards and punishments per se need not work in opposition to internalization, however. Discipline methods may promote internalization by communicating expectations about appropriate behavior, by providing alternative and more acceptable modes for reaching goals, and by sensitizing the child to effects of actions on others (Aronfreed, 1963, 1969, 1976; Hoffman, 1970a,b). A discipline style that utilizes inductions—explanations of the reasons for following rules in terms of consequences to others—appears to be a highly effective strategy for producing internalization. Such a style induces a humanistic orientation rather than a conventional orientation to rule violation and focuses on the spirit of the rule rather than the letter of the law (Hoffman, 1970a). Overall then, the consistent, judicious, and inductively-oriented use of sanctions would appear to be crucial to the internalization process.

Given the importance of inductions in a social learning approach to student role socialization, social learning proves to be relevant to understanding the impact of teacher expectations as well as sanctions. Inductive explanations are a subcategory of all explanations; and as long as the explanations focused on are those involving why students should or should not behave in a particular way, then they are logically prescriptive or expectation statements that simply provide further reasons or rationales. In terms of the role/responsibility model, social learning thus may provide the key to implementing the prescriptive and sanctioning portions of the model. Therefore, we have chosen to focus on all teacher sanctions—or their threat or promise—and on all teacher communication regarding expectations, including further "why" information. Social learning theory and findings would suggest that either or both of these may affect children's learning and internalization of the student role.

Management and Task Structure: Macrolevel Social Learning Problems

When looking at teacher behavior within a particular classroom, or even at comparisons among teachers, educators and psychologists often utilize some version of the social learning approach. The overwhelming importance of maintaining classroom order and effective discipline naturally leads toward that perspective. A further step in that direction has also been made relatively recently. As evidence emerged that effects of such variables as classroom "climate" or teacher "warmth" on children's academic and social outcomes were apparently slight, researchers began to pay serious attention to Kounin's (1970) argument that maintaining orderly procedures for learning by the *group* is necessary for achievement by individuals within it (see also reviews by Dunkin & Biddle, 1974). Organizational questions therefore begin to emerge, and researchers turn more attention to sociological literatures on groups, organizations, management, and authority (Duke, 1979).

It is a relatively simple matter to bridge the apparent conceptual gap between teacher-child dyadic reinforcement and the group-level issues. First, looking within a given classroom, teacher reinforcers to the group can readily be viewed in terms of direct and vicarious reinforcement to given individuals. More importantly, the sociological concepts of the *role structure* within which the teacher operates as a manager or authority figure and the *task structure* which she sets up for carrying out the role can be viewed as environmental constraints that may govern reinforcement patterns. The role structure is a constraint on the teacher; the task structure is a constraint both on students and on the teacher herself, insofar as it governs the allocation of time and mode of teaching. Investigation of socialization into the student role should thus attempt to take into account the macrolevel problems of the constraints of role and task structure. Fortunately, there are helpful guidelines available in recent educational literatures on "classroom management" and "teacher effectiveness."

An excellent historical and conceptual overview of the question of the teacher's role is provided in Johnson and Brooks (1979). They first outline the development of the American school from the undifferentiated "one room schoolhouse" to the modern bureaucratic organization, a change achieved in many areas by the turn of the last century. Such bureaucratization, of course, is generally characteristic of industrialization and its accompanying urban migrations. The theoretical and practical importance of this change is that the modern school must properly be considered as a bureaucracy in which teacher behaviors may be governed by formal role constraints. The teacher is in a hierarchy, acting both under the supervision of the principal and other administrative figures and *as* supervisor of the behavior and productivity of the students taught. Thus in a very real sense even the child entering school faces an organization in which the teacher is structurally a manager and the student a worker.

There are a number of ways in which the school is an unusual bureaucracy, of course, including the key fact that the child is simultaneously worker and "product" (a general characteristic of socializing institutions). The teacher's managerial task is also complex in that society expects both scholarship and citizenship to be part of this final product. As Johnson and Brooks describe this latter tension,

All managers have to arrange working conditions so that workers are at least minimally satisfied, through having basic personality needs met, but teachers are additionally expected to manage the situation in such a way that the workers (pupils) learn to assume increasing responsibility for carrying out, with diminishing supervision, both the work of the classroom and activities outside of school. *The most distinctive feature of the classroom may be this dual concern with both discipline for learning and learning of discipline.* (1979, p. 28, emphasis added)

In our terminology, scholarship and citizenship can make a difficult managerial mix.

Evidence ranging from Kounin (1970) to other more recent sources suggests that a teacher's effectiveness as a manager has payoffs in students' academic progress as well as their conduct (see review by Brophy, 1979). Despite the apparent difficulty of the managerial mix involved in the teacher's role, some of the payoff from good management results because ''good managers also tend to be good instructors, and vice versa,'' given the similar skills in preparation and organization involved in both (Brophy, 1979, p. 736). What remains to be seen is the extent to which indicators of managerial effectiveness may also relate to children's thoughts and feelings about the student role itself.

The teacher's managerial role and especially control behaviors are also differentiated and shaped by the types of tasks employed during instruction (e.g., Bossert, 1977, 1978, 1979; Doyle, 1978). This is not surprising, for to the extent that different instructional patterns involve different managerial tasks, then teachers may attend to and respond to different student behaviors. For example, in situations where all children are required to sit quietly, face front, and direct undivided attention on the teacher, such acts as squirming, whispering, day-dreaming, and other minor disruptive behaviors are likely to meet with disapproval. In a less structured setting, teachers may be freed from such procedural concerns to attend more to purely academic or general citizenship issues. Alternatively, teachers in traditional and ''open'' classrooms may divide their concerns similarly between the issues of scholarship and citizenship but attend to different aspects of these. It is clear, however, that the what, when, where, and how of work organization can influence specific teacher expectations for classroom life. Thus, what actually constitutes acceptable student role behavior may vary with task structure, and teacher communication concerning that role should vary concomitantly.

The question of task structure has, of course, been a subject of much debate in recent years, as advocates of ''traditional'' versus ''open'' instruction have debated their merits—often in the absence of clear definitions of either or without clear-cut dependent variables in mind (Horowitz, 1979; Marshall, 1981; Wright, 1975). Some recent research suggests, however, that a more structured or traditional approach is more effective for academic performance, particularly in the early grades where children have difficulty managing learning on their own (see review by Brophy, 1979). Yet for children's internalization of classroom norms, their feelings about these norms, and the whole arena of citizenship as opposed to scholarship, the effects of task structure are still open questions. Thus task structure appears to be a potentially important determinant of student role socialization, one that is logically distinct from managerial effectiveness per se and one whose impact cannot yet be predicted.

Differentiating Components of the Student Role

The management and task structure literatures suggest that we should look at how the teacher defines the student role itself; and the social learning and attribution literatures suggest that we look at particular types of communication about that role as theoretically important socializing tools. Yet a variety of clues within each of these literatures also indicates that the student role should be examined in terms of a number of distinct components or domains of classroom life. We have already noted the fundamental dichotomy between scholarship and citizenship in the student role, but a more fine-grained view is needed.

The central defining characteristic of the student role is clearly an academic one. However, the teacher must impart means as well as ends, training the child in how to learn as well as what to learn. Thus even academic instruction can profitably be divided into content versus procedures for operation. On the citizenship side, given that the classroom is a group setting, social procedures for working with or in the presence of others must be instilled. And moral norms must be enforced, in the classroom just as anywhere else in the society. Ranging from those most specific to the setting to those most general to society, the expectations to be conveyed by the teacher can thus be conveniently divided into four categories or domains: *academic performance, academic procedure, social procedures, and social/moral norms.* Important empirical questions include the extent to which teachers emphasize one type of issue versus another, the extent to which socializing strategies in one domain resemble those in another, and the extent to which teachers have impacts on students across domains. Thus we have chosen to look at structural determinants of "teacher talk," at information carried in teacher talk, and at its effects on student thought in terms of these different domains of classroom life.

Differentiation Among Students

Whatever the teacher's understanding of components of the student role, and however she is influenced by managerial concerns or task structure in communicating it, the recipients of that communication are not interchangeable blank slates. Children are cognitively and socially differentiated in ways that may influence both the teacher's behavior and the child's understanding of the student role. The variables that we chose to focus on were the child's age, sex, and social class. We discuss these and present results pertaining to them in this order, as we anticipated the largest differences would be due to age and the smallest to social class.

The child's *age* may affect both the teacher's behavior, because the teacher makes different assumptions about what the child has already learned about the role, and the child's understanding, because of the child's level of cognitive development. Taking two grade levels where children are reasonably separated in both school experience and cognitive development, first versus fifth grades, we can explore both teacher behavior and children's comprehension of the student role.

Teacher behaviors and expectations are likely to differ across grade levels. Teachers in early grades, especially first grade, might be forced to spend a relatively large proportion of effort on instilling procedural norms, both academic and social. Teachers in higher grades may be spared this since children will have had several years of experience in the general setting. Teacher expectations may accordingly be less stringent in the first steps of socialization, as the teacher employs "shaping" by rewarding children for conformity to basic role expectations. Teachers in upper grades may be less likely to reward for simple conformity to role behavior or more hasty to punish for nonconformity. These differences in expectations may also lead teachers in upper grades to make somewhat different attributions, in that they have more information available to enable them to make internal attributions for failure or misbehavior. In general, the expectation that the child has the ability and knowledge to conform to the role should be related positively to attributions to personal factors as causes of nonconformity; thus as expectations shift upwards, attributions may shift inwards, toward assuming stable personal inclinations in the child.

The child's understanding of all this communication, of course, undergoes potentially dramatic shifts with cognitive development. The child entering school is probably thinking at a preoperational or early concrete operational level. The experienced student, the fifth grader, is probably thinking at a concrete operational or early formal operational level (e.g., Piaget & Inhelder, 1969). Sheer cognitive differences plus concomitant shifts in moral judgment should affect what the student absorbs and how that information is organized.

Basically, the child's differentiation of the domains of classroom life and assessments of their importance may be a function of cognitive/moral development. Differentiation and categorization of issues should be more developed in the older child. It is known that even preschool children can make some distinction between moral and purely conventional issues and understand the greater importance of moral issues (Nucci & Turiel, 1979; Turiel, 1978); but prior studies have not explored a range of classroom-relevant issues, such as concern for the procedural convenience of others, that represent an area of both importance to teachers and potential confusion to children. Further, studies of how children judge academic as opposed to moral successes and failures have just begun (e.g., Parsons, 1974; Weiner & Peter, 1973). Thus it is important to explore how children of different ages may assess the various aspects of the student role.[3]

In both first and fifth grades, of course, one finds that most ubiquitous differentiator of humans: the child's *sex*. So far, the primary attention in the educational literature has been on sex differences in disruptive behavior, with girls coming out as "sugar and spice" by that criterion of fulfilling the student role (see Brophy & Good, 1974). More fine-grained socialization such as that provided by teacher attributions or expectations has only recently received research attention (e.g., Blumenfeld, Hamilton, Wessels & Falkner, 1977; Dweck et al., 1978; Parsons, Kaczala, & Meece, in press). What remains undone is detailed examination across grade levels with respect to both teacher differences in type and quality of communication to boys and girls and sex differences in what children *think* is involved in being a student, given what teachers try to tell them.

The children's *social class* background also appears likely to mold how and what the teacher communicates about the student role. The educational literature indicates that teachers hold lower expectations for children from lower social class backgrounds, often differentially allocate instructional assistance, and employ more negative sanctions against lower and working class children for social behaviors (e.g., Davis & Dollard, 1940; Rist, 1970; review by Brophy & Good, 1974). The child's own preparation for school is also likely to be differentiated by class, given that middle class parents are likely to have socialized with more verbal interchanges, more verbal and induction-oriented moral training, and higher general expectations that the child act independently and self-reliantly (e.g., Boocock, 1972; Hess, 1970; Katz, 1968; Kerckhoff, 1973; Kohn, 1969). What is not known in any detail is the pattern of day-to-day interaction between the lower or working class student who may be ill-prepared and the teacher whose expectations for him or her may be low. Detailed examination of both teacher talk about the student role and children's understanding of that role is necessary for exploring effects of the subtle class boundaries of American society.

---

[3]The domains of classroom life studied here have varied relationships to the moral/conventional dichotomy. Two domains, social/moral and social procedural norms, fall into the realm of citizenship; two domains, academic performance and procedure, into the realm of scholarship. The rationales for in-role behavior in the two realms are likely to differ, with citizenship issues involving consequences to others and scholarship issues consequences to the self. Overall, social/moral norms emerge as clearly moral, as the label implies. Social procedural norms are conventional, entailing behaviors designed to facilitate classroom management and to keep children in crowded rooms from interfering with one another. Academic procedural norms are also conventional, but differ from previously examined conventional norms in frequently involving consequences to self. Finally, academic performance issues have thoroughly individual consequences and in that sense differ from both the moral and conventional norms previously studied, although it is unclear the extent to which they may have moral overtones (Weiner, 1979).

Summary of the Study Design and Goals

The goal of the overall study is a detailed map of socialization into the student role. We use a model which asserts that roles are learned by learning their boundaries—those things that lie within the role and those that exceed the expectations of others either positively or negatively. The key "other," from the child's point of view, is clearly the teacher. Thus we emphasize teacher communication about the role, "teacher talk," as the potential cause of children's judgments about the role, "student thought."

The original study design was also intended to examine variations in student role socialization produced by classroom task structure and by children's age, sex, and social class. Thus the plan called for choice of two open and two traditional classrooms in each of first and fifth grades in predominantly working versus middle class schools—for a total of 16 classrooms.[4] In the conveniently located working class schools, however, officially open classrooms were abolished before we could begin data collection. Thus we adjusted to a more mixed design, in which our predominantly middle class school district contributed two open classrooms and two not so designated classrooms at each of the two grade levels; and two predominantly working class districts were tapped for a total of ten rather than eight classrooms (five at each grade level), to obtain as much variability in task structure as possible. The measures used for structure of task organization, described later, are then based on our own observations rather than official designations and produce a continuous gradation rather than the official dichotomous labels. An indicator of managerial effectiveness is also provided from our observations.

The fundamental questions to be answered in part involve simple descriptions of teacher talk and student thought about the student role. Thus initial questions concern the distribution of teacher attention among the domains of classroom life and, to the extent feasible, among particular issues within those domains; the extent to which potentially key socializing information (expectations, attributions, and sanctions) is provided in teacher remarks; and, given social learning theory concerns, the extent to which communication is proactive or reactive, positive or negative in evaluative tone, and of low or high salience, or intensity. The differentiation of teacher talk depending on either teacher variables— managerial effectiveness and task structure—or target variables—children's age, sex, or social class—can then be explored. Children's thought about the student role can then be described, and its differentiation by children's own characteristics and by aspects of teacher talk can be examined. At that point we will have completed a first broad sweep at exploring what is in the student role as com-

---

[4]Class composition of the schools was determined by conversations with principals about the class backgrounds of students, as well as by the general industrial characteristics of the communities concerned.

municated by the teacher, what is there from the child's point of view, and what—if any—relationship exists between the two.

METHOD

Measures of Teacher Talk

The coding scheme for teacher communication is summarized in Table 7.1. The universe of statements that was coded consisted of all remarks that communicated directives about performance or feedback on performance, whether that performance was of an academic or social nature. The only teacher remarks thereby excluded were social talk, such as complimenting a student on a new dress, and sheer academic instruction, in which no statements of either role expectations or feedback were being made.[5] All remarks were recorded verbatim and subsequently coded at the level of *clauses* containing information.

All such clauses were first coded regarding the *domain* of the remark: academic performance, academic procedure, social procedure, or social/moral norms. Issues considered as falling into each domain are found in the table. Clauses were also coded for the *time* at which the remark was made (i.e., before or after child's behavior); for the *quality* of the behavior from the teacher's point of view (positive, negative, ambiguous, or not applicable—i.e., when the remark occurred before a behavior); for the *target* of the remark (girl, boy, small group, or whole group); for the *structure* of the activity being engaged in by the child and teacher; and for the *salience* of the teacher's remark (essentially whether she appeared to be upset or excited and deliberately drew class attention to it).

Within this universe of communication, some embedded further information to the target: expectations, attributions, or sanctions. These were differentiated as described in the table. Categories used for expectations and sanctions were derived from our prior observational experience, whereas categories for attributions followed closely from the literature in that area. The sole exception to the clause-level analysis is also a new attributional category, *mixed*, in which the teacher made two linked attributions at once, one of which was positive and one negative in implication. We felt that use of this combination category represented a more accurate reflection of the information imparted than would be obtained were those attributions treated as independent bits of information.

[5]It is important to note that we were interested in teachers' efforts to socialize children into a role rather than in the content or method of academic instruction. Thus, whereas other observational codes (see Dunkin and Biddle, 1974) focus on lessons and subject-matter teaching (e.g., providing examples, asking questions, explaining facts) as well as on socialization practices like praise and criticism, we exclude the former as not related specifically to role socializing activity.

TABLE 7.1
Categorization Scheme for "Teacher Talk"

Domain and Issue. Each piece of information was categorized as to the area of classroom life referred to and the specific subject of the remark.

1. Academic performance: Statements concerning the quality or correctness of intellectual performance or referring to rationales for particular assignments. Subject matter of math, reading and other was noted as well.

   a) Format (math, reading, other): Statements related to the "correctness" of the form or format of the student's academic work.
   Example: "You forgot to put your name on the paper." "I can't read your answers, your work is so sloppy."
   b) Content (math, reading, other): Statements related to the correctness of the student's work.
   Example: "You only missed one problem, very good." "You have to have fractions to be able to do fifth grade work."
   c) Ambiguous (math, reading, other): No specific referent to correctness or incorrectness of either content or format.
   Example: "That's nice. Okay, next." (Teacher fishes for more information)– "Yes, but what about . . ."

2. Academic procedure: Statements pertaining to academic routines. These included comments about what work the children were assigned and how, when, and where they were expected to complete it. Statements in this domain were differentiated into one of eight categories.

   a) Assignment: Reference to expectations concerning what assignments students should do and how they should do them.
   Example: "Read two chapters in the green book today." "Use a pen to write this letter, not a pencil." "Everyone should try to do at least six problems on this page."
   b) On-task: Any reference to not listening when the teacher is trying to give an assignment, instructions, or information; failure to use work periods constructively.
   Example: "Please pay attention, stop chattering, you won't know how to do this later." "Get back to work now. You've almost wasted the whole period."
   c) Completion: Specifications of when work is to be finished or statements of expectations that students should complete, do so on time, and know what to do after completing an assignment.
   Example: "Try to finish this work sheet before recess." "You didn't finish the last six problems on this page."
   d) General routine: Statements concerning what students should be doing when.
   Example: "Do your math first, then spelling." "You should be working on your reading now, not your science."
   e) Assistance: Reference to expectations that students should follow proper procedures for getting help with work or complete assignments independently.
   Example: "Put your name on the board, if you need help." "You can ask someone who is finished for help."
   f) Persistence: Reference to expectations that students should not give up easily on a difficult task.
   Example: "This is hard, so you'll have to try." "These problems are tough; you'll have to work hard."

(continued)

TABLE 7.1 (*Continued*)

g) Readiness: Reference to expectations that students should be prepared for work by having the correct materials (e.g., pencils, paper, books, etc.) or by having the prerequisite assignment or homework completed.
Example: "This is the fifth time you forgot your math book, you'd better remember it tomorrow."

h) General academic procedure issues: Reference to other types of expectations related to academic procedures (e.g. where to put assignments) that do not fit into one of the above categories.

3. Social procedure: Statements pertaining to classroom social rules and routines. These included comments about conduct that facilitated or interfered with the teacher's, other students', or one's own activities by failure to adhere to common organizational practices. These were differentiated into five issues.

a) Care of classroom and classroom materials: Reference to expectations that students should keep the classroom neat, take care of classroom materials, and use them properly.
Example: "Keep the floor under your desk neat." "Put the library books back on the shelves where they belong." "Stop wasting that paper, that is all we have for the rest of the year."

b) Place: Reference to expectations concerning where students should perform certain activities or where students should be in the classroom at a particular time.
Example: "That's right, you can use the glue in the art area." "What are you doing wandering around back here? You should be at your seat." "Karen, I called your reading group to come up to my desk, why aren't you up here?"

c) Role: Reference to expectations that students should perform tasks associated with an assigned job (e.g., line captain, librarian, sanitation engineer) or that they should not overstep the boundaries of the student role.
Example: "This is the second time you forgot to check the bathrooms, I guess I'll give the job to someone else." "It's not your place to tell the janitor about this, I'll take care of it."

d) Talking: Reference to (1) high level of noise; (2) following procedures for raising hands or interrupting; (3) opening mouths when it is quiet time; etc.
Example: "Shh. I can't hear because you're so loud." "Don't interrupt, be careful to raise your hand." "It's not your turn to recite."

e) General social procedural issues: Reference to other types of expectations related to the social organization of the classroom that do not fit into one of the above categories (e.g., lining up, closing the door, hanging up coats).

4. Social/moral: Statements referring to behaviors of an interpersonal nature which involve the rights and welfare of others, either physical or psychological. Statements in this domain were differentiated into four categories.

a) Sharing: Reference to the expectation that students should share their personal property with others.
Example: "Billy, you can't eat the candy in your desk unless there is enough for everyone."

b) Lying or cheating: Reference to the expectation that students should be fair and not lie or cheat.
Example: "You had four turns; it's against the rules to have more than two." "Look at your own paper, or I'll take it away. This is a test."

c) Physical aggression: Reference to the expectation that students should be fair and not bite, hit, push, kick, or otherwise physically hurt others.

(*continued*)

156

TABLE 7.1 (*Continued*)

d) Respect for others: Reference to expectations that students should be thoughtful towards others and should not tease, provoke, or otherwise hurt the feelings of others.
Example: "Don't call her "four eyes," it's not nice." "That was nice of you to help Billy fix the model."

Time. All statements were differentiated into one of two categories:

1. Proactive (before): Statements made prior to an event which served to encourage appropriate behavior and define and explain expectations.

2. Reactive (after): Statement made subsequent to an event or in response to a particular action.

Quality of Behavior. Statements were differentiated into one of four categories:

1. Positive: Statements referring to expected or accomplished good performance or appropriate behavior.

2. Negative: Statements made in anticipation of or in reaction to poor academic performance, failure to adhere to classroom procedure, or antisocial behavior.

3. Ambiguous: Statements referring to academic performance that do not communicate clearly whether the outcome was positive or negative such as, "Uh, huh."

4. Not applicable—neutral statements which communicate what work is to be done.

Target: Statements were differentiated according to the person(s) to whom they were addressed (a female, a male, a small group, or the whole group) and whether the target was working or not working with the teacher at the time.

Child Activity: The organization of activity (activities) of the class when the statement was made were delineated into five categories.

1. Class: Students are engaged in discussion or recitation as a group.

2. Individual Seatwork (same): Students are working individually on the same assignment.

3. Individual Seatwork (different): Students are working individually on different assignments.

4. Small Group: Students working in small groups for a common product (game, play).

5. Free Time: Students have free time/choice.

6. Combinations were noted when the children were engaged in a variety of different activities.

Teacher Activity. What the teacher was doing when the remark was made was coded as:

1. Recitation: Teacher is working with the whole class, reviewing old material, instructing or giving out assignments, organizing the day.

2. Small group: Teacher is working with a small group evaluating, reviewing old material, instructing, giving out assignments.

3. Teacher check: Teacher is moving about the room working with individuals, or students are coming up individually to her desk for assistance or checking, or the teacher is doing administrative work.

4. Class: Teacher is observing whole class activity, such as show and tell or free time, without much participation herself.

(*continued*)

TABLE 7.1 *(Continued)*

Salience. All statements were differentiated as to the amount of attention they commanded. They were categorized as:

1. Low: Statements made in normal tone of voice.

2. Medium: Statements where the teacher raised her voice somewhat.

3. High: Statements where the teacher was clearly angry, screamed, or shook a child.

Informatives. Each communication that contained further information—expectations, attributions, or sanctions—was further coded at the clause level according to the following categories:

1. Expectations. Reasons for behavioral expectations or evaluative feedback which did not include attributional reference were coded into four categories:

   a) Rule: Statement of social or procedural norms that offer no rationale beyond the fact that the norm is to be followed.
   Example: "Nice people don't call names." "First graders must learn to spell correctly."

   b) Consequences: Rationale for expectation by reference to effect of behavior on others or oneself.
   These are divided in five categories.

      1. Self: "If you learn to sound out words, you won't have to ask anyone for help."
      2. Others: "It makes Janey feel good when you share with her."
      3. Group: "The class is being delayed because you're talking."
      4. Teacher: "I get tired of having to pick up after you. It hurts my back to keep bending."
      5. Object: "The book will get messed up if you leave it on the floor."

   c) Circumstances: Reference to present or future conditions as the basis for requests, expectations, or evaluations.
   Example: "We're almost out of paste so be careful to use just a little bit."

   d) Authority: References to administrative ease or teacher preference.
   Example: "Do it this way. I like it better." "The principal says you must bring in slips tomorrow or no trip."

2. Sanctioning practices. Statements or actions which served to promote compliance were categorized as one of five types:

   a) Reward
   b) Promise
   c) Punishment: e.g., removal of privileges, giving extra work.
   d) Threat
   e) Redirection of action: e.g., changing a child's seat, confiscating an object, providing the child with another task.

3. Attributions. Explicit contingent or prior feedback referring to factors contributing to success or failure, including four basic categories:

   a) Motivation: Success or failure attributed to effort. These were further differentiated as to mention of positive or negative motivation (presence or absence of effort).
   Examples: "Your spelling is good. You certainly were *careful*." "You keep *forgetting* to read the instructions."

   b) Ability: Success or failure attributed to the presence or absence of stable skills or personal traits. These were divided into positive (desirable) and negative (undesirable) traits or abilities.

(continued)

158

TABLE 7.1 (*Continued*)

Examples: "You're *not mature* enough to behave yourselves." "Your stories are *always so interesting and funny.*"

c) Mixed: Success or failure attributed to atypical performance. Comments about successful performance which imply the child usually fails or about failure which imply the child usually succeeds.
Examples: "This work is not as good as you can do." "You've been having a lot of trouble with math; I'm glad to see you got these right."

d) Unstable: Success or failure attributed to presence of some factor outside the child's control, such as illness or fatigue.

e) Task: Success or failure attributed to difficulty of the assignment or type of undertaking without negative implications for the child's ability or effort.
Examples: "They're making it *hard* on you. Now you need to multiply three columns." "This is *third grade work.*"

Observers were trained in two ways. First, sample transcripts of teacher statements taken from previous work were prepared. Observers were taught to code from these transcripts to familiarize themselves with the categories. Second, to be certain that they gathered accurately the set of teacher statements that were of interest for our purposes, each observer was accompanied by one of the experimenters familiar with the codes for a 30-minute session in a classroom. Later, agreement between observer and experimenter was assessed both for inclusion of remarks into the universe of socialization statements and for recording of basic context information necessary for more detailed coding (i.e., reactivity, quality of remark, and target). Reliability for recording the correct information was .92. Reliability for correctly coding *all* categories (domain, issue within domain, time, quality, target, child and teacher activity structures, salience, expectation, attribution, and sanction) subsequently ranged from .75 to .90 with an average of .85. Given that the verbatim records of teacher statements were available for checking, it was readily possible to ensure that this more detailed information was coded correctly after actual data gathering. First, one of the experimenters reviewed all statements recorded for the first three hours of classroom observation and checked all categorizations with observers individually. Weekly meetings were then held to spot check coding and discuss any problems. Spot checks of the coding against the verbatim teacher statements indicated that after three hours of data collection all coders had reached at least .85 accuracy.

Ten hours of statements made by teachers were collected in each classroom. Only statements made by the adult with primary responsibility for the classroom were recorded, eliminating remarks by student teachers, substitute teachers, or parents. Insofar as possible, statements were recorded verbatim, given that actual coding was done from the notes taken in class.

Observations were scattered throughout the school day. At least two hours of observations were done while the teacher conducted reading lessons or reading groups except in those rooms where reading instruction was not carried out in group fashion. The remaining hours included periods devoted to other subjects such as math as well as less academically oriented periods such as show-and-tell.

Managerial Effectiveness and Task Structure

Managerial effectiveness was not originally built into the design as a potential determinant of student role socialization. Instead, we turned to this literature for guidelines when some of the variables initially thought important proved to be relatively unimportant parts of teacher talk or unimportant determinants of either that talk or student thought, as is discussed later. As it emerged that managerial issues might be important, we were able to include a questionnaire for observers in the second year's data gathering so that managerial issues could be directly assessed. Here, however, we must rely on an *indicator* of such effectiveness rather than an explicit *measure*. There is always the possibility, therefore, that the indicator chosen is really "something else," and readers should assess relevant results accordingly.

Given that the central official task in the teacher role is to encourage scholarship, what we chose as an indicator of managerial effectiveness is what might be seen as the teacher's "work orientation": the proportion of socializing communication devoted to academic performance as opposed to procedural or social/moral issues. As a measure of managerial effectiveness, the danger of using such a variable is that high proportionate attention to academic performance could result either because the teacher has procedural issues under control and is able to do her job, *or* because she is simply ignoring procedural and social chaos and plodding onward with the lesson. Thus we examined observers' comments about the rooms as well as their transcripts, finding consistent evidence that the rooms high in proportionate attention to academic performance were also generally characterized by high student productivity and good behavior. This may provide further support for Brophy's conclusion, quoted earlier, that good managers tend to make good teachers because the requisite skills overlap; but in any case, it clearly refutes the notion that high proportionate attention to academic performance entails ignoring social chaos. Overall, then, a teacher's relative attention to academic performance, at least in these data, seems a reasonable indicator of managerial effectiveness.

Given that all clauses of teacher communication were coded for the domain addressed, obtaining a score for each teacher of attention to academic performance was simple. We merely calculated the percentage of all clauses coded as dealing with academic outcome. Although certain questions cannot legitimately be addressed using this variable—such as, for example, teachers' relative attention to social procedure, because it would have to be negatively correlated—most of the potentially relevant research questions can be addressed. Differences between teachers on attention to academic performance and correlates of these differences are presented later in the results section.

In contrast to the question of managerial effectiveness, we had a number of possible measures of task structure. As noted in footnote one, extensive ethnographic records were available for 12 of the rooms; these were coded for task structure and typified into categories of low to high openness of task structure based on the teacher's degree of use of multitask teaching activities. This typification is highly related, however, to our measures of the child's activity structure and the teacher's activity structure, both of which were obtained for all clauses of teacher communication for all rooms.

Because the child's activity variable was more finely differentiated and reflected the organization of the class at a given time, we used that variable for constructing the task structure measure. We simply took all activities in which the children were doing the same thing at the same time, coding those as traditional, and all activities in which children were doing different things (essentially multitask structures, in terms of the relevant literature), coding those as open. Then, we derived a score for each teacher of "percent openness" by looking at the distribution of the resulting dichotomy across all clauses recorded. The resulting variable provides a continuous gradation of degree of openness of the actually observed task structure for all classrooms studied.

Student Thought

In order to assess how students react to norms the teacher tries to impose, children responded to pictures illustrating conformity and nonconformity to norms on each issue for each domain coded in the teacher statements. To facilitate presentation, issues were divided into "good" books and "bad" books, where the good books concerned doing deeds that one should do and omitting deeds that one should not do, and the bad books concerned the reverse. No more than ten issues were included in any one book, with three books containing 28 issues presented in one session for the good books and three books containing 30 issues presented in a single session for the bad books. The large number of issues was necessary because we wanted to ask about both sides of each norm (e.g., doing a bad deed would go into a bad book, while omitting it would go into a good book). The additional issues in the bad books included teasing and tattling, which were side issues not represented in the teacher codes and for which comparable mirror images were difficult to construct. Order of presentation of issues was randomized within one set of books and then kept the same for the second set. Which set was tested first was then alternated within grades, and booklet order was varied according to a Latin Square design to control for possible effects of order of presentation. A full list of the issues used will be presented in the results section below.

Two measures were included for each issue in order to tap both cognitive and affective responses to classroom norms. Children were asked to assess how bad (or good) each thing was to do and then asked to indicate "how they feel when they do'' what was pictured. All children had first responded to a training task in which a very bad (good) and mildly bad (good) extra-classroom deed had been depicted and the interviewer had ascertained that they could differentiate the importance of issues. To assess the importance—degree of goodness or badness—of an action, fifth graders drew a line within preset boundaries of 250 millimeters. First graders, for whom such a task was deemed too difficult, moved a marker on a ''magic line maker'' where a red line was revealed when the marker was pushed. To indicate how they would feel when doing an action depicted, all children marked one of four faces that ranged from neutral to a large frown for bad acts and neutral to a large smile for good acts. Fifth graders were interviewed in groups, usually of five students at a time; first graders were interviewed individually. Since the fifth graders simply filled out booklets, there was no interference or sharing of answers between children.

Because different children might calibrate the scale for importance in different ways, we used a data transformation for the dependent variable. This transformation uses the lines as measures of *relative* importance on a child-by-child basis. Indices of importance—degree of goodness or badness—were constructed for each issue by assigning the value of 1.0 to the longest line drawn by each individual child and the value 0 to the shortest, with intermediate lengths transformed according to the formula (length - minimum length) / (maximum length - minimum length). For each issue, therefore, average importances reported across children can also theoretically range from 1.0 to 0, and results reported can be read essentially as proportions of the maximum range.[6]

RESULTS

Overall Flow of Teacher Talk

If the teacher is to transmit the student role, then the first and most basic question concerns what she says when communicating what we have characterized as socializing information: directives and feedback about role behaviors. How much is said? How proactive or reactive? How positive or negative? How informative is it? About what? We therefore turn first to a general account of socializing communication before exploring the effects of structural variables on that communication.

The overall flow of communication averaged 585 clauses per classroom, ranging from 270 to 1126 clauses. This communication was largely reactive, negative, and procedural in nature. Fully 78% of the clauses occurred after rather than before student behaviors. Evaluative tone, which could be positive, nega-

---

[6]Thanks are extended to our computer and statistical consultant, John Gray, for suggesting this transformation as the most appropriate for these data.

tive, ambiguous, or not applicable (for "before" statements), was 49% negative to 28% positive. Salience of remarks, however, was low, indicating that the degree of affectivity displayed by the teacher was slight; fully 98.5% of all clauses were rated as of low salience. A majority of the overall communication was procedural, either academic (31%) or social (26%), with a smaller proportion devoted to academic performance issues (41%) and a miniscule proportion devoted to social/moral concerns (2%).

Characteristics of communication varied dramatically between domains. Academic performance was heavily reactive (98%), academic procedure least reactive (53%), and the other domains intermediate (social procedure: 78%; social/moral: 81%). This is predictable given that performance communication by definition is primarily after a behavior, while academic procedure communication tended to be linked to instructions about work. More interestingly, the evaluative tone also dramatically differed, with academic performance standing out as only 30% negative, in contrast to the more negative tone of academic procedure (49%), social procedure (76%), and social/moral (81%) communications. This combination suggests in part the obvious point that reactivity per se should not necessarily be characterized as negative or bad, but may be an inevitable part of the domain in question.

From the viewpoint of attribution or social learning theories, the presence of clauses that communicated further socializing information—expectations, attributions, or sanctions—might be of equal importance in predicting effective transmission of the student role. For convenience in discussion, we will refer to these types of communication as *informatives,* although they in fact simply embed further information of a theoretically relevant nature. A small proportion of the role-relevant communication, only 14%, consisted of informatives. This ranged from a low of 5% to a high of 27% of all clauses recorded, yielding a total ranging from 22 to 126 informatives for 10 hours of observation. Particularly given that our universe of communication already excluded social talking and simple instruction, one message of these data is that potentially key informatives occur but rarely in a sea of other speech.

Informatives were dramatically more negative and procedurally-oriented than was the overall flow of socializing communication, although they were about equally reactive. An overwhelming 71% of informatives were negative, as opposed to 8% positive, in evaluative tone; some 79% occurred after rather than before student behaviors. Procedural concerns clearly dominated, with 37% of informatives devoted to academic procedure and 40% to social procedure, as opposed to 20% devoted to academic performance and 3% to the social/moral domain. Table 7.2 summarizes comparisons between overall communication and informatives.

Given that informatives were predominantly negative, reactive, and procedural, a further question concerns differences in quality of this information between domains. Table 7.3 presents comparisons between overall communication and informatives by domain. It shows that, first, relatively *few* informatives are provided in the academic performance domain—hardly what one would see a priori as beneficial. Among informatives, academic performance is again the most reactive and academic procedure the least reactive domain. Somewhat hearteningly, academic performance also again stands out from the other domains in involving dramatically more positive feedback, although positive feedback is outweighed more than double by negative among informatives even in this domain.

Perhaps surprisingly, a single issue dominated the informatives for each domain. Over half of the miniscule quantity of social/moral informatives (57%) concerned respect for others, while over half of the social procedure informatives (51%) concerned talking; nearly half of academic procedure informatives concerned keeping on task (46%), and nearly half of academic performance informatives concerned language content (45%). The dominance of language content over other academic issues may well be a function of our care in sampling reading and writing periods. But the heavy single-issue emphasis in the two procedural domains—which themselves accounted for 77% of informatives— would appear to be clearly a "real" result, meaning that over one-third of the overall total of expectations, attributions, and sanctions transmitted simply concerned talking or keeping on task.

Further questions concern the distribution of informatives by types among domains, as well as their breakdown into the finer categorizations actually coded. Table 7.4 shows the overall distribution of informatives among all categories of expectations, attributions, and sanctions, as well as this same distribution for each domain. Given the large number of categories and the high variation in

TABLE 7.2
Characteristics of Overall Teacher Communication
Versus Informatives

	Overall	*Informative*
Reactivity		
Before	22%	21%
After	78	79
Evaluative tone[a]		
Positive	28%	8%
Negative	49	71
Distribution		
Academic Outcome	41%	20%
Academic Procedure	31	37
Social Procedure	26	40
Social/Moral	2	3
N (clauses)	10,526	1416

[a]Ambiguous or not applicable (before) communication not presented.

TABLE 7.3
Domain Differences in Reactivity and Quality
of Overall Communication and Informatives

	Academic Performance	Academic Procedure	Social Procedure	Social/ Moral
Overall Communication				
Percent Informative[a]	10%	21%	24%	31%
Reactivity[b]				
Before	2%	47%	22%	15%
After	98	53	78	85
Evaluative tone[c]				
Positive	64%	4%	3%	6%
Negative	30	49	76	81
N(clauses)	4300	3299	2755	167
Informatives				
Reactivity[d]				
Before	8%	34%	16%	21%
After	92	66	84	79
Evaluative tone[e]				
Positive	29%	4%	2%	2%
Negative	62	63	82	81
N(clauses)	276	525	568	47

[a]χ^2 from table including informatives and all other communication = 1607, d.f. = 6, $p < .0001$.
[b]$\chi^2 = 2251$, d.f. = 3, $p < .0001$.
[c]Ambiguous or not applicable (before) communication not presented. Overall $\chi^2 = 6130$, d.f. = 9, $p < .0001$.
[d]$\chi^2 = 90$, d.f. = 3, $p < .0001$.
[e]Ambiguous or not applicable (before) communication not presented. Overall, $\chi^2 = 271$, d.f. = 9, $p < .0001$.

amount of information by domain, comparisons must be made with care. But a number of differences are instructive. The domain of academic performance shows heavy use of attributions, and these have a relatively positive cast.[7] In particular, negative ability is rarely communicated to students, there or in other domains of communication. The procedural domains show heavier reliance on

---

[7]An overall chi-square test for domain differences in kind of information (with subcategories collapsed) did show highly significant differences, with dramatic reliance on attributions in academic performance, and expectations and sanctions dominating the other domains, as would be expected from examining the more finely differentiated table.

TABLE 7.4
Distribution of Expectations, Attributions, and Sanctions
in Teacher Talk Overall and by Domain[a]

Information:	Overall	Academic Performance	Academic Procedure	Social Procedure	Social Moral
Expectations					
Rule	6%	2%	3%	7%	30%
Consequences to self	12	6	17	11	4
Consequences to group	2	0	2	3	0
Consequences to other	7	2	3	13	21
Consequences to teacher	4	2	2	6	0
Consequences to object	2	0	1	4	0
Circumstances	10	2	13	10	6
Authority	2	1	2	3	4
Attributions					
Positive effort	4	14	3	1	2
Negative effort	7	21	7	1	0
Positive ability	3	9	3	1	0
Negative ability	3	4	3	2	2
Unstable	1	2	2	0	0
Task	5	11	6	0	0
Mixed	4	13	2	1	0
Sanctions					
Reward	1	1	2	1	0
Promise	0	0	1	0	0
Punishment	6	7	3	9	11
Threat	15	3	16	20	13
Redirection	7	0	11	7	6
N (clauses)	1414	275	524	568	47

[a]χ^2 for domain differences = 685, d.f. = 57, $p < .0001$.

expectations, with a preponderance of intrinsic (consequences-oriented) communication. Socialization concerning social/moral issues presents possibly the
bleakest picture: The exceedingly rare informatives in this area are essentially
negative sanctions or extrinsic explanations in terms of rules. But sanctions in
general, it is strikingly clear, *are* essentially negative in this data set.

The initial picture of teacher talk regarding the student role is thus mixed at
best. It is reactive, negative, and procedural. Informatives—expectations, attributions, or sanctions—occur but rarely and are even more negative and procedural in emphasis than the overall flow of talk. Socialization concerning the
core task of academic performance, although outweighed by procedural communication, does offer the most positive picture; but it is perhaps most honestly
characterized as simply less negative than the other socialization that occurs.

Teacher talk may depend, however, on structural factors. The picture may be
more or less bleak when one looks at teachers of differential managerial effectiveness or at classrooms with different degrees of openness of task structure.

Further, features of the children that differ across or within classrooms may affect teacher talk; such talk may be affected by whether it is an older or younger, male or female, and working or middle class target who sits waiting to be socialized. Thus we now turn to an overview of these structural effects on teacher communication about the student role.

Teacher Talk: Managerial Effectiveness and Task Structure

Before summarizing these results we should emphasize that both managerial effectiveness and openness of task structure are correlational rather than causal variables with respect to teacher talk, although in somewhat different ways. As noted in the methods section, our indicator of managerial effectiveness was percentage of communication devoted to academic performance. Thus, as noted, certain comparisons, like distribution of remarks among domains, are ruled out. But it is also true that features that emerged as characteristic of the academic procedure domain are likely to correlate with "managerial effectiveness" because of the choice of indicator; we shall attempt to sort out in our discussion of results the extent to which such findings might actually be part of an overall package of effective management, given evidence from the previous literature. The degree of openness of task structure, in contrast, is defined independently of any of the other measures of interest. It presents a correlational problem only in the sense that a teacher both chooses to operate within a task structure and talks to students. It is thus possible that some (unmeasured) teacher characteristic causes both the selection of task structure and characteristics of teacher talk. We would agree with this argument, although we tend to believe that task structures, once set up, have causal effects in molding what the teacher says and how it is said. To partially sort out this latter correlation/causation question, we also examine differences in teacher talk during more differentiated and less differentiated instructional activity, for since all teachers in fact engaged in both open and traditional types of activity, this strategy effectively uses teachers as their own controls.

Aspects that characterize speech in the academic performance domain have already been summarized both for overall communication and for informatives above and in Table 7.3. Overall, such teacher talk was less negative, more reactive, and contained fewer informatives than that for other domains. When the variables are all transformed to percentages for individual teachers, and the n thus becomes 18, only one significant correlate of percent academic performance remains: negativity. Teachers' percentage of communication devoted to academic performance and the percentage negativity of their talk correlated a substantial $-.77$, highly significant even with teacher as the unit of analysis.

For the measure of openness, we first characterized the various categories of the child activity code as either differentiated, multi-task or undifferentiated, single-task, with the former considered as open and the latter as traditional. It is then possible both to look at the level of clauses for relationships with other variables and to characterize teachers overall and seek relationships at that level. At the level of clauses, several significant relationships emerged. When the teacher talk was occurring in an open activity structure, it was significantly less negative (43% versus 53% for traditional); more likely to involve academic performance and less likely to involve social procedure (by 11% in each case); and contained fewer informatives (14% to 21%). At the level of teachers' overall percentages, no relationships were significant. For example, although speech occurring in an open activity structure tended to involve more academic performance, it was not the case that teachers who had more open classrooms had any significant tendency to emphasize academic performance. Finally, teachers' degree of openness was checked for relationships with grade or social class. Although no relationship was found with grade, there was a significant difference between working and middle class in openness. It is not surprising that working class schools were significantly less open, given that, as noted in the methods section, officially open rooms had been abandoned in those schools prior to the study.

Teacher Talk: Differences in Target

We have seen thus far certain differences in teacher communication as a function of teacher-carried structural variables, especially with respect to the negativity of teacher talk. The theoretical section noted, however, that we might expect differences particularly between grade levels in the type and quality of communication, but also possibly between remarks addressed to boys and girls and between communication to working class and middle-class students.

Grade Differences.   Surprising similarity between first and fifth grades was observed, especially given that teachers theoretically should engage in somewhat different role socialization for optimal results. Overall communication to the two grade levels was about equally reactive. In the first grade positive communication did form a significantly higher proportion of talk, by 62% to 50%, as would be expected from the assumption that first-grade teachers are trying to instill norms rather than enforce already-instilled norms. Teachers differed across grades, however, in what was being instilled or talked about, with emphasis in the first grade on academic performance and social procedures and in the fifth grade on academic procedure. Yet these differences, while statistically significant, were small—suggesting that overall emphasis on procedural issues characterizes both grade levels equally well.

Although informatives were found in roughly equal proportions across grades, and were again about equally reactive, they differed both in again being more positive in the first grade and in the *kind* of communication being made. First-grade teachers provided proportionately fewer expectations than fifth-grade teachers (39% to 48% of informatives). When expectations were broken down into extrinsic versus intrinsic (consequences-oriented) types, first-grade teachers were also significantly less likely to provide intrinsic expectation information. These differences suggest that the first-grade teacher may presume less about what her students can or will understand of their action, focusing more on telling and doing than on explaining, relative to her fifth-grade counterpart. Overall, however, grade had a generally slight impact on the flow of communication or of informatives within that communication.

Sex of Student. A much more dramatic socialization difference emerged within classrooms than across classrooms of different grades. Very simply, there was a sizeable sex difference in distribution of overall communication: it was substantially more likely to be made to boys (39%) than to girls (29%). The remainder of communication was addressed to small groups or to the whole group.[8] This imbalance is even more pronounced in looking at informatives only, for 39% of these were addressed to boys as opposed to 21% to girls. Both differences are highly significant.

One question that arises in considering such lopsided communication is the problem that the target of communication may be such for a positive reason (e.g., the teacher likes boys better) or a negative reason (e.g., the teacher finds boys to be behavior problems). Thus we examined overall communication received by boys, girls, small groups, and whole groups to explore its quality and the distribution of concerns addressed. Results, presented in Table 7.5, indicate that reactive communication was addressed heavily to individuals, although about equally to boys and girls. There was a slight but not overwhelming tendency for boys to receive proportionately more negative feedback than girls, a difference that may be explicable in terms of the concerns addressed to the two sexes. Girls received an appreciably higher proportion of their communication regarding academic performance, while communication to boys involved more of both procedural areas. As we have already seen, academic performance communication tends to be more positive than that about procedural concerns.

The picture of informatives for boys and girls resembled that for overall remarks. Informatives were again almost identically reactive, but more similar in their negativity than was true of overall communication: 81% of informatives to boys were negative in comparison to 78% to girls. Distribution of these informatives among domains was somewhat more skewed, with girls receiving an even higher relative proportion of their informatives about academic performance (37%) than was true for boys (22%). Given these differences in concerns addressed to the two sexes, it is not surprising that only 17% of the negative

---

[8]Very small amounts of communication were addressed to small groups made up entirely of girls or boys. Because these mirrored the results for boys and girls individually, they were combined with those for individuals in these analyses.

TABLE 7.5
Characteristics of Overall Communication to
Boys, Girls, and Groups of Students

	Boys	Girls	Small Group	Whole Class
Reactivity[a]				
Before	11%	10%	51%	46%
After	89	90	49	54
Quality of Feedback[b]				
Positive	33%	41%	15%	6%
Negative	54	45	34	49
Distribution[c]				
Academic Performance	49%	61%	17%	7%
Academic Procedure	27	23	48	44
Social Procedure	22	15	35	47
Social/Moral	2	2	1	2

[a]$\chi^2 = 1851$, d.f. = 3, $p < .0001$.
[b]Ambiguous or not applicable (before) communication not presented. Overall $\chi^2 = 2247$, d.f. = 9, $p < .0001$.
[c]$\chi^2 = 1863$, d.f. = 9, $p < .0001$.

informatives addressed to boys concerned academic performance, in contrast to 33% of the negative informatives to girls. The *kind* of information provided also differed in congruent ways. Comparing the overall distribution of informatives among expectations, attributions, and sanctions, girls proved to receive proportionately more attributions among their informatives (40% versus 28% for boys). This is also not surprising given that attributions were found earlier to be concentrated more heavily in the academic performance domain.

Despite some differences between the sexes in the nature and distribution of teacher talk received, the overall message of these data is similar to that from our pilot investigation (Blumenfeld et al., 1977, 1979). The striking difference in teacher handling of girls versus boys concerns the amount of attention paid to them in the first place. Within that background fact, there are relatively more subtle tendencies for girls to receive disproportionately more academic performance communication, and quite slight evidence of more positive communication to girls. Teachers do *not* appear to be attending to boys because they are disruptors—although of course they might be attending to boys so as to prevent them from *becoming* disruptors. In any case, although a simple explanation does not emerge from these data, the simple fact remains: the sheer amount of both overall communication and informatives addressed to boys substantially outweigh those to girls.

Social Class.   In contrast to those for grade or sex, the effects of social class on teacher talk can be readily summarized: there were almost none. Teachers in working- versus middle-class schools did not differ significantly in the reactivity or negativity of overall communication; in its distribution among domains; in the number of informatives provided; or in their reactivity and negativity. They addressed essentially the same issues within domains and gave the same kinds of attributions and expectation information. The sole difference of any import found is a tendency toward more sanctioning—which essentially means more punishing and threatening—in the working-class schools. Some 34% of informatives were sanctions for the working class, while the percentage for middle-class schools was only 24%. Although managerial effectiveness was uncorrelated with social class, recall that openness was substantially related to class. Thus we examined the relationship between class and distribution of informatives controlling for whether the teacher talk occurred in an open or traditional structure. The class difference proved to hold only during traditional communication (which occurred to some extent in all rooms). Thus with the caveat that it is limited to traditional communication, this sanctioning difference would appear to be a "real" social class difference. But the overall similarity in teacher communication to working- and middle-class students is far more impressive than this one rather slender difference.

Children's Thought about the Student Role

The student role as communicated in teacher talk is one of conformity to procedural demands, enforced through largely reactive and negative means, and rarely accompanied by further informatives that might guide internalization of classroom norms. Structural differences in this communication were relatively few, with the effects of our indicator of managerial effectiveness and the differences in attention paid to boys versus girls standing out in a general picture of cross- and within-classroom similarity. The issues then remaining are, first, what students think about the relative importance of the domains of classroom life or issues within them; second, how they would feel if they met or failed to meet expectations; third, how different the children's responses are depending on their grade, sex, or social class; and, crucially, the potential impact of differences in teacher talk, managerial effectiveness, or task structure on children's thought about the student role.

Table 7.6 presents average importance and feelings ratings summaries for each issue as well as for each domain overall, separately for good and bad books. Grade differences, also presented here for convenience, are discussed later. In examining results or in particular in comparing importance and feelings data, recall that the measure of importance is a transformation of the continuous line data that ranges between 0 and 1.0; feelings data represent assignment of numbers, ranging from 1 to 4, to the neutral face through large smile (or large frown) stimuli.

Certain general patterns appear across domains, as well as, predictably, differences among domains. A first general pattern concerns how students react to meeting an expectation ("good books") versus failing to meet one ("bad

TABLE 7.6
Student Thought about Classroom Norms by Domain: Importance (lines) and Feelings (faces) for Each Norm

	Issue	Importance				Feelings			
		Overall	First Grade	Fifth Grade	Significance level	Overall	First Grade	Fifth Grade	Significance level

A. Academic Performance

	Issue	Overall	First Grade	Fifth Grade	Sig.	Overall	First Grade	Fifth Grade	Sig.
G	OVERALL	.66	.74	.59	d	3.23	3.45	3.01	d
O	Math Content	.74	.80	.70	c	3.50	3.58	3.42	a
O	Language Content	.70	.75	.65	c	3.30	3.47	3.14	d
D	Other Content	.63	.70	.57	d	3.26	3.47	3.08	d
B	Language Format	.57	.68	.47	d	2.90	3.27	2.57	d
O	Math Format	.66	.76	.58	d	3.11	3.44	2.81	d
O	OVERALL	.46	.57	.37	d	2.74	3.12	2.39	d
K	Math Content	.54	.61	.48	d	3.07	3.27	2.90	c
S	Language Content	.55	.62	.49	c	2.92	3.14	2.72	d
	Other Content	.40	.52	.29	d	2.64	3.12	2.21	d
	Language Format	.34	.48	.21	d	2.29	2.80	1.82	d
	Math Format	.52	.64	.40	d	2.76	3.25	2.31	d

B. Academic Procedure

	Issue	Overall	First Grade	Fifth Grade	Sig.	Overall	First Grade	Fifth Grade	Sig.
G	OVERALL	.68	.76	.60	d	3.09	3.43	2.79	d
O	On-Task	.68	.78	.59	d	3.06	3.47	2.69	d
O	Assistance	.65	.76	.55	d	3.01	3.38	2.68	d
D	Persistence	.75	.82	.68	d	3.78	3.48	2.92	d
B	Readiness	.64	.69	.59	b	3.07	3.42	2.76	d
O	Routine	.65	.75	.56	d	2.96	3.37	2.58	d
S	Completion	.70	.76	.64	c	3.27	3.47	3.08	d

B OVERALL	.59	.68	.51	d	2.91	3.23	2.63	d
A On-Task	.64	.75	.53	d	2.99	3.36	2.66	d
D Assistance	.57	.67	.47	d	2.85	3.23	2.49	d
B Persistence	.68	.76	.61	d	3.07	3.31	2.85	d
O Readiness	.51	.56	.47	b	2.72	2.91	2.55	c
K Routine	.62	.71	.53	d	2.99	3.36	2.65	d
S Completion	.53	.63	.44	d	2.87	3.22	2.55	d

C. Social Procedure

G OVERALL	.62	.73	.53	d	2.93	3.36	2.55	d
O Materials	.69	.78	.60	d	3.12	3.50	2.78	d
O Place	.55	.68	.44	d	2.79	3.27	2.35	d
D Lining Up	.57	.69	.45	d	2.82	3.30	2.39	d
B General	.59	.68	.50	d	2.81	3.25	2.41	d
O Turn Taking	.64	.73	.55	d	2.97	3.34	2.63	d
O Role	.64	.71	.57	d	3.00	3.42	2.63	d
K Late	.63	.73	.54	d	2.93	3.38	2.53	d
S Cleaning Up	.70	.81	.60	d	3.06	3.47	2.71	d
Noise	.62	.72	.53	d	2.89	3.32	2.50	d

B OVERALL	.58	.69	.47	d	2.82	3.21	2.47	d
A Materials	.64	.77	.52	d	3.03	3.44	2.65	d
D Place	.43	.57	.31	d	2.42	2.88	2.00	d
B Lining Up	.56	.70	.44	d	2.74	3.26	2.25	d
O General	.67	.77	.58	d	2.99	3.35	2.66	d
O Turn Taking	.61	.71	.51	d	2.89	3.26	2.56	d
K Role	.63	.71	.56	d	3.04	3.25	2.85	d
S Late	.39	.48	.31	d	2.44	2.80	2.11	d
Cleaning Up	.66	.79	.53	d	3.03	3.40	2.69	d
Noise	.60	.75	.48	d	2.84	3.25	2.47	d

(continued)

TABLE 7.6 (Continued)

A. Academic Performance

		Importance				Feelings			
	Issue	Overall	First Grade	Fifth Grade	Significance level	Overall	First Grade	Fifth Grade	Significance level
	D. Social/Moral								
G	OVERALL	.73	.81	.66	d	3.21	3.50	2.95	d
O	Comforting	.78	.84	.72	d	3.33	3.55	3.14	d
O	Aggression	.70	.83	.59	d	3.13	3.45	2.84	d
D	L_ing	.77	.83	.71	d	3.18	3.51	2.87	d
	Sharing	.70	.76	.65	c	3.21	3.45	3.00	d
B	Include Others	.68	.77	.60	d	3.19	3.56	2.84	d
O	Playing Fair	.65	.75	.57	d	3.09	3.47	2.74	d
O	Cheating	.76	.82	.70	c	3.24	3.52	2.99	d
K	Stealing	.79	.83	.75	b	3.33	3.50	3.18	c
S									
B	OVERALL	.69	.76	.63	d	3.14	3.40	2.91	d
A	Comforting	.65	.74	.56	d	3.12	3.47	2.80	d
D	Aggression	.78	.86	.71	d	3.30	3.57	3.05	d
	Lying	.84	.89	.80	c	3.55	3.68	3.42	c
B	Sharing	.57	.69	.46	d	2.91	3.39	2.47	d
O	Include Others	.63	.73	.54	d	2.96	3.24	2.72	d
O	Playing Fair	.54	.60	.49	b	2.84	3.10	2.60	d
K	Cheating	.83	.84	.82	n.s.	3.45	3.51	3.41	n.s.
S	Stealing	.89	.89	.90	n.s.	3.66	3.68	3.64	n.s.
	Tattling	.55	.64	.46	d	2.72	3.03	2.44	d
	Teasing	.63	.74	.53	d	2.93	3.32	2.56	d

a) t – test $p \leq .05$
b) $p \leq .01$
c) $p \leq .001$
d) $p \leq .0001$

books''). Overall averages for good versus bad books show, across all domains, that children rate it to be better to meet an expectation than it is bad to fail at one. In addition, they are consistent in rating that they would feel more good in meeting a role expectation than they would feel bad in failing to meet one. This pattern is somewhat surprising, given that such a high proportion of teacher communication concerns essentially the ''bad books'' version of issues; in addition, children are supposed to absorb learning about doing and not doing ''bads'' earlier than they do about ''goods'' (Keasey, 1978).

Relative importance of the domains shows that the domain receiving least emphasis in the classroom—that of social/moral issues—is the most important one, at least by the criteria of how children responded to these lines and faces measures. This both again illustrates children's ability to distinguish moral from other issues (e.g., Turiel, 1978) and suggests that moral concerns might be most fruitfully considered as outside the student role per se. They are something that is learned in the child's daily life, rather than in the classroom itself, and are carried into the classroom as into any other setting the child encounters.

Responses within social moral issues do suggest clues to how different types of norms may be learned. In this domain there are clear distinctions between issues where children are taught ''thou shalts'' and issues where they are taught ''thou shalt nots.'' Norms like comforting another, sharing, including others, and playing fairly call for the *commission* of behavior. Norms about such issues as aggression, lying, and cheating, in contrast, call for the *omission* of behavior. For the commission norms here, children consistently reported that it was more good to do the act than it was bad to omit it; for the omission norms, they reported that it was more bad to do the act than it was good to omit it. There could be a variety of reasons for this pattern of differences, including the perceptual and conceptual simplicity of human action (versus inaction), as well as possibly the reinforcement patterns employed for the different types of norms. In any case, the overall result that ''good books'' tended to receive generally higher ratings than ''bad books'', discussed earlier, may be a function of the fact that most classroom norms are either clearly commission norms or ambiguous rather than omission norms.[9] The kind of norm asked about may determine what one finds concerning children's comprehension or their assessments.

The three domains specifically related to classroom life look very similar with regard to how good it is to meet an expectation. Teachers' relative lack of emphasis on academic performance may be reflected in the results for the bad books that it was rated *least* bad not to fulfill academic performance norms and that children indicated they would feel least bad about not doing so. Norms in this domain are also clearly and uniformly commission norms, however, while

---

[9]By ambiguous norms we mean ones in which the socialization might readily be phrased in terms of either commission or omission (e.g., ''don't be late'' versus ''be on time''; ''be neat'' versus ''don't be messy'').

some norms in the two procedural domains are ambiguous or omission norms. Thus it is not entirely clear whether to attribute such results to the domain of activity or to the type of norm involved.

Among the procedural issues, one essentially ''moral'' norm stands out: persistence, trying to do one's academic work. Weiner (1979) has suggested that effort is seen by children as a moral imperative. It is clear that children here perceived persistence as the best of the academic or social procedural activities when fulfilled, and failure to persist as the worst violation; their feelings data were congruent with these important ratings. These patterns suggest that Weiner's argument is correct.

Group Differences.   The one truly overwhelming set of group differences is presented in Table 7.6: the consistent difference between first and fifth graders. For every norm except cheating and stealing, first graders rated the actions as more extremely good or bad and indicated that they would feel better or worse, respectively, than was true of fifth graders. Grade differences for importance might possibly be attributed to use of a different measuring instrument for first and fifth graders, as described in the methods section above. But the congruence of the reactions for feelings suggests that first graders were simply reacting with greater conformity to any and all norms. This pattern is consistent with our cognitive development-based expectation that responses of first graders would be less discriminating and more global.

Many fewer differences emerged between boys and girls and between working- and middle-class students, and in both cases they tended to involve ratings of feelings rather than importance. For both of these variables, tests were made using regressions with grade controlled by entering it first hierarchically; the interaction of each variable with grade was also entered and is discussed where significant. Tables therefore report partial correlations rather than means for both sex and social class. Because there are multiple nonindependent statistical tests made for such data, we adopted the decision rule that issues only be examined individually when the overall summary variable for the domain showed a significant group difference. (This rule was obviously unnecessary for grade differences, where almost all tests were highly significant.) Table 7.7 shows the results that emerge for sex differences using this selection criterion.

The consistent patterns of sex differences emerge in response to the bad books only, and involve feelings only, in the academic procedure, social procedure, and social/moral domains. Results are quite easy to summarize: Girls always reported that they would feel worse about violating the norm. The other dozen-odd scattered significant effects, for lines or for faces in the good books, might not be ones that could be individually trusted; but their pattern was also consistent with that found for feelings, in that girls always reported that it was better to fulfill an expectation and that they would feel better doing so, or worse to fail an expectation and (as shown) that they would feel worse. Thus sex differences are simply sharpest with regard to feeling bad about norm violations.

TABLE 7.7
Partial Correlations for Significant Sex Differences
in Feelings Ratings

	Domain and Issue	Partial r's	Significance Level
Bad Books	Academic Procedure		
	Overall	.14	.01
	On Task	.16	.002
	Routine	.11	.04
Bad Books	Social Procedure		
	Overall	.15	.005
	Lining Up	.14	.009
	General Social		
	Procedure	.12	.03
	Late	.14	.01
	Cleaning Up	.12	.03
	Noise	.15	.007
Bad Books	Social/Moral		
	Overall	.21	.0001
	Comforting	.14	.01
	Aggression	.15	.007
	Lying	.16	.004
	Sharing	.15	.005
	Tattling	.12	.03
	Teasing	.14	.008

The pattern of sex differences bears no direct relationship to the differential treatment the sexes received from the teacher. Girls reported greater conformity to the norms, despite receiving much less socializing attention than that received by boys. Girls were also most different from boys in the social/moral area, at least as indexed by number of significant differences found, and that area barely appears in classroom life. They were least different in the area of academic performance, the domain where teachers target the highest proportion of effort at girls. In general, evidence from student thought about the role supports a relatively "sugar and spice" picture of girls—certainly more so than is true of the teacher talk data, and in ways not particularly consistent with it.

Surprisingly, there were more significant differences between working and middle class students than between the sexes. These were also primarily concentrated in the feelings ratings, as Table 7.8 shows, but did involve importance ratings for both good and bad books in the academic performance realm. In contrast, for feelings ratings there were significant class differences in six of the eight possible areas, everywhere except in the good books for academic performance and procedure. Results can be readily summarized, as they were consistent across all tests: Working-class children always indicated it was better to meet a normative expectation and that they would feel better doing so, or that it was worse to fail an expectation and that they would feel worse doing so. Thus

TABLE 7.8
Partial Correlations for Significant Social Class Differences
in Importance or Feelings Ratings

Domain and Issue	Importance		Feelings	
	Partial r	*Significance*	*Partial r*	*Significance*
Good Books				
Academic Performance				
Overall	.12	.02		n.s.
Language Content	.12	.03		
Other Content	.18	.0006		
Bad Books				
Academic Performance				
Overall	.20	.0003	.20	.0002
Other Content	.24	$<.0001$	.20	.0002
Language Format	.11	.05	.15	.007
Math Format	.14	.01	.19	.0005
Bad Books				
Academic Procedure				
Overall		n.s.	.17	.002
On Task			.14	.01
Assistance			.12	.02
Routine			.19	.0006

Good Books	Social Procedure			
	Overall	n.s.	.11	.05
Bad Books	Social Procedure			
	Overall	n.s.	.20	.0002
	Materials		.11	.05
	Place		.15	.005
	Lining Up		.18	.001
	Turn Taking		.15	.007
	Cleaning Up		.16	.003
	Noise		.16	.003
Good Books	Social/Moral			
	Overall	n.s.	.12	.03
	Aggression		.24	<.0001
	Including Others		.11	.05
	Playing Fair		.12	.03
Bad Books	Social/Moral			
	Overall	n.s.	.11	.04
	Sharing		.14	.008

despite little if any evidence of differential socialization by teachers, working-class children—even more so than girls overall—exhibited greater conformity to the norms involved in the student role.

A couple of interactions between social class and grade level did emerge. For the social procedure bad books, the working class children gave higher importance ratings in the first grade, while in fifth grade the two social classes were essentially equal. For the social/moral bad books, in the first grade working class children gave higher importance ratings, whereas in the fifth grade, middle-class children did so by a very similar margin. These patterns give some indication of reduction with age in working class conformity to the norms in question, but do not involve the feelings ratings where most of the class differences lie.

Effects of Teacher Talk on Student Thought

Thus far we have seen a series of differences involving children's judgments of the importance of classroom norms and their feelings about them, differences that bear but little relationship to any patterns uncovered in teacher talk itself. One natural question, then, is whether any aspects of teacher communication do affect children's views of the student role. Given the theoretical foundations in social learning and attribution theories, a number of possible candidates for appropriate "aspects" emerge. The reactivity of the communication is not particularly appropriate, given, as we have seen, that it can be simply a part of a classroom activity—like feedback about academic performance—rather than really serving as an indicator that the teacher is failing to shape behaviors. The negativity of communication is a much more plausible candidate, but given its correlation with the teacher's emphasis on academic performance, it is more reasonable to consider negativity as itself an effect of that structural variable.[10] We are then left with aspects of the informatives provided by teachers as possible determinants of children's thought about the student role. It is to these that we then look for teacher effects.

Information per se would be a category so broad as to be useless, for results showed that informatives of different types were distributed across the domains of classroom life in very different patterns and were also of differential negativity. Thus we chose to look at three different indices for informatives: the teacher's percentage of attributions provided in the academic performance domain, for that was where attributions were concentrated; and the teacher's percentage of expectation and sanction information in each of the academic procedure and social procedure domains, for those domains were where expectations and sanctions were chiefly found. In addition to controlling for domains in-

---

[10]It appears more plausible that the domain or topic determines the affective tone than the reverse. Thus, given their high intercorrelation, we chose to use the more structural (and probably causal) variable of the two.

volved, this division also separates a relatively positive category (attributions) from the more generally negative expectation and sanctioning information.

Each of the measures of perceived importance or feelings was regressed on these information measures separately, using hierarchical regressions in which grade was entered first, then the information measure, and finally the interaction between the two. Again the decision rule was employed to look at specific issues only when a variable had an effect on a summary variable (such as "good books" responses for academic performance). Table 7.9 presents the results of these regressions for all three variables for the importance data only, given that there were generally many fewer effects on children's feelings ratings. Where there were significant relationships to feelings, these are discussed later in text.

As Table 7.9 reveals, the effects of the teacher's percentage of attributions in academic performance were quite specific to academic areas, and within those, to judgments of the good books, or meeting of normative expectations. There was an overall positive relationship for the academic performance domain itself, tempered by an interaction between percentage of attributions and grade; examination of that interaction revealed that there was no impact of attribution percentage in the first grade, but only in the fifth grade. In the good books for the academic procedure domain, only an interaction with grade emerged. Examination showed that it was similar to the previous interaction, in that there was a negligible negative effect of attribution percentage in the first grade and a substantial positive one in the fifth grade.

The most dramatic news in these analyses of teacher information, obvious from Table 7.9, concerns the difference between the impacts of expectations and sanctions from the two procedural domains. Although we have seen that the realm of academic procedure is a relatively negative one, and there is no reason to believe that the expectations and sanctions being tapped by the present variable differ from those in the social procedure domain in this respect, they have opposite effects on children's ratings of importance. Expectations and sanctions in the academic procedure domain, as a percentage of overall communication in that domain, had simple *positive* relationships to children's importance ratings for both academic performance and academic procedure. The chief difference from the pattern for attributions is that the expectations/sanctions variable affected ratings of the bad books, or failures to meet normative expectations, rather than the good books. In addition, there was also a significant positive relationship to ratings of the faces, or feelings data, for the academic procedure bad books. Attributions, in contrast, had no relationship whatsoever to feelings ratings.

Percentage of expectations and sanctions in the social procedure domain, in contrast, had quite diffuse effects on children's ratings across all domains. For academic performance, both good and bad books, there was a negative effect of teacher's percentage of social procedure expectations/sanctions on children's ratings. In the academic procedure realm, a similar main effect appeared for good

TABLE 7.9
Partial Correlations for Significant Main Effects of
Teacher Talk Variables on Children's Importance Ratings

	A.	Domain and Issue	Percent Academic Performance Attributions	Significance Level
Good Books		Academic Performance		
		Overall	.12	.02
		Math Content	.16	.002
		Math Format	.11	.05

	B.	Domain and Issue	Percent Academic Procedure Expectations/ Sanctions	Significance Level
Bad Books		Academic Performance		
		Overall	.15	.005
		Other Content	.18	.002
		Language Format	.12	.03
Bad Books		Academic Procedure		
		Overall	.12	.03
		On Task	.11	.04
		Assistance	.13	.02

	C.	Domain and Issue	Percent Social Procedure Expectations/ Sanctions	Significance Level
Good Books		Academic Performance		
		Overall	-.20	.0002
		Math Content	-.14	.008
		Language Content	-.12	.02
		Other Content	-.15	.006
		Language Format	-.18	.001
		Math Format	-.15	.005
Bad Books		Academic Performance		
		Overall	-.16	.003
		Math Content	-.12	.02
		Language Format	-.12	.03
Good Books		Academic Procedure		
		Overall	-.14	.009
		On Task	-.15	.005
		Assistance	-.12	.03
		Completion	-.12	.02
Good Books		Social Procedure		
		Overall	-.18	.001
		Materials	-.12	.02
		Place	-.19	.0006
		Lining Up	-.13	.01
		General Social Procedure	-.24	< .0001
		Role	-.11	.05

books, plus an interaction with grade; similarly to the previous interactions, this now indicated that there was a bigger negative relationship in the fifth grade than in the first. In social procedure itself there were again relationships with the good books, both a negative main effect of expectation/sanction percentage and an interaction with grade. The interaction again involved a larger negative relationship in the fifth grade than in the first. Results for the social/moral domain were the only ones that differed from the general pattern at all, in that an interaction with grade was the only general effect in the importance data; that interaction showed no effect of social procedure expectations/sanctions in the first grade, and a negative effect in the fifth. Further, the only relationships to feelings ratings appeared in this area for the bad books—and involved a different interaction, with a small negative relationship in first grade and no relationship in fifth grade. Given that this was the only link of this variable to feelings ratings and that the pattern differed from that of all the other interactions—which each showed larger negative effects in the fifth grade—the results should probably be discounted. Even including it in the overall pattern, that pattern clearly involves a negative impact of teachers' use of expectations or sanctions in the social procedure domain: The more those were used, the lower the children's importance ratings of a whole series of norms across the full range of norms tapped. Further, this relationship was generally stronger, and sometimes appeared only among fifth graders.

Overall, then, teachers' use of attributions in the academic performance domain had a positive impact on children's ratings of academically-related norms. This is reasonable given that such attributions are both informative per se and, as we have seen, relatively positive in tone. Surprisingly, use of expectations and sactions in the academic and social procedure realms had divergent effects on children's ratings, with academic procedure expectations/sanctions relating positively to ratings in the two academic domains and social procedure expectations/sanctions having diffuse negative effects on ratings. In general, however, all three teacher communication variables affected importance rather than feelings ratings, in contrast to the effects of sex or social class on judgments. It would appear that the more cognitive measure was more susceptible to teacher influence, whereas the more affective measure was more closely linked to differences children bring to the classroom. Some speculation about reasons for divergent effects among the teacher variables is made in the conclusions section.

Effects of Managerial Effectiveness and Task Structure on Student Thought

Either our indicator of managerial effectiveness or the openness of task structure might also affect children's thought about the student role, both because these indicators had some relationship to teacher talk and because they might reflect aspects of classroom life not necessarily captured in our teacher talk measures themselves. Simple direct effects of either variable were assessed in separate regressions where grade and classroom social class composition were entered first hierarchically; interactions of each with these control variables were also entered and are discussed in the text where significant. Interactions between academic performance as a percentage of a teacher's overall communication and percent openness were assessed in an equation in which grade was entered first, followed hierarchically by percentage academic performance and percent open, followed by all interaction terms. These interactions appear in Table 7.10 below, along with summaries of each set of main effects.

In a pattern resembling that for the teacher talk variables, both of these structural variables had effects on importance judgments only. The managerial effectiveness indicator had a significant positive effect on all four sets of "good books" ratings, but no effect on "bad books" ratings. For the social/moral good importance ratings there was also a small but significant three-way interaction with grade and social class such that in the first grade, there was an effect of percent academic performance for working class children only; in the fifth grade there was a positive relationship for both social classes. The only effects of percent academic performance on the feelings ratings appeared in interaction with social class for the academic procedure good books and the social procedure bad books. In the case of academic procedure, the social classes showed no differences in first grade, but in the fifth grade the working-class children showed a negative effect of percent academic performance; the middle-class children, a positive effect. For social procedure, at both grade levels the working-class children showed a negative effect of percent academic performance and the middle-class children a positive effect.

Main effects of the percentage of teacher talk occurring in open structures were even more specific than effects of percent academic performance. There were no effects whatsoever on the feelings ratings, and effects on only three groups of importance ratings: those for the academic performance good and bad books and for social procedure good books. The most interesting feature of the results is their negative sign, however, for the greater the teacher's degree of openness the *lower* the importance ratings given to the norms shown in Table 7.10.

Interactions are what make the results for percent openness truly interesting, however. The only interaction with a structural variable was one with social class for the academic performance bad books; it indicated that in the middle-class schools, openness had a positive effect in first grade and a negative effect in the fifth; in the working-class schools, the openness effect was uniformly negative. The key feature, shown in Table 7.10, was the interactions with percent academic performance (typically also accompanied by three-way interactions with grade). When graphed these showed that, in general, when percent academic performance was *low*, the effect of openness on children's ratings was negative; when percent academic performance was *high*, the relationship reversed and the effect of openness was positive. This flip-flop pattern appeared

TABLE 7.10
Partial Correlations for Main Effects of Percentage
Academic Performance, Percentage Openness, and Their Interaction[a]

Domain and Issue		Percent Academic Performance	Percent Open	Academic Performance X Open
Good Books	Academic Performance			
	Overall	.13	-.15	.19
	Math Content	n.s.	-.18	.16
	Language Content	.13	n.s.	.15
	Language Format	.12	-.11	.13
	Math Format	n.s.	n.s.	.19
Bad Books	Academic Performance			
	Overall	n.s.	-.14	n.s.
	Language Content		-.14	
	Language Format		-.15	
Good Books	Academic Procedure			
	Overall	.20	n.s.	.16
	On Task	n.s.		.19
	Assistance	.12		.13
	Persistence	.18		n.s.
	Readiness	.15		n.s.
	Routine	.22		n.s.
	Completion	.11		.14
Good Books	Social Procedure			
	Overall	.15	-.12	.13
	Materials	.12	n.s.	n.s.
	Place	n.s.	-.19	.12
	Lining Up	n.s.	-.12	n.s.
	General Social Procedure	n.s.	-.17	n.s.
	Turn Taking	.12	n.s.	.12
	Role	.14	n.s.	n.s.
	Late	.20	n.s.	.11
	Cleaning Up	.11	n.s.	n.s.
	Noise	.17	n.s.	n.s.
Good Books	Social/Moral			
	Overall	.17	n.s.	.16
	Comforting	.15		n.s.
	Aggression	n.s.		.15
	Lying	n.s.		.11
	Sharing	.11		.13
	Including Others	.15		n.s.
	Playing Fair	n.s.		.13
	Cheating	.13		n.s.
	Stealing	.17		.13

[a] Partials for percent academic performance and percent open are reported from equations in which grade and social class were entered first hierarchically as controls. To simplify the number of terms involved, the partials for the interaction were obtained from an equation in which just grade, the two independent variables, and their interactions were entered hierarchically.

more strongly, or only, in the fifth grade, yielding three-way interactions. One way of making sense of this pattern is to suggest that when a teacher is not an effective manager (i.e., when percent academic performance is low), greater openness may simply mean greater chaos, such that it has a negative impact on children's views of classroom life; when the teacher is an effective manager, greater openness may accomplish some of the benefits its proponents have suggested. Thus effects of task structure need to be considered in the context of the teacher's managerial effectiveness. The fact that this interactive effect for openness appeared only in the fifth grades does, however, lend support to recent cautionary notes about open structures in the very early grades (e.g., Brophy, 1979), in that openness in the first grade simply had negative or at best nil effects on children's ratings.

CONCLUSIONS

As a socializing institution, the school is the arena from which the larger society expects scholars and citizens to emerge. However, as Jackson (1968) suggested, our data so far indicate that it is the everyday demands of the *institution* rather than the long-term goal of *socializing* that receive emphasis in teacher communication to children about the student role. The teacher is a manager of activities, and immediate institutional imperatives of conducting those activities and preventing chaos override what might be ideal-typical socializing practices. Instead, the teacher is a manager who mainly reacts, and reacts to things she does not like. Those things are mostly violations of the procedures that probably must be maintained if the show is to go on. Relatively rarely, and primarily when spurred by a negative event, is the teacher prompted to provide further socializing information involving her expectations, attributions of causality, or sanctions themselves. The student is essentially a socializee who absorbs on-the-job experience geared to passive citizenship in an ongoing institution.

Two kinds of potential differences in teacher talk were examined: those flowing from differences in teacher managerial effectiveness and the structure of tasks in the classroom, and those flowing from differences among the recipients of the communication themselves. Few effects of either type of variable were found, perhaps because of the fundamental similarity of managerial demands across classrooms. Our indicator of managerial effectiveness, the percentage of communication devoted to academic performance, was powerfully related to the negativity of teacher talk, with better managers less negative. While this result must provisionally be considered simply an empirical association, we tend to believe that managerial effectiveness and positivity are organically linked. Procedural issues, although they form the bulk of teacher communication, are essentially about interferences with the core task of instruction itself—and hence relatively negative. When the teacher is able to talk about academic performance, it indicates that she is doing the core task of the job. Such talk is also neither positive nor negative by necessity, and hence emerges as more positive than communication about the interferences themselves. In contrast to managerial effectiveness, the degree of openness of task structure did not relate significantly to differences in teacher talk.

Differences among students—grade, sex, and social class—were linked to few differences in teacher communication. Teachers of first and fifth graders behaved quite similarly, with only slight tendencies for first-grade teachers to be more positive and for fifth-grade teachers to be more expansive with information about expectations. Given that from a socialization standpoint rather substantial differences might be optimal, as noted earlier, it would appear here that managerial imperatives work against the long-term goal. The most striking difference, the greater attention paid to boys, may reflect perceived managerial demands of averting classroom disruption. Our data, however, clearly do not paint boys as sheer classroom disruptors; they are instead primarily sheer attention-getters. The final structural difference, social class of students, proved to have almost no impact on teacher talk, with teachers in middle- and working-class schools behaving quite similarly. In this last case, at least, the apparent fundamental similarities in management needs produced a heartening result, insofar as we might have expected a still more procedurally or punitively oriented socialization pattern in the working-class schools than was observed overall.

Children's thoughts about the student role were more sharply differentiated by these latter structural variables than was the teacher talk directed at them. First graders were uniformly more eagerly conforming to classroom norms, whether in terms of their thought about the importance of these norms or their feelings regarding conformity/nonconformity. Girls and working-class children were also more conforming, although in the case of girls this was entirely in the realm of their feelings and in the case of working-class children it was predominantly so. These would appear to be differences imported to the classroom by the children, rather than produced by teachers' treatment, given the relative absence of differential treatment for either first graders or working-class children and the striking lack of attention paid to girls.

Both teacher structural differences—managerial effectiveness and openness—and features of teacher talk itself affected children's thought about the student role. All of these teacher variables, however, had effects on children's ratings of the importance of norms rather than on their ratings of feelings about the norms, suggesting that the more emotional/motivational area is less susceptible to teacher influence. The pattern of results generally suggests that although all students are absorbing on-the-job experience in the student role, the meaning of being ''on-the-job'' differs across classrooms in systematic ways.

The indicator of managerial effectiveness, degree of attention to academic performance, essentially reflects differential effectiveness in ability to organize and monitor academic work. Managerial effectiveness as defined by this criterion appears congruent with descriptions of good teachers (Anderson, Evertson, & Emmer, 1980; Brophy & Putnam, 1979), in that such teachers seem to monitor student progress, provide feedback that is more oriented to work than to conduct, and keep the classroom running smoothly. In addition to previous findings that this type of environment influences actual achievement (Brophy, 1979; Rosenshine, 1976), our data show a positive impact on students' ratings of the importance of conforming to the role. In classrooms where teachers attended heavily to performance, children thought it was more important to adhere to the conventions of the classroom and to do work both properly and well.

The pattern of results found for openness of task structure also suggests something of the meaning of task structure for children's on-the-job experience. Openness per se had a generally negative effect on children's ratings of importance of various norms. However, it also interacted with managerial effectiveness such that, for the older children, teacher's low managerial effectiveness produced a negative impact of openness and high managerial effectiveness a positive impact of openness. Such a pattern is sensible in terms of the managerial demands of different structures. The more differentiated the organization, the greater the degree of management needed to coordinate students' efforts successfully (Brophy & Putnam, 1979). Monitoring, organizing, and managing a class in which a variety of tasks are going on simultaneously place great demands on the teacher. Thus as the degree of openness increases, the potential for disorganization increases—and hence so does the necessity for effective management. Although proponents of differentiated activity structures (Bossert, 1978; Horowitz, 1979; Walberg & Thomas, 1972) claim that they improve the potential for student involvement, interaction, and independence, this may only be true where the teacher is an effective enough manager. Yet a combination of good management and a relatively differentiated structure can lead to greater commitment to good quality work on the part of the student.

Children's experience of the student role was also affected by explicit socializing information provided by the teacher. In the present data set, three types of such information proved to affect children's thought about the role: percentage of academic performance communication devoted to attributions, percentage of academic procedure devoted to expectations/sanctions, and percentage of social procedure devoted to expectations/sanctions. The divergent impacts of these kinds of information on children's thought prove explicable in terms of the day-to-day communication they probably reflect. First, attributions about performance increased children's (and particularly older children's) ratings of the importance of academic performance and procedure. This may reflect the fact that most attributions were made after poor quality performance and generally referred to lack of effort, an issue which children perceive as very serious. Thus, it appears that the communication "you can do better" has the effect of focusing children on the idea that they must work and must persist.

In contrast, expectations and sanctions in the realm of academic procedure were likely to concern being off task and often communicated the negative consequences of not working or the likely punishments to be imposed. It is not surprising that teachers who provided proportionately more information about why it is bad not to work properly had students who in fact thought it was bad not to do so. It is possible that the additional effects of such information on children's ratings of academic performance reflect children's tendency to see work procedure and outcome as related (Blumenfeld, Wessels, Pintrich, & Meece, 1981; Stipek, 1981; Weinstein, 1981).

The divergent impact of social procedure expectations/sanctions, which had a negative impact on a variety of children's ratings, illustrates that frequency or type of communication per se has no necessary relation to outcomes. Most of this social procedure information concerned talking, an issue generally of low importance to the children. We would suggest that a series of relatively low affect and predominantly negative communications about an unimportant issue are likely to be defined as nagging and hence discounted. Certainly neither the negativity per se nor the procedural focus per se can account for the effect, given that academic procedure information, also negative, had positive impacts on children's ratings. It would appear that the meaning of the information to the child may be crucial.

Thus, despite the bleak picture of the student role as it appears in the overall outlines of teacher communication, the pattern of effects of teacher variables on children's thought about the role provides to some extent a prescription for hope. We should emphasize that the effects found were generally significant but small, possibly reflecting the overall similarities among teachers in carrying out their role. But it appears that the teacher who focuses on the central task to be done, who emphasizes issues of effort, who insists on keeping on task—such a teacher produces students more convinced of the importance of the central academic aspects of the role. The citizenship thus presented might be a relatively passive one, but the scholarship will get accomplished. Such a picture is probably relatively similar to that of a good manager in any area. The American school is thus much like the American factory, in that the small workers whose product is themselves need good managers in order either to turn out a good product or to care about the production process.

ACKNOWLEDGMENT

The research reported here was supported by Grant NIE-G-78-0190 from the National Institutes of Education.

REFERENCES

Anderson, L., Evertson, C., & Emmer, E. Dimensions in classroom management. *Journal of Curriculum Studies,* 1980, *12,* 343–356.

Aronfreed, J. The effect of experimental socialization paradigms upon two moral responses to transgression. *Journal of Abnormal and Social Psychology,* 1963, *66,* 437–448.

Aronfreed, J. The concept of internalization. In D. A. Goslin (Ed.), *Handbook of socialization theory and research.* New York: Rand-McNally, 1969, 263–324.

Aronfreed, J. Moral development from the standpoint of a general psychological theory. In T. Lickona (Ed.), *Moral development and behavior*. New York: Holt, 1976, 54-69.

Bandura, A. *Principles of behavior modification*. New York: Holt, 1969.

Bandura, A. *Social learning theory*. Englewood Cliffs, N.J.: Prentice-Hall, 1977.

Bar-Tal, D & Saxe, L. (Ed.). *Social psychology in education: Theory and research*. Washington, D.C.: Halsted Press, 1978.

Biddle, B. J., & Thomas, E. J. (Eds.) *Role theory: Concepts and research*. New York: Wiley, 1966.

Biddle, B. J. *Role Theory: Expectations, identities and behaviors*. New York: Academic Press, 1979.

Blumenfeld, P., Hamilton, V. L., Wessels, K., & Falkner, D. *"You can," "you should," and "you'd better": Teacher attributions regarding achievement and social behaviors*. Paper presented at American Psychological Association, San Francisco, 1977.

Blumenfeld, P., Hamilton, V. L., Wessels, K., & Falkner, D. Teaching responsibility to first graders. *Theory into Practice*, 1979, *28*, 174-180.

Blumenfeld, P., Wessels, K., Pintrich, P., & Meece, J. *Age and sex differences in the impact of teacher communication on self-perception*. Paper presented at the Meetings of the Society for Research in Child Development. Boston, Mass, 1981.

Boocock, S. *Introduction to the sociology of learning*. New York: Houghton-Mifflin, 1972.

Bossert, S. T. Tasks, group management, and teacher control behavior. *School Review*, 1977, *85*, 552-565.

Bossert, S. T. *Activity structures and student outcomes*. Paper presented at NIE Conference on School Organization and Effects, San Diego, 1978.

Bossert, S. T. *Tasks and social relationships in classrooms*. American Sociological Association, Arnold and Caroline Rose Monograph Series. New York: Cambridge University Press, 1979.

Brophy, J. Teacher behavior and its effects. *Journal of Educational Psychology*, 1979, *71*, 733-750.

Brophy, J., & Good, T. *Teacher-student relationships: Causes and consequences*. New York: Holt, 1974.

Brophy, J., & Putnam, J. Classroom management in the elementary grades. In D. Duke (Ed.), *Classroom management*. The seventy-eighth yearbook of the Society for the Study of Education, Part II. Chicago: University of Chicago Press, 1979.

Cartledge, G., & Milburn, J. F. The case for teaching social skills in the classroom: A review. *Review of Educational Research*, 1978, *48*, 133-156.

Clarizio, H. F. *Toward positive classroom discipline*. New York: Wiley, 1971.

Cooper, H. Pygmalion grows up. A model for teacher expectation communication and performance influence. *Review of Educational Research*, 1979, *49*, 389-410.

Covington, M., & Beery, R. *Self-worth and school learning*. New York: Holt, Rinehart & Winston, 1976.

Davis, T., & Dollard, J. *Children of bondage*. Washington D.C.: American Council on Education, 1940.

deCharms, R. *Personal causation*. New York: Academic Press, 1968.

Doyle, W. Paradigms for teacher effectiveness research. In L. Shulman (Ed.), *Review of educational research*. Itasca, Ill: Peacock, 1978.

Duke, D. (Ed.). *Classroom management*. The seventy-eighth yearbook of the Society for the Study of Education, Part II. Chicago: University of Chicago Press, 1979.

Dunkin, M., & Biddle, B. *The study of teaching*, New York: Holt, Rinehart & Winston, 1974.

Dweck, C. S., Davidson, W., Nelson, S., & Enna, B. Sex differences in learned helplessness: (II) The contingencies of evaluative feedback in classroom and (III) An experimental analysis. *Developmental Psychology*, 1978, *14*, 268-276.

Hamilton, V. L. Who is responsible? Toward a *social* psychology of responsibility attribution. *Social Psychology*, 1978, *41*, 316-328.

Hamilton, V. L., & Rytina, S. On measuring a norm: Should the punishment fit the crime? *American Journal of Sociology,* 1980, *85,* 1117–1144.

Hamilton, V. L., & Sanders, J. The effect of roles and deeds on responsibility judgments: The normative structure of wrongdoing. *Social Psychology Quarterly,* 1981, *44,* 237–254.

Harvey, J., Ickes, W., & Kidd, R. *New directions in attribution research* (Vol. 1). Hillsdale, N.J.: Lawrence Erlbaum Associates, 1976.

Harvey, J., Ickes, W., & Kidd, R. *New directions in attribution research.* (Vol. 2). Hillsdale, N.J.: Lawrence Erlbaum Associates, 1978.

Heider, F. *The psychology of interpersonal relations.* New York: Wiley, 1958.

Hess, R. Class and ethnic influences upon socialization. In P. H. Mussen (Ed.), *Carmichael's manual of child psychology* (Vol. 2). New York: Wiley, 1970.

Hoffman, M. L. Conscience, personality and socialization techniques. *Human Development,* 1970, *13,* 90–126. (a)

Hoffman, M. L. Moral development. In P. H. Mussen (Ed.), *Carmichael's manual of child psychology* (Vol. 2). New York: Wiley, 1970 (b).

Horowitz, R. Psychological effects of the "open classroom." *Review of Educational Research,* 1979, *49,* 71–86.

Jackson, P. *Life in classrooms.* New York: Holt, Rinehart & Winston, 1968.

Johnson, M., & Brooks, H. Conceptualizing classroom management. In D. Duke (Ed.), *Classroom management.* The seventy-eighth yearbook of the National Society for the Study of Education, Part II. Chicago: University of Chicago Press, 1979.

Jones, E. E., & Davis, K. E. From acts to dispositions: the attribution process in person perception. In L. Berkowitz (Ed.), *Advances in experimental social psychology* (Vol. 2). New York: Academic Press, 1965.

Katz, I. Academic motivation and equal educational opportunity. *Harvard Educational Review,* 1968, *38,* 57–84.

Keasey, C. Children's developing awareness and usage of intentionality and motives. *Nebraska symposium on motivation* (Vol. 25). Lincoln, Nebraska: University of Nebraska Press, 1978, 219–260.

Kelley, H. Attribution theory in social psychology. In D. Levine (Ed.), *Nebraska symposium on motivation* (Vol. 15). Lincoln: University of Nebraska Press, 1967.

Kelley, H. The process of causal attribution. *American Psychologist,* 1973, *28,* 107–128.

Kerckhoff, A. *Socialization and social class.* Englewood Cliffs, N.J.: Prentice-Hall, 1973.

Kohn, M. *Class and conformity.* Homewood, Ill.: Dorsey, 1969.

Kounin, J. *Discipline and group management in classrooms.* New York: Holt, Rinehart & Winston, 1970.

Larkin, R. Contextual influences on teacher leadership styles. *Sociology of Education,* 1973, *46,* 471–479.

Lepper, M. R. & Green, D. Turning play into work: Effects of adult surveillance and extrinsic rewards on children's intrinsic motivation. *Journal of Personality and Social Psychology,* 1975, *31,* 479–486.

Marshall, H. Open classrooms: Has the term outlived its usefulness? *Review of Educational Research,* 1981, *51,* 181–192.

Miller, R. L., Brickman, P., & Bolen, D. Attribution versus persuasion as a means for modifying behavior. *Journal of Personality and Social Psychology,* 1975, *31,* 430–441.

Mischel, W., & Mischel, H. N. A cognitive social-learning approach to morality and self-regulation. In T. Lickona (Ed.), *Moral development and behavior.* New York: Holt, Rinehart & Winston, 1976, 84–107.

Nucci, L., & Turiel, E. Social interactions and the development of social concepts in preschool children. *Child Development,* 1978, *49,* 400–407.

Parke, R. D. Effectiveness of punishment as an interaction of intensity, timing, agent nurturance and cognitive-structuring. *Child Development,* 1969, *40,* 213–235.

192   BLUMENFELD, HAMILTON, BOSSERT, WESSELS, MEECE

Parke, R. D. The role of punishment in the socialization process. In R. A. Hoppe, G. A. Milton, & E. C. Simmel (Eds.), *Early experiences and the processes of socialization*. New York: Academic Press, 1970.

Parsons, J. *Causal attribution and the role of situational cues in the development of children's evaluative judgments*. Unpublished Ph.D. dissertation. University of California, Los Angeles, 1974.

Parsons, J. E., Kaczala, C. M., & Meece, J. L. Socialization of achievement attitudes and beliefs: Classroom influences. *Child Development*, in press.

Piaget, J., & Inhelder, B. *The psychology of the child*. New York: Basic Books, 1969.

Posner, G. The extensiveness of curriculum structure: A conceptual scheme. *Review of Educational Research*, 1974, *44*, 401–407.

Rest, J. Developmental psychology as a guide to value education: a review of Kohlbergian programs. *Review of Educational Research*, 1974, *44*, 241–259.

Rosenshine, B. Classroom instruction. In N. Gage (Ed.), *The psychology of teaching methods*. The seventy-seventh yearbook of the National Society for the Study of Education. Chicago: University of Chicago Press, 1976.

Rist, R. C. Student social class and teacher expectation: The self-fulfilling prophecy in ghetto education. *Harvard Educational Review*, 1970, *40*, 411–451.

Seligman, M. E. P. *Helplessness: On depression, development and death*. San Francisco: Freeman, 1975.

Silberman, C. *Crisis in the classroom*. New York: Random House, 1970.

Simon, S., & Kirschenbaum, H. *Readings in values clarification*. Minneapolis, Minn.: Winston Press, 1973.

Stipek, D. Children's perceptions of their own and their classmates' ability. *Journal of Educational Psychology*, 1981, *73*, 404–410.

Thomas, E. J., & Biddle, B. J. Basic concepts for classifying the phenomenon of role. In B. J. Biddle & E. J. Thomas (Eds.), *Role theory*. New York: Wiley, 1966.

Turiel, E. Distinct conceptual and developmental domains: Social conventions and morality. In C. B. Keasey (Ed.), *Nebraska Symposium on Motivation* (Vol. 25). Lincoln: University of Nebraska Press, 1978.

Walberg, H. J., & Thomas, S. C. Open education: An operational definition and validation in Great Britain and the U.S. *American Educational Research Journal*, 1972, *9*, 197–207.

Walker, D. & Schaffarzick, J. Comparing curricula. *Review of Educational Research*, 1974, *9*, 83–111.

Weiner, B. *Theory of motivation: From mechanism to cognition*. Chicago: Markham Publishing Co., 1972.

Weiner, B. A theory of motivation for some classroom experiences. *Journal of Educational Psychology*, 1979, *71*, 3–25.

Weiner, B., & Peter, N. A. A cognitive-developmental analysis of achievement and moral judgments. *Developmental Psychology*, 1973, *9*, 290–309.

Wright, R. The affective and cognitive consequences of an open education elementary school. *American Educational Research Journal*, 1975, *4*, 449–464.

Weinstein, R. *Student perspectives on "achievement" in varied classroom environments*. Paper presented at the Annual Meetings of the American Educational Research Association. Los Angeles, California, 1981.

8 Communication of Teacher Expectations to Students

Harris M. Cooper
University of Missouri—Columbia

In the late 1960s, the fields of social and educational psychology found an intersection which generated enormous professional and public interest. Involved was the possibility that teacher beliefs about student performance could operate as what Merton (1957) called self-fulfilling prophecies. More specifically, interest was taken in whether teacher beliefs about student future achievement could actually influence how students eventually performed. Public concern centered around Kenneth Clark's (1963) assertion that ghetto youths were sometimes victims of poor expectations held by their teachers. The most visible investigation into teacher prophecy was Rosenthal and Jacobson's (1968) *Pygmalion in the Classroom*. The *Pygmalion* study reported evidence affirming the existence of classroom self-fulfilling prophecies, and a lively debate ensued. The debate focused mainly on differences of opinion among educational researchers concerning the inferential power of isolated studies and the methodological problems associated with in vivo educational research.

By the early 1970s, this intersection of social and educational psychology had essentially disappeared. Social psychologists interested in the educational context had substituted attributions as the cognition of choice and had returned to their more traditional workplace, the laboratory. At the center of social psychological interest was Weiner and colleagues' theory of attribution and achievement (Weiner, Frieze, Kukla, Reed, Rest & Rosenbaum, 1971). Educational psychologists, meanwhile, maintained a keen interest in expectation effects and, for the most part, continued to investigate the question in naturalistic settings. In fact, interest in teacher prophecies remained so high that in the past four years four papers on the topic have appeared in the *Review of Educational Research* (Braun, 1976; Cooper, 1979 a; Dusek, 1975; West & Anderson, 1976).

A reading of this literature, which conforms to several earlier reviews (cf. Brophy & Good, 1974; Cooper, 1979 a; Rosenthal, 1974), leads to a conclusion that, although influences on student performance are multiple and complex, teacher expectations do play a role in student achievement. The research evidence, however, suggests some important qualifications to this contention. First, expectations probably serve more to *sustain* student achievement at a particular level, rather than to radically alter achievement away from a prior course. The reason for this sustaining role seems to be that expectations which depart dramatically from a student's actual achievement are difficult to maintain in the ongoing classroom. This leads to the second necessary qualification: The relation between teacher expectation and student achievement is *bidirectional*. A student's actual performance serves as the primary influence on the expectation held by the teacher, and a cyclical process of mutual influence seems best supported by the literature. Finally, it is evident that *not all teachers* are prone to expectation effects and teachers possess individual differences that mediate the appearance of these effects.

Having made this assessment, it was natural for educational researchers next to ask, "How are teacher expectations communicated?" and "How do they come to influence student performance?" Regrettably, answers to these questions were not rapidly forthcoming. Although the attribution research of social psychologists had a firm theoretical underpinning, the expectation research of educational psychologists proceeded mainly without conceptual framework. This atheoretical approach meant that research concerning the expectation communication process was largely based on a scattering of unrelated hypotheses. The only focus which was apparent in the literature involved a methodological commonality, use of the Teacher-Child Dyadic Interaction System (Brophy & Good, 1968). This low inference, multivariate instrument for coding classroom behaviors proved perfectly suited to expectation research and to the coming generation of educational investigations. In 1974, some attempts at a formal integration of expectation research did appear. Brophy and Good (1974) suggested a sequence of relations underlying expectation communication, and Rosenthal (1974) suggested four types of teacher behavior that might be involved in the sequence. What generally prevailed as the 1970s closed, however, was the classic scientific juxtaposition: Attribution researchers had a strong theory rarely tested without laboratory control, whereas expectation researchers had weak theory but abundant evidence collected in the exact context to which it applied.

The overriding purpose of the efforts I am about to describe has been the reintegration of social psychological theory and educational expectation research. Specifically, attribution theory is used to provide the explanatory links needed to make the expectation communication process understandable. In addition, by testing attribution theory in actual classroom settings, a determination is possible as to whether modifications are needed to make the theory generalizable to this obviously relevant context. To begin, then, a brief summary of some previous research relating teacher expectations to classroom behavior is needed. With this research as background, a model for teacher expectation communication is presented which uses attribution theory and concepts as explanatory links in the process. Then, a data analysis strategy is described which addresses some of the knottier problems arising in naturalistic classroom research. The strategy has evolved out of an ongoing investigation aimed at testing the communication model. Finally, to draw the theoretical and methodological discussions together, a set of data is presented which illustrates the analytic strategy and which addresses both the expectation communication process and the generality of attribution theory to in-class, face-to-face, teacher-student relations.

Teaching Behaviors Related to Expectations for Student Performance

Rosenthal (1974) suggested four behavioral categories which have produced reliable associations with teacher expectations.

First, teachers appear to create warmer *socioemotional environments* for high expectation students. Videotapes of simulated tutorial sessions have found that teachers who were interacting with students believed to be bright smiled and nodded their heads more often than teachers interacting with presumably slow students. Teachers also leaned towards brights and looked brights in the eyes more frequently. Classroom observers have also found teachers with induced high expectations were most supportive and friendly toward bright-labeled students. It seems, then, that nonverbal behaviors associated with positive emotional attraction are displayed by teachers most frequently in interactions with students believed to be intelligent.

There is also evidence indicating that teachers' *verbal inputs* to students are dependent on performance expectations. Students labeled as slow have been found to receive fewer opportunities to learn new material and to have less difficult material taught to them. Thus, the quantity and quality of teacher attempts at instruction seem associated with expectations.

The third factor, *verbal output,* can be operationally defined as the teacher's persistence in insuring that interactions end in a satisfactory way. Observational data indicate that teachers tend to engage in more clue giving, more repetition, and more rephrasing when highs answer a question incorrectly than when lows answer incorrectly. Teachers have also been found to pay closer attention to responses of students described as gifted and to allow allegedly bright students more time before redirecting unanswered questions to other class members.

The final factor is *affective feedback.* This factor involves the teacher's use of praise and criticism after an academic exchange. As with teacher persistence, a fairly consistent pattern of teacher use of reinforcement is found. Teachers generally praise high expectation students more and also praise these students proportionately more per correct response, while lows are generally criticized more and receive proportionately more criticism per incorrect response. This result is based on some studies which simply count positive and negative use of affect and some which, allowing for the greater opportunity available to be positive toward highs, adjust praise and criticism use by the number of correct and incorrect responses the students made.

For some of the behavior differences just outlined, the relation to performance seems fairly straightforward. Students who are taught less difficult material and who are presented with less instruction should eventually possess correspondingly less information. In addition, a student given less time to respond will less often answer correctly. The remaining differences, however, in socioemotional climate and teacher feedback seem less clearly linked to performance effects. The purpose of the model I now present is to integrate the climate and feedback factors into a single process culminating in sustained student performance.

A Model for Teacher Expectation Communication

Figure 8.1 summarizes how the expectation communication process might proceed. The model begins with the contention that, based on student ability and background, teachers form differential expectations for student performance (Cooper, 1979 b; Cooper, Baron, & Lowe, 1975). The fact that performance expectations vary is beyond argument. The point is made here to insure that we begin with the teacher's "raw data" and that the process' non-recursive nature is made explicit. People are always asking "Isn't the figure missing arrows? Couldn't an arrow run from here to here and here to here?" The answer is "Yes, but only those arrows pertinent to the present formulation are given."

The model next proposes that not only do teachers form differential perceptions of students, but they also cognitively distinguish between classroom interaction contexts. Specifically, classroom situations differ in the amount of personal control they allow a teacher, and teachers are aware that such differences exist (Cooper, Burger, & Seymour, 1979; Cooper, Hinkel, & Good, 1980). In teacher-initiated interactions, for instance, the teacher has chosen the question and the student who is to respond. In student-initiated interactions, on the other hand, the child has at least phrased the question and has determined to some extent that he or she will be involved. Presumably, then, most teachers will feel the greatest degree of personal control over what an interaction will be about and when it will occur when they themselves are the initiators.

The magnitude of situational distinctions in control should depend on student characteristics as well. In particular, high expectation students are probably viewed by teachers as generally more controllable. Control of low expectation students by the teacher may be more situationally dependent than control of highs. Teachers may feel their own initiations toward slow students provide perceptibly more control for themselves than when slow students do the initiat-

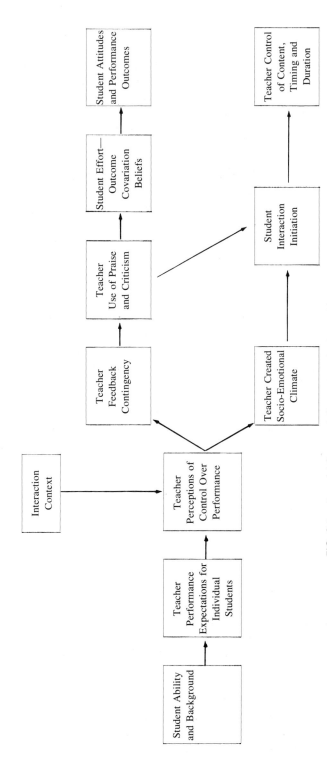

FIG. 8.1. A model for expectation communication and behavior influence.[2]

[2]Taken from Cooper, H. Pygmalion grows up: A model for teacher expectation communication and performance influence. *Review of Educational Research*, 1979, *49*, 389–410. (a)

ing. More important, teachers may believe that the more control over slow students a context affords them, the more likely it is that the exchange will be fruitful. Therefore, because slow students' initiations are least controllable they may also be viewed as least desirable.

This personal control notion provides the link between expectations and observed patterns of classroom feedback and climate. Specifically, teachers can maximize control over slow students by inhibiting slows' initiations (Cooper, 1977). Such a strategy would entail the use of simple reinforcement principles. The teacher increases personal control through the creation of an unrewarding socioemotional environment and the relatively infrequent use of praise and freer use of criticism in interactions with slows.

The use of feedback and climate to control interactions has other implications, however. A control strategy means high and low students are evaluated using different contingencies. Some teachers may tend not to praise good performances from lows because praise will reduce future personal control by encouraging slow students' initiations. Teachers may also tend to be more generally critical of low students' poor performances since criticism increases future control. In evaluating highs, teachers may dispense praise and criticism more in response to the degree of effort the student exhibited since future control of highs' behavior is less of an issue. As has been argued elsewhere (Cooper & Baron, 1977; 1979), this differential contingency hypothesis has implications for attribution theory. Specifically, the communication model implies that in face-to-face classroom situations the use of reinforcement as a control device supersedes its use as an indicant of effort. Reinforcement will be used by a teacher as an aid in classroom management until the teacher believes students will behave in a "satisfactory" manner without it. Only then will reinforcement use reflect the contingency prescribed by broader social values, namely that strong effort is good and weak effort bad. The empirical demonstration I describe shortly addresses the question of what attributions covary with in-class reinforcement.

It is argued, then, that the climate, feedback, and output factors may be causally linked. The three factors are integrated if their relation to teacher personal control is taken into account. Negative climate and feedback patterns for low expectation students increase teacher control over when interactions with these students will occur. However, the control strategy also means lows will seek less interaction with the teacher and teacher feedback to lows will be less effort-contingent than feedback to highs. The sustaining of low expectation student performance is viewed as a result of these different feedback contingencies.

For achievement motivation to be maintained it is necessary that students believe they can influence their academic outcomes. Numerous studies report that students who are high in achievement motivation believe that effort and performance outcome covary (e.g., Kukla, 1972). They believe the harder they try the more likely they are to succeed. Students low in achievement motivation perceive less effort-outcome covariation. No matter how hard they try, these students perceive themselves as less able to influence the outcomes of their performance. This perception on the part of *low expectation students* may be an accurate reflection of their classroom environment. High expectation students may be criticized when the teacher perceives them as not having tried and may be praised when efforts are strong. Low expectation students, however, may be praised and criticized more often for reasons independent of their personal efforts, namely, the teacher's desire to control interactions. A greater use of feedback by teachers to control interactions may lead to a lesser belief on the part of the student that his or her effort can bring success.

To complete the expectation communication process, the attitude and performance effects of perceived noncontingent reinforcement need to be stated. Most of the research associated with learned helplessness phenomena would be relevant here. Let me just say that much research indicates at least three effects of feeling little personal control over academic performance. Little perceived effort-outcome covariation leads to negative affect and attitudes towards tasks presented, less persistence in the face of failure, and, finally, a greater incidence of failure. With the translation of student beliefs into student performance, the expectation communication model is completed.

Most of the evidence supporting the communication model comes from studies which were not originally designed for this purpose. Also, very few of the existing studies test more than one model link at a time. We have recently completed the first year of a study which attempts to test most of the links in a single sample of classrooms. However, before I can describe our sample and some of the data we have collected, a digression is necessary. The digression involves the problem of how to analyze data collected in naturally occurring classrooms. The proper treatment of this type of data has troubled educational researchers for some time, and the pros and cons of differing analysis strategies have been debated (e.g., Page, 1975). It is important that these issues be readdressed with particular reference to social psychological phenomena. The remarks that follow, then, have a considerably broader focus than teacher expectation effects, though my struggles with expectation-related data crystallized the problems and suggested solutions.

Methodology: The Importance of Analytic Level Specification

The social psychology of education has one primary attribute which distinguishes it from other fields: The social relations of interest are embedded within a context called "the classroom." To ignore the classroom when one studies social relations in schools robs the subdiscipline of its unique character. More important, it ignores the fact that individuals' responses are dependent on facets of the broader environment in which they occur.

Cronbach, in 1976, suggested three reasons why individuals' responses in classrooms cannot be viewed as independent of their general setting. First, students within a class are typically more alike at the outset of instruction than

students randomly sampled from the relevant population. The nonrandom placement of students into classrooms means classrooms exhibit *differing levels of
traits found in the population,* for example, differing average achievement levels
or average frequencies of particular behaviors. As an example of how nonrandom
grouping would affect interpretations of social research, let us speculate that
American students are not randomly placed into classrooms with regard to social
class. Therefore, a middle-class student's social responses in school are likely to
be elicited by other middle-class students, while lower-class students are likely to
be responding to lower-class others. Therefore, not only does a student's social
class distinguish him or her from other students, it also distinguishes the nature of
the stimuli presented to the student.

A second reason why persons within a given classroom will be similar to one
another, but potentially different from persons in other classrooms, involves
intended difference in the way classrooms are treated. Such treatments include
variations in the textbooks that are used or in the way seating is arranged. Of
more importance, the teacher can be conceptualized as just such an intended
treatment. Teacher "treatments" would include characteristics like teaching experience, educational philosophy, global perceptions of the class, and the frequency of particular teaching behaviors.

The final context effect suggested by Cronbach is *unintended treatments.*
Though these influences are not specifically planned, they serve to increase the
similarity of persons in the same classroom, relative to others. These variations
would include things like room temperature and room location.

It can be said, then, that the classroom is an undeniable aspect of education's
social fabric. Now we must ask, "How does one go about studying classroom
social relations in a manner which captures the contextualized nature of these
relations?" One approach readily presents itself: Psychologists can study
classrooms as whole groups, or as units that have characteristics which exist at a
group level of analysis. Specifically, it might be of interest to determine how
classroom variations, in trait samplings and intended and unintended treatments,
relate to one another. These lines of investigation would include questions like,
"Is a teacher's choice of presentation style related to the average achievement
level of students in the classroom?" or "Does a class's average attitude toward
school relate to the average frequency with which classroom rules are broken?"
These kinds of questions can be said to examine relations which exist at the
whole-class level. Answering these questions involves examining the variations
between entire classrooms.

While whole-class characteristics are certainly important, they do not encompass all the questions psychologists typically find interesting. Also of concern is
the examination of relations *between individuals within the same class.* For
example, we often want to know if a teacher's attitude toward a particular
student, or a student's attitude toward the teacher, relates to the way the teacher
and student interact. This type of question, addressing a teacher's relative treat-

ment of different students in the same class, is of paramount importance in the expectation communication process. Of interest here are relations that exist at a *within-class level*. They are concerned with how persons within classrooms relate to one another.

Since it is possible to identify two levels of classroom analysis, we must next ask if it is necessary for the researcher to choose to study one level or the other. We find that it is possible to study within-classroom relations and certain types of between-classroom relations with a single set of data. Since this strategy is used in the example that follows, some attention to its details will prove valuable. Figure 8.2 presents the strategy.

First, let us assume we are interested in the relation between a teacher's use of praise and performance attributions. At a whole-class level, then, we would investigate how a teacher's overall frequency of praise relates to his or her general citation of different causal attributions for success. To answer this question we might correlate a sample of teachers' average praise use and average frequency of particular causal citations. If an ANOVA-type analysis is preferred, we might divide teachers into high and low praiser groups and use a t-test to assess the difference in the two groups' use of different attributions. At a within-class level, on the other hand, we would investigate how the particular amount of praise a student receives from a teacher relates to the teacher's attributions for that student's successes. To answer this question, we might correlate praise and attributions *within each class separately* and then test to see if any relations are consistently found across classrooms. Alternatively, students within each class could be grouped into relatively high and relatively low praise receivers. The group means on attributions could then be tested for consistency across classrooms with a paired observation t-test. This strategy views the teacher as the unit-of-analysis and the two groups of students as repeated stimulus conditions

	Unit of Analysis	Students in Class Who Receive the Most Praise	Students in Class Who Receive the Least Praise	
Teachers Who Use The *Most* Praise	Classroom 1	Mean Score of Attribution	Mean Score of Attribution	
	Classroom 2	$\bar{Y}$	$\bar{Y}$	$\bar{\bar{Y}}$
	Classroom 3	$\bar{Y}$	$\bar{Y}$	$\uparrow$
	Classroom 4	$\bar{Y}$	$\bar{Y}$	Between-
		$\bar{\bar{Y}}$	$\bar{Y}$	Classroom
Teachers Who Use The *Least* Praise	Classroom 5	$\bar{Y}$	$\bar{Y}$	Comparison
	Classroom 6	$\bar{Y}$	$\bar{Y}$	$\downarrow$
	Classroom 7	$\bar{Y}$	$\bar{Y}$	$\bar{\bar{Y}}$
	Classroom 8	$\bar{Y}$	$\bar{Y}$	

$\bar{\bar{Y}}$ ← Within-Classroom Comparison → $\bar{\bar{Y}}$

FIG. 8.2.   An analysis of variance approach to studying classroom relations at the two analytic levels.

(cf. Page, 1975).[1] As these examples make apparent, it is possible to ask both the whole- and within-class questions as part of a single analysis. This is accomplished by creating a 2×2 analysis of variance with one between-classrooms factor and one repeated measurement factor. The between-classrooms factor distinguishes among teachers according to their relative use of praise (high versus low). The within-classrooms factor distinguishes students according to their relative reception of praise (high versus low), with "relative" meaning in relation to classmates. This ANOVA model has the nice feature of allowing a test of analytic level interaction. In the present example this question would be, "Are the relations between praise and attributions found within classrooms similar at all levels of average teacher praise usage?"

The ANOVA model also serves to highlight the importance of identifying the analytic level to which a result applies. Specifically, the two sources of variance in the ANOVA model, between- and within-classrooms, are entirely statistically independent of one another. Knowing an average classroom score on X *by definition* tells us nothing about the deviations around X in any given classroom. This statistical independence reveals that no a priori grounds exist for believing that a relation found at one level will also be found at the other. Without knowing the analytic level to which research evidence relates, therefore, we may confuse our literature and may suggest reforms which interfere with good educational practice.

There are several other consequences to the adoption of the analytic level specification approach. The most important is that choosing the classroom to be the smallest data unit makes the analysis low in power. In the present investigation, for example, measurements were obtained on 192 students. However, the students were drawn from only 16 different classrooms so only 15 degrees of freedom were available for any error term. Accepting and dealing with low power is inevitable, however, since alternatives to the analytic level specification approach, most notably using raw data and the student as unit, do not meet the assumptions of parametric inference testing (Lindquist, 1953; Page, 1975).

Can anything be done to counter the low power of legitimate classroom data analyses? Cronbach takes an exceptionally pessimistic view of the role of inference testing in classroom research. He states that inference testing is prohibitively costly and can rarely be used. A slightly more hopeful alternative can be suggested, however. Researchers with small numbers of classrooms might interpret relations falling below, say, the 1 in 5 level of significance as "deserving

---

[1]Between- and within-class variables need not be continuous, as they are in this example. Teachers and students can be categorized according to qualitative traits such as gender, race, or whatever. The ANOVA model accommodates these variables as it would any other group identity. Interestingly, the examination of, say, male/female differences within a class can be paired with (a) the difference in class ratios of boys to girls, (b) the teacher's gender, or (c) both (a) and (b) as the between classrooms factor(s).

further study.'' With small samples these significance levels will be associated with large amounts of variance explained. This convention is employed in the analyses that follow, with one added restriction. Since each attribution-feedback relation was tested at three times of the school year, the relation direction must have been similar over all three replications for the result to be reported as reliable. This convention has several implications. First, because the reported relations are consistent over time we have greater confidence that a Type 1 error has not been committed and that the effect has some temporal generality. On the other hand, the convention might also lead us to overlook interesting shifts in relations over time. This loss of information is regrettable, but the first set of considerations are more closely related to internal validity and, therefore, were given more weight.

Researchers with very small sample sizes, say less than 8 or 10 classrooms, might be advised to report raw data and interpret it descriptively. As evidence in the literature accumulates, raw data from separate studies can be combined for purposes of inference testing.

An Illustration: Attribution-Feedback Relations in Naturalistic Classrooms

I would like to refer, then, to a set of data which asks the question, "Do teacher attributions correlate with the use of affective feedback in naturally occurring classrooms, and, if so, what attributions are involved?" I would like to try to answer this question using a level specification analysis. The data involved were obtained from 16 third-, fourth-, and fifth-grade classrooms, with 12 students studied in each class. The 16 classrooms were drawn from five schools serving mostly white, middle- and lower middle-class families. All 16 classrooms had female teachers, and teachers averaged over 8 years of teaching experience. Student and teacher participation was voluntary. Each classroom was observed for about 8 hours at three times of the school year, during Fall, Winter, and Spring. Among many behaviors observed and recorded (cf. Cooper et. al., 1979) were the frequency of students' appropriate and inappropriate responding and the frequency of teachers' praise, criticism, and ignoring of these responses. A student's response to a teacher's question or a student's initiation was categorized as appropriate or inappropriate based on the teacher's stated reaction. In the absence of a reaction, the coders inferred the teacher's evaluation. Praise and criticism were coded when the teacher used positive or negative affect in her reactions. Interactions were coded only when the teacher and an individual student communicated. Instances of chorus-type answers and group praise or criticism were ignored. At three corresponding times during the year the teacher was asked to provide causal attributions for the observed student's successes and failures. In the fashion described by Cooper and Burger (1980), teachers provided open-ended attributions. They then assigned percentages to each cause

I. Attribution Categories
1. *Internal Stable Causes*
   Ability
   Previous Experience
   Acquired Characteristics
      (habits, attitudes, self-perception)
2. *Stable Effort Causes*
   Stable Effort
   Interest in the Subject Matter

3. *Immediate Effort Causes*
   Immediate Effort
   Attention
4. *Teacher-Related External Causes*
   Directions and Instruction
   Task
5. *Other External Causes*
   Family
   Other Students

II. Affective Feedback Categories[3]

		Student's Relative Reception of Affective Feedback Following a Response	
		High	Low
Teacher's Relative Use of Affect Following a Student Response	High		
	Low		

[3]Teachers and students were categorized separately for praise and criticism and for each time of the school year.

FIG. 8.3.   Categories used to relate teacher attributions and affective feedback.

dependent on how frequently the attribution explained the student's performance. Causes were then placed by two coders into one of 11 categories, as shown in Figure 8.3. For the analyses that follow, these 11 categories were reduced to five more substantive types. The five categories referred to the frequency with which the teacher felt the student's successes and failures were caused by (1) internal stable, (2) stable effort, (3) immediate effort, (4) teacher-related external, or (5) miscellaneous external causes. The internal stable and immediate effort (internal, unstable) categories have the meanings traditionally associated with them in achievement attribution theories. The stable effort category acknowledges that a substantial portion of teacher attributions are to a student's general propensity toward laziness and industry. These attributions are more similar to ability than to effort attributions on the stability dimension. External attributions, the vast majority of which are stable, were divided into two categories. Teacher-related causes were those implying the largest teacher involvement in the outcome (Cooper & Burger, 1980). All other attributions were placed in a miscellaneous external category. The ten percentage scores (five for success and five for failure) for each student were calculated separately for each of the three observation periods.

To investigate the relations between success attributions and praise, classrooms were grouped according to whether the teacher used a relatively large amount or a relatively small amount of *praise per appropriate response.* That is, teachers were not classified according to absolute frequency of praise. Instead, teachers' average praise usage was first residualized with the average appropriate responses in the classroom used as predictor. Residuals were then used to assign teachers to high and low praising groups. A similar procedure was used to classify students within each classroom into relatively high and low praise-receivers. For failure attribution analyses, criticism and ignoring of responses provided a composite residualized measure to place teachers and students into groups. The residualization procedure means comparisons are between the relative likelihood, *on any single response,* of giving or receiving affect (see Figure 8.3).

The analysis revealed several consistent feedback-attribution relations. Let us examine between-classroom relations first. Table 8.1 presents the only attribution category whose percent citation was related to the teachers' average "freeness" with praise. Specifically, teachers in the higher praising group reported successes were due to external teacher-related causes less often than did the low praising teachers (in Winter $F(1,13) = 3.84$, $p < .08$). This result is consistent with Weiner's and colleagues' (1971) theorizing. They reasoned that a reinforcing agent will view reinforcement as incapable of affecting the future frequency of an act if the act is perceived as caused by the environment (external) or by an internal stable characteristic of the actor. Since external factors already under teacher control will not be facilitated or inhibited through praise to the child, the attribution model would predict our finding that high praising teachers were less likely to see success as externally caused than were low praising teachers. Table

TABLE 8.1
Between-Classroom Comparisons Showing Teachers'
Average Attributions for Success as a Function
of Teachers' Average Use of Praise

		Teachers' Use of Praise	
Student Successes Attributed to:		Less Than Other Teachers	More Than Other Teachers
Teacher-Related Causes (followed directions;	Fall	12.7	9.4
good instruction;	Winter	15.2	7.9
appropriate tasks)	Spring	20.5	14.1

Note. Entries are the percent of successful outcomes attributed to the stated cause.

TABLE 8.2
Between-Classroom Comparisons Showing Teachers'
Average Attributions for Failure as a Function
of Teachers' Average Use of Negative Feedback

Student Failures Attributed to:		Teachers' Use of Negative Feedback	
		Less Than Other Teachers	More Than Other Teachers
Internal Stable Causes (lack of ability; inexperience; bad habits and attitudes)	Fall	20.8	10.0
	Winter	27.8	13.9
	Spring	32.9	14.7
Immediate Effort Causes (lack of attention; not being prepared for the task)	Fall	36.8	47.9
	Winter	32.9	60.5
	Spring	35.6	37.6

Note. Entries are the percent of failure outcomes attributed to the stated cause.

8.2 presents the between-classroom relations of failure attributions and negative feedback. Here, two attribution categories were found to be related to the teacher's freeness with negative affect. Teachers in the high criticizing group less often cited internal stable causes (in Fall (F1,14) = 3.69, p < .09; in Winter F(1,13) = p < .08; in Spring F(1,14) = 3.47, p < .09) and more often cited immediate effort causes (in Winter F(1,13) = 5.60, p < .04) for their students' performance. This result is exactly as the Weiner et al. (1971) model predicts, since immediate effort is an internal but unstable characteristic. Criticism to students whose efforts are weak may affect how frequently the students fail in the future because students are capable of altering their level of effort.

Now, let us turn to within-class relations. Table 8.3 shows the consistent relations between students' reception of praise in the class and the teacher's attributions for the particular students' success. Students who were in the most freely praised group were also those whose successes were less often attributed to internal stable causes (in Winter F(1,13) = 3.80, p < .08) and *more* often attributed to teacher-related causes (in Fall F(1,14) = 4.21, p < .07; in Winter F(1,13) = 6.73, p < .02). This last relation is *opposite* to that found for the same attributions at the between-class level. That is, the average freeness of praising by the teacher is negatively related to the general perceived frequency of teacher-related successes. However, how a teacher deviates around this mean toward different students within the class is positively related to teacher involvement. The more frequently a student's successes are seen as implying a positive teacher influence, the more freely the student is praised, relative to classmates.

Turning finally to the within-class relations of negative affect and failure attributions, teacher-related causes again proved most consistent. As Table 8.4 indicates, students in the group who were given the freest negative feedback were also those whose failures were more often attributed to teacher-related causes (in Fall $F(1,14) = 4.02$, $p < .07$). If a student's failures were often seen as due to not following directions, poor instructions, or inappropriate tasks, the student was also more often criticized, relative to classmates.

The data revealed no consistent interactions crossing the two levels of analysis. A visual inspection of the data lead to the impression that within-classroom relations might have been strongest in classrooms where teachers used more affect.

Implications for Attribution Theory and Expectation Communication

From these data, what conclusions can be drawn about attribution theory and expectation communication? First, with regard to achievement attributions, laboratory results were found to be consistent with teachers' average or general reinforcement strategy. The between-classroom results seem to clearly support several aspects of Weiner et al's (1971) attribution model. Teacher average negative feedback was inversely related to the stability of internal causes. Teacher average praise use was negatively related to the frequency of external causality. Other attribution model predictions did not appear, however (i.e., a

TABLE 8.3
Within-Classroom Comparisons Showing Teachers'
Attributions for Particular Students' Success
as a Function of Students' Reception of Praise

Student Successes Attributed to:		Students' Reception of Praise	
		Less Than Other Students	*More Than Other Students*
Internal Stable Causes (high ability;	Fall	40.1	37.2
previous experience; good habits and	Winter	35.1	29.0
attitudes)	Spring	32.9	31.8
Teacher-Related Causes (followed directions;	Fall	9.0	13.5
good instruction;	Winter	6.7	15.9
appropriate tasks)	Spring	16.0	18.7

Note. Entries are the percent of successful outcomes attributed to the stated cause.

positive immediate effort-praise relation). It is also significant to note that no result inconsistent with attribution theory was found for between-classroom relations. The utility of the attribution model is further underscored by the likelihood that the model also applies to written, as opposed to verbal, evaluations (cf. Cooper & Baron, 1979).

The data demonstrate, however, that the achievement-attribution model cannot predict teacher reinforcement behavior universally across contexts. When one examines how teachers distribute reinforcement within a class, there is little evidence that these deviations from the mean follow the pattern predicted by Weiner et al. (1971). Rather, students whose causes for success most often imply the teacher has had a positive influence are given freest praise, while students whose failures imply a negative teacher influence are given freest negative affect. In both cases, the positive relation between external causes and frequency of reinforcement is contrary to the attribution model. It seems, then, that a fruitful strategy for future attribution-behavior research would be to ask, "What attributional dimensions relate to behavior X *in context* Y?" Many dimensions underlying attributions have been suggested and even more, no doubt, exist. I suspect that a social context can be found in which each attribution dimension holds sway over some behavior. The recognition of the importance of context to social relations should be manifested through a careful examination of context characteristics. In this way we will eventually be able to address the question of what *contextual characteristics* mediate the appearance of different attribution-behavior relations. This approach, whether theory directed or inductive, is most likely to provide conclusions applicable to real world social phenomena.

The data also indirectly supported the expectation communication model. The model is based on the assumption that teachers have a fundamental and overriding concern with classroom management. Evidence that this is the case emerged from the data. The positive teacher-role relation to feedback is a clear indication

TABLE 8.4
Within-Class Comparisons Showing Teachers'
Attributions for Particular Students' Failure
as a Function of Students' Reception of Negative Feedback

Student Failures Attributed to:		Students' Reception of Negative Feedback	
		Less Than Other Students	More Than Other Students
Teacher-Related Causes (didn't follow directions;	Fall	26.6	30.5
poor instruction;	Winter	9.6	12.0
inappropriate task)	Spring	24.9	27.5

Note. Entries are the percent of failure outcomes attributed to the stated cause.

of the salience of management issues. However, this relation appeared only when within-class deviations were compared. Finally, recall that the model proposed that reinforcement to high expectation students might be more effort contingent than reinforcement to lows. This prediction was not tested in the data analysis, but results do suggest it might also be fruitful to examine whether highs' reinforcements are *less* contingent on teacher-related causes. If this is the case, lows may be learning that their successes are caused more often than highs' successes by help from and obedience to the teacher. Clearly, this cognition would lead to the same difference in sense of control between highs and lows that is contained in the proposed model. The present data, then, suggested some additional potential avenues the expectation communication process might take.

Implications for Instructional Design

Great caution must be exercised whenever one attempts to translate an educational theory into concrete recommendations for instructional design. Some boldness is called for in the present instance, however. After all, one objective of the way the model was constructed and the way supporting evidence was gathered was to make this leap as natural as possible.

The communication model proposes that classroom management concerns are at the heart of expectation phenomena. More specifically, it appears that the management concerns which accompany low performance expectations are the crucial links in the teacher's cognitive nexus. Therefore, classroom designs which serve to disassociate performance and management concerns ought to serve also to mitigate expectation effects. For instance, classes with fewer students ought to be less prone than large classes to producing teacher prophecies. With fewer students competing for the teacher's time, the teacher's sense of control over slower students ought to be generally greater.

It is more difficult to make a recommendation concerning the effects of ability tracking. This is because tracking has implications for both within and between class processes. Within classrooms, it would appear that creating homogeneous groups would have positive expectation effects: The lack of variety in students would inhibit distinctions in how teachers treated students. On the other hand, tracking will necessarily create more distinct general classroom expectations between teachers. This may set in motion processes detrimental to the achievement of the students in the lower ability classrooms. Tracking, then, is a complex issue. Its implications for teacher prophecies must await some estimation of the relative impact on achievement of between and within classroom expectation processes.

Finally, classroom designs which consciously transfer responsibility for learning from the teacher to the student ought to mitigate expectation effects. An example of such a design would be the self-scheduling system described by Margaret Wang in this volume. As long as these systems are available to all students (and not used to reward brighter students) they should afford the teacher less opportunity to express expectations.

In addition to classroom design considerations, it might also be possible to intervene in the expectation process by changing the teacher's cognitive set. Teachers can be directly made aware of expectation and attribution research and can be asked to highlight effort in their evaluations of students and to positively reward strong effort *regardless* of prior expectations. It is questionable, however, whether these conscious strategies are implementable by teachers without accompanying supportive environmental changes.

Since the expectation communication model is temporally sequenced, interventions at any point ought to "short circuit" the remainder of the sequence. I have suggested several points, and others will suggest more. Hopefully, tests of intervention points will be constructed so that the dialogue between theory and practice continues.

ACKNOWLEDGMENT

Portions of this chapter were presented to the 87th meeting of the American Psychological Association, New York City, 1979. The research reported was facilitated by a grant from the National Science Foundation, Social and Developmental Psychology Directorate (BNS 78-08834), to Harris M. Cooper, Principal Investigator.

REFERENCES

Braun, C. Teacher expectation: Sociopsychological dynamics. *Review of Educational Research,* 1976, *46* (2), 185–213.

Brophy, J., & Good, T. *Teacher-child dyadic interaction: A manual for coding classroom behavior.* Austin: Research and Development Center for Teacher Education, 1968.

Brophy, J., & Good, T. *Teacher-student relationships: Causes and consequences.* New York: Holt, Rinehart & Winston, 1974.

Clark, K. B. Educational stimulation of racially disadvantaged children. In A. H. Passow (Ed.), *Education in Depressed Areas.* New York: Teachers College, Columbia University, 1963.

Cooper, H. Pygmalion grows up: A model for teacher expectation communication and performance influence. *Review of Educational Research,* 1979, *49* (3), 389–410. (a)

Cooper, H. Some effects of preperformance information on academic expectations. *Journal of Educational Psychology,* 1979, *71,* 375–380. (b)

Cooper, H. Controlling personal rewards: Professional teachers' differential use of feedback and the effects of feedback on the student's motivation to perform. *Journal of Educational Psychology,* 1977, *69,* 419–427.

Cooper, H., & Baron, R. Academic expectations and attributed responsibility as predictors of professional teachers' reinforcement behavior. *Journal of Educational Psychology,* 1977, *69* (4), 409–418.

Cooper, H., & Baron, R. Academic expectations, attributed responsibility and teachers' reinforcement behavior: A suggested integration of conflicting literatures. *Journal of Educational Psychology,* 1979, *71* (2), 274–277.

Cooper, H., Baron, R., & Lowe, C. The importance of race and social class information in the formation of expectancies about academic performance. *Journal of Educational Psychology,* 1975, *67,* 312-319.

Cooper, H., Blakey, S., Burger, J., Good, T., Hinkel, G., & Sterling, J. Teacher-child dyadic interaction: Coding modifications for social and educational research in attribution theory, teacher expectations and learned helplessness theory. *Technical Report No. 167,* Center for Research in Social Behavior, University of Missouri–Columbia, Columbia, Mo., 1979.

Cooper, H., & Burger, J. How teachers explain students' academic performance. A categorization of free response academic attributions. *American Educational Research Journal,* 1980, *17,* 95-109.

Cooper, H., Burger, J., & Seymour, G. Classroom context and student ability as influences on teacher perceptions of classroom control. *American Educational Research Journal,* 1979, *16,* 189-196.

Cooper, H., Hinkel, G., & Good, T. Teachers' beliefs about interaction control and their observed behavior correlates. *Journal of Educational Psychology,* 1980, *72,* 345-354.

Cronbach, L. *Research on classrooms and schools: Formulation of questions, design and analysis.* Stanford Evaluation Consortium, Stanford University, Stanford, Calif., 1976, Eric Document No. ED 135 801.

Dusek, J. Do teachers bias children's learning? *Review of Educational Research,* 1975, *45,* 661-684.

Kukla, A. Attributional determinants of achievement-related behavior. *Journal of Personality and Social Psychology,* 1972, *21,* 166-174.

Lindquist, E. F. *Design and analysis of experiments in psychology and education.* Boston: Houghton Mifflin, 1953.

Merton, R. K. *Social theory and social structure* (Rev. Ed.). New York: The Free Press, 1957.

Page, E. Statistically recapturing the richness within the classroom. *Psychology in the Schools,* 1975, *12,* (3), 339-344.

Rosenthal, R. *On the social psychology of the self-fulfilling prophecy: Further evidence for Pygmalion effects and their mediating mechanisms.* New York: MSS Modular Publications, 1974.

Rosenthal, R., & Jacobson, L. *Pygmalion in the classroom: Teacher expectation and pupils' intellectual development.* New York: Holt, Rinehart & Winston, 1968.

Weiner, B., Frieze, I., Kukla, A., Reed, L., Rest, S., & Rosenbaum, R. *Perceiving the causes of success and failure.* New Jersey: General Learning Press, 1971.

West, C., & Anderson, T. The question of preponderant causation in teacher expectancy research. *Review of Educational Research,* 1976, *46,* 185-213.

9 Development and Consequences of Students' Sense of Personal Control

Margaret C. Wang
University of Pittsburgh

The development and consequences of students' perception of personal control over their school learning has for some time been a focus of educational research on social-psychological determinants of individual differences in student learning. In recent years, data suggesting a close relationship between students' sense of personal control and their learning processes and outcomes have intensified this interest (e.g., Coleman, Campbell, Hobson, McPartland, Mood, Weinfeld, York, 1966; Crandall, Katkovsky, & Crandall, 1965; Nowicki & Walker, 1974; Shaw & Uhl, 1971; Stallings & Kaskowitz, 1974; Uguroglu & Walberg, 1979; Wang & Stiles, 1976a). The twofold purpose of this chapter is (a) to examine the above relationship from both psychological and educational perspectives in the context of existing theories and research, and (b) to discuss the instructional design implications of the relationship for school programs designed to maximize student learning.

First, a general overview is presented of theories and research dealing with the consequences of students' perception of personal control over the school learning environment and the effects of educational practices designed to foster such a perception. This overview is followed by a brief explication of a conceptual model of students' sense of personal control. Next, the critical design characteristics of learning environments conducive to the development of a sense of personal control are discussed. Finally, the Adaptive Learning Environments Model is described, and research concerning the efficacy of this innovative educational environment is presented.

THEORIES AND RESEARCH ON LOCUS OF CONTROL

Perception of personal control is defined in this chapter as students' belief that they are personally responsible for their school learning. Rotter's concept of locus of control (Rotter, 1966) has greatly influenced research in this area. According to Rotter, an individual's locus of control is his or her perception of the location of the force responsible for the development of an experience. Rotter distinguishes between two types of locus of control, internal and external. Individuals with an internal locus of control perceive themselves as the causal factor in determining events in their environment. Those with an external locus of control perceive forces outside themselves as determining such events. Locus of control is viewed as relevant for both positive and negative events. Although there have been variations on how locus of control is defined in specific studies, Rotter's basic concept has served as the basis for most of these definitions.

Extensive research on locus of control suggests that internal locus of control tends to be associated with positive attitudes toward mastery and competence behavior in both children and adults. It has been suggested that persons who believe they can control their destinies are likely to use previously learned skills in acquiring new ones (Holden & Rotter, 1962; James & Rotter, 1958; Lefcourt, 1976; Phares, 1957; Rotter, Liverant, & Crowne, 1961). Furthermore, such persons actively try to change their environment (Gore & Rotter, 1963), make realistic intermediate-probability bets in situations involving risk (Liverant & Scodel, 1960), resist group pressures (Crowne & Liverant, 1963), and remain aware of information that might affect their behavior in the immediate future (Seeman, 1963).

Studies designed to investigate students' locus of control in school situations also show that internality is positively related to such outcomes as degree of classroom participation, academic performance, scores on academic achievement tests, and ability to delay gratification (Bialer, 1961; Mischel, Zeiss, & Zeiss, 1974; Wolfgang & Potwin, 1973). In addition, evidence suggests that students' sense of personal control is related to cognitive styles and dispositions that aid learning and performance. For example, internal locus of control is related to the tendencies to seek information and use information in problem-solving (Davis & Phares, 1967; Phares, 1968) and to persist in difficult intellectual tasks (Crandall, 1966). Students with an internal locus of control demonstrate greater reflectivity and attentiveness as well as better performance and higher rates of knowledge acquisition than do students with an external locus of control (Chance, 1968). Results from Stephens' (1971) observational study of children's school behavior suggest that students with an internal locus of control are active and assertive and exhibit a high degree of exploratory behavior and excitement about learning. In contrast, students with an external locus of control tend to be relatively passive, compliant, non-exploratory, and inattentive.

Parallel to the above investigations on the locus of control process is recent work investigating the implications of locus of control for instructional design and behavioral management. It is hypothesized in these studies that students who believe they can influence their learning are more likely to succeed in school than those who believe their learning is controlled by powerful others (e.g., teachers and other relevant adults). In recent years, research evidence supporting this theory has accumulated rapidly (e.g., Cellura, 1963; Coleman, et al., 1966; Crandall, Katkovsky, & Preston, 1962; Felixbrod & O'Leary, 1974; Kanfer, 1971; Mahoney & Thoreson, 1974; McLaughlin & Malaby, 1974; Stallings & Kaskowitz, 1974; Wang & Stiles, 1976a).

One influential stimulus for current interest in the implications of locus of control for instructional design was the publication of *Equality of Educational Opportunity* (Coleman et al., 1966). Although several aspects of this work have been criticized, results suggesting a close relationship between certain attitudinal measures and school achievement have received strong empirical support (Mosteller & Moynihan, 1972). Students' interests and attitudes contributed more to variations in school achievement than did eight other variables (e.g., student background factors, teacher characteristics, school variables) included in the study. Furthermore, students' feelings about their ability to control their destinies were found to be a significantly more important correlate of school achievement than was the curriculum.

Assuming that locus of control is important in school learning and that it is desirable to incorporate this variable into the design of learning environments, then the question of the extent to which locus of control is a stable disposition must be addressed. Extensive research has shown that locus of control can be modified by a variety of environmental factors. Mischel and his colleagues, for example, have suggested that "social behavior, rather than being determined by global, broadly generalized personality traits, depends on the person's specific response capabilities and his expectations concerning the consequences of alternative courses of action in the situation" (Mischel, Zeiss, & Zeiss, 1974, p. 266). Furthermore, in studying the relationship between behaviors in different situations and individual differences in locus of control orientation, Mischel et al. found that the correlations between locus of control and various behaviors were high only when the sampled behaviors were related to the exercise of control by the subject.

Results from a number of studies have shown that special instructional interventions can change an individual's locus of control. Shore, Milgram, and Malasky (1971) reported that their enriched educational program, as compared to programs in regular classrooms, contributed to changes in children's feelings of control over the environment. Children 5 to 7 years of age who participated in the enriched program showed a clear and significant change toward an internal orientation. In a similar study, Hunt and Hardt (1969) reported that adolescents from low-income families became more internally oriented as a result of their participation in an Upward Bound program. deCharms (1972) also reported changes in behavior related to locus of control as the result of "personal causation" training designed to promote "origin" rather than "pawn" behavior. In a study of inner-city adolescents, Nowicki and Barnes (1973) showed that a highly structured summer camp experience, which focused on the relationship between behavior and reinforcement, tended to enhance internal control tendencies. These findings are supported by data from Reimanis' (1974) investigations in which deliberate attempts were made to alter the locus of control of students in different age groups. Finally, in an investigation of the effects of an instructional intervention program, Wang and Stiles (1976a) found that students in the early elementary grades who were taught to assume responsibility for their learning not only showed a significant increase in task completion rates but also developed a greater sense of personal control.

In summary, research on the development and consequences of sense of personal control generally suggests that locus of control orientation can be modified. It appears that instructional intervention programs can shift students' perception of locus of control toward the internal orientation. Moreover, research shows a relationship between changes in student perceptions of locus of control and improvements in school performance. In light of these research and development efforts, it seems that the next appropriate step is to design and study the processes and effects of learning environments that attempt to maximize student learning through the development of students' sense of personal control. It is in this context that our model was developed (Wang, 1979c).

A MODEL OF STUDENTS' PERCEPTION OF PERSONAL CONTROL

Briefly, the model is based on two assumptions. First, students' sense of personal control greatly affects their school learning processes and outcomes; second, students' sense of control can be modified through instructional intervention. Figure 9.1 shows a hypothesized sequence for the development and consequences of students' sense of personal control in classroom settings.

Implicit in the model is the transactional influence between the teacher and student in the classroom. The interactive sequence, as shown in Figure 9.1, begins with the teacher's implementation of an educational intervention program (in this case, a program designed to foster the student's sense of personal control). As the implementation proceeds, the teacher, influenced by the program's philosophy and approach, formulates (or alters) achievement expectancies for individual students based on either evidence about a specific student or experience on students in similar situations. Expectations are formed for each student's ability to achieve the program's goals and to function effectively in the school

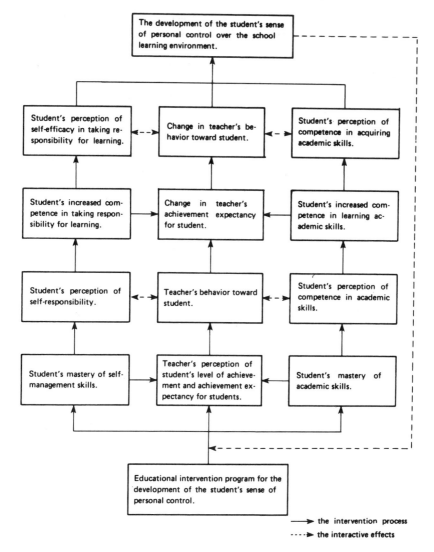

FIG. 9.1. A conceptual model of the development and consequences of the student's sense of personal control.

learning environment. These expectations, in turn, affect the teacher's behavior toward individual students and, consequently, also affect each student's learning as well as his or her perception of self-efficacy and sense of personal control.

It is hypothesized that students are more likely to increase their competence in academic and self-management skills when in an educational intervention program that provides opportunities to master these skills. As a reaction to an increase in student competence, the teacher's perception of the student's ability to achieve the program's goals is likely to be modified. As the teacher's perception of each student's competence changes, the teacher's behavior toward and expectations for each student are also affected. Positive alterations in the teacher's behavior and expectations, in turn, result in changes in the student's perception of his or her competence and efficacy in acquiring academic and self-management skills. From the student's perspective, the development of competence in academic and self-management skills results in an increased sense of personal control. Furthermore, this newly developed competence also affects the nature and patterns of the teacher's and the student's classroom behaviors. Therefore, the relationship between a student's mastery of academic and self-management skills and his or her development of a sense of personal control is a central feature of the conceptual model.

CRITICAL DESIGN CHARACTERISTICS

Two design characteristics are postulated as critical to school learning environments that facilitate students' success in mastering both academic and self-management skills: (a) instruction in and opportunities to practice self-management skills, and (b) instruction in and opportunities for mastery of academic skills.

Instruction in Self-Management Skills and Opportunities for Self-Managed Learning

Self-management skills are defined herein as skills related to management of the learning environment and the learning process. Included are skills required (a) to plan and carry out routine classroom management tasks (e.g., obtaining and returning learning materials and equipment); (b) to search for, order, and organize information for learning and retention; (c) to break complex tasks into meaningful and manageable subparts; (d) to set realistic goals and learning tasks; and (e) to estimate the amount of time and effort required to complete a task. Few attempts have been made to develop self-management skills through instructional intervention, even though the development of students' motivation and ability to exercise control over their learning environment has often been a major goal of educational programs. It is usually assumed that self-management skills are present in more "socially mature" and "academically able" students and are developed in other students as they become "socialized" during the process of schooling. It may be, however, that self-management skills need to be fostered through direct instructional intervention, just as do basic academic skills, such as reading and math (Wang, 1979b).

A major concern of researchers interested in the implications of instructional design for learner-controlled instruction is the identification of effective strategies and alternative programs that provide opportunities to develop students' sense of personal control. Research in this area generally has been conducted by three groups: developers of computer-assisted (CAI) and computer-managed (CMI) instruction, concerned with using computer technology to increase instructional resources; behavioral psychologists, concerned with developing instructional intervention procedures to increase students' self-management of classroom learning; and program developers, concerned with designing school learning experiences that develop students' beliefs in their ability to control their behaviors and enhance their sense of competence in school learning (Wang & Schorling, 1977).

The close relationship between academic performance and self-management has been supported by results from a number of experimental and field studies (e.g., Broden, Hall, & Mitts, 1971; Davis & Phares, 1967; Glynn, Thomas, & Shee, 1973; McLaughlin & Malaby, 1974; Pines & Julian, 1972). In general, the data show that students with highly developed self-management skills tend to use previously learned concepts in problem solving and tend to be persistent in seeking information necessary for solving problems. In contrast, students low in self-management skills tend to adopt a given problem-solving strategy regardless of whether or not the strategy is effective. The performance of this latter group improves only when students know they will be given evaluative feedback by the teacher. These findings are also supported in studies conducted by Ross and Zimiles (1974) and Wang (1976) on specific instructional programs. Ross and Zimiles reported that students in classrooms designed with "learner-controlled instruction" features were more autonomous, engaged in more conceptually based information exchanges, and asked more questions than students in traditional classrooms. Wang conducted a series of studies designed to investigate the effects of a program that focused on teaching children to manage their learning. Data obtained from these studies showed that when children were taught self-management skills and provided with opportunities to use them, they became more independent, and their task completion rates increased significantly. Finally, Arlin and Whitley (1978) conducted a study that varied the amount of opportunity for students to exercise self-management. Data from this study suggested that the number of opportunities students were given to control their learning was causally related to their perceptions of the amount of control they had over their learning outcomes.

Analyses of research findings in this area show that the implementation of instructional programs that encourage the development of self-management skills requires fundamental changes in the traditional classroom authority structure and instructional-learning processes. The conventional role of the teacher as the manager of students needs to be modified so that a greater amount of routine classroom management and management of student learning is transferred to the students. The teacher in such classrooms, to use Bloom's terms, should become more a "manager of instruction" and less a "manager of students" (Bloom,

1976). Classroom environments designed to foster self-managed learning should provide opportunities for students (a) to carry out individual learning plans with increasing independence, (b) to evaluate their learning, (c) to select subject matter from among a wide array of learning options and alternatives, (d) to learn to work with others and share classroom resources, and (e) to take responsibility for helping one another in carrying out learning plans. There is evidence that when students are provided with such opportunities, they tend to score higher on measures of self-esteem and internal locus of control (e.g., Arlin & Whitley, 1978; Sagotsky, Patterson, & Lepper, 1978; Stallings & Kaskowitz, 1974; Stephens, 1971; Tuchman, Cochran, & Travers, 1973; Wang & Stiles, 1976a).

Instruction in and Opportunities for Mastery of Academic Skills

A variable that influences whether students perceive that they are in control of their learning outcomes is the extent to which school learning environments provide opportunities for each child to experience success in acquiring academic as well as social and personal skills. Evidence supporting the close relationship between skills acquisition and perception of personal control has been reported by many, particularly those who assume that skills mastery and competence are essential to the development of the student's sense of self-efficacy and self-confidence (e.g., Bandura, 1977; Bloom, 1976, 1980; Covington & Beery, 1976; Covington & Omelich, 1979; Lefcourt, 1976; Weiner, 1979).

Bandura's (1977) theory of self-efficacy is relevant to the development and consequences of students' sense of personal control in classroom settings. Self-efficacy, according to Bandura, is the ability to process information conveyed by an event, weigh all elements of the prospective situation, and then make judgments about how to organize and carry out the necessary actions to deal with that situation (Bandura, 1981). A student's perception of self-efficacy is seen to influence the student's choice of activities, the situations under which he or she chooses to work, the persons with whom the student chooses to interact and work, and the amount of effort, vigor, and persistence with which the student carries out learning tasks. Bandura stresses that academic successes strengthen students' perceptions of control over learning outcomes, while repeated failures weaken such perceptions. Thus, mastery-based instructional approaches tend to produce higher, stronger, and more generalized perceptions and expectations of personal efficacy (Bandura, Adams, & Beyer, 1977).

Educational programs most likely to foster skills acquisition are those that focus on adapting learning experiences to student differences. Such programs can be characterized as including (a) built-in provisions for permitting students to enter a given subject area at entry points based on analyses of their individual competencies and learning needs; (b) provisions for alternative approaches to instruction, including options for selecting learning tasks and learning objectives that provide a good match between the student and the learning environment; (c) explicit statements of student performance standards, as well as alternative ways of succeeding and of assessing success; (d) hierarchical groupings of learning objectives in small subsets with built-in checkpoints that allow frequent opportunities for teachers to give formal and informal feedback to students about their performance; and (e) required student acquisition of each prerequisite subset of skills before proceeding to the next level to insure a steady rate of success. When functioning under programs with these features, each student should be able to make continuous progress toward mastery of the curricular content at his or her own rate. The student should also be able to plan his or her learning based on what has been accomplished and what skills need improvement as well as be able to evaluate his or her learning based on performance and teacher feedback (Wang, 1980).

To summarize, if students function in carefully structured learning environments where opportunities are provided for skills acquisition and where continuous emphasis is placed on self-direction, self-initiative, and self-evaluative behaviors, it is postulated that students should gain an increased sense of self-efficacy and personal control. Furthermore, it is assumed that academic successes are more likely to increase students' perception of personal control if the successes are achieved without a high degree of dependence on external agents, such as teachers. Similarly, if failures are minimal and not attributed to external agents, students are more likely to persist and to view momentary conflicts and failures as challenges or signals to modify their behaviors rather than as indications of low ability. This discussion will take on more meaning by illustrating how the characteristics of an educational intervention program designed to develop students' sense of personal control can be incorporated into the schooling process. In the following section, a brief description is provided of the Adaptive Learning Environments Model, a program designed to maximize student learning by fostering the development of a sense of personal control and the acquisition of basic academic and self-management skills. Next, a synopsis is presented of several studies that investigated the relationship between selected instructional design variables and the development of students' sense of personal control. The resulting impact on instructional-learning processes and student learning outcomes is discussed.

THE ADAPTIVE LEARNING ENVIRONMENTS MODEL

The Adaptive Learning Environments Model (ALEM) is an educational program designed with the implicit goal of fostering the development of students' sense of personal control through school learning experiences that are adaptive to individual differences. ALEM has been developed and field-tested during the past decade at the Learning Research and Development Center of the University of Pittsburgh (Glaser, 1977; Wang, 1980). The program combines (a) aspects of highly structured prescriptive instruction that are effective in assuring student acquisition of basic academic skills, and (b) aspects of informal education that are effective in generating inquisitiveness regarding new learning tasks and situations, independence, and social cooperation.

Basic Program Features

Mastery of Basic Academic Skills

In ALEM student mastery of basic academic skills is achieved through two basic curricular components, a prescriptive learning component and an exploratory learning component. The prescriptive component is designed explicitly to teach basic academic skills. It includes a series of individualized learning experiences in academic subject areas (e.g., math, reading). These learning experiences, diagnostically tailored to each student's competencies and learning needs, are based on a continuum of instructional objectives that have been hierarchically sequenced and empirically validated to ensure the acquisition of simple skills necessary in acquiring more complex skills (e.g., Wang & Resnick, 1979; Wang, Resnick, & Boozer, 1971). An integral feature of the prescriptive learning component is the diagnostic and skills mastery testing program. The testing program provides teachers and students with evaluative feedback that can be used to monitor and reinforce student learning progress. Based on the results of the diagnostic and skills mastery tests, teachers are able to place students at curricular levels where they can complete their learning tasks with increasing independence (Wang & Resnick, 1979).

In the exploratory learning component, students are encouraged to assume responsibility for structuring and defining their learning tasks. Unlike prescriptive learning tasks, exploratory learning tasks generally are selected and designed by students themselves, with teacher assistance when needed. As a way of helping students assume responsibility for structuring and defining their learning tasks, they are taught the skills needed for choosing, planning, and carrying out learning tasks with minimal teacher supervision. As they work on exploratory learning tasks, students are encouraged to plan, explore, risk mistakes, and apply their skills and knowledge in new situations. Learning tasks can involve topics related to academic subject areas such as reading, math, science, and social studies. They can also be designed in such areas as creative writing, block construction, creative arts, perceptual skills, music, and socio-dramatic play. The range of different exploratory learning tasks is largely determined by students' interests, teachers' expertise, and material and space constraints (Wang & Resnick, 1979).

Development of Self-Management Skills

A unique feature of ALEM is that it explicitly provides for the development of self-management skills. Student self-management is taught through the implementation of an instructional-learning management system known as the Self-Schedule System (Wang, 1974a). This component of ALEM was designed to help teachers and students function more proficiently in learning environments where student self-management is a requirement for successful program implementation. The Self-Schedule System is based on a multifaceted approach that (a) develops teachers' competencies by training them to maximize the use of school time for instructional purposes, (b) teaches students skills needed to assume responsibility for planning and carrying out their learning activities, and (c) helps students use their ability to control the reinforcements that shape their learning behaviors. While students are provided with the flexibility to schedule their learning activities, they must also assume certain responsibilities under the Self-Schedule System. Students, for example, are expected to budget their time in order to complete all their teacher-assigned prescriptive learning tasks and a number of self-selected exploratory learning tasks within a specified amount of time (e.g., an hour, a day, a week). They are also expected to take the responsibility to ask for teacher or peer assistance when needed (Wang, 1974a).

Encouragement of spontaneous socializing and cooperative interaction and the flexibility for maximum use of teacher and student school time differentiate the Self-Schedule System from the traditional Block-Schedule System. The Block-Schedule System, used in most schools, schedules instruction in each subject for a specific time. Even though the development of self-management skills is a desired outcome of the Block-Scheduling System, block scheduling provides little, if any, opportunity for students to assume responsibility for planning and carrying out their learning. Under the Block-Schedule System, the way learning activities take place is generally predetermined and directed by the teacher. Students are not given the opportunity to make learning decisions or to manage their learning time. Therefore, it is hypothesized that ALEM, with its Self-Schedule component that combines the development of a sense of self-responsibility for learning with the mastery of basic academic skills, can more effectively foster students' sense of personal control over their school learning.

RESEARCH

In this section, an overview of several studies designed to investigate the development and consequences of students' sense of personal control in ALEM is presented. Findings from these studies provided, in part, the data base for the formulation of the conceptual model discussed above. The review of our research is organized into three major sections. First, the basic types of data collected are discussed. Second, research designed to document the impact of the Self-Schedule System, the component of ALEM designed specifically to develop self-management skills, on students' sense of personal control is presented. Third, research investigating the effects of the Self-Schedule System on various classroom processes and student learning outcomes is discussed. In the latter section, attention is also given to the relationship between sense of personal control and selected processes and outcomes. It is important to point out that although mastery of academic skills is an important outcome of ALEM, the present discussion focuses primarily on the development of self-management skills. This is done because of space limitations and because studies on the capability of the ALEM to foster acquisition of academic skills have been discussed in detail elsewhere (e.g., Resnick & Wang, 1974; Wang, Leinhardt, & Boston, 1980; Wang, 1981a,b).

Types of Data

Three basic categories of information were collected in the present studies: measures of students' self-responsibility and sense of personal control, descriptions of classroom processes and student and teacher behaviors, and student learning outcomes. The specific measures included in each of the categories are now briefly described.

Measures of Students' Self-responsibility and Sense of Personal Control. Two instruments were used to obtain information on students' self-responsibility and perception of personal control: the Self-Responsibility Interview Schedule (SRIS), developed by Wang (1974b), and the Intellectual Achievement Responsibility Questionnaire (IAR), developed by Crandall, Katkovsky, and Crandall (1965).

The SRIS includes 21 questions designed to obtain four categories of information on individual students: knowledge about the learning environment, ability to evaluate one's learning, preference for a management system that requires students to take responsibility for their learning versus a system that places this responsibility with the teacher, and perception of personal control. The IAR, which consists of 34 forced-choice items, assesses children's internal-external perceptions of academic success or failure. Each item describes either a positive or a negative achievement experience that routinely occurs in children's daily lives.

Descriptions of Classroom Processes. Descriptive information on classroom processes was obtained through systematically-sampled narrative recordings of teacher and student behaviors and through the use of the Student Behavior Observation Schedule (SBOS) developed by Wang (1974c). Data obtained through narrative recordings were analyzed to provide information on the person(s) with whom a specific child interacted, the reason for each interaction, and the nature of the situation in which the interaction occurred. The SBOS was designed specifically to gather information on (a) the frequency and purposes of student-teacher interactions; (b) the frequency and purposes of interactions among students; (c) the percentage of time students spent working in group interactive, group parallel, or individual settings; and (d) the manner in which learning took place (e.g., the extent to which children exhibited on-task versus distracted behaviors).

Student Learning Outcomes.   Task completion rates were used as the primary measure for assessing student learning outcomes. Detailed daily records were kept on the number of prescriptive tasks assigned by teachers and the number of prescriptive and exploratory tasks completed by students. Task completion rates were calculated by dividing the number of tasks completed correctly by the number of tasks assigned.

There are two reasons for using task completion rates rather than achievement test scores, the most frequently used measure of student learning. First, task completion rates seem to be a more appropriate indicator of student learning performance in the studies reported here. Since the overall goal of these studies was to investigate the extent to which students' sense of personal control affects their learning, a direct behavioral measure of student learning, such as the rate of tasks completed correctly, is likely to be more meaningful than measures of learning outcomes such as standardized achievement test scores, which may be influenced by other intervening variables (e.g., the quality of the curricular materials used). Second, although task completion rates are likely to be highly related to standardized achievement test results, the extent to which they correlate depends not only on what the students do in the classroom but also, and perhaps to an even greater degree, on (a) the extent to which the learning task is effective in teaching the skills measured by the standardized achievement test, and (b) the ability of the teacher to prescribe appropriate tasks for the individual students. Therefore, task completion rates are used as central measures to avoid confusing the central issues that the studies were designed to address.

Impact of Self-Schedule System on Sense of Self-Responsibility and Personal Control

The two experimental studies described below were conducted to investigate the effectiveness of the Self-Schedule System as an instructional intervention that fosters students' sense of personal control. Study I (Wang & Stiles, 1976a) was an experimental study conducted in four second grades in each of two schools with differing SES backgrounds. One of four second-grade classes in an inner city school was designated as the experimental group. The remaining second-grade classes from the same school served as the comparison Group A, and all second-grade classes in a suburban school served as comparision Group B. Basically the study was a repeated measures design that combined (a) an experimental-reversal design with four treatment periods (baseline-experimental-reversal-experimental), and (b) an experimental-control group design. The prescriptive and exploratory components of ALEM were used in all participating classes. The Self-Schedule System was adopted during the experimental periods by the experimental class; the Block-Schedule System was used by the experimental class during the baseline and reversal periods and by comparison Groups A and B during all four periods.

Results indicated that the SRIS responses of the experimental group did not differ significantly from those of either comparison group during the baseline period when the Self-Schedule System was not implemented. However, differences between SRIS responses of the experimental and the comparison groups were statistically significant during the experimental periods. During both periods, the experimental group showed higher scores, indicating more personal control. Moreover, for the experimental group, significant differences in SRIS scores were found when the two experimental periods were compared with the baseline reversal periods. These results showed that the SRIS scores were very closely tied to the treatment conditions. The experimental group attained high SRIS scores during both experimental periods, while their SRIS scores were significantly lower during the baseline and reversal periods. This is an interesting and important finding because it indicates that although students' sense of self-responsibility changed through instructional intervention, this change was not permanent. The fact that SRIS scores dropped in the reversal period suggests that students' sense of self-responsibility and perception of personal control reflect a situational response, rather than an enduring disposition.

Differences were also found in the IAR scores of the experimental and the comparison groups during the experimental periods. The IAR scores for the experimental group were higher than those for the comparison groups. However, statistically significant differences were found only between comparison Group A and the experimental group. Since comparison Group A was from the same school as the experimental group, it is reasonable to assume that the students in these two groups shared similar academic and personal characteristics. Thus the differences in the IAR scores may be attributed to the Self-Schedule System. Comparison Group B, on the other hand, differed in a number of student characteristics. It may be speculated, therefore, that the nonsignificant difference in the IAR scores is more a reflection of the differences in student characteristics, which may be tapped by the IAR items, rather than the difference in the treatments (the Self-Schedule System).

To further investigate the impact of the Self-Schedule System on students' sense of self-responsibility and personal control, a replication study, Study II (Wang & Richardson, 1977), was conducted using different classrooms in the same schools as Study I. Two first-grade and four second-grade classes from

School A (the inner city school) and one first-grade and one second-grade class from School B (the suburban school) participated in the study. A multiple baseline design was used. The prescriptive and exploratory learning components of ALEM were used in all participating classes. The Self-Schedule System was added to the program as each class moved into the experimental condition. The SRIS was administered twice, for pre- and post-measures, to all students.

To assess more directly the effects of the Self-Schedule System on student perception of personal control, the four categories of the SRIS items were analyzed separately. Items directly related to the locus of control category were used to assess the impact of the Self-Schedule System on students' sense of personal control. As expected, no significant differences in the locus of control subscores of the SRIS were found during periods when the Block-Schedule System was implemented. However, significant differences within and across classes were found between periods when the Block-Schedule System and the Self-Schedule System were implemented. Except for two second-grade classes where the Self-Schedule System was not fully implemented prior to the end of the study, locus of control subscores were statistically higher when the Self-Schedule System was implemented.

The results of these two experimental studies suggest that, when fully implemented, the Self-Schedule System is generally effective in fostering the development of students' sense of self-responsibility for school learning and personal control over such learning. Furthermore, and perhaps more importantly, the data suggest that this sense of self-responsibility and perception of personal control is situation-specific.

Impact of Self-Schedule System on Classroom Processes and Outcomes

A series of studies was designed to investigate the effects of the Self-Schedule System on classroom processes and student learning outcomes. The studies included classrooms implementing the Self-Schedule System as a component of ALEM (Wang, 1980, 1981c; Wang & Brictson, 1973; Wang, Mazza, Haines, & Johnson, 1972; Wang & Richardson, 1977; Wang & Stiles, 1976b; Weisstein & Wang, 1978, 1980) and classrooms where the component was used in conjunction with other instructional programs (Wang, 1979c). An underlying assumption in the design of these studies, based on the results of the studies described above, was that the impact of the Self-Schedule System on classroom processes and outcomes is mediated to a large extent by students' sense of personal control.

Classroom Processes.   Data on the effects of the Self-Schedule System on classroom processes were obtained from a series of classroom observation studies designed to collect systematic information on how students and teachers spent their time in the classroom. The data on classroom processes under the

TABLE 9.1
Summary of Data on Classroom Processes Under the Self-Schedule System
(SBOS Data)

| | | Mean Percent of Observed Frequencies Reported | | | | | | | | | | | | | | | |
| | Wang & Brictson Note 12 | Wang & Stiles (1976 b) Experimental | | Wang & Richardson Note 8 | | | | | | Weisstein & Wang Note 9 | Wang Note 5** | | | | Median of Means Across Studies |
Variable		Period 1	Period 2	Class S	Class D	Class E	Class G	Class L	Class J		Class A	Class B	Class C	Class D	
Manner in which activities were carried out															
On-task	.81	.82	.84	.81	.89	.90	.82	.94	.74	.70	.78	.90	.81	.93	.82
Waiting for teacher help	.08	.06	.06	.12	.09	.07	.04	.01	.16	.07	.01	.01	.01	.01	.06
Distracted	.13	.10	.10	.07	.01	.03	.14	.03	.10	.24	.20	.08	.18	.05	.10
Active type															
Prescriptive	.66	.80	.69	.80	.65	.80	.66	.75	.59	.74	.73	.85	.77	.87	.74
Exploratory	.31	.19	.31	.19	.35	.20	.34	.24	.41	.15	.09	.12	.08	.11	.20
Other	.02	.01	.00	.00	.00	.00	.00	.00	.00	.11	.18	.03	.15	.02	.01
Setting in which students worked															
Group interactive	.09	.08	.04	.07	.15	.08	.16	.08	.21	.19	.17	.22	.15	.15	.16
Group parallel	.15	.03	.03	.00	.00	.04	.00	.03	.00	.03	.39	.44	.31	.49	.03
Individual	.76	.87	.93	.92	.85	.88	.84	.87	.79	.78	.44	.33	.53	.36	.82

228

Interactions with teachers initiated by														
Student	.60	*	.20	.10	.40	.23	.50	.54	.63	.60	.50	.75	.33	.50
Teacher	.40	*	.40	.20	.20	.31	.50	.31	.18	.40	.50	.25	.66	.32
Unknown	.00	*	.40	.70	.40	.46	.00	.15	.18	.00	.00	.00	.00	.00
Purpose of interaction														
Instructional	.50	.90	.87	1.00	.83	.92	1.00	.93	.64	.80	.80	.66	.75	.81
Management	.18	.10	.13	.00	.17	.08	.00	.07	.27	.20	.20	.33	.25	.18
Other	.32	.00	.00	.00	.00	.00	.00	.00	.09	.00	.00	.00	.00	.00
Interactions with peers														
Constructive (sharing)	.96	*	1.00	1.00	1.00	1.00	1.00	.94	.96	.86	1.00	1.00	1.00	1.00
Disruptive (disagreement)	.04	*	.00	.00	.00	.00	.00	.06	.04	.14	.00	.00	.00	.00

Note. * Information was not collected.
  ** In these classrooms, the Self-Schedule System was implemented in conjunction with the school district's curriculum instead of the prescriptive component of the Adaptive Learning Environments Program.

Self-Schedule System are summarized in Table 9.1. The table includes the mean percent of observed frequencies for each classroom process variable as well as the median across all studies.

Although the absolute frequencies for particular variables vary from study to study, the overall pattern of results is quite consistent. Results from the majority of comparisons show that students functioning under the Self-Schedule System tended to interact with teachers more frequently for instructional than for management purposes. They tended to interact with peers for constructive purposes most of the time, and there were very few discipline problems. Disruptive behaviors such as arguing or fighting occurred very infrequently, if at all, and students in general seemed to be on-task most of the time (observed on-task behavior ranged between .70 and .94 with a median of .82). Interestingly, this rate is quite high when compared with the statistics reported in a number of nationwide studies of classroom processes (e.g., Berliner, Filby, Marliave, & Weir, 1976). Note that students given the responsibility to manage their learning, as required under the Self-Schedule System, tended to spend little time waiting for teacher help, a behavior cited as one of the management problems in many individualized instructional programs (Wang & Yeager, 1973).

Table 9.2 summarizes the data from several experimental studies designed to investigate the extent to which classroom processes differed under the Self-Schedule System and the Block-Schedule System (Wang & Brictson, 1973; Wang & Richardson, 1977; Wang & Stiles, 1976b). While some of the differences were not statistically significant, a generally consistent pattern of results was evident. Students were found to be on-task more when functioning under the Self-Schedule System than under the Block-Schedule System, and they tended to spend less time waiting for teacher help. In addition, the nature of interactions among students tended to be more constructive and less disruptive under the Self-Schedule System.

In summary, the classroom processes data reported in Tables 9.1 and 9.2 support our thesis that as students learn to use the Self-Schedule System (i.e., as they acquire self-management skills and are provided with opportunities to practice these skills), they exhibit behaviors which suggest competence in managing their learning. When functioning under the Self-Schedule System, students show high rates of on-task behavior. Furthermore, across all the studies and in the majority of classrooms, students exhibited purposeful and attentive behaviors and spent relatively little time waiting for instruction or directions from the teachers.

Student Learning Outcomes.   Analyses of the effects of the Self-Schedule System on student learning outcomes were based on students' task completion rates. Table 9.3 provides a summary analysis of the task completion rates from the various studies. Data from the experimental studies show that students' task completion rates were significantly higher when functioning under the Self-

TABLE 9.2

Summary Analysis of Data Comparing Classroom Processes Under the Block-Schedule System and the Self-Schedule System

	Comparisons of Percent of Observed Frequencies Reported								
	Wang & Bricson, Note 11 First Grade			Wang & Stiles, 1976 b Second Grade					
				Period 1			Period 2		
Variables	Block-Schedule System	Self-Schedule System	t-test*	Block-Schedule System	Self-Schedule System	t-test*	Block-Schedule System	Self-Schedule System	t-test*
Manner in which activities were carried out									
On-task	.57	.81	$< .05$	.77	.82		.71	.84	$< .05$
Waiting for teacher help	.25	.08	$< .05$	.08	.06		.10	.06	
Distracted	.19	.13		.13	.10		.16	.10	
Activity type									
Prescriptive	.87	.66	$< .05$	.70	.80	$< .05$	.68	.69	
Exploratory	.05	.31	$< .05$	.30	.19		.31	.31	
Other	.04	.02		.00	.01		.00	.00	
Settings in which students worked									
Group interactive	.04	.09		.05	.08		.06	.04	
Group parallel	.01	.15	$< .05$	.08	.03	$< .05$	.14	.03	$< .01$
Individual	.93	.76	$< .05$	.87	.87		.78	.93	$< .01$
Interactions with teachers initiated by									
Student	.58	.60	$< .05$	**	**		**	**	
Teacher	.42	.40	$< .05$	**	**		**	**	
Unknown	.00	.00		**	**		**	**	
Purpose of interaction									
Instruction	.48	.50		.82	.90	$< .05$	.69	.71	$< .05$
Management	.21	.18		.18	.10		.31	.29	$< .01$
Other	.00	.00		.00	.00		.00	.00	

(continued)

TABLE 9.2 (*Continued*)

Comparisons of Percent of Observed Frequencies Reported

| | Wang & Brictson, Note 11 First Grade | | | Wang & Stiles, 1976 b Second Grade | | | | | | |
| | | | | Period 1 | | | Period 2 | | |
Variables	Block-Schedule System	Self-Schedule System	t-test[*]	Block-Schedule System	Self-Schedule System	t-test[*]	Block-Schedule System	Self-Schedule System	t-test[*]
Interaction with peers									
Constructive (sharing)	.88	.96	<.05	**	**		**	**	
Disruptive (disagreement)	.12	.04	<.05	**	**		**	**	

Note: [*]Only statistically significant p-values are reported.
[**]Information was not collected.

TABLE 9.2 (Continued)

Comparisons of Percent of Observed Frequencies Reported

Wang & Richardson, Note 8

| | First Grade | | | | | | Second Grade | | | | | | | | | | | | Median of Means Across Studies | |
| | Class S | | | Class D | | | Class E | | | Class G | | | Class L | | | Class J | | | | |
Variables	Block-Schedule System	Self-Schedule System	p<	Block-Schedule System	Self-Schedule System	p<	Block-Schedule System	Self-Schedule System	p<	Block-Schedule System	Self-Schedule System	p<	Block-Schedule System	Self-Schedule System	p<	Block-Schedule System	Self-Schedule System	p<	Block-Schedule System	Self-Schedule System
Manners in which activities were carried out																				
On-task	.85	.81		.73	.89	<.05	.80	.90	<.05	.89	.82	<.05	.75	.95	<.01	.72	.74		.75	.82
Waiting for teacher help	.11	.12		.16	.09	<.05	.14	.07	<.05	.01	.04	<.05	.10	.01	<.01	.20	.16		.11	.07
Distracted	.04	.07		.11	.01	<.01	.06	.03		.10	.14		.16	.03	<.01	.07	.10		.11	.10
Activity type																				
Prescriptive	.66	.80		.65	.65		.64	.80	<.01	.65	.66		.67	.75		.66	.60		.66	.69
Exploratory	.33	.19		.35	.35		.36	.20	<.01	.33	.34		.33	.24		.34	.41		.33	.31
Other	.00	.00		.00	.00		.00	.00		.01	.00		.00	.00		.00	.00		.00	.00
Settings in which students worked																				
Group interactive	.17	.07	<.01	.17	.15		.06	.08		.04	.16	<.01	.09	.08		.28	.21		.06	.08
Group parallel	.00	.00		.01	.00		.07	.04		.05	.00	<.05	.01	.03		.00	.00		.01	.03
Individual	.83	.92	<.01	.81	.85		.87	.88		.91	.84	<.05	.90	.87		.71	.79		.87	.87
Interactions with teachers initiated by																				
Student	.46	.20	<.05	.62	.10	<.01	.17	.40	<.01	.50	.23	<.01	.33	.50	<.01	.38	.54	<.05	.46	.40
Teacher	.08	.40	<.01	.19	.20		.33	.20	<.05	.00	.31	<.01	.22	.50	<.01	.19	.31		.19	.31
Unknown	.46	.40		.19	.70	<.01	.50	.40		.50	.46		.44	.00	<.05	.43	.15	<.01	.44	.40
Purpose of interaction																				
Instruction	.85	.87		.90	1.00	<.01	1.00	.83	<.01	1.00	.92	<.01	1.00	1.00		.90	.93		.90	.90
Management	.08	.13		.07	.00	<.05	.00	.17		.00	.08		.00	.00		.06	.07		.07	.10
Other	.08	.00		.03	.00		.00	.00		.00	.00		.00	.00		.06	.00		.00	.00
Interactions with peers																				
Constructive (sharing)	1.00	1.00		.88	1.00	<.01	1.00	1.00		.86	1.00		.66	1.00	<.05	1.00	.94		.88	1.00
Disruptive (disagreement)	.00	.00		.12	.00	<.05	.00	.00		.14	.00	<.05	.33	.00	<.05	.00	.06		.12	.00

Note. *Only statistically significant p-values are reported.

233

TABLE 9.3
Summary of Task Completion Rates from Studies on the
Effects of the Self-Schedule System

Studies	Mean Task Completion Rates		t-test
	Block Schedule System	*Self-Schedule System*	
Experimental Studies			
Wang, Mazza, Haines, & Johnson, 1972	86%	97%	p <.01
Wang & Stiles, 1976b			
Experimental 1	55%	65%	p <.01
Experimental 2	52%	74%	p <.01
Descriptive Studies			
Weisstein & Wang, Note 9		105%	
Wang, Note 5			
Class A		78%	
Class B		94%	
Class C		81%	
Class D		95%	

Schedule System than the Block-Schedule System. Furthermore, data from the descriptive studies show that the students functioning under the Self-Schedule System achieved high absolute task completion rates.

Relationship Between Students' Sense of Self-Responsibility and Personal Control and Their Learning Processes and Outcomes. The foregoing data indicate that students functioning under the Self-Schedule System exhibit different behaviors and outcomes than students in the traditional Block-Schedule System. Furthermore, those behaviors and outcomes have been postulated as reflecting students' competence in self-management and their sense of personal control. To test this hypothesis, the relationship between SRIS scores and a selected number of outcome and process variables believed related to students' sense of personal control was examined.

Table 9.4 shows the results of correlational analyses of the SRIS scores and selected process and outcome variables from an experimental study conducted to investigate the effects of the Self-Schedule System (Wang, 1979b). Student behaviors indicative of competence in self-management (e.g., task completion rate, on-task behavior) are positively related to students' sense of self-responsibility and personal control (SRIS scores). On the other hand, behaviors indicative of lack of self-management skills (e.g., distracted behavior, management interactions with teachers) are negatively related to SRIS scores. Under the Self-Schedule System, for example, students' sense of self-responsibility and

TABLE 9.4

Correlation Between SRIS Scores and Selected Classroom Processes and Student Learning Outcome Variables

(N = 21)

	Variable					
SRIS Scores	Task Completion Rate	On-Task Behavior	Distracted Behavior	Minutes Spent Completing the Task	Instructional Interactions with Teacher	Management Interactions with Teacher
Block-Schedule System	.23	.22	-.50*	.07	-.17	-.20
Self-Schedule System	.51*	.30	-.17	.14	.04	-.03

Note. *p $<$ .05

235

personal control for learning, as measured by the SRIS, is significantly related to their task completion rates. The correlation between the two variables under the Block-Schedule System, however, was not statistically significant. On the other hand, a significant negative correlation was found between students' distracted behavior and their SRIS scores when functioning under the Block-Schedule System.

Teacher Behaviors and Expectations.   One of the hypothesized outcomes of the Self-Schedule System is that students' competence in taking responsibility for their learning not only will increase their sense of personal control, but also will produce changes in teacher expectations for them. Furthermore, these changes are assumed to affect the classroom behaviors of both teachers and students. In line with this hypothesis, two questions related to teacher expectations were raised. Do teachers functioning under ALEM and its component Self-Schedule System interact with students differentially as a result of their expectancies for students' achievement? If so, does this differential pattern of teacher behavior influence student behavior and learning performance? These two questions were addressed in the following two studies.

The studies were conducted during two consecutive school years in a multi-age primary classroom where the Self-Schedule System was implemented as a component of ALEM. The classroom included 46 children when the first study (Study A) was conducted. Forty-two students were enrolled in the classroom during the subsequent year when the second study (Study B) was conducted. For both studies, children ranged in age from 5 through 8 years. The classroom staff included two teachers, one research assistant, and one instructional aide. There was one teacher change between Study A and B. All of the adults and children enrolled in the classroom served as subjects. However, the method for identifying high and low achievers for study differed in Study A and Study B.

In Study A (Wang, 1981), high- and low-achieving students were identified on the basis of math and reading scores on standardized achievement tests. Students performing at or below the 25th percentile were identified as low achievers; those scoring above the 95th percentile were identified as high achievers. Using this criterion, four children in Study A were identified as low achievers, and eight were identified as high achievers. The identities of these children, however, were not revealed to either the instructional staff or the students. Although, it is important to note that by the very nature of the individualized instructional approach, teachers in such an individualized program are likely to be even more conscious of students' achievement levels. In Study B (Weisstein & Wang, 1980), students were classified as high, moderate, and low achievers on the basis of the teachers' perceptions of students' achievement levels rather than on the basis of achievement test results. At the beginning of the study, the staff was asked to identify students they believed were in the top 1/3, middle 1/3, and bottom 1/3 of the achievement continuum for the class. A student was included in the sample only if all the adults agreed on the achievement category for that student. On this basis, 16 students were selected for intensive study. Within this subsample, six students were identified as high achievers, three as moderate achievers, and seven as low achievers. For both studies, a scoring procedure that takes into account the distributions of both the observed frequencies and the frequencies which could be expected by chance was used to control for differences in grouping (Wang, 1981c).

Results of Study A. In analyzing the data, we were interested in investigating four categories of potential teacher expectation effects: patterns of classroom interactions between high and low achievers and their teachers, effects of teacher-student interaction patterns on student learning processes, effects of teacher-student interaction patterns on student learning outcomes, and patterns of classroom interactions between high and low achievers and their peers.

1. *Patterns of Classroom Interactions Between High and Low Achievers and Their Teachers.* The SBOS data were first examined to determine the overall frequency and purpose of the interactions between teachers and students. Some contrasting trends in teacher-student interaction patterns as a function of students' achievement level were observed. While 76% of teachers' interactions with high-achieving students were for instructional purposes, only 52% of their interactions with low-achieving students were instructional. In addition, the percentage of management interactions between teachers and low achievers was much higher (47%) than the percentage of management interactions between teachers and either high achievers (13%) or the class as a whole (27%).

Contrary to our assumptions, these findings are similar to those from studies of teacher behavior in traditional programs (e.g., Brophy & Good, 1970; McDermott, 1977). Our data suggest that teachers interact differentially with high- and low-achieving students even when functioning under ALEM. Because this program requires teachers to develop and implement learning plans for individual students based on student progress data instead of teacher perceptions, it was assumed that the program would have a minimizing effect on differential treatment of high- and low-achieving students.

2. *Effects of Teacher-Student Interaction Patterns on Student Learning Processes.* The SBOS data were analyzed to investigate the extent to which the observed differences in how teachers responded to high- and low-achieving students affected students' learning processes. Our main question was whether the effects of differences in teacher interactions with low- and high-achieving students could be minimized through instructional design. It was hypothesized that these differences would not significantly affect student learning processes in our learning environment, which was designed explicitly to teach students to assume responsibility for their learning.

In general, the data showed no major learning-process differences between the high- and low-achievement student groups. The only observed difference was in the type of instructional setting in which students preferred to work. More low achievers (64%) worked in individual settings than did high achievers (29%). In contrast, more high achievers (60%) worked in group interactive settings than did low achievers (28%). On the basis of informal observations, we believe that these findings might reflect differences in the nature of the learning tasks assigned by the teachers rather than differences in high- and low-achieving students' preferences for particular instructional settings. Overall, the data suggest that while patterns of teacher interaction with high and low achievers differed, these differences did not have important effects on high- and low-achieving students' learning processes.

3. *Effects of Teacher-Student Interaction Patterns on Student Learning Outcomes.* To examine the extent to which the differential teacher-student interactions affected student learning outcomes, the high- and low-achieving students' task completion rates and perceptions of self-responsibility were examined. If the amount of student on-task behavior is highly related to task completion rates, the completion rates of high- and low-achieving students would not be expected to differ. In contrast, if task completion rates are highly related to the pattern of teacher-student interactions, higher task completion rates among high achievers would be expected. No significant differences in task completion rates were found between the high- and low-achieving groups. The low-achieving students achieved mean task completion rates of 115% in reading and 125% in math. The mean task completion rates of the high achievers were 107% in reading and 125% in math. These results indicte that both the high- and low-achieving students were able to complete correctly more tasks than assigned, which is consistent with the findings from other studies conducted in classrooms where the Self-Schedule System is implemented. Children in the ALEM routinely select additional tasks on their own or ask the teacher for more assignments, after correctly completing teacher-prescribed tasks and the required number of self-selected tasks.

The task completion rates suggest that, although the pattern of interaction between teachers and low-achieving students may not have been as conducive to learning as the pattern between teachers and high-achieving students, low achievers were able to complete nearly as many assigned tasks as their high-achieving peers. One possible explanation for this finding may lie in low-achieving students' ability to plan and manage their learning. A major goal of ALEM is to insure that when teacher assistance is needed, all students are able either to seek teacher assistance or to find other ways to get the help they need.

IAR scores were examined to determine any differences between high- and low-achieving students' perceptions of locus of control over their school learning. Since the low-achieving students, like their high-achieving peers, were taught to manage their learning with minimum teacher direction, it was expected that low achievers would be as competent as high achievers in meeting the program's self-responsibility requirements and, therefore, would be likely to perceive themselves as having control over their school learning. The IAR scores for low-achieving students ($M = 23$) were almost identical to those for high achievers ($M = 22.3$). Thus, differential patterns of teacher interaction with high- and low-achieving students did not substantially affect students' perception of personal control.

4. *Patterns of Classroom Interactions Between High and Low Achievers and Their Peers.*   Narrative recordings of students' classroom behaviors were used to examine the extent to which students utilized their peers as resources, especially when they failed to get the assistance they needed from teachers. The data suggest that low achievers tended to initiate interactions with high achievers more frequently than with other peers in the class. That low-achieving students obtained instructional help from their high-achieving peers may account for why differences in the patterns of teacher interactions with high- and low-achieving students did not affect students' task completion rates.

To summarize, the data from Study A suggest two major findings. First, teacher interactions with students of different achievement levels did differ, even though the names of high- and low-achieving students were not revealed to the teachers. This finding is consistent with previous descriptions of teacher behavior in traditional classrooms. This was somewhat surprising, however, since implicit in the design of the ALEM are features which theoretically should minimize the effects of teacher expectations on teacher behaviors. Second, although teachers interacted with students differentially as a function of student achievement level, concomitant differences in students' learning processes, task completion rates, and locus of control over learning were not observed. Thus, although the program, as implemented in Study A, did not influence, as anticipated, teacher behaviors known to be associated with teacher expectancy effects, the effects of differences in teachers' interactions with high- and low-achieving students seem minimal. Students with different achievement levels functioned similarly in spite of the differences in the ways teachers interacted with them. Low achievers were able to accomplish as much as their high-achieving peers. In addition, they, like high-achieving peers, also perceived a sense of personal control over their learning. This finding suggests the potential utility of instructional interventions, such as the Self-Schedule System, in shaping student behaviors which may indirectly minimize teacher expectancy effects. Similar findings have been obtained in several related studies. The results of Fiedler's (1975) study, for example, showed that in classrooms encouraging self-responsibility for learning, students tended not to comply with teachers' attempts to influence their learning performance.

Results of Study B.   Study B was designed to test more directly the relationship between teacher expectations and student learning. Study B investigated (a) whether there are significant differences in the way teachers interact with children in three achievement expectancy groups defined by the teachers, and (b) whether students in the groups differ significantly in their learning behaviors, learning processes, and learning outcomes. We reasoned that teacher perceptions of students' achievement would not substantially influence teacher interactions with students in a learning environment where (a) mastery of self-management and academic skills is emphasized, and (b) teachers receive formal feedback (e.g., curriculum-embedded diagnostic test results, task completion rates) and informal feedback (e.g., behavioral indicators that reflect students' self-management competence) on a frequent and systematic basis. To insure that the teachers were aware of students' learning progress in academic and self-management skills, weekly discussion sessions were held between teachers and researchers. These weekly meetings, and the fact that students' achievement groups were defined by staff members rather than by test results, were the major differences between Studies A and B.

1. *Effects of Teacher Expectations on Teacher-Student Interaction Patterns.* Contrary to the findings of Study A and several teacher expectation studies conducted in traditional school learning environments (e.g., Brophy & Good, 1970, 1974; Cooper, 1977, 1979; McDermott, 1977), no significant differences in the frequency of teacher-initiated interactions for either instructional or management purposes were found among the three achievement expectancy groups. This finding supports the central hypothesis of Study B. That is, differences in teacher interactions with students of different achievement expectancies may be minimized when teachers receive feedback that low achievers are making steady progress in the program and that their classroom behavioral patterns and task performance rates are similar to those of students in higher achievement expectancy groups. In comparing the interaction data from Studies A and B, it appears that the added design feature in Study B (i.e., giving the teachers regular feedback on the students' learning progress) may have influenced the teachers' behaviors.

2. *Effects of Teacher Expectations on Student Learning Processes.* Analyses were also performed to determine any differences in the learning behaviors and processes of the low, moderate, and high achievement expectancy students. Results showed that the low achievement expectancy students displayed behaviors and learning processes that were very similar to those displayed by moderate and high achievement expectancy students. No significant differences were observed in the frequencies with which each group worked on learning tasks assigned by the teachers. Moreover, there were no statistical differences among the three groups regarding on-task behaviors, time spent waiting for teacher assistance, or distracted behaviors.

3. *Effects of Teacher Expectations on Student Learning Outcomes.* No significant differences were found among the low, moderate, and high expectancy

students in math and reading achievement gains, task completion rates, or SRIS scores. Several specific results are worth noting, however. First, students in all groups completed more learning tasks in math and reading than teachers assigned. Second, an apparent inconsistency exists between students' task completion rates and achievement gains as measured by standardized achievement tests. Although no statistically significant differences were observed in reading and math achievement gains, closer examination of the data suggest that differences among those gains might have been statistically significant if a larger sample had been used, since the average gains of high achievement expectancy students were twice as large as those of low (and moderate) achievement expectancy students. Thus, while students in the low achievement expectancy group completed as many teacher-assigned tasks as those in the high expectancy group, their mean achievement gain was substantially (though not significantly) lower. Perhaps, tasks assigned to low-achieving students were not as effective (i.e., appropriate for teaching a prerequisite skill) as tasks assigned to high-achieving students. If so, tasks assigned to low-achieving students may not have been as effective in helping these students to acquire mastery of relevant skills, even though they completed correctly all of the tasks assigned.

Some support for the above hypothesis is gained through an examination of task assignment patterns. Teachers tended to assign more review tasks and smaller tasks (e.g., fewer workbook pages) to low achievement expectancy students than to students in the other two groups. In questioning teachers about these differences, we learned that they consciously differentiated the nature and size of assignments on the basis of their expectations of what each student could successfully accomplish. Thus, it appears that teacher expectations may have influenced their task assignment patterns. Furthermore, it may be speculated that teacher expectations might play an even greater role in student learning in conventional classrooms, where students are given little if any opportunity to exercise control over their learning.

In addition to basic skills acquisition, the extent to which students in each achievement expectancy group perceived that they had control over their learning environment and behaviors was examined. No significant differences among groups were observed. This is not surprising, since no differences in task completion rates were found among students of different achievement expectancy groups and since all students were given feedback on their competence in completing daily tasks. Thus, even though there were differences in students' achievement levels, the message apparently conveyed to high-, intermediate-, and low-expectancy students on a daily basis was that they were capable of taking on self-responsibility for their school learning.

4. *Changes in Teacher Expectations.*   The extent to which the built-in feedback system of ALEM regarding students' learning progress affected teacher expectations for student achievement levels was also examined. This analysis investigated whether teacher expectations changed when the teachers were pro-

vided with evidence that students in all achievement expectancy groups were able to master academic and self-management skills.

Since low achievement expectancy students in Study B displayed learning processes and outcomes similar to those of their peers with higher achievement expectancies, it was predicted that teachers would increase their expectations for low expectancy students. To test this hypothesis, teachers' initial and end-of-year expectancies for low achievement expectancy students were compared. Results showed no significant change in teachers' ratings for the low expectancy group (or the other two groups). This finding raises an obvious and important question: Given that the low achievement expectancy group showed as much gain in learning outcomes as the other two groups, why did teachers not increase their expectations for the low group? One answer to this question is based on the relative placement of the three groups on the achievement continuum at the end of the year. Since students from all groups displayed similar progress during the school year, the relative positions of the groups (placement on the achievement continuum) at the beginning of the school year remained unchanged at the end of the year. A change in teacher expectations for low expectancy students would not be anticipated unless significantly higher achievement gains were made by these students. Since teachers were asked to rate the achievement levels of students according to their *relative* rather than *absolute* achievement gains, there was no reason, based on available data, for the teachers to increase their achievement expectations for the low expectancy group.

Although not directly tested, the added treatment in Study B of regular discussions with teachers concerning students' progress and teachers' use of student progress data for instructional planning may have contributed to the differences between Study A and Study B in the patterns of interaction between teachers and students with different achievement expectancies. These results, together with results such as those obtained by Brophy and Good (1974), support our contention that when teachers are provided with information which shows that the academic performance of low-achieving students is better than expected, teachers' interactions with these students are altered. Clearly, however, further validation of these findings through experimental studies with adequate control groups is necessary before a firm conclusion can be drawn regarding the impact of ALEM on teacher expectancy effects.

SUMMARY AND DISCUSSION

Results from this series of studies support several of the processes suggested by the model regarding the development and consequences of students' sense of personal control. Among the more important findings are that (a) when students are taught the prerequisite skills for managing their learning behaviors and learning situations, they can successfully take on self-management responsibilities;

(b) as students gain increasing capability to exert control over their school learning, their task performance improves; (c) it is possible to design intervention programs to foster the development of students' sense of personal control; (d) students' belief in their personal control may be an important factor in allowing them to resist the adverse effects of teacher expectations; and (e) learning environments that are effective in fostering perceptions of self-responsibility need organizational and curricular structures that allow students to acquire both academic and self-management skills.

Although the data are generally in accord with the assumption that students' sense of personal control is important to school learning, much work is needed to test specific aspects of the model of the development and consequences of students' sense of personal control. Additional research, for example, must be done on the relationship between teacher expectations and student behaviors in both traditional and innovative educational settings. One area that requires particular attention is the nature of the causal link between teacher expectations and student learning. Although our data suggest that the effect of teacher expectations on student learning is minimal when the Self-Schedule System is operating, no clear causal link has been established in regard to the mediating role of students' sense of personal control. Another major area not yet addressed is the relationship between the development of students' sense of personal control and the development of their achievement expectations as they gain increased competence in planning and managing their learning. Finally, efforts should be made to develop training programs that allow teachers to create and maintain learning environments of the type believed to foster students' sense of personal control. Such programs will likely produce fundamental changes in teachers' beliefs about what students are capable of handling and in their perceptions of the role and function of teachers.

ACKNOWLEDGMENTS

The research reported herein was supported by the Learning Research and Development Center, supported in part as a research and development center by funds from the National Institute of Education (NIE), United States Department of Health, Education, and Welfare. The opinions expressed do not necessarily reflect the position or policy of NIE, and no official endorsement should be inferred. The author would like to extend her sincere appreciation to John Levine and Lauren Resnick for their comments and suggestions to an earlier draft of this chapter, and to Ellen Cooper for her editorial assistance.

REFERENCES

Arlin, M., & Whitley, T. W. Perceptions of self-managed learning opportunities and academic locus of control: A causal interpretation. *Journal of Educational Psychology*, 1978, *70*(6), 988–992.

Bandura, A. *Social learning theory*. Englewood Cliffs, N.J.: Prentice-Hall, 1977.

Bandura, A. Self-referent thought: A developmental analysis of self-efficacy. In J. H. Flavell, & L. R. Ross (Eds.), *Cognitive social development: Frontiers and possible futures*. New York: Cambridge University Press, 1981.

Bandura, A., Adams, N. E., & Beyer, J. Cognitive processes mediating behavioral change. *Personality and Social Psychology*, 1977, *35*(3), 125-139.

Berliner, C. C., Filby, N. N., Marliave, R., & Weir, C. D. *Proposal for Phase III-B of the BTES*. San Francisco, Calif.: Far West Laboratory for Educational Research and Development, 1976.

Bialer, I. Conceptualization of success and failure in mentally retarded and normal children. *Journal of Personality*, 1961, *20*, 303-320.

Bloom, B. *Human characteristics and school learning*. New York: McGraw-Hill, 1976.

Bloom, B. *Are our children learning?* New York: McGraw Hill, 1980.

Broden, M., Hall, R. V., & Mitts, B. The effect of self-recording on the classroom behavior of two eighth-grade students. *Journal of Applied Behavior Analysis*, 1971, *4*, 191-199.

Brophy, J., & Good, T. Teachers' communication of differential expectations for children's classroom performance: Some behavioral data. *Journal of Educational Psychology*, 1970, *61*, 365-374.

Brophy, J., & Good, T. Promoting proactive teaching. In J. Brophy, & T. Good (Eds.), *Teacher-student relationships: Causes and consequences*. New York: Holt, Rinehart & Winston, Inc., 1974, 280-291.

Cellura, A. R. *Internality as a determinant of academic achievement in low SES adolescents*. Unpublished manuscript, University of Rochester, 1963.

Chance, J. Mother-child relations and children's achievement. *Terminal Report*, USPHS—Grant No. MHO 5260, 1968.

Coleman, J. S., Campbell, E. Q., Hobson, C. J., McPartland, J., Mood, A. M., Weinfeld, F. D., & York, R. L. *Equality of educational opportunity*. Report from the Office of Education, Washington, D.C.: U.S. Government Printing Office, 1966.

Cooper, H. Controlling personal rewards: Professional teachers' differential use of feedback and the effects of feedback on the student's motivation to perform. *Journal of Educational Psychology*, 1977, *69*(4), 419-427.

Cooper, H. Pygmalion grows up: A model for teacher expectation communication and performance influence. *Review of Educational Research*, 1979, *49*(3), 389-410.

Covington, M. V., & Beery, R. *Self-worth and school learning*. New York: Holt, Rinehart & Winston, 1976.

Covington, M. C. & Omelich, C. L. The double-edged sword in school achievement. *Journal of Educational Psychology*, 1979, *71*, 169-182.

Crandall, V. C. Personality characteristics and social and achievement tendencies. *Journal of Social Psychology*, 1966, *4*, 477-486.

Crandall, V. C., Katkovsky, W., & Crandall, V. J. Children's belief in their control of reinforcement in intellectual-academic achievement situations. *Child Development*, 1965, *36*, 91-109.

Crandall, V. J., Katkovsky, W., & Preston, A. Motivational and ability determinants of young children's intellectual academic behaviors. *Child Development*, 1962, *33*, 643-661.

Crowne, D. P., & Liverant, S. Conformity under varying conditions of personal commitment. *Journal of Abnormal and Social Psychology*, 1963, *66*, 547-555.

Davis, W. L., & Phares, E. J. Internal-external control as a determinant of information-seeking in a social influence situation. *Journal of Personality*, 1967, *35*, 547-551.

deCharms, R. Personal causation training in the schools. *Journal of Applied Social Psychology*, 1972, *2*, 95-113.

Felixbrod, J. J., & O'Leary, K. D. Self-determination of academic standards by children: Toward freedom from external control. *Journal of Educational Psychology*, 1974, *66*, 845-850.

Fiedler, M. L. Bidirectionality of influence in classroom interaction. *Journal of Educational Psychology*, 1975, *67*, 735-744.

Glaser, R. *Adaptive education: Individual diversity and learning.* New York: Holt, Rinehart & Winston, 1977.

Glynn, E. L., Thomas, J. D., & Shee, S. H. Behavioral self-control of task behavior in an elementary classroom. *Journal of Applied Behavior Analysis,* 1973, *6,* 105–113.

Gore, P. M., & Rotter, J. B. A personality correlate of social action. *Journal of Personality,* 1963, *31,* 58–64.

Holden, K. B., & Rotter, J. B. A non-verbal measure of extinction in skill and chance situations. *Journal of Experimental Psychology,* 1962, *63,* 519–520.

Hunt, D. E., & Hardt, R. H. The effect of Upward Bound programs on the attitudes, motivation, and academic achievement of Negro students. *Journal of Social Issues,* 1969, *25*(3), 117–120.

James, W. H., & Rotter, J. B. Partial and 100 percent reinforcement under chance and skill conditions. *Journal of Experimental Psychology,* 1958, *55,* 397–403.

Kanfer, F. H. Maintenance of behavior by self-generated stimuli and reinforcement. In A. Jacobs, & L. B. Sachs (Eds.), *The Psychology of Private Events.* New York: Academic Press, 1971, 39–59.

Lefcourt, H. *Locus of control: Current trends in theory and research.* New York: Wiley, 1976.

Liverant, S., & Scodel, A. Internal and external control as determinants of decision making under conditions of risk. *Psychological Reports,* 1960, *7,* 59–67.

Mahoney, M. J., & Thoresen, C. E. *Self-control: Power to the person.* Monterey, California: Brooks/Cole Publishing Co., 1974.

McDermott, R. P. Social relations as contexts for learning. *Harvard Educational Review,* 1977, *47,* 198–213.

McLaughlin, T. F., & Malaby, J. E. Increasing and maintaining assignment completion with teacher and pupil controlled individual contingency programs: Three case studies. *Psychology,* 1974, *11*(3), 45–51.

Mischel, W., Zeiss, R., & Zeiss, A. Internal-external control and persistence: Validation and implications of the Stanford Preschool Internal-External Scale. *Journal of Personality and Social Psychology,* 1974, *29,* 265–278.

Mosteller, F., & Moynihan, D. P. (Eds.). *On equality of educational opportunity.* New York: Random House, 1972.

Nowicki, S., & Barnes, J. Effects of a structured camp experience on locus of control orientation of inner-city children. *Journal of Genetic Psychology,* 1973, *122,* 247–262.

Nowicki, S., & Walker, C. The role of generalized and specific expectancies in determining academic achievement. *Journal of Social Psychology,* 1974, *94,* 275–280.

Phares, E. J. Expectancy changes in skill and chance situations. *Journal of Abnormal and Social Psychology,* 1957, *54,* 339–342.

Phares, E. J. Differential utilization of information as a function of internal-external control. *Journal of Personality,* 1968, *36,* 649–662.

Pines, H. A., & Julian, J. W. Effects of task and social demands on locus of control differences in information processing. *Journal of Personality,* 1972, *40,* 407–416.

Reimanis, S. Effects of locus of reinforcement control modification procedures in early grades and college students. *Journal of Educational Research,* 1974, *68,* 124–127.

Resnick, L. B., & Wang, M. C. *Improvement of academic performance of poor-prognosis children through the use of an individualized instructional program* (LRDC Publication 1974/2). Pittsburgh, Pa.: University of Pittsburgh, Learning Research and Development Center, 1974.

Ross, S., & Zimiles, H. The differentiated child behavior observational system. In M. C. Wang (Ed.), *The use of direct observation to study instructional-learning behaviors in school settings* (LRDC Publication 1974/9). Pittsburgh, Pa.: University of Pittsburgh, Learning Research and Development Center, 1974.

Rotter, J. B. Generalized expectancies for internal versus external control of reinforcement. *Psychological Monographs,* 1966, *80* (1, Whole No. 609).

Rotter, J. B., Liverant, S., & Crowne, D. P. The growth and extinction of expectancies in chance controlled and skilled tasks. *Journal of Psychology,* 1961, *52,* 161–177.

Sagotsky, G., Patterson, C. J., & Lepper, M. Training children's self-control: A field experiment in self-monitoring and goal setting in the classroom. *Journal of Experimental Child Psychology,* 1978, *25,* 242–253.

Seeman, M. Alienation and social learning in a reformatory. *American Journal of Sociology,* 1963, *69,* 270–284.

Shaw, R. L., & Uhl, N. P. Control of reinforcement and academic achievement. *Journal of Educational Research,* 1971, *64,* 226–228.

Shore, M. F., Milgram, N. A., & Malasky, C. The effectiveness of an enrichment program for disadvantaged young children. *American Journal of Orthopsychiatry,* 1971, *41,* 442–449.

Stallings, J. A., & Kaskowitz, D. H. *Follow Through classroom observation evaluation, 1972–1973.* Stanford Research Institute, Report prepared for Division of Elementary and Secondary Programs, Office of Planning, U.S. Office of Education, 1974.

Stephens, M. W. *Cognitive and cultural determinants of early IE development.* Paper presented at the annual meeting of the American Psychological Association, Washington, D.C., 1971.

Tuchman, B., Cochran, D., & Travers, E. *Evaluating the open classroom.* A paper presented at the annual meeting of the American Educational Research Association, New Orleans, 1973.

Uguroglu, M. E., & Walberg, H. J. Motivation and achievement: A quantitative syntheses. *American Educational Research Journal,* 1979, *16*(4), 375–389.

Wang, M. C. *The rationale and design of the Self-Schedule System* (LRDC Publication 1974/5). Pittsburgh, Pa.: University of Pittsburgh, Learning Research and Development Center, 1974.(a)

Wang, M. C. *The self-responsibility interview schedule.* Pittsburgh, Pa.: University of Pittsburgh, Learning Research and Development Center, 1974.(b)

Wang, M. C. The use of observational data for formative evaluation of an instructional model. In M. C. Wang (Ed.), *The use of direct observation to study instructional-learning behaviors in school settings* (LRDC Publication 1974/9). Pittsburgh, Pa.: University of Pittsburgh, Learning Research and Development Center, 1974.(c)

Wang, M. C. (Ed.). *The Self-Schedule System for instructional-learning management in adaptive school learning environments* (LRDC Publication 1976/9). Pittsburgh, Pa.: University of Pittsburgh, Learning Research and Development Center, 1976.

Wang, M. C. Maximizing the effective use of school time by teachers and students. *Contemporary Educational Psychology,* 1979, *4,* 187–201. (b)

Wang, M. C. *The development and consequences of the student's sense of personal control: Implications for designing mainstreaming programs for exceptional children.* Working paper, 1979.(c)

Wang, M. C. Adaptive instruction: Building on diversity. *Theory into Practice,* 1980, *19*(2), 122–128.

Wang, M. C. *Providing effective "special education" In regular classrooms: A possibility in the 1980's.* Invited paper presentation at the Northeast Regional Deans' Grants Conference, New York, December 1981. (a)

Wang, M. C. *Maximizing the use of school time: Some program design implications for adaptive instruction.* Paper presented at the national invitational conference on "Instructional Time and Student Achievement," Chicago, Illinois, May 1981, conference proceedings in preparation. (b)

Wang, M. C. Mainstreaming exceptional children: Some instructional design considerations. *Elementary School Journal,* 1981, *81*(4), pp. 195–221. (c)

Wang, M. C., & Brictson, P. *An observational investigation of classroom instructional-learning behaviors under two different classroom management systems.* A paper presented at the annual meeting of the American Educational Research Association, New Orleans, 1973.

Wang, M. C., Leinhart, G., & Boston, M. E. *The Individualized Early Learning Program* (LRDC Publication 1980/2). Pittsburgh, Pa.: University of Pittsburgh, Learning Research and Development Center, 1980.

Wang, M. C., Mazza, M., Haines, J., & Johnson, M. *Some measured effects of a classroom management model designed for an individualized early learning curriculum.* Paper presented at the annual meeting of the American Educational Research Association, Chicago, 1972.

Wang, M. C., & Resnick, L. B. *The primary education program (PEP).* Johnstown, Pa.: Mafex Associates, Inc., 1979.

Wang, M. C., Resnick, L. B., & Boozer, R. The sequence of development of some early mathematics behaviors. *Child Development,* 1971, *42* (6), 1767-1778.

Wang, M. C., & Richardson, B. L. *The Self-Schedule System: Its effects on students' and teachers' classroom behaviors and attitudes.* Paper presented at the annual meeting of the American Educational Research Association, New York, 1977.

Wang, M. C., & Schorling, L. *Learner control of instruction: Student choice and behavior characteristics.* A paper presented at the annual meeting of the American Educational Research Association, New York, 1977.

Wang, M. C., & Stiles, B. An investigation of children's concept of self-responsibility for their school learning. *American Educational Research Journal,* 1976, *13*(3), 159-179. (a)

Wang, M. C., & Stiles, B. Effects of the Self-Schedule System on teacher and student behaviors. In M. C. Wang (Ed.), *The Self-Schedule System for instructional-learning management in adaptive school learning environments* (LRDC Publication 1976/9). Pittsburgh, Pa.: University of Pittsburgh, Learning Research and Development Center, 1976. (b)

Wang, M. C., & Yeager, J. L. The evaluation of student progress under individualized instruction. *The Elementary School Journal,* 1971, *71*(8), reprinted by Educational Technology Publications, 1972, also Halstead and Bradley, *The Beginning Elementary School Teacher in Action.* Texas: North Texas State University Press, 1973.

Weiner, B. A theory of motivation for some classroom experiences. *Journal of Educational Psychology,* 1979, *71*(1), 3-25.

Weisstein, W. J., & Wang, M. C. *An investigation of classroom interactions between academically gifted and learning disabled children with their teachers.* Paper presented at the annual meeting of the American Educational Research Association, Toronto, 1978.

Weisstein, W. J., & Wang, M. C. *An investigation of the effects of teacher perceptions on high and low achievers.* A paper presented at the annual meeting of the American Educational Research Association, Boston, 1980.

Wolfgang, A., & Potwin, R. Internality as a determinant of degree of classroom participation and academic performance among elementary students. *Proceedings of the 81st Annual Convention of the American Psychological Association,* Montreal, Canada, 1973, *8,* 611-612. (Abstract)

10 Modeling Young Children's Performance Expectations

Doris R. Entwisle
The Johns Hopkins University

Leslie Alec Hayduk
University of Alberta

Pupils, teachers, learning. Today schooling occupies a dominant place in children's lives in almost all societies. This chapter is chiefly about how early school experiences may affect young children's ideas about their own academic competence.

Schooling, in addition to providing a vocation for persons too young to work, is a cornerstone of stratification. The question of the extent to which schooling supports occupational stratification has not been answered to everyone's satisfaction, but clearly it could have some substantial role in the process. Knowledge is lacking, however, about exactly how schooling effects occur and under what conditions children can better or worsen their chances for success in school, even though such knowledge is essential for understanding stratification in industrial and developing societies more generally.

It is a fact that relatively few lower-class persons use education as a route to upward mobility. To review the many explanations put forward to account for the correlations between social class and school achievement is a huge task, far too big a task for us to undertake here, because it is one that would take a book in itself. We can note, however, that explanations tend to polarize around either a genetic or an environmental base. To focus directly on these issues may be premature, however, until one looks carefully at the schooling process to see what, in fact, it actually consists of. If well understood, schooling might be turned in a direction to counteract *either* hereditary or environmental deficits.

It appears that a promising route to improving the life chances of underachievers lies in the direction of a better understanding of the schooling process. The problem is not a "minority" problem; it is a scientific problem. The folly of focusing narrowly on black-white differences, or any other majority-minority difference, should be apparent from the observation that some minorities, notably Orientals, as a group do well in school. The same conclusion is suggested by the observation that some individual blacks, some individual Indians, and some individual Hispanics do well in school. Schooling occurs in schools. The process of schooling, however, and not schools themselves should be the target of study, as Heyns (1978) points out.

Later success or failure in school, and even general life chances, could be shaped by children's experiences in the early grades. National (Krause, 1973) and cross-national (Husen, 1969) data testify that by the end of third grade, children have sorted themselves into achievement trajectories that they will more or less pursue for the rest of their lives. Other data at the classroom level, now beginning to appear, suggest that the way children are treated in first grade affects their progress in second grade (Rist, 1970) and even their functioning as adults many decades later (Pederson, Faucher, & Eaton, 1978).

We suspect that self-expectations are critical for academic development, because forecasts for the self likely filter, color, and even determine a child's experiences. In most classrooms a child is repeatedly compared with 20 or 30 children of the same age. The net residue of these comparisons is thought to shape the child's self-evaluation, variously termed the self-concept, self-image, or "expectations." If children think they will do well, they will be glad to try. If, however, they think they will do poorly, they are apt to hang back and avoid doing the very things that will help them learn. Low expectations, furthermore, are infectious. Persons who hold low expectations for themselves encourage others to do likewise.

The Case Studies

In order to develop and test our ideas about schooling we undertook three extensive case studies in which we followed a large number of children through the first three grades of three different elementary schools. Each case study focused on a particular school: a white middle-class suburban school, a lower-class urban integrated school, and a lower-class black urban school. Each school is unique, yet in our view each serves as an exemplar of a kind of school presently found in many areas of the United States. Since it seems plausible that long-term cultural learning opportunities may lead to stable differences in both attainment and self-image, we hoped to gain insight into what affects young children's early school experience by looking in detail at what happened to children as they progressed through the first three grades in the distinct environment that each of these schools provided. We wanted to see, among other things, whether the process of schooling was different depending on the social context. Our choice of variables and hypotheses was based on a number of considerations arising from theory and from identification of particular gaps in the empirical literature in sociology and education, but was mainly motivated by our wish to understand the basic nature of the schooling process for children beginning their school careers.

There is little information available on young children's expectations, however, or on such things as the expectations parents have for their first-grade children or how parents' expectations relate to children's characteristics. Even precisely how first-grade children's gender relates to their performance is unclear. Reading failures in first grade are often estimated to be 90% male and 10% female, but to our knowledge there is no literature addressing the issue of a possible sex bias in teachers' early evaluations. Findings reported in this chapter, based on case studies of single schools, cannot necessarily be generalized to the population at large. Hopefully, however, the data will shed some light on process: how expectations of significant others and expectations of children themselves may affect the children's achievement and academic self-image in the early grades.

This chapter focuses mainly on children's self-expectations and the modeling strategies we used to examine the impact of children's expectations on the schooling process. The discussion concerns mainly two of the schools, the white middle-class school and integrated lower-class school.

The Research Strategy

This research began with pilot studies of children's expectations in the late '60s. Work from 1971–74 is summarized in *Too Great Expectations* (Entwisle & Hayduk, 1978) and the entire project will be covered in a book by the same authors (Entwisle & Hayduk, in press (b)). Much of the research effort over the years has been directed at devising models to represent the process of early schooling. Although these models are reminiscent of those used by sociologists for research on secondary-school educational attainment, the resemblance is more apparent than real because our models are cyclic and the process of schooling, rather than levels of attainment, is the target of explanation.

The models conceptualize a child's self-expectations as affective outcomes and also consider a child's mark in conduct as an affective outcome. Performance in reading and arithmetic (cognitive outcomes) are also considered. The purpose of the models is to explain both kinds of outcomes. A critical feature of the models is that the two kinds of outcomes are assumed to act upon each other. It seems reasonable that a child's expectations should affect performance or achievement; but the reverse may also occur—achievement should affect expectations. And conduct must affect reading and arithmetic achievement—the child who is behaving cannot attend to the lesson of the day—and there could be effects *from* reading and arithmetic to conduct. A child whose marks lead him to feel he is not doing well may misbehave either because of frustration or boredom.

The models are "mid-range"—the individual is nested in a classroom, and significant others include the teacher and classroom peers. This focus differs from macro-studies (where the school is taken as the unit of analysis) and from micro-studies (where individuals are the unit of analysis with no notice taken of the social structure in which the student functions). Recent literature suggests this strategy may be important. Lately several studies have appeared suggesting that effects in elementary school show teacher differences (e.g. Berkeley, 1978; Brookover et al., 1978; Murnane, 1975; Pedersen et al., 1978; Summers & Wolfe, 1977) which we take as indication of the need to preserve the social context in which the student functions. Also secondary-school researchers are saying that a time earlier in the life cycle than the secondary level may be a better place to look for school effects (Alwin and Otto, 1977) and that models conceptualized in terms of two-wave panels are unlikely to mirror the process of schooling (see Hauser, 1978; Sorenson & Hallinan, 1977 and related commentary). Multi-wave data like ours are probably essential. Fortunately, as these reports began to surface, we were completing work with the large longitudinal sample of first-, second-, and third-grade children reported on here which explicitly addresses all these issues.

THE DATA

In the space available it is impossible to provide a complete description of the sample and its characteristics, or complete definitions of the variables that were measured. (More complete information is available in Entwisle and Hayduk, in press (a), and Entwisle and Hayduk, in press (b).) However, as mentioned previously, all children enrolling in first grade for several years in the case-study schools were followed, insofar as possible, to the end of third grade.

At several points in the school year we obtained data pertaining to each child from several different respondents within a time frame dictated by substantive concerns (see Figure 10.1). For instance, we asked parents in the early fall of the first-grade year how well they expected their children to perform in reading, arithmetic, and conduct before any formal school evaluations were given to parents about children's performances in those areas and before we asked children for their own expectations. Other measures were likewise taken at points in the school year dictated by consideration of the schooling process. The models are summarized by semester (Figures 10.2, 10.3 and 10.4) but the measures were obtained at times corresponding to positions along the time line in Figure 10.1.

Our research was undertaken with the realization that some of its methodological features are not ideal. The sample is purposive, not random. However, we felt that to have any hope of understanding the interplay of events and outcomes for such young children, rich data would be needed and measurements would have to be taken as close as possible to the time when critical events occurred. Children, for instance, have been asked about how well they expected to do in reading and arithmetic *before* they received their first marks in those subjects. At the end of the school year one could not ask first-grade children to recall, let alone verbalize, exactly how they felt about their first marks when they had been in school only 2 months. And it is probably wise to ask parents about their expectations early in the first-grade year as well.

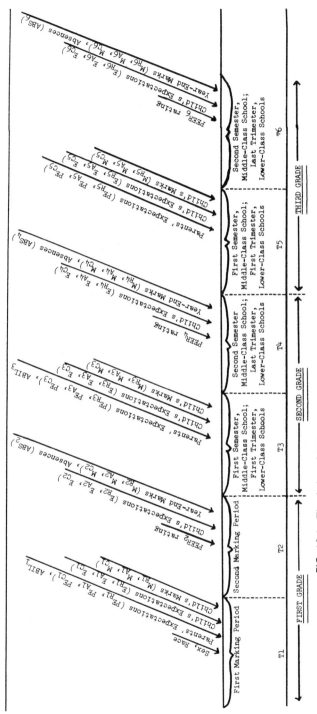

FIG. 10.1 The timing of data collection

253

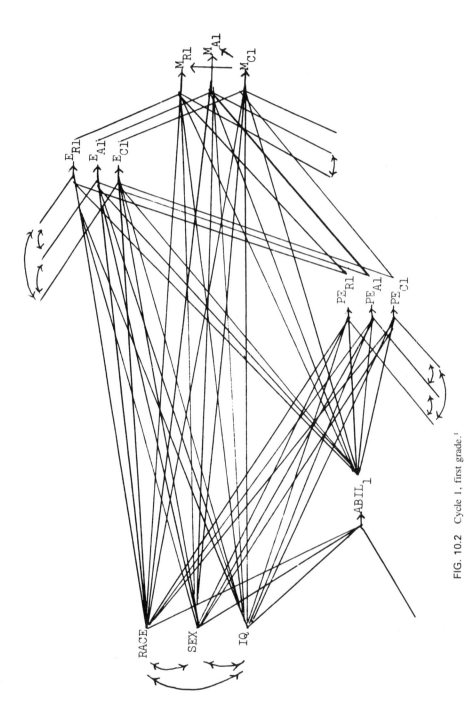

FIG. 10.2   Cycle 1, first grade.[1]

[1]Only in the irtegrated lower-class school was Race included as an exogenous variable.

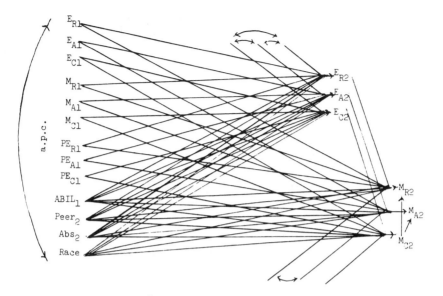

FIG. 10.3   Cycle 2, first grade.[2]

[2]Only in the integrated lower-class school was Race included as an exogenous variable. a.p.c. denotes the inclusion of all the possible correlations between these variables.

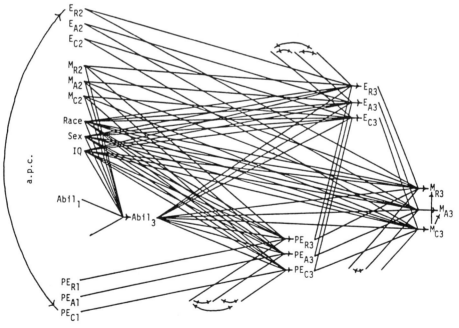

FIG. 10.4   Cycle 3, second grade[a]

[a]Only in the integrated lower-class school was Race included as an exogenous variable. a.p.c. denotes the inclusion of all the possible correlations between these variables.

TABLE 10.1
Maryland Accountability Program Report Statistics

	School Enrollment	Pupil Staff Ratio	Average Daily Attendance (%)	Average Experience of Teachers (Years)	Staff Masters Degree or Above (%)	% Disadvantaged	Mother's Median Education	Median Family Income
1973-1974								
White Middle-Class School	659	20.7	97.1	10.1	28.3	2.2	12.5	$14,869
Integrated Lower-Class School	784	24.9	88.8	11.1	28.6	29.3	10.0	7,435
Black Lower-Class School	776	25.0	92.3	14.1	19.3	26.8	10.0	7,952
1974-1975								
White Middle-Class School	644	21.6	96.4	11.4	26.8	2.1	12.4	$14,868
Integrated Lower-Class School	742	22.8	87.5	9.4	18.5	29.4	9.9	7,434
Black Lower-Class School	720	22.1	91.7	14.0	24.5	26.8	10.0	7,951

TABLE 10.2
Number of Students Entering and Departing from Study

	Time Interval				
	T1-T2	T2-T3	T3-T4	T4-T5	T5-T6
White Middle-Class School					
Enter	423	8	56	8	46
Depart	13	35	9	20	1
Integrated Lower-Class School					
Enter	438	33	65	22	30
Depart	22	65	24	49	17
Black Lower-Class School					
Enter	285	19	49	6	38
Depart	11	33	10	32	6

The age of the respondents has many implications for data collection. It was usually necessary to secure written permission in advance from the child's parent to include the child in the study. Since all participation at every level is voluntary, an enormous amount of time was invested in public relations, answering parents' and teachers' questions and the like, and in making sure that the rights of these small children were respected. When young children are studied there has to be a trade-off between "independent" units and validity or completeness of response. Our sample, which consists of all children enrolled in first grade of three schools for 5 successive years, has obvious drawbacks. It also had advantages. For research at this stage and of this type, we felt we had no real alternative.

The socioeconomic characteristics of the case-study schools can be judged from Table 10.1. The integrated and black schools were closely matched in terms of clients. All schools were similar in quality of staff. Table 10.2 summarizes sample composition. Yearly cohorts of students were aggregated to provide a case base of sufficient size to support estimation of the models.

THE MODELS

Models for the first three cycles, given in Figures 10.2, 10.3, and 10.4, are roughly matched to the first three semesters of elementary school. Three more models, matched to the fourth, fifth, and sixth semesters of elementary school, are not shown here but are analogous in every respect.

These structural models are designed to explicate the process of early schooling. Data to estimate the models were procured from children nested in classrooms. In Cycle 1, which is matched to the time the child begins first grade, three exogenous variables (Race, Sex, and IQ) are identified. The variables are presumed to have direct effects on all endogenous variables, including ABIL (the parent's conception of the child's general ability to do school work), PE (the parent's expectation for the quality of the child's school performance in reading, arithmetic, and conduct), E (the child's own expectations in reading, arithmetic, and conduct), M_C (the child's mark in conduct) and ultimately on performance in reading and arithmetic as measured by teachers' marks (M_R and M_A). Figure 10.1 makes it clear that each of these variables was measured at a time consistent with its position in the set of structural equations. For example, status characteristics of children (race, sex), present before the child enters first grade, could affect the child's earliest expectations. They are inserted in the model ahead of children's expectations.

To measure children's expectations, just before their earliest report cards were issued in first grade, children were queried about their expectations for their forthcoming marks in reading, in arithmetic, and in conduct. Children were presumed to have some notion of how well they would perform in each area. During an individual interview the children were asked to "play a game" guessing the marks their forthcoming report card would show in reading, in arithmetic, and in conduct. Great care was taken that the children understood the task and understood the meaning of both "marks" and "report cards." This interview provided data for Time 1 (T1) expectations. Later in first grade, just before the year-end report card was issued, children were again individually interviewed and asked to make the same kinds of guesses concerning the marks they expected to receive on the last report card of that school year. The second interview provided Time 2 (T2) children's expectations.

Parents filled out a questionnaire which, among other things, asked the parent to rate the child's general ability to do school work compared to other children in his class. In addition the parents of each child were also presumed to have expectations for how well the child would perform in each of three areas, and parents were asked to "guess the mark your child will receive in reading, in arithmetic, and in conduct." Data were gathered only once a year from parents, usually by interviewers, shortly before the first report card was issued. (Children were interviewed twice a year.) Parents recorded their guesses on stylized replicas of the report cards in use in the school at the time. When necessary, interviewers interpreted to the parents the marking standards used by the school and answered parents' questions.

Children's gender, their marks in reading, arithmetic, and conduct, and their IQ scores, were ascertained from school records.

Marks on the first report card in first grade are "T1 marks." Marks on the last report card in first grade are "T2 marks." Both marks and expectations were recorded on a scale from 1 to 4, with 1 indicating a high mark or expectation.

The first-cycle model (Figure 10.2) sets the stage for a second model showing how expectation levels and marks change over the rest of the first-grade year (Figure 10.3). The outputs of Figure 10.2 serve as inputs for Figure 10.3.

This division of the school year into two separate time periods allows successive linear models to be used for investigating feedback. Note particularly that the models, as well as being adapted for modeling causal processes, allow for non-stationarity. (See Huggins & Entwisle, 1968.) That is, there is no assumption that the structural coefficients linking similar variables, say expectations and marks, are non-varying at every stage in the schooling process. The position of each variable in the model is exactly specified by time. Parents' expectations appear before children's expectations and were measured ahead of them. Children's expectations appear before marks and were measured before report cards were issued, and so on.

At the end of each cycle, two different cognitive measures, marks in reading and arithmetic, were examined.

Reading and arithmetic are the core areas of the elementary curriculum, but they differ from each other in the kinds of capabilities presumed to underlie competence and in the socialization practices (say in sex-role expectancies) that may affect early performance. The conduct mark directly precedes the marks in reading and arithmetic in the model on the assumption that deportment in the classroom affects performance in at least two ways: (1) the child who is not sitting still or attending to the lesson may not learn as well. (2) The teacher may be biased in her evaluation of reading or arithmetic performance according to the child's classroom conduct. Conduct represents non-cognitive factors that may affect performance in the two academic subjects, but it is also of interest in itself as an indicator of affective development. Furthermore in the first cycle this mark precedes the other two marks because it is reasonable to assume that conduct affects performance (rather than the other way around) until the time the first mark is issued. Later effects of marks in reading and arithmetic on conduct are indirect, being mediated through either children's or parents' expectations.

The exogenous variables, sex and IQ, are assumed to exert separate direct effects on parents' general ability estimates (ABIL), on parents' expectations (PE) in each area, on children's expectations in each of the three areas (E_R, E_A, E_C) and on each mark (reading (M_R), arithmetic (M_A), conduct (M_C)).

The possibility for sex and/or IQ to exert separate causal effects is clear. Gender effects, for example, could arise because parents and teachers often expect girls to learn to read more easily than boys (Palardy, 1969). IQ effects may occur because tested mental ability could be seen as relevant to performance in arithmetic but not to performance in conduct.

The paths starting from the parents' general ability estimate indicate that these estimates may affect parents' expectations in particular areas (parents who think their children have high ability to do schoolwork in general need not expect their children to be particularly well in arithmetic). Also the parents' general ability estimate is presumed to affect children's expectations and children's marks. Parents who have high general ability estimates may convey this impression to the child and thus encourage high expectations in the child; also they may convey this impression to the teacher and thus influence her evaluation (the child's mark).

The paths starting from parents' expectations indicate that parental expectations may influence both children's expectations and their marks. This could come about either by direct socialization or by parents and children sharing the same home environment, or by both. For instance, parents who hold high reading expectations for their children may provide books for their children. Likewise, parents can influence performance (as reflected in marks) through direct coaching or by way of an otherwise supportive home environment.

No direct effects are assumed to exist among the triplicate variables (reading, arithmetic, and conduct) within clusters of children's or parents' expectations. That is, children's expectations in reading are not assumed to affect their expectations in arithmetic, or the reverse. But, as previously mentioned, direct effects are assumed between marks in conduct and marks in reading and arithmetic. (The implied lack of causal ordering among the triplicate expectation variables and between marks in reading and arithmetic prevent the model from being fully recursive.)

There are no across-area effects of parental expectations on later endogenous variables. The lack of direct effects from parents' expectations for reading to arithmetic marks, for example, reflects a contention that parental expectations are "area specific." The triplicate paths leading from the exogenous variables to parental expectations provide for the development of three distinct expectations, and the parallel paths arising from parental expectations maintain the distinct causal efficacy of these separate expectations. This distinct-area assumption, maintained throughout the models with respect to expectations in the three academic areas, was adopted because there is considerable prior evidence of its validity (see Entwisle & Hayduk, 1978) and also because parents' expectations for reading or arithmetic may respond rather differently to gender.

This assumption greatly simplifies the model and reduces the number of free parameters to be estimated. The clustered disturbance terms indicate that greater consistency is expected between areas than can be accounted for by the exogenous variables, however. Teachers, for example, do tend to assign similar marks in reading and arithmetic. Sets of expectations of all actors might also be made similar by internalized demands for psychological consistency. Additionally, since the clustered variables were measured at a single time, the correlated disturbance terms would also capture any situational consistency produced by the single measurement situation.

A child's marks and expectations may remain constant or change over time, namely from T1, the time of the first report card in first grade, to T2, the time of the last report card in first grade. One way to model such over-time data is to allow each of the earlier observations on marks and expectations to influence the later observations on these variables directly, as indicated in Figure 10.3. That is, marks at T1 are assumed to influence marks at T2 (teachers tend to give similar marks from one time to the next and/or children's performance tends to be of the same quality over the year) and marks at T1 also influence expectations at T2 (children who do better than they expected may raise their expectations; children who do worse than they expected may lower their expectations). In addition, expectations at T1 may influence expectations at T2 (children may be consistent) and expectations at both T1 and T2 may influence marks (if children expect to do well this may cause them to do well).

In Figure 10.3 two additional variables, a within-classroom popularity rating (PEER$_2$) and the number of times the child was absent during first grade (ABS$_2$), are also included. Peer popularity was measured late in the school year, but prior to the time year-end expectations were procured. The number of absences for each child pertains to the entire school year, but most absences obviously had occurred prior to the year-end expectation measurements because expectations were obtained in late May-early June.

The inputs shown in Figure 10.3, which is matched to the latter part of the first-grade year, include all the endogenous variables of Figure 10.2 plus the measures of peer ratings and absences.

The inputs shown in Figure 10.4, for the first part of second grade, include a repetition of the exogenous variables of the first cycle, i.e. Race, Sex, and IQ. The rationale is that a new teacher in second grade may be affected by these characteristics in a quite different way from the grade one teacher. For example, the first-grade teacher may have biased her evaluations in line with gender (giving girls higher marks in conduct) whereas the second-grade teacher could be blind to gender. In addition parent variables from the first cycle plus expectation and mark variables from the second cycle appear as inputs.

This brief overview is enough to indicate some of the models' important features, and the major ones of interest in this chapter are that children's initial expectations are assumed to shape performance but that subsequently expectations and performance are linked in feedback loops—expectations affect performance, but after the initial cycle performance affects expectations. In addition, by studying childrens' expectations over time and evaluating their response to parents' expectations, the child's gender, and so on, changes in expectations are evaluated net of these variables. If children's expectations change from the first to the second cycle, for instance, that change is evaluated net of the influence of background factors. The measurement error structure is not shown in the diagrams, but reliability estimates were attached to every variable in the models and incorporated in the estimation process since parameter estimates can be biased unless errors in measurement are acknowledged. (See Entwisle & Hayduk, in press (b), for details of the measurement model.)

The main point of the discussion in this chapter is the structure of the models and the light this structure sheds on the process of expectation formation and maintenance in young children. The impact of expectations upon children's early performance is also of interest. With models estimated separately for each school it is possible to get some idea of whether the process of expectation development is different from one school to the other. Interest is *not* directed at differential achievement levels (impossible to consider with teachers' marks as the criterion) but rather is directed at how school experience may shape children's expectations differently in various schools.

A word is in order about how models were estimated and the advantages these models enjoy compared to other alternatives.

LISREL (Jöreskog & Sörbom, 1978), a program that provides maximum likelihood estimates of the parameters in sets of structural equations, was the major strategy used in data reduction. This program is extremely versatile since it allows for correlation among the input variables, measurement error, and correlations among disturbance terms. It also will provide estimates geared to reciprocal causation so that, for example, it was possible for us to explore the reasonableness of assuming that initial marks responded to initial expectations rather than the other way around.

The LISREL program is marvelously adapted to exploratory work like ours. The matter of reciprocal causality has already been mentioned. Other changes in structure are also easy to evaluate. For one example, all of the preliminary runs were carried out without putting in the measurement structure, but it was easy to insert when final models had been picked. For another example, in early work we conceived of children's marks in reading, arithmetic, and conduct as triplicate variables with correlated disturbance terms, but later altered the model so as to conceive of performance in conduct as a cause of the other marks in any one cycle (children's performances in reading and arithmetic may be interfered with if they are misbehaving and/or teachers may bias their evaluations of academic performance in line with children's deportment). The LISREL program also facilitated an analytic strategy of random subsample replicates that can only be mentioned here in passing. All pruning of models was carried out on only one half of the data, reserving the second half as a "fresh" set to test the models finally decided upon. This strategy greatly strengthens our confidence in the structure of the models.

A FEW FINDINGS

To the extent one may place confidence in the findings, the process of schooling does look somewhat different across schools. On the other hand, there is a comforting consistency from school to school in that the variables included in the model turned out to be the same from school to school and from year to year. There is thus consistency over time as well as across schools.

As Table 10.3 shows, children's expectations for their own performance are increasingly responsive to prior variables with the passage of time. At the beginning of first grade, very little of the variance in expectations can be accounted

TABLE 10.3
Coefficients of Determination

	T1			T2			T3			T4			T5			T6		
	Read.	Arith.	Cond.	Read.	Arith.	Cond.	Read.	Arith.	Cond.	Read.	Arith.	Cond.	Read.	Arith.	Cond.	Read.	Arith.	Cond.
Children's Expectations (E)																		
White Middle-Class School	5.1	8.8	6.3	12.6	15.8	14.5	11.3	28.7	21.3	16.9	14.1	17.8	19.3	35.0	29.0	35.5	29.4	22.4
Integrated Lower-Class School	6.0	6.3	1.6	12.5	15.0	16.6	20.7	37.0	30.0	18.3	24.1	16.6	20.2	13.3	31.0[b]	7.6	12.7	27.6[b]
Black Lower-Class School	3.5	14.1	5.6	27.0	11.3	23.0	[c]	[c]		[a]	13.0	31.2[b]	28.8	12.1	10.0[b]	18.1	25.3	29.5
Marks (M)																		
White Middle-Class School	18.4	20.4	31.4	37.4	44.2	57.3	43.0	37.0	31.0	52.4	55.5	59.0	38.0	22.2	19.9	47.9	39.9	48.2
Integrated Lower-Class School	57.5	35.1	23.9	76.5	64.4	64.2	88.8	51.5	52.5	56.6	69.8	64.8	77.8	48.2	35.5[b]	44.5	59.1	55.1[b]
Black Lower-Class School	24.3	63.0	18.0	34.1	56.9	63.6	[c]	[c]		82.0	74.7	52.7[b]	62.8	50.7	6.7[b]	85.1	73.8	62.6
Parents' Expectations (PE)																		
White Middle-Class School	56.8	55.3	19.8				50.5	44.4	48.7				64.4	47.9	40.2			
Integrated Lower-Class School	35.3	36.1	4.7				39.8	22.7	29.8				34.3	34.7	33.3[b]			
Black Lower-Class School	36.4	25.1	25.5				[c]	[c]					52.8	54.9	22.0[b]			

[a] E_{R4} had to be eliminated.

[b] These parameters are from a model that did not provide a satisfactory χ^2.

[c] Model could not be estimated because covariance matrix was singular.

263

for. Expectations are largely amorphous. Expectations are better explained by the end of the year, however. This suggests that children's expectations may not be well-formed at the start of school, and more importantly, perhaps, that children's expectations develop as a consequence of school experience. The amount of explained variance in children's expectations does not appear to differ across schools. It seems reasonable also that much more of the variance in parents' expectations than in children's expectations should be explained by prior variables.

The picture for marks is different from the picture for expectations. For one thing, all along much more variance is being explained—by the end of first grade around 50% of the variance in arithmetic marks is being explained in all three schools (Table 10.3). For another thing, the amount of explained variance differs by school, with generally less mark variance explained in the middle-class school compared to the other two schools.

Space does not permit more than one limited example of the results of the analyses as far as the determinants of children's expectations are concerned. Figures 10.5 and 10.6 provide estimates of the models given in Figures 10.2 and 10.3 separately for the white and integrated schools. In Figures 10.5 and 10.6 only paths exceeding 1.5 times their standard error are drawn, although all parameters shown in Figures 10.2 and 10.3 were included in the maximum likelihood solutions.

In these models, as mentioned above, children's initial expectations are not very responsive to prior variables. However, as the second-cycle models for both schools reveal, expectations early in the school year are determinants of expectations later in the year. There are paths for middle-class children from E_{R1} and E_{C1} to E_{R2} and E_{C2}. There are also paths for lower-class children from E_{A1} and E_{C1} to E_{A2} and E_{C2}, respectively.

Children's expectations are linked to marks only occasionally, however, implying that in both these schools, first-grade children's expectations for themselves are erratic predictors of performance. If these findings are taken at face value, the implication is that children's ideas about their own capability are not strong determinants of performance level at this age.

Among the many implications of Figures 10.5 and 10.6, and a critical one, is that in the diagram for the middle-class school there are paths from both of the first marks in reading and conduct (M_{R1} and M_{C1}) to year-end expectations (E_{R2} and E_{C2}). By contrast, none of the parameters linking first marks to later expectations is significant in the integrated school. (This finding is seen in every cycle). In the middle-class school, feedback from marks modulates children's expectations, and in the lower-class integrated school it does not. Children in the lower-class school are apparently not using feedback from teachers' marks to modify their own expectations for the future. Without taking notice of evaluations in relation to ideas of their own competence, these children can maintain unrealistic ideas about their capabilities, and, in fact, in this school children's expectations remain

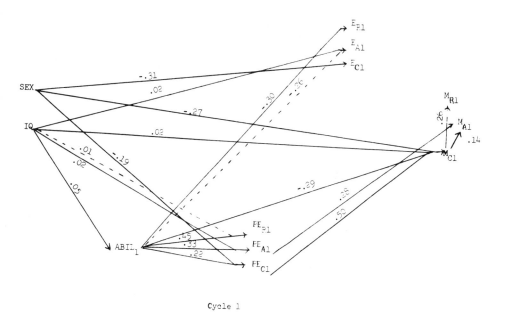

Cycle 1

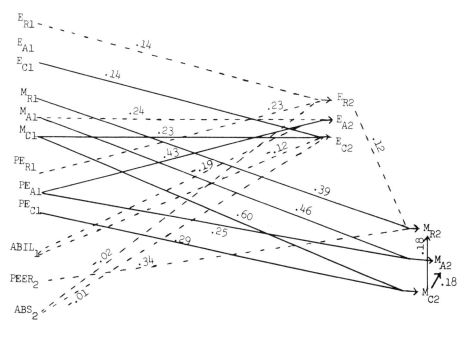

Cycle 2

FIG. 10.5 Models for two cycles, first grade white middle-class school.

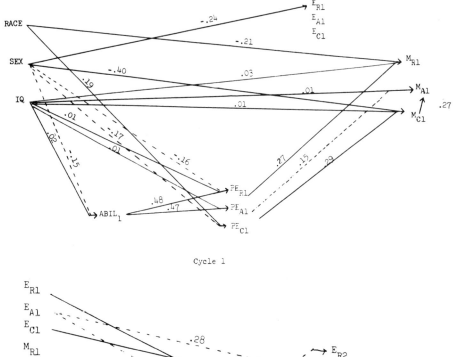

Cycle 1

Cycle 2

FIG. 10.6 Models for two cycles, first grade integrated lower-class school.

266

much higher than their marks over the first three grades. By contrast, in the middle-class school, children's expectations decline somewhat and come into line with their marks.

In *Too Great Expectations* we note that expectations of lower-class and/or minority-group children are higher than expectations of their middle-class counterparts and that, perplexingly, these expectations do not decline much in spite of very discouraging feedback. The structural models shown here in Figures 10.5 and 10.6 suggest that children's expectations respond to different forces in the two schools.

Insofar as it can be examined, the influence of race on expectations appears unimportant.

A little discussion is now provided based on the entire data set, that is on the full set of findings, not just Figures 10.5 and 10.6.

In some respects the relationships among expectations and marks lie at the heart of the models. The impact of expectations on marks and the subsequent feedback from marks to expectations we see as key elements in a dynamic process shaping achievement. Obviously by sampling marks and expectations twice a year we used only a few discrete points in time in order to sample variables that are continuously interacting. But the careful timing of our observations helped considerably in the specification of causal orders. Furthermore, both the first order partial derivatives and some estimation of backward paths (from M_1 to E_1, for example) suggest that the model is properly specified, with children's expectations acting as a causal force on marks within the first time period rather than the other way around. After the first cycle, of course, there is opportunity in every cycle for marks to impact on expectations at any subsequent time as well as for expectations to influence marks.

In the overall analysis for the entire set of data, two themes stand out: first, in the middle-class school, children's expectations come increasingly into line with marks, but this is not the case in the lower-class schools; second, a lack of paths from marks at one time to expectations at the next time is characteristic of the structural models for both lower-class schools, but such paths are consistently present in the middle-class school. The implication is that feedback is processed in one place but not in the others.

The difference between the schools in how marks at one time affect expectations at a subsequent time is striking. In the middle-class school it is the rule that previous marks shape later expectations, especially within any one year. In other words, mark feedback is processed. In the lower-class schools, on the other hand, there are only a few borderline-size coefficients connecting marks with subsequent expectations and several reversals in sign. In the middle-class school children get better and better at anticipating their marks in all three areas, with the errors of being too optimistic or too pessimistic being about equally frequent. From about the end of second grade on, most children in the middle-class school forecast their mark correctly, and the proportion of those expecting to do better than they actually do is about equal to the proportion of those who expect to do worse than they do.

This kind of symmetry around a set of frequently-correct estimates is not seem in the data for the lower-class schools. There, few children make correct estimates, and a very large proportion of children do worse than they expected, particularly in reading. Furthermore, although the number displaying the maximal discrepancies between expectations and marks decreases over time, at the end of third grade more than 25% of the children are still off by two units or more in their forecasts in both reading and arithmetic in these schools. For example, 28% of the children in the integrated school either expect an A while getting a C, or expect a B while getting a D. This information, together with the information derived from the parameter estimates showing how marks affect subsequent expectations, suggests that marks are being well-processed by children in the middle-class school and that marks are poorly processed in the two lower-class schools.

All in all, the models clarify the nature of some of the psychological processes that may govern achievement. One implication of the models is that children's expectations have different determinants in different social settings. Expectations persist to about the same degree in all three schools, but achievement predicts expectations in only the middle-class school. It turns out that IQ and gender (but not race) are more influential in determining expectations in the lower-class schools.

The discussion so far has focused mainly on how marks affect expectations. But the question can be turned around. Expectations of children affect marks modestly in the middle-class school. In the lower-class schools effects of children's expectations on marks are much weaker and are manifest mainly in connection with conduct marks.

The overall patterns seen in the lower-class schools suggest how children in the lower-class schools could develop feelings of low efficacy. Their initially high expectations are not damped by subsequent low evaluations. Since forecasts do not improve in accuracy, children could conclude that their thinking or actions are of little consequence. The patterns across the schools suggest that, contrary to much speculation in the literature, minority-group children do not have low expectations for themselves relative to other children that damp achievement. In these schools expectations of lower SES children consistently exceeded those of their higher SES counterparts. Paradoxically, however, too-high expectations damp achievement rather than encourage it. Apparently mark feedback is so negative in comparison with expectations that children fail to process it. Two explanations of the relation between low SES children's expectations and their performance are suggested and both are quite different from the one usually proposed, namely that such children have low expectations which cause them to make low forecasts for themselves and that these low forecasts limit achievement.

Another matter of practical importance upon which these models shed light is the developmental history of children's expectations. Some authors (e.g. Rist, 1970) have proposed that children's academic expectations crystallize very early, perhaps in kindergarten, and that expectations remain rather stable thereafter. Our data contradict these notions. At least for the children in the present study, expectations appear to be unformed until well into the first-grade year. They tend to acquire form through the first grade and into the next grade, at least. Also middle-class children's low expectations seem malleable. Most of those who had very pessimistic expectations at the beginning of first grade quickly learned that few children in their school received low marks and raised their expectations. On the other hand, the lower-class children's expectations seemed stuck at the high end of the scale.

Much further research is required to fully understand the complex process that shapes early achievement in school. But these data and the models proposed in this chapter point to the feasibility and usefulness of collecting multi-wave data from very young children.

SUMMARY

This research is an extensive case study of all children enrolled in the first three grades at three elementary schools and focuses on the schooling process. Children entering first grade in a middle-class white school, an integrated lower-class school, and an all black lower-class school were followed continuously to the end of grade three.

Cyclic structural equation models are proposed to explain affective and cognitive outcomes of schooling in the three social milieux. FIML estimates of the models, taking measurement error into account, suggest that marks in reading and marks in arithmetic (cognitive outcomes) as well as children's marks in conduct and academic self-images (affective outcomes) can be rather well accounted for in all three schools and also that somewhat different processes lead to achievement and to affective development in the three places. On the other hand consistency in the basic structure of the models from one year to another, and from one school to another, as well as agreement between subsample replications, document the reasonableness of the models. The research points to both the feasibility and the usefulness of studying schooling early in children's school careers.

ACKNOWLEDGMENT

This research was supported by NIE Grant NIE-G-74-0029 and a Guggenheim fellowship to Doris Entwisle. Preparation of this report was facilitated by support from the Center for Social Organization of Schools through NIE Grant NIE-G-80-0113.

REFERENCES

Alwin, D. F., & Otto, L. B. High school context effects on aspirations. *Sociology of Education,* 1977, *50,* 259–273.

Berkeley, M. V. Inside kindergarten. *Unpublished doctoral dissertation,* Johns Hopkins University, 1978.

Brookover, W. B., Schweitzer, H. H., Schneider, J. M., Beady, C. H., Flood, P. K., & Wisenbaker, J. M. Elementary school social climate and school achievement. *American Educational Research Journal,* 1978, *15,* 301–318.

Entwisle, D. R., & Hayduk, L. A. *Too great expectations.* Baltimore: Johns Hopkins Press, 1978.

Entwisle, D. R., & Hayduk, L. A. Schooling of young children. In S. A. Mednick & M. Harway (eds.), *Longitudinal research in the United States,* in press. (a)

Entwisle, D. R., & Hayduk, L. A. *The schooling of young children,* The Johns Hopkins Press, in press. (b)

Hauser, R. M. On 'A reconceptualization of school effects.' *Sociology of Education,* 1978, *51,* 68–72.

Heyns, B. *School learning.* New York: Academic Press, 1978.

Huggins, W. H., & Entwisle, D. R. *Introductory systems and design.* Waltham, Mass.: Wiley (formerly Ginn/Blaisdell), 1968.

Husen, T. *Talent, opportunity and career.* Stockholm: Almqvist & Wiksell, 1969.

Jöreskog, K. G., & Sörbom, D. *LISREL: Version IV.* Chicago: International Educational Resources, 1978.

Kraus, P. E. *Yesterday's children.* New York: Wiley, 1973.

Murnane, R. J. *The impact of school resources on the learning of inner city children.* Cambridge: Ballinger, 1975.

Palardy, J. M. What teachers believe—What children achieve. *Elementary School Journal,* 1969, *69,* 370–374.

Pederson, E., Faucher, T. A., & Eaton, W. W. A new perspective on the effects of first-grade teachers on children's subsequent adult status. *Harvard Educational Review,* 1978, *48,* 1–31.

Rist, R. C. Student social class and teacher expectations: the self-fulfilling prophecy in ghetto education. *Harvard Educational Review,* 1970, *40,* 411–451.

Sorenson, A. B., & Hallinan, M. T. A reconceptualization of school effects. *Sociology of Education,* 1977, *50,* 273–289.

Summers, A. A., & Wolfe, B. L. Do schools make a difference? American *Economic Review,* 1977, *65,* 639–652.

11 What Is An Attribution, That Thou Art Mindful Of It?

Donald M. Baer
The University of Kansas

From one point of view, it may seem strange to have these four papers discussed in the terms of radical behaviorism (which is what is about to happen). From another point of view, though, it is quite apposite: these papers can be seen as thoroughly dedicated to the discipline of behavior analysis, especially applied behavior analysis, sometimes called behavior modification. For the most part, these arguments and reports suggest that a process called attribution or expectation controls the function of—what? Reinforcement contingencies! Sometimes, they suggest that it is the reinforcer-giver's attributions and expectations that control whether or not anything will be given, and whether the stimuli given will be positive or negative reinforcers, and for what behaviors they will be given contingently. Sometimes, they suggest that the function of reinforcers received can be augmented, weakened, or canceled altogether by the recipient's expectations or attributions. Few other functions of attributions and expectations are examined here. If an area of nonbehavioral psychology is now concerned with the mediation of reinforcement contingencies—with what controls their use, and what controls their effectiveness—then it must be that this area explicitly acknowledges the importance of reinforcement contingencies. To a discipline accustomed mainly to accusations of triviality, inappropriateness, and unhumanistic mechanism from other areas of psychology, this is indeed flattering validation. That it comes from so important an intersection of psychological areas as cognitive and social psychology is even more impressive (and surprising). A simplistic worker in applied behavior analysis might be tempted to wonder if these other areas have no theory or discipline of behavior change themselves, such that they must attend to and thereby endorse this one.

Given some endorsement of the best-known premise of behavior analysis—that contingencies can control behavior—then perhaps it will be instructive to apply a few other quite basic premises from the same discipline, and to apply them specifically to the thesis that there are processes called expectations and attributions that can mediate both the use and effectiveness of reinforcement contingencies.

If attributions and expectations were to be discussed from the point of view of methodological behaviorism, the adventure would be quite brief. As described here, these processes are mainly private, covert events directly observable only by their hosts. In methodological behaviorism, events that cannot be directly observed by any investigator desirous of doing so are thereby debarred from further consideration. Their existence is not denied; the possibility of saying anything both useful and verifiable about them is. (Methodological behaviorists know that they themselves are host to such covert events; their point is simply the apparent impossibility of one individual establishing objectively the important characteristics of such events in any other individual.) But, since attributions and expectations are to be discussed from the point of view of radical behaviorism, the adventure can be both longer and more complex. Radical behaviorism is willing to agree to both the existence and the possibility of function of covert events. It does so, distinctively, from the vantage point of a crucial assumption about them: that they are homogeneous with other behaviors that are not covert. In other words, covert events like attributions are behaviors; they respond to environmental contingencies just as do overt behaviors, and are capable of filling the same functions—but only the same functions—as overt behaviors do. The fact that they are typically unobservable except by their host[1] makes it difficult to characterize them further. There are only two things to do with them: infer their characteristics as strongly as possible, or teach them experimentally to subjects to see what the consequences of doing so are.

Skinner provides an exemplar of the first tactic in his book, *Verbal Behavior* (1957). It is an inferential account of what language functions could be like, given the principles of behavior analysis known to be valid for a wide range of observable behaviors; thus, it is strong inference. (More than one behaviorist has characterized it as necessarily unproven, yet as the inevitable behavioral account of language.) Meichenbaum has exemplified the second tactic: he and his colleagues taught children certain self-instructions about how to learn, and did so in an experimental design that allowed us all to see the consequences of doing so (e.g., Meichenbaum and Goodman, 1971). The self-instructions became covert; indeed, the children were taught to make them covert (as if there were some virtue in removing these self-instructions from observability). But some of the children's observable behaviors changed, nevertheless; interestingly, those

---

[1]And sometimes not even by their hosts, except by unusual instrumentation: consider blood pressure, EEG potentials, and the other events now often transduced as "biofeedback".

changes were seen primarily in psychometric tests often taken as measures of children's ability to learn (IQ), rather than in the children's actual classroom learning performances. Thus, the Meichenbaum and Goodman study did not prove that self-instructions (which are like attributions) can control classroom learning; that might be because they taught the wrong self-instruction for that purpose, or because they considered the wrong measures of that outcome, or because mere self-instructions do not have that strong a function in the teeth of actual-problem difficulties and contingencies that make the child wrong just as often whether these self-instructions are followed or not. Thus, the question is hardly settled—but the tactic remains a very attractive one for settling the question in the future.

Teaching attributions to see what their consequences are has manifold advantages over inferring their existence and their characteristics. It is a more powerful method of discovery; it is a more convincing method of proof; it allows making a wide variety of attributions to see what each of them is worth, rather than settling for those that can be found in the cases at hand; and if it ever shows desirable outcomes, it is already a technology of accomplishing those outcomes, in that it is necessarily a collection of successful teaching methods. Given all these advantages, it is remarkable that the method is not used more often, especially in preference to the tactic of attempting even strong inferences. Yet these chapters show a thorough abstention from the tactic, although Wang, on her last page, very creditably proposes it for the case of students' attributions of personal control over their learning environments: ". . . efforts should be made to develop training programs that allow teachers to create and maintain learning environments of the type believed to foster students' sense of personal control. Such programs will likely produce fundamental changes . . ."

Wang's assertion of "likely" is a bold one: A consideration of the possible relations between a behavior called an attribution, and any teaching and learning correlates of it, shows an impressive variety of potential arrangements, only one of which is likely to produce fundamental changes.

Take as a case in point a teacher's attributions that some students are not interested in learning, will not work hard or even attend to instructions, do not value either teacher praise or high marks, and thus might as well be ignored when they occasionally attend to instructions or manage a correct performance; whereas other students are interested in learning, do attend to instructions and work hard at complying with them, are responsive to both praise and high marks, and thus deserve and profit from teacher attention and individualized grading. Cooper shows that such teachers are likely to give the latter students more nods, smiles, leans-toward, and praise; more cues to support the correct answer and more repairs of an incorrect or partially incorrect answer; longer durations of attention; and more criticisms followed closely by challenges and opportunities to do better. Furthermore, the teachers do all that in better contingencies (for the furtherance of academic behaviors) than characterize their occasional efforts with the former group. What relations might explain this correlation between teachers' attributions of student characteristics and teachers' performances with those students?

1. Perhaps the teachers' attributions about their students control their teaching performances with those students. If so, then the process of attribution has great importance for education, and for any theory of behavior that incorporates a process of mediation of one behavior by another (which certainly includes radical behaviorism, operant conditioning, social learning theory, and all the behavior therapies).

2. Perhaps the teachers' already existing teaching performances control their attributions about their students. Then why do teachers teach different students differently, if not because of the different attributions that they make about their students? Perhaps because the students' learning performances contort the teachers' teaching performances, and these teaching performances, once established, are noticed by the teacher who is their host and thus provoke explanation or justification by the teacher. If so, then the process of attribution is interesting, but not educationally important: rather than mediating teaching technique, it is a result of it.

3. Perhaps the teachers' attributions about their students are brought into existence by researchers' questions, which either stimulate self-description of differential teaching performance, or, by pointing to differential teaching performances, demand justification of them. If so, attributions are still interesting behaviors, but again are not educationally important—unless, now that they exist mainly to explain and justify, they will control future teaching performances. (But how long could that last?)

4. Perhaps the teachers' attributions about their students and their teaching performances with those students are both controlled by some third factor, such as the students' previous and/or current records as good or poor students, or the socioeconomic levels of their families. That is, students known or supposed to be poor students are neither expected to do well nor taught well (in terms of the teaching performance that Cooper specified, noted above); students known or supposed to be good students are both expected to do well and taught well. (They might be taught well because their reputation, acting as a discriminative stimulus, evokes good teaching, and/or because they reinforce good teaching by responding well to it in the ways that "good" students do.) In that case attributions are parallel behaviors to teaching, not mediators of it; again, they are interesting but educationally unimportant behaviors.

Of these four major possibilities, each of which represents an entirely plausible social learning process, only the first one elevates attributions to an educationally important role (although all of them place attributions in at least analytically interesting relationships with common environmental factors in the world of teaching). If the only research evidence available is a pattern of correlation between attribution and teaching performance (or learning performance), then no certain choice can be made among these four archetypes of cause-and-effect relationship. Inference is all that is possible, and the nature of these four archetypes is such that only weak inference is possible.

(This analysis was constructed in terms of attributions and teaching. A parallel analysis could be constructed in terms of attributions and learning, primarily from the students' vantage point. It would indeed be parallel, would result in the same pattern of archetypal cause-and-effect relationships to choose among, and would again represent a situation allowing only weak inference. Its construction is left as an exercise for the reader.)

Thus, the most striking characteristic of the research presented here is its abstention from the alternative research tactic for analyzing private events: experimentally teaching them, and only them, to see what happens as a result (e.g., Dweck, 1975). That tactic is experimental, not correlational; in consequence, it narrows to one the number of directions in which cause-and-effect relationships may flow. To decide whether or not attributions ever constitute educationally important processes, it is precisely the direction of their cause-and-effect relationships that must be established—attributions as anything other than mediators of teaching or learning are theoretically interesting, but educationally trivial: modifying them will do nothing for educational outcomes, in three of the four possible processes just sketched.

This is the point in a critical argument where qualifications of criticism should enter. A significant one operates here in this argument; it is a corollary of the Law of Large Numbers. Recall that three paragraphs back, each of the four major archetypes of inference about cause-and-effect relationships between attribution and teaching (or learning) was characterized as "an entirely plausible social learning process." In other words, each is possible and realistic; the essential question is its probability, not its realism. The Law of Large Numbers states that even very unlikely events will occur with a probability approaching certainty as the opportunities for their occurrence increase. In a world full of very Large Numbers of teachers and students, surely each of those four cases actually occurs at least sometimes, in at least some teachers and at least some students. We ought not to proceed as if only one of those four cases were correct; we ought to proceed as if the problem were to describe the probability of each of them. That moderates the current criticism of much of the research presented here: its inability to determine the direction and nature of the cause-and-effect relationships it suspects now seems not quite so crucial, if they all operate at least sometime. But it also translates that criticism into a different but equally severe one: these studies for the most part seem unable to estimate the relative probabilities of the multiple and various cases with which they must be dealing. To some extent, they attempt to approach that ability by segregating their subjects into categories, such as SES (Entwisle and Hayduk), achievement levels (insistently attended to by Wang), sex, SES, and grade levels (Blumenfeld, Hamilton, Bossert, Wessels, and Meece), and, intriguingly, educational contexts (wisely acknowledged and emphasized by Cooper). More of this kind of attention to the variables that might control which of the four cases operates in each teacher and student ought to advance the problem significantly. Thus, taking that tactic to its ultimate suggests that single-subject designs should be used in this problem area to display when individuals are operating stably under which (or how many, depending on context) of the four cases in question, and thus eventually estimate their separate and conjoint probabilities. Wang already embodies some of those designs, yet on groups rather than on individuals. Why not take them one step farther as an act of individual diagnosis?

A behavioral analysis of these studies suggests another very important dimension, as well; this time, radical and methodological behaviorists alike will enter the discussion, since it is not specific to private events. In these studies, attributions are supposed to mediate teaching and learning. Teaching is most often presented as the giving of stimuli discriminative for reinforceable behaviors and the giving of appropriate reinforcers when those behaviors are academically correct: and learning most often is seen as behavior modified under just those contingencies. Thus, Cooper describes in excellent detail the behavioral anatomy of a teaching performance; Wang and others measure carefully the actual academic achievements of students (rather than their grades, which, being partly teacher behavior, can represent the attribution process as much as one of its ultimate outcomes). When Cooper dissects teaching into those components, how does he know that each of them or any of them actually functions as a discriminative stimulus or as a reinforcer? The underlying premise is only actuarial: stimuli like those have been shown to be functional (sometimes) for other students in other classrooms interacting with other teachers at other times; why should they not be functional this time, too? Those of us who actually try to use those events as putative reinforcers for modifying student behavior know that, often, they do work "this time, too." Unfortunately, we also know, from direct experience, that often they do not work "this time, too." One student's discriminative stimulus to answer the question is another's discriminative stimulus to sass the teacher and yet another's nonevent; one student's reinforcer is another's punisher and yet another's nonevent. Thus, any studies attempting to show that attributions mediate teaching need to know first that the teaching that is being mediated is indeed *functional* teaching, if the research is to have any educational significance. If the teacher's performance is not functional, then of the four possible cases relating attribution and teaching, not even the presumably educationally significant case of attributions mediating teaching is actually educationally significant. This is only putative, not functional, teaching; knowing what mediates it may interest social and cognitive psychologists, but it will not improve actual teaching and subsequent learning.

In this context, the study by Blumenfeld, Hamilton, Bossert, Wessels, and Meece takes on considerable significance. It suggests that teachers devote their primary effort to maintaining order, good citizenship, and school system function, rather than to teaching academic substance. Even putative teaching is something that happens mainly when order and procedure are being maintained without threat or disruption, and students seem to reflect this fact in their own (at least putative) values. Taking these data seriously suggests that the possibility that attributions mediate teaching is less educationally significant than the possibility that attributions mediate order-keeping and institutional management.

(I take the Blumenfeld et al. data seriously because of a personal, nonobjective, unproven suspicion. I am the father of three daughters, all products of the usual public school system, all endowed with the highest of academic honors. Throughout their schooling, I would ask them what they learned in school that day. Uniformly, they would look at me with that expression that the years would teach me meant that I had asked the wrong question. Even so, they answered as cooperatively as they could, and the essence of their answer was that they had homework to do. Finally, I realized that what they regarded as ''learning something'' was the interaction that took place between them and their textbooks in the evening when they did their homework. From the substance, explanations, and especially the examples that their textbooks presented, they read, deduced, or induced the solution, meaning, substance, or completion of their homework assignments. Occasionally, they asked their mother or me to help them with one of those textbooks; occasionally, they telephoned a friend for advice. Sometimes, after finishing a homework assignment, they would say, in effect, that *now* they had ''learned something.'' Thus, my suspicion, which grows stronger every year, even with my daughters now all into their university educations, is that schools and school teachers do not teach: they *assign*. Publishers teach more directly than teachers. Teachers assign homework and also conduct activities, and to do all that, they maintain order and system. The data of Blumenfeld et al. seem both soft and exactly correct to me.)

It would be profitable to apply the methods of the Blumenfeld et al. study to more classrooms, at more grade levels, across more social classes, in more regions of this country and others, and for some period of time, to see how general its findings are. They may very well prove quite general. In that case, the next book on attribution processes in education, in addition to incorporating some radically different research tactics, would do well to target a radically different set of behaviors to analyze: not so much teaching as maintaining institutional order. Meanwhile, researchers concerned with attributions more than with education might reasonably at least take note of a radical-behaviorist view of processes like attribution: There are such processes; they are behaviors, difficult to observe after they have been acquired but perhaps not so difficult to teach; they fill any of the functions that observable behaviors can fill, which includes mediation of other behaviors; like observable behaviors, there is no necessity that they serve a mediating function, only a possibility; the most powerful research tactic for their study is to teach them experimentally to see what the consequences of doing so may be; and—if anyone decides to join the currently rather small band of researchers who are doing just that—teaching attributions ought to be done with the best teaching technology that the field knows, and with the best programs for their maintenance once they are taught, for, like any other behaviors, they are subject to extinction if they do not work for their host. Teaching a school child to say, "If I try harder I'll get it right" had better be true if it is to go on mediating adaptive learning performances.

ACKNOWLEDGMENT

I am indebted to Dr. Lauren Resnick for some of the ideas expressed here: When I asked her why in the world her colleagues had asked me to serve as a discussant on *this* topic, she immediately outlined a logically cogent case. For the most part, I have responded to that case in developing this discussion. But it would not be accurate to say that because she provoked it, she agrees with it; that would be logically invalid attribution.

REFERENCES

Dweck, C. W. The role of expectations and attributions in the alleviation of learned helplessness. *Journal of Personality and Social Psychology,* 1975, *31,* 674-685.
Meichenbaum, D. H., & Goodman, J. Training impulsive children to talk to themselves: A means of developing self-control. *Journal of Abnormal Psychology,* 1971, *77*(2), 115-126.
Skinner, B. F. *Verbal behavior.* New York: Appleton-Century-Crofts, 1957.

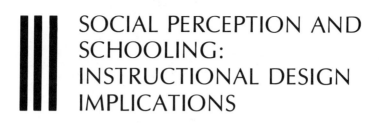

SOCIAL PERCEPTION AND SCHOOLING: INSTRUCTIONAL DESIGN IMPLICATIONS

12
Extrinsic Reward and Intrinsic Motivation: Implications for the Classroom

Mark R. Lepper
Stanford University

The question of how to instill interest and motivate children in the classroom has been a central concern of educators and a focus of pedagogical controversy since, at least, the advent of compulsory schooling over a century ago. In earlier days, the frequent use of corporal punishment and other punitive measures was considered part and parcel of the educational system; negative sanctions were viewed as essential ingredients in eliciting compliance with classroom dictates and in maintaining "interest" in academic pursuits. Only in the relatively recent past (and not without opposition) have techniques of punishment in the school fallen into general disfavor, to be supplanted by an increased reliance upon more humane means of social control involving the use of contingent rewards and privileges to control behavior and motivate academic performance in the classroom.

As times and social traditions have changed, however, issues of classroom motivation and conduct have remained critical. As schools have come to rely more upon systems of rewards and principles of reinforcement to motivate and control students, debates concerning fundamental issues of control and motivation have come to revolve around the issue of how and when rewards may best be used to enhance interest and promote learning and performance in the classroom. It is this continuing controversy that I wish to address in this chapter.

Somewhat incongruously, the last decade has witnessed the growth of two quite different and, at least superficially, antithetical research traditions—each concerned with the effects of tangible rewards on children's conduct, task performance and subsequent behavior. Both have potentially significant implications for our understanding of how rewards may be best employed in schools and other educational contexts. Both have proven controversial and have been a source of considerable debate, as well as a stimulus to considerable empirical research.

The first of these traditions derives quite directly from the application of traditional techniques of functional analysis and operant reinforcement procedures—initially developed in the animal laboratory—to issues of motivational and conduct problems that occur in and often plague children's classrooms. Although this general approach also includes attempts to analyze and alter systematically the social contingencies prevailing in classrooms, it is perhaps best exemplified in the use of "token economy" programs in the school. Such programs typically involve the introduction of a system of highly attractive, extrinsic rewards into the classroom, with access to these rewards made strictly contingent in an essentially arbitrary fashion upon specified desirable or "appropriate" behavior patterns. Such token economy systems take their name from the practice of providing children with frequent feedback and reinforcement in the form of "tokens" (e.g., stars, points, pennies, or poker chips) which may, in turn, be accumulated and used by the children to purchase attractive "back-up" rewards in the form of food, special privileges, or access to highly preferred activities.

The dramatic proliferation of such token economies in educational and classroom settings is amply documented in a number of recent reviews of controlled experimental research in this area (e.g., Kazdin, 1975; Kazdin & Bootzin, 1972; O'Leary, 1978, O'Leary & Drabman, 1971; Winett & Winkler, 1972). Their increasing popularity in classroom practice, apart from experimental research, is undeniable, as the numerous publications available to the practitioner who might wish to institute such a program in his or her own classroom attest. The obvious attraction of such approaches, moreover, is due in large part to the striking success of such systematic reward programs in producing dramatic changes in students' behavior. Across a wide variety of specific programs, token economy systems have proven remarkably successful in producing decreases in disruptive and inappropriate behavior and increased attention to (and occasionally performance on) academic tasks or exams. At least as long as these programs remain in effect, the positive effects of such contingent reward programs are indisputable.

By contrast, the second research tradition I wish to consider—concerned with what have been termed the "hidden costs" of rewards—will be considerably less familiar to most educators. In part this lesser familiarity may stem from the fact that this work is more recent and has focused on theoretical rather than applied issues; more importantly, I suspect, this research is less familiar because the message it carries is both more complex and less encouraging for the practitioner. This line of investigation has involved the study of the potential deleterious effects of the inappropriate use of extrinsic rewards on task performance and subsequent intrinsic interest in the previously rewarded activity. Again, although the issues raised by this approach are relatively new, the last 5 years have witnessed the growth of a large empirical literature in this area, as a number of recent reviews indicate (e.g., Condry, 1977; Deci, 1975; Lepper, 1981, in press; Lepper & Greene, 1978a, 1978b; Maehr, 1976). Although the questions involved are perhaps more complex than they may seem (Lepper & ⌣. 1978c), the assertion that extrinsic rewards may have negative, as well as positive, effects on subsequent behavior provides a clear challenge to the uncritical acceptance of contingent reward systems as a universal answer to questions of motivation and interest in the classroom.

This seeming clash in findings and the possible implications of this controversy for classroom practice have occasioned heated debate. Although there have been a few attempts to delineate the conditions under which these different effects of rewards are likely to occur and to consider the conditions under which each might be relevant to educational practice (e.g., Lepper & Greene, 1978c; O'Leary, 1978; Vasta, in press), extreme claims have been made on both sides of the debate. Vociferous proponents of systematic reinforcement programs have not only argued that demonstrations of negative effects of contingent reward programs are irrelevant to educational practice, but have suggested that such research is likely to prevent the alleviation of human suffering and is of little scientific value. Equally extreme critics of the traditional reinforcement approach have extrapolated far beyond the existing evidence to proscribe broadly the use of systematic reward systems to modify children's behavior in educational contexts. Both sets of claims are, I believe, exaggerated; but the issues underlying this debate remain of critical significance.

In the remainder of this chapter, I wish to consider these questions more fully. In particular, I wish to begin by reviewing briefly the current literature concerning the potential detrimental effects of the inappropriate use of extrinsic rewards and the conditions under which such negative effects appear to occur in the laboratory. I would then like to consider the relevance, or irrelevance, of these findings to classroom practice, in terms of three basic questions. The first of these we might term the "engineering" question: Can we, by simple changes in design, create more effective reinforcement programs that will have none of the potential negative consequences that we know improperly designed programs may produce? The second might be described as the "ecological relevance" question: Are there common situations in current classroom practice where rewards seem to be employed inappropriately, or might be employed more effectively? Finally, I wish to raise the question of "evaluation" of reward programs. In so doing, I hope to illustrate the complex interaction of factors that must be considered in determining when rewards are likely to have positive versus negative effects and to suggest that our evaluations must depend, in part, on the relative value we place on the different functions such programs must serve.

THE HIDDEN COSTS OF REWARD

Let us consider, then, the hidden costs of reward—the potential deleterious effects of the inappropriate use of extrinsic rewards—and the conditions under which they may occur. Such detrimental effects, I wish to argue from the outset, fall into two conceptually distinct classes. Rewards may first have negative effects on measures of performance (e.g., learning, recall, creativity, or even enjoyment) at an activity in the situation in which rewards have been offered contingent upon task engagement or task performance. These effects I would like to classify as "immediate" performance effects. Rewards may also have negative effects on subsequent intrinsic interest in or attitudes towards the previously rewarded activity in later situations in which extrinsic rewards and constraints are no longer available or salient. These results I will describe as effects on subsequent interest. This distinction, I believe, is important to our understanding of the conditions under which detrimental effects will result, and seems to me mandated by existing data that suggest that these two classes of effects are at least partially independent (Lepper, 1981; Lepper & Greene, 1978b). Both, however, may have important social implications.

Both sorts of effects have also remained, until quite recently, "hidden" by a widespread theoretical approach to the study of the effects of rewards in which "reinforcers" are literally defined in terms of their demonstrable positive effects on subsequent behavior. Thus, traditional research on the effects of rewards on subsequent behavior has been dominated for many years by a standard paradigm that has served to define both the questions addressed and the appropriate means for addressing those questions (Krantz, 1971; Kuhn, 1970). In this approach the goal is generally clear: to establish functional control over some response or class of responses in some particular setting through the application of contingent reinforcement procedures. The analysis assumes that response variability in the organism is a function of response variability in the environment and that any behavior can be explained in terms of the organism's desire to maximize reinforcement. Although in practice the decision as to what sorts of events or outcomes will serve as a reinforcer may be informed by our common-sense notions about what events are rewarding, the actual definition of some event or outcome as a reinforcer depends upon an empirical demonstration that the subsequent probability of the response upon which that event or outcome has been made contingent is increased over baseline levels (and, in most cases, that response probability will correspondingly decrease when this contingency is removed). The demonstration of functional control, therefore, defines the existence of a "reward" or reinforcer (cf. McCullers, 1978) and insures both that reinforcement will have positive effects on subsequent behavior and that the underlying premise that reinforcement increases response probability cannot be questioned or disproved.

In the following sections, however, we wish to consider a quite different set of questions that may be raised concerning the effects of rewards on behavior. Let us start, in particular, with a set of events or outcomes that most of us would classify, and might be likely to use, as rewards, on the basis of our everyday experience or our knowledge of their use in prior studies in the reinforcement literature. One might then ask what effects would result from making these "rewards" contingent upon task performance or task engagement—with the possibility of discovering that particular rewards, or rewards presented in particular ways, might have *either* positive or negative effects on behavior in that setting in which we have imposed this contingency. Indeed, we might go one step further and ask what the effects of prior receipt of such rewards for task engagement or performance are on later behavior in contexts where the person who has been rewarded believes that the same behavior will no longer prove instrumental in producing further extrinsic rewards.

It is to these more unorthodox questions concerning the effects of rewards on immediate task performance in the face of salient extrinsic contingencies and on subsequent intrinsic interest in the absence of salient extrinsic constraints that the study of the hidden costs of reward has been addressed; and it is to these issues that we will now turn. Because most of our own work and a majority of the research that has followed in this tradition have been primarily concerned with the second of these categories—the effects of extrinsic rewards and constraints on subsequent intrinsic interest—we shall address this issue first.

Undermining Intrinsic Interest with Extrinsic Rewards

The basic proposition that the imposition of superfluous extrinsic rewards or constraints on one's engagement in an activity of initial interest might have adverse effects on later intrinsic interest in that activity and the earliest studies in this area (Deci, 1971; Kruglanski, Friedman, & Zeevi, 1971; Lepper, Greene, & Nisbett, 1973) derived, in various ways, from an analysis of the effects of rewards within a general attribution or self-perception framework (Bem, 1967, 1972; deCharms, 1968; Kelley, 1967, 1973). In our own work, this derivation was relatively direct and stemmed from previous research concerned with the effects of mild versus severe threats of punishment on children's later internalization of the prohibited activity and related more general values (Lepper, 1973; Lepper, Zanna, & Abelson, 1970; Zanna, Lepper & Abelson, 1973). In this work, it had been suggested that the use of minimal, but sufficient, pressure to induce a child to refrain from engaging in an inherently attractive activity was more likely than the use of more powerful, but incrementally superfluous, pressure to produce subsequent adherence to this and related prohibitions in later situations in which external pressures were lacking.

Within an attributional account the results of these and other "insufficient justification" (Aronson, 1966) studies were seen as a function of the extent to which the use of differentially powerful and salient external constraints would lead children to view their previous actions as either intrinsically or extrinsically motivated. If an individual were induced to engage in a particular behavior in the face of clear, salient, and powerful extrinsic constraints, this account suggested, he or she would be likely to view that behavior as a response to those constraints and to see that action as extrinsically motivated. If the same individual were induced to engage in the same behavior in the absence of extrinsic constraints sufficiently salient, powerful, or psychologically "sufficient" to provide a ready explanation of his or her actions, the person would be likely to view that behavior as intrinsically motivated—to attribute it to his or her own desires, preferences, or dispositions. Evidence of greater "internalization" of the behavior performed in the face of minimal justification in these studies, therefore, was interpreted as a consequence of differential attributions concerning one's reasons for engaging in the behavior under these different conditions.

Although such an account was in many respects indistinguishable from the original dissonance model that spawned this research, its major heuristic value was to suggest that such processes might be quite general and might occur, in particular, even if the initial activity one was asked to undertake was not inherently aversive or inconsistent with one's beliefs. This attributional model suggested, in particular, that the use of overly sufficient extrinsic pressure to induce an individual to engage in an activity of initial interest in its own right, as a means to some extrinsic goal, might lead that individual to view his or her actions as extrinsically motivated and to find that activity, in the later absence of further extrinsic rewards or constraints, to be of less intrinsic interest. This proposition—that inducing engagement in an activity of initial interest in order to obtain some extrinsic goal or reward might undermine subsequent intrinsic interest—we termed the "overjustification" hypothesis, to emphasize its conceptual relationship to prior work on insufficient justification.

To examine this hypothesis, David Greene, Dick Nisbett and I undertook a deceptively simple experimental demonstration under conditions designed to maximize the likelihood that such an undermining effect might be apparent (Lepper, Greene, & Nisbett, 1973). In this effort, our first task was to find a setting in which we felt that children's choices among activities would legitimately serve as an index of their relative intrinsic interest in these activities in the absence of extrinsic pressures. For this purpose, we turned to the Bing Nursery School, a preschool research facility on the Stanford campus that seemed to afford a nearly ideal setting for the assessment of intrinsic interest. First, the school's program was structured so that children were presented daily with large blocks of time devoted explicitly to "free play," during which children were free to choose among a wide array of alternative activities without external pressures from the teachers to select any particular activity over another. Second, because the school had been designed as a research facility, it was possible to secure the cooperation of teachers for introducing experimental activities into the classroom as part of children's regular program, without interference by unfamiliar research personnel, and to observe children's choices, without their knowledge, through one-way mirrors into the classrooms. Under these conditions, we felt that it would be possible to draw inferences about children's relative intrinsic interest—their interest in an activity for its own sake—from their choices among classroom options.

We began our study, then, by having a target art activity introduced into the children's classrooms over a one-week period, during which we covertly observed children's engagement with this activity; and we selected for our study only those children who had shown an initial interest in this activity in this unconstrained classroom setting. These children were then seen in subsequent individual experimental sessions in a separate room, where they were presented with this activity under one of three conditions. In the Control condition, children were simply shown the experimental materials and asked if they would like to draw some pictures with these materials. Since we had selected as subjects only those children with an initial interest in this activity, all of them agreed to do so and engaged in the activity without expectation or receipt of any tangible reward for their efforts. In the Expected Award condition, on the other hand, children were first shown a sample Good Player Award and asked if they would like to win such an award. After the children had expressed a desire to win the award, they were told that they could win this award by drawing pictures with the target materials and were asked explicitly to agree to draw pictures with our materials in order to win this award. At the completion of the experimental period, these subjects were given the award and the same verbal feedback as children in the control condition. Finally, in a third, Unexpected Award condition, children were asked initially, as in the Control condition, to engage in the activity without expectation of reward. After they had finished, however, these children were shown and given, unexpectedly, the same reward and feedback as chidren in the Expected Reward condition. These three conditions, then, allowed us to compare the effects of a procedure in which an initially interesting activity had been made an explicit means to an extrinsic reward—a procedure designed to make salient the instrumentality of one's actions—with otherwise comparable conditions in which the same reward was received unexpectedly or in which no tangible reward was received.

Our central concern, of course, was with the effects of these procedures on later intrinsic interest in the activity in the subsequent absence of any further expectation of reward or other extrinsic constraints. Hence, several weeks later, this same experimental activity was returned to children's classrooms during free play periods and children's choices of this activity were covertly monitored. During these postexperimental observations, as anticipated, Expected Award subjects played with the target activity significantly less, indeed half as much, as they had during baseline periods; whereas subjects in the Control and Unexpected Award groups showed no significant change from baseline interest levels. Similarly, in between-groups comparisons, Expected Award subjects showed significantly less interest than Control or Unexpected Award subjects, who did not differ in later interest.

These initial findings, and early studies with adult populations by other investigators, stimulated a great deal of further research that has provided evidence of conceptually comparable effects across a wide variety of specific experimental tasks, particular tangible rewards, and contingent systems. Likewise, analogous effects have been obtained across an unusually wide age range—from preschoolers (Anderson, Manoogian & Resnick, 1976; Boggiano & Ruble, 1979; Greene & Lepper, 1974; Lepper & Greene, 1975; Lepper, Sagotsky, Dafoe & Greene, in press; Lepper, Sagotsky & Greene, 1981a, 1981b; Loveland & Olley, 1979; McLoyd, 1979; Reiss & Sushinsky, 1975; Ross, 1975; Wells & Shultz, 1980) and elementary school students (Blackwell, 1974; Boggiano & Ruble, 1979; Brownell, Colletti, Ersner-Hershfield, Hershfield & Wilson, 1977; Colvin, 1971; Dollinger & Thelen, 1978; Greene, Sternberg & Lepper, 1976; Karniol & Ross, 1977; Kruglanski, Alon & Lewis, 1972; Perry, Bussey & Redman, 1977; Ross, Karniol & Rothstein, 1976; Sorenson & Maehr, 1976; Swann & Pittman, 1977) to high school pupils (Harackiewicz, 1979; Kruglanski, Friedman & Zeevi, 1971; Kruglanski, Riter, Amatai, Margolin, Shabtai & Zaksh, 1975) and college students (Amabile, 1979; Amabile, DeJong & Lepper, 1976; Calder & Staw, 1975; Deci, 1971, 1972, 1975; Enzle & Look, 1980; Enzle & Ross, 1978; Folger, Rosenfield & Hays, 1978; Johnson, Greene & Carroll, 1980; Pinder, 1976; Pittman, Cooper & Smith, 1977; Pittman, Davey, Alafet, Wetherill & Kramer, 1980; Pritchard, Campbell & Campbell, 1977; Scott & Yalch, 1978; Smith & Pittman, 1978; Smith, 1976; Upton, 1974; Wilson, Hull & Johnson, 1981).

These further studies extend greatly the generality of our initial findings. They provide us, as well, with considerable evidence concerning the conditions under which detrimental effects of extrinsic rewards on subsequent intrinsic interest are likely to be observed and the conditions under which extrinsic rewards may be likely to have positive effects on subsequent interest. To provide a conceptual background for our further consideration of the potential implications of these results, let me attempt to summarize briefly the major themes of this further literature, as I see them.

Perceptions of Constraint and Competence

By far the largest portion of this subsequent literature has been devoted, generally, to an attempt to specify the conditions under which extrinsic rewards may have adverse effects on later interest—in terms of variations in the nature or the manner of presentation of extrinsic incentives or constraints imposed upon task engagement or performance. These studies, I will argue, suggest two central parameters that determine the effects of extrinsic contingencies on subsequent intrinsic interest: perceptions of external constraint and perceptions of personal competence.

Recall that our initial analysis had suggested that it is the perceived instrumentality of one's actions as a means to some extrinsic goal that should lead children to view the activity subsequently as less inherently interesting. Consistent with this analysis, a number of studies have demonstrated that the provision of extrinsic rewards in a manner that makes salient the instrumentality of one's actions will produce decreases in later interest that are not obtained when the same rewards are presented in a fashion that does not promote perceptions of one's engagement in the activity as instrumental. Thus, extrinsic rewards presented unexpectedly after task engagement (Enzle & Look, 1980; Enzle & Ross, 1978; Greene & Lepper, 1974; Lepper et al., 1973; Lepper et al., 1980; Smith, 1976) or presented as contingent upon waiting for a specified time period while incidentally engaged in the activity (Ross et al., 1976; Swann & Pittman, 1977) appear not to produce the decreases in later intrinsic interest that can be shown to result when these same rewards are presented as explicitly contingent upon task engagement. Similarly, direct manipulations of the salience of a proffered contingent reward (Ross, 1975) and direct attempts to induce subjects who have been offered a reward for task engagement to label their actions as either "intrinsically" or "extrinsically" motivated (Johnson et al., 1980; Pittman et al., 1977) indicate that detrimental effects are more likely to occur when instrumental motives have been made salient than when one's interest in the activity itself has been emphasized.[1]

At the same time, other research suggests that such findings are not limited to cases in which extrinsic rewards are employed to induce perceptions of instrumentality, but apply more generally, as an attributional model would suggest, to cases in which superfluous extrinsic constraints of many sorts are imposed on engagement in an activity of initial interest. For example, the imposition of unnecessarily close surveillance (Lepper & Greene, 1975; Pittman et al., 1980), temporal deadlines (Amabile et al., 1976), "forced rehearsal" of modeled actions (Rosenhan, 1969), and threats of punishment (Deci, 1975; Lepper, 1973) have all been shown to reduce the probability of the behavior previously under constraint in the later absence of comparable external pressures. Even the mere imposition of a purely nominal contingency—the presentation of two equally attractive activities in an explicit means-end relationship—may prove sufficient to decrease later interest in the activity one had been constrained to undertake in order to obtain the opportunity to engage in the other (Lepper et al., in press).

Hence, a first conclusion that one might draw from this work is that the perception of one's actions as extrinsically constrained is a critical element in the demonstration of subsequent decreases in intrinsic interest. These findings also help to rule out a variety of potential alternative explanations of these findings in terms of the simple distracting, arousing, or frustrative effects of salient extrinsic rewards per se (cf. Lepper, 1981, in press; Lepper & Greene, 1976, 1978b; Ross

---

[1]It is worth being clear that the conceptual variable of interest here is the child's perception of constraint or, in the case of rewards, instrumentality. Thus, under appropriate circumstances, it is possible to show both that deemphasizing perceptions of instrumentality in the face of an expected reward may eliminate detrimental effects on later interest (e.g., Johnson et al., 1980) and that leading children to believe that they had engaged in an activity in order to obtain a reward that was, in reality, unexpected may produce detrimental effects (e.g., Kruglanski, Alon, & Lewis, 1972).

et al., 1976). A second and equally important conclusion that might be drawn from this further literature, however, suggests a need for attention to the effects of extrinsic rewards on perceptions of competence as well as perceptions of constraint.

The findings that prompt this second general conclusion derive from attempts to compare the effects of two sorts of contingent reward procedures: "task-contingent" rewards, presented to subjects as contingent simply upon engagement in the activity without regard to the quality of one's performance versus "performance-contingent" rewards, presented to subjects as contingent upon specified levels of excellence at the activity, in terms of either successful solutions or normatively superior performance. In the first case, characteristic of most of the above research, perceptions of constraint appear highly likely, but the receipt of reward conveys little information to the individual concerning his or her competence at the activity; in the second case, both perceptions of constraint and competence may be aroused, since receipt of reward also provides evidence of one's superior competence at the activity.

Assuming that procedures that enhance perceptions of competence will be likely to enhance intrinsic interest (deCharms, 1968; Deci, 1975; Hunt, 1961, 1965), it would be expected that performance-contingent rewards should be less likely than task-contingent rewards to produce later decrements in intrinsic interest. This, indeed, seems to be the case. In several studies that have directly compared tangible extrinsic rewards presented as contingent upon either mere task engagement or superior task performance, performance-contingent rewards proved less likely than task-contingent rewards to have adverse effects on later intrinsic interest, relative to nonrewarded control conditions (Boggiano & Ruble, 1979; Enzle & Ross, 1978; Karniol & Ross, 1977; Ross, 1976). Interestingly, from a developmental standpoint, young children appear quite unresponsive to social comparative feedback: Although they may respond less negatively to rewards contingent upon absolute task success than to task-contingent rewards, the effects of rewards that convey evidence concerning their task competence relative to peers do not seem to differ from the effects of task-contingent rewards (Boggiano & Ruble, 1979; Greene & Lepper, 1974). Only later will comparative feedback produce positive effects (Boggiano & Ruble, 1979). Other studies providing further, though more tangential, support for this distinction with older children and adults have compared tangible task-contingent and social performance-contingent rewards, with the reasonably consistent finding of decreased interest in the former case and increased interest in the latter case, relative to appropriate control conditions (Anderson et al., 1976; Blanck, Reis & Jackson, 1980; Deci, 1971, 1972, 1975; Dollinger & Thelen, 1978; Harackiewicz, 1979; Swann & Pittman, 1977; Weiner & Mander, 1978).[2]

---

[2]Two additional points deserve mention in this context. First, it is important to note that there is reason to believe that people may be much less likely to see their actions as instrumentally governed by social rewards and approval than by more tangible rewards and incentives (cf. Deci, 1975; Kelley,

On the basis of the evidence presented to this point, then, it appears that the likelihood that extrinsic rewards will undermine later intrinsic interest depends, at least, on two potentially competing processes—perceptions of one's actions as extrinsically constrained, hypothesized to decrease subsequent interest, and perceptions of personal competence at the activity, hypothesized to increase subsequent interest. In those cases in which extrinsic rewards may convey both sorts of information, the net effect of the procedure should depend upon the relative strength of these two effects. With the single exception of one study presented by Pittman, Boggiano, and Ruble (this volume), however, it is of interest to note that in none of these studies has the use of extrinsic rewards, even performance-contingent rewards conveying salient evidence of one's normative superiority at the task, been shown to significantly increase later intrinsic interest in the activity.

Relationships between Task Performance and Subsequent Intrinsic Interest

Let us turn, then, to a second general issue addressed by this subsequent literature on the conditions under which extrinsic rewards and constraints will have either positive or negative effects on later interest. This issue—which I wish to touch on only briefly here—concerns the potential mediation of later decreases in intrinsic interest by earlier detrimental effects of the reward manipulation on task performance during the initial treatment period.

If, as we shall see shortly, the inappropriate use of extrinsic incentives may produce not only detrimental effects on subsequent intrinsic interest in other settings in the later absence of further rewards, but may also have adverse effects on immediate task performance in the setting in which rewards are available, the question naturally arises as to whether the later effects of these manipulations in other settings depend upon prior differences in performance during the treatment phase. If this were so, obviously one would wish to view these subsequent effects in quite different theoretical terms.

The basic conclusions I wish to draw from the subsequent literature in this regard are relatively straightforward. Superfluous extrinsic rewards can clearly produce a variety of detrimental effects on measures of immediate task perfor-

---

1967; Kruglanski, 1978; Lepper & Greene, 1978b). This would imply that social contingencies should, in general, prove less likely than tangible contingency systems to produce adverse effects of subsequent intrinsic interest (Deci, 1975), unless efforts are taken to make the social contingency particularly explicit (cf. Smith, 1976). In the present analysis, therefore, we have concentrated on literature concerned with more palpable and salient tangible constraints. Second, as we will note later in this chapter, there are some cases in which even performance-contingent tangible rewards may decrease later interest (Deci, 1975; Harackiewicz, 1979; Sorenson & Maehr, 1976), suggesting that even the use of tangible rewards that provide information regarding one's competence at the activity may not provide a complete solution of the problem of how to use rewards without later negative effects on intrinsic interest.

mance; and, under conditions where such performance decrements are observed, these effects may themselves contribute to later decreases in subsequent intrinsic interest in the activity. At the same time, such performance impairments do not appear to be a necessary condition for the demonstration of later decreases in intrinsic interest in the absence of further rewards (cf. Lepper, 1981; Lepper & Greene, 1976, 1978b). A wide variety of studies, for example, has shown detrimental effects on later interest measures in the absence of previous performance decrements (Amabile et al., 1976; Boggiano & Ruble, 1979; Calder & Staw, 1975; Dollinger & Thelen, 1978; Enzle & Ross, 1978; Harackiewicz, 1979; Lepper & Greene, 1975; Lepper et al., in press; Ross, 1975; Ross, et al., 1976; Smith & Pittman, 1978). Likewise, experimental procedures that do produce significant negative or positive effects on immediate task performance do not necessarily produce corresponding decreases and increases in later intrinsic interest (Amabile, 1979; Lepper et al., 1981b; Ross et al., 1976). Performance decrements, in short, appear to depend much more precisely upon the nature of the activity and the contingency imposed upon one's engagement in that activity (i.e., the specific aspects of performance presented as relevant to attainment of the reward) than do subsequent decreases in later intrinsic interest in the absence of extrinsic rewards or constraints. The greater specificity of these performance effects makes theoretical sense, moreover, because these effects necessarily occur in a setting in which the subject is confronted with potentially conflicting motives based on the interest value of the task itself versus a desire to attain the extrinsic reward.

Multiple-Trial Reward Procedures and the Assessment of Intrinsic Interest

The third, and final, set of major issues this further literature has raised relates to both of the preceding concerns. It involves the question of whether the detrimental effects of extrinsic rewards observed in these previous studies will also occur following the use of multiple-trial and objectively effective reinforcement programs that can be shown to have increased response probability (i.e., task engagement) during the treatment phase. The question arises because most of the preceding studies—in order to rule out alternative explanations of decreases in later interest in terms of processes involving boredom, satiation, and the like—employed single-trial reward procedures that did not result in demonstrable increases in task engagement during treatment, relative to performance in non-rewarded control conditions. Hence, one may wonder whether the detrimental effects observed in these studies are limited to the use of such reward procedures.

Indeed, several authors have suggested that this may be the case and have provided a number of studies in which demonstrably effective, multiple-trial reinforcement procedures have been imposed on children's engagement in an activity of initial interest without subsequent detrimental effects on later task engagement, and often with positive effects on later behavior (Davidson &

Bucher, 1978; Feingold & Mahoney, 1975; Reiss & Sushinsky, 1975; Vasta, Andrews, McLaughlin, Stirpe, & Comfort, 1978; Vasta & Stirpe, 1979). These authors have typically explained their results in terms of either the habituation of distraction or frustration responses upon repeated presentation of rewards or the assumption that detrimental effects in prior studies are the result of immediate performance decrements or the use of rewards that are not objectively reinforcing to subjects. Other explanations are also possible: increased task engagement produced in these studies may itself affect factors, such as familiarity with (Zajonc, 1968, 1980), proficiency at (Bandura, 1978), or perceived competence regarding (Harter, 1978b) the activity, that may independently enhance later interest. A closer examination of the procedures employed in these studies in terms of our fundamental conceptual distinction between intrinsic and extrinsic motivation, however, suggests an even more general interpretative problem posed by these studies.

Specifically, in these studies children are presented with a small set of two to four activities during baseline periods in some experimental setting. Next they are exposed to a differential contingency in which engagement with one of these activities is rewarded and the others are not. Following this treatment phase, children are told that tangible rewards are no longer available. During this extinction period, however, these children continue to be confronted with this same limited set of activities in the same or a closely related situation. In this context, children appear more likely to continue to play with the previously rewarded item in the set of activities.

Perhaps these results indicate that detrimental effects do not occur when demonstrably effective multiple-trial reward systems are employed. Other investigations in which detrimental effects have been obtained following the use and withdrawal of demonstrably effective reinforcement programs, however, suggest that this is not the entire story (Brownell et al., 1977; Colvin, 1971; Greene et al., 1976; Lepper et al., 1981b; Smith & Pittman, 1978; Sorenson & Maehr, 1976). A second possibility, suggested by our distinction between intrinsic and extrinsic motivation, is that these different patterns of results are as much a function of differences in the measurement of subsequent task engagement as they are a function of differences in the effects of the reward procedure per se.

Simply put, the question from an attributional perspective is whether children in these studies—when confronted with the same set of activities during extinction, in a setting identical or similar to that in which they had received prior differential rewards for a specified target activity—believed that the experimenter expected them to, or would be more pleased if they were to continue to, engage in the previously rewarded activity. If children continued to engage in the activity in order to please the experimenter, just as if they had continued to engage in the activity to obtain further tangible rewards, we would not wish to infer that their behavior reflected "intrinsic" interest in the activity. Hence, the relevant experimental test would involve an examination of children's choices of the target activity in a dissociated setting, in which they were not aware that their behavior was being monitored or was of interest to adults in the environment.

To provide such a test, Lepper, Sagotsky, and Greene (1981b) examined the effects of a demonstrably effective multiple-trial reward procedure on children's subsequent engagement in the target activity in two different situations designed to vary in their potential social demands for continued engagement in the previously rewarded task. In the conditions of greatest interest, children preselected for an initial interest in a target activity in their classrooms were exposed to a set of four activities in individual experimental sessions and were offered either a differential reward for engaging in one of these four activities or a nondifferential reward for engaging in any of the activities. During these treatment sessions, children were rewarded with tokens on a fixed-interval schedule, with these tokens being redeemable at the end of the session for an attractive prize; and this multiple-trial reward procedure proved highly effective in producing increased task engagement when the reward was made contingent upon engagement in only the target activity. Other conditions, involving contingent or noncontingent rewards for engagement in the activity in the absence of other alternatives, provided a control for the effects of increased task engagement per se.

Subsequently, these children's reactions to the target activity were assessed in two quite different settings—when the activity was again presented in children's classrooms, in the clear absence of further constraints and where children were not aware that their behavior was under observation; and upon their return to the experimental setting, in which they were confronted with the same set of alternatives as during the treatment phase and in which they knew their responses were being observed (although these sessions were conducted by a different experimenter who informed the children specifically that there would be no further tangible rewards). The contrasting results obtained from the same set of children on these two measures were informative. When subsequent intrinsic interest was assessed unobtrusively in children's classrooms, as in our previous studies, subjects exposed to the contingent reward procedure showed significantly less interest than subjects presented with noncontingent rewards or no rewards during treatment. When subsequent task engagement was assessed upon children's return to the experimental room when confronted with the same set of activities, the above findings were reversed and contingent-reward subjects continued to engage more in the previously rewarded activity than appropriate controls. That these data may, indeed, be a function of the presence of perceived demand characteristics in this latter setting is suggested by additional data gathered in a subsequent study, in which different children were presented with a description of another child going through our experimental procedure and were asked to indicate whether they felt that the adults in the classroom or in the experimental room would be more pleased if this child were to play with the target activity or other available activities. Children who witnessed an enactment of our contingent-reward condition with this procedure appeared to distinguish clearly between the social contingencies that prevailed in these two settings: Most felt that the new experimenter in the game room would be most pleased if the child continued to play with the target activity, but very few felt that the teachers in the classroom would care whether the child played with this or other activities.

Without further data concerning children's perceptions of the settings in which subsequent task engagement has been assessed in previous studies, it would be inappropriate to conclude that this distinction provides a sufficient explanation of previous conflicting results. The data from this study do suggest, however, that the demonstration of detrimental effects on subsequent interest in the task are likely to be observed only under conditions in which children do believe that their continued engagement in the target activity will no longer be instrumental to the attainment of further tangible, or social, rewards. They also indicate, along with other studies cited above, that the mere use of an objectively effective, multiple-trial reinforcement procedure is not itself sufficient to eliminate detrimental effects on later intrinsic interest.[3]

Summary: Detrimental Effects of Extrinsic Rewards on Subsequent Intrinsic Interest

Our review of the literature on the conditions that determine when the use of extrinsic rewards will have detrimental effects on subsequent intrinsic interest, then, suggests that one needs to take into account at least three potentially distinct effects that rewards may have on subjects' perceptions of continued instrumentality, personal competence, and external constraint.

Thus, provision of extrinsic rewards contingent upon task engagement or performance may affect subjects' *perceptions of continued instrumentality*, to the extent that the receipt of reward leads the individual to believe that further tangible, or social, rewards may follow continued task engagement in the future. The result of such changes should be increased task engagement in those situations in which the activity is perceived to be of continued instrumental value; but these effects should not influence behavior in settings in which this is not assumed to be so.

At the same time, the provision of extrinsic rewards contingent upon the quality of one's performance at an activity may influence subjects' *perceptions*

---

[3]Without some direct attempt to measure children's expectations concerning the social demands inherent in particular experimental situations, of course, it is difficult to draw unequivocal conclusions regarding the prevalence of such demands across different experiments. Presumably, perceptions of continued social instrumentality will depend upon a number of factors—the continuity of treatment and testing phases, the nature of the contingency employed and the alternative activities presented, the child's awareness of being observed, and the specific instructions given to children during the posttest phase—and the issue requires further explicit attention. The procedural controls included in at least some of the studies (e.g., Davidson & Bucher, 1978) reporting a positive effect of multiple-trial reward procedures on later task engagement, however, do suggest that these effects are not solely a function of differences in the dependent measures employed.

of personal competence at the activity. Under most circumstances, increases in perceived competence are predicted to increase subsequent interest in the activity for its own sake.

Finally, the provision of contingent, and particularly superfluous, extrinsic rewards may lead to *perceptions of external constraint,* as may other forms of salient social control. The consequence of such perceptions, other factors held constant, will be decreases in subsequent intrinsic interest, as assessed in subsequent situations in which further extrinsic constraints are no longer salient.

Predictions of the effects on subsequent task engagement of any particular reward system will, therefore, depend upon the effects that program has on each of these factors, as well as the situation in which subsequent behavior is observed (cf. Lepper & Gilovich, 1981, for a more detailed discussion).

Adverse Effects on Immediate Task Performance

Excluded from this brief summary, of course, are the possible effects of variations in task performance, produced by the imposition of extrinsic rewards, on subsequent interest. Let us turn now to this second class of potential detrimental effects that the inappropriate use of extrinsic rewards may have and the conditions under which they occur. Historically, I might note, my own interest in such effects began with the discovery of performance decrements in our own early studies on the effects of extrinsic rewards (Greene & Lepper, 1974; Lepper et al., 1973) that were purely incidental to our primary interest in the effects of these rewards on later interest. Because these effects occurred in the setting in which rewards were offered and seemed readily explained by traditional and well-documented analyses of reward effects, moreover, such findings seemed of lesser theoretical interest. As the evidence concerning adverse effects of rewards on task performance has accumulated, however, it seems clear to me that these traditional models have at least underestimated the range and prevalence of such effects and that these effects ought to be considered of interest in their own right (Condry, 1977; McGraw, 1978). Let us review briefly the evidence that bears on such claims in terms of the effects that extrinsic rewards may have on subjects' goals in undertaking the activity, the control of subjects' attention, and subjects' learning from task engagement.

Effects on Goal Selection and Approach to the Activity

Consider, first, the effects of the offer of contingent extrinsic rewards on subjects' goals in undertaking an activity and their approach to the activity. When an activity is undertaken explicitly in order to attain some extrinsic reward, a number of authors (Condry & Chambers, 1978; Kruglanski, 1978; Lepper & Greene, 1978b) have suggested that those features of task engagement that are perceived as relevant to attainment of that reward will define a set of goals or criteria that will guide subjects' approach to and engagement in the activity. In fact, these authors have suggested, the presence of such goals is likely to lead subjects to respond by seeking the least effortful and most perfunctory way of insuring reward attainment, even if that means that task engagement will itself be less inherently interesting to the subject. Kruglanski, Stein, and Riter (1978) describe this tendency in terms of a "minimax" principle: Subjects are motivated to maximize reward with a minimum of effort. It appears in studies on the effects of rewards on performance in several areas.

Perhaps the most obvious evidence of such a process is apparent in children's attempts to circumvent contingency systems in which effortful problem-solving would normally be required for reward attainment. There is both a wealth of anecdotal evidence (cf. Holt, 1964) and some experimental evidence (Condry & Chambers, 1978) to suggest that the offer of a reward contingent upon the solution of a complex task will lead subjects to guess repeatedly at the solution without doing the work involved to examine the correctness of their guesses. Alternatively, if attention has not been paid to the possibility in designing the system, imposition of an attractive reward system may lead children to find ways of cheating to arrive at answers that will produce the reward without doing the required work (Silberman, 1970; cf. Kazdin & Bootzin, 1973; Turkewitz, O'Leary & Ironsmith, 1975).

Similar adverse effects have been observed when extrinsic reward systems have been imposed on task performance with activities that permit the subject to select particular problems to work on from a larger set containing problems of varying difficulty levels. In the absence of extrinsic rewards, as we know from a variety of evidence on achievement and intrinsic motivation (Hunt, 1961, 1965; Weiner, 1974), subjects confronted with such a choice will typically show a preference for problems of moderate, or intermediate, difficulty—choices that have been hypothesized to maximize challenge and intrinsic interest in the task. When confronted with such a task under conditions where extrinsic rewards have been offered contingent upon correct problem solutions, however, both adults (Condry & Chambers, 1978; Shapira, 1976) and children (Blackwell, 1974; Harter, 1978a) will show marked shifts toward the choice of less difficult and challenging problems, which are more likely to insure the attainment of the proffered rewards. These shifts appear to occur, frequently, at the expense of one's enjoyment of the activity per se. Harter (1978a), for example, found grade-school children told that they would be graded on their performance on an anagrams task smiled less upon solving each problem, both as a function of their choice of less challenging problems and as a function of the presence of an extrinsic incentive within each level of difficulty, than did subjects not exposed to this contingency. Similarly, Blackwell (1974) found that an increased choice of easier problems during the reward phase was accompanied by subsequent decreases in later intrinsic interest in the activity in the absence of further constraints.

Effects on the Control of Attentional Processes and Task Engagement

Closely related to the effects described above is a second class of findings suggesting potential detrimental effects of extrinsic rewards on task performance as a function of effects that contingent rewards and the goals of activity they imply may have on the allocation of subjects' attention during task engagement. That is, when an individual is engaged in an activity in order to obtain a reward, his or her attention is likely to be centered on those parameters or goals of task performance that are seen as instrumentally relevant to the receipt of reward. With tasks sufficiently complex to demand a substantial investment of attention, this focusing will result in correspondingly less attention devoted toward aspects of the activity that are not perceived to be instrumentally relevant (Condry & Chambers, 1978; Lepper & Greene, 1978b; McGraw, 1978; Simon, 1967). Such a shift in attention, depending upon the nature of the task employed and the contingency imposed, may result in a number of potentially adverse effects on performance.

It has long been recognized in the learning literature, for example, that salient rewards may simultaneously enhance task performance along dimensions central to reward attainment but impair incidental learning along dimensions not relevant to receipt of reward (McCullers, 1978; McGraw, 1978). More recent studies examining the effects of extrinsic rewards on later intrinsic interest provide added evidence of the potential adverse effects of rewards on incidental learning (Harackiewicz, 1979; Kruglanski et al., 1971). Similar effects also appear when the effects of rewards on central versus incidental dimensions of performance, rather than learning, are examined (Kruglanski, 1978; Kruglanski et al., 1978). In two of our own early studies, for instance, children offered a reward for drawing pictures during a given time period produced more pictures, but pictures that were rated by independent judges as lower in average quality (Greene & Lepper, 1974; Lepper et al., 1973).

Perhaps more surprisingly, there is also evidence that the inappropriate use of extrinsic rewards may have deleterious effects, with certain sorts of activities, even on measures of performance designated as central to reward attainment. In independent studies using measures of literary and artistic creativity, respectively, Kruglanski, Friedman, and Zeevi (1971) and Amabile (1979) have shown decreases in creativity to result from the imposition of extrinsic constraints on task performance, even when the tasks were explicitly presented as involving creative performance. Likewise, McGraw and McCullers (1979; McGraw, 1978) provide and review evidence to suggest that the offer of extrinsic rewards may impair performance on tasks that require "insight" or the ability to "break set" for their solution.

In two rather more complex studies, Garbarino (1975) and Condry and Chambers (1978) illustrate further, more qualitative, adverse effects of rewards on task performance. In the Garbarino study, sixth-grade girls were engaged to serve as tutors for a first-grade child, either with or without promise of a reward based on their tutoring effectiveness. Subjects offered a reward conducted tutoring sessions that involved more criticism, impatience, and negative affect and made less efficient use of their time. As a result, rewarded subjects were less successful in achieving their primary goal, in that their tutees learned the material significantly less well. In the Condry and Chambers study, college subjects were presented with a complex concept-attainment task under contingent-reward or no-reward conditions. In addition to attempting to guess the answer earlier and more persistently, subjects expecting a reward made less efficient use of their time on task as indexed by a variety of different measures.

In an extensive review of these and other findings, McGraw (1978) has suggested that these detrimental effects on central performance measures are most likely to occur when the activity in question is both of initial interest to subjects in its own right and of sufficient complexity as to require a ''heuristic'' rather than an ''algorithmic'' approach for successful performance—conditions under which a narrow preoccupation with those parameters of performance most obviously relevant to task solution may have negative instead of positive results. Such an account is generally consistent with earlier work by Easterbrook (1959) on the narrowing of cue utilization and by Spence (1956) on the increased reliance on well-rehearsed and overlearned responses hypothesized to result when contingent incentives are present—at least in that each of these accounts implies that the appearance of such detrimental effects will depend upon the interaction of task demands and subjects' skills (cf. Lepper & Greene, 1978b).

Effects on Subsequent Learning and Performance

The final class of potential adverse effects of improperly designed contingency systems that I wish to consider concerns the possible negative effects of extrinsic rewards on subsequent learning or subsequent performance in the later absence of further constraints. Unfortunately, I raise these issues largely to signal their importance, on both theoretical and practical grounds, and to indicate that very little relevant research has been conducted on this topic.

We have already considered a number of cases in which detrimental effects obtained during treatment sessions may relate to decreases in subsequent intrinsic interest and a diminished probability that the individual will subsequently choose to engage in that activity in the later absence of further rewards or constraints. There are, however, a number of other questions that might be raised concerning subsequent learning and performance. If the offer of extrinsic rewards in a particular setting, for example, leads children to selectively choose to attempt only problems that they are certain they can already answer correctly, one might expect them to learn less, in the long run, from their engagement in the activity than children who have attempted more difficult and challenging problems during this period. Perhaps such a system, over some period of time, might teach children to avoid challenging problems. We do not, at this time, have any evidence on these sorts of questions.

Indeed, only the Condry and Chambers study provides a clear example of a subsequent performance deficit, although it is an elegant and potentially important finding. Their subjects, it will be recalled, were asked to attempt a concept-attainment task, with or without the expectation of a reward contingent upon successful discovery of the underlying concept; and subjects in the reward condition of this study showed a propensity for guessing at the answer and made less efficient use of their time on task. The further, and more striking, result I wish to highlight here is that when these subjects were subsequently confronted with a similar activity but were explicitly instructed not to guess or give an answer until they could be sure that it was correct, those subjects who had previously undertaken the task in order to obtain a reward were significantly more likely to assert that they had discovered the correct solution before they could logically have ascertained its correctness.

Summary: Detrimental Effects of Extrinsic Rewards on Task Performance

In summary, this recent literature reveals a variety of potential adverse effects of extrinsic rewards on immediate task performance, which are of theoretical interest and clear educational relevance in their own right. Such performance deficits, when they occur, may contribute to later decreases in intrinsic interest; but they appear not to be a precondition for such subsequent effects. Instead, these detrimental effects appear to depend much more specifically on the particular structure of the activity involved and the precise nature of the contingency imposed on one's engagement in the activity—as one might expect when subjects' behavior is observed in settings in which those instrumental contingencies are present.

Although a comprehensive explanation of the conditions under which these adverse performance effects will occur is undoubtedly more complex (cf. Condry & Chambers, 1978, Deci & Porac, 1978; Lepper & Greene, 1978b), this brief review suggests that much of this work can be understood in terms of the effects of imposed contingencies on subjects' goals in approaching and undertaking the activity and on the focus of subjects' attention as they engage in the activity. Thus, the imposition of salient extrinsic contingencies on performance appears to define a set of minimally effortful criteria designed to insure the attainment of reward. These *instrumentally-directed goals and criteria* for task performance may, as we have indicated elsewhere (Lepper & Greene, 1978b), influence task engagement and performance in a hierarchical sense on a number of levels. These goals may serve to define the conditions under which one will approach the task, the standards one will set in monitoring one's ongoing performance, and the point at which one will terminate engagement with the task. The results may include a preference for less challenging, less complex, and less risky alternatives, a search for ways of circumventing the imposed contingency entirely, or performance geared to reward attainment with the minimal investment of effort and involvement in the task. Such effects may, further, result in less satisfaction from task engagement per se.

In a closely related vein, the offer of contingent extrinsic rewards may also result in a *focusing of attention on dimensions or parameters of task performance seen as instrumental to receipt of reward*. In cases where our limited attentional capacities are at all taxed by the task at hand, this will result, as well, in corresponding decreases in attention devoted to parameters or aspects of the activity that are not perceived as instrumentally relevant. The consequences of this attentional shift may include both general decrements in incidental learning or performance on incidental task parameters, across a variety of tasks, and detrimental effects even on measures of central task performance, when the task itself is complex and not easily amenable to solution through the application of well-learned algorithms or responses.

In predicting the ultimate effects of any reward program, therefore, a complete account will need to consider not only the effects the program may have on perceptions of continued instrumentality, personal competence, and extrinsic constraint. It must deal as well with the subsequent effects of either positive or negative effects of rewards on task engagement and task performance.

IMPLICATIONS FOR THE CLASSROOM

The preceding section provides an overview of what I take to be the central themes of the research literature concerned with the potential detrimental effects of extrinsic rewards and constraints on task performance and subsequent intrinsic interest. I would like to turn at this point to a consideration of the possible implications of this literature for the classroom setting. In the best of all worlds, the section to follow would contain a clear set of prescriptive dicta regarding the use of extrinsic rewards in classrooms, but I do not believe that the present literature is sufficient to warrant such a summary. Instead the best I believe I can fairly offer is an indication of the further questions we would need to be able to answer to determine the actual significance of these findings for classroom practice and a few bits of data that may be relevant to some of these issues.

The Engineering Question

Let us consider, then, the first of these questions—what might be called the engineering issue. Clearly the preceding literature establishes that the inappropriate use of extrinsic rewards can have detrimental effects on task performance and subsequent intrinsic interest. Yet we also know, from years of laboratory research on reinforcement processes (e.g., Glaser, 1971) and the application of systematic reward programs in classrooms (e.g., O'Leary, 1978), that the appearance of such effects is not a necessary or routine consequence of the use of extrinsic rewards. Hence, a reasonable proponent of a more traditional reinforcement model might well argue that the foregoing results provide no fundamental challenge to that model, but instead indicate only that it is possible to design reward programs sufficiently ill-conceived that they will seem to show detrimental effects. With slight, and largely technical, changes in the procedures used, this argument runs, we should be able to show that rewards will have positive effects on these same indices in these same contexts. The evidence of adverse effects of rewards is thus viewed as a problem in engineering and application, rather than an indication of some potentially more fundamental limitations on the contexts in which the traditional model is applicable. Let us examine this thesis, first in the context of adverse effects of rewards on task performance, and then in the context of detrimental effects on later interest.

Effects on Task Performance

If one considers the literature on adverse performance effects in this light, there is, I think, considerable merit to the engineering argument, although there are some cases in which it may not apply. Take the findings that the imposition of a reward system may lead to attempts to circumvent that system, by guessing, cheating, or other means. This clearly is a classic issue in applied behavior analysis (Kazdin, 1975; Kazdin & Bootzin, 1973), and one that, for practical purposes, has a simple engineering solution in most cases. One simply needs to be sufficiently clever in designing the contingency system to take into account this possibility and to include such possible responses in the contingency system itself: if children appear to be cheating to obtain the rewards, for example, the imposition of some additional monitoring system and negative sanctions for cheating may be sufficient to eliminate this problem (e.g., Turkewitz et al., 1975).

Consider as well the finding that the offer of rewards may lead children to select only problems they are certain they can already solve, in order to insure receipt of the reward. Although this finding has been obtained across a number of studies, all of these demonstrations share a common contingency system, in which one is rewarded equally for correct problem solutions regardless of the difficulty of the problem attempted. In this case it makes instrumental sense for children to select only easy problems. On the other hand, relatively minor variations in the contingency system, we have found, may eliminate or reverse this effect. In one dissertation, for example, Blackwell (1974) compared the effects of two sorts of contingency procedures to a nonrewarded control condition: in one case, as in other research, children were offered rewards for each problem solved; in the other, children were told that they would later be tested on what they had learned from the activity and that the rewards they received would depend on their performance on that test. Children offered rewards for problem solutions showed the expected shift toward the selection of less challenging problems; children offered rewards contingent upon "learning" did not.

Other performance effects seem amenable to a similar analysis. We have found, for example, that the detrimental effects of rewards on the quality of children's art work obtained in our own earliest studies (Greene & Lepper, 1974; Lepper et al., 1973) can be easily eliminated by simply making the contingency more specific concerning the amount of work required to obtain the reward. Thus, when we asked children in later studies to make a specific number of drawings or to engage in the activity for a specified period of time in order to obtain the reward, detrimental effects of rewards on quality of performance were no longer apparent. Even in more complex cases, there may be some truth to the engineering analysis. A recent dissertation by Amabile (1979), for example, provides some conceptually related data regarding the effects of intrinsic constraints on judged creativity of artistic products. In the conditions most relevant to present concerns, Amabile compared two sorts of contingency systems with an appropriate control condition. In the first group, subjects were told that their performance would be evaluated in terms of its creativity, but were given no specific instructions on how this goal might be achieved; in the second condition, subjects were told that their performance would be evaluated in terms of its creativity, and were given a set of quite specific instructions concerning the dimensions of performance along which creativity would be judged. In the former case, evaluation contingent upon creativity led to less creative efforts; in the latter case, in which subjects were provided with specific criteria, expected evaluation along these dimensions led to products that were rated as higher in creativity.

The findings I have just described, then, suggest that the adverse effects of extrinsic rewards on task performance may be viewed, in many cases, as a problem in the design of appropriate contingency systems. In terms of our earlier analysis, the key to eliminating or reversing these performance effects seems to lie in the use of contingencies that are (1) designed to encompass the range of performance dimensions seen as important for learning (i.e., to transform previously "incidental" task parameters into "central," instrumentally-relevant parameters), and (2) sufficiently specific to allow subjects to meet performance standards through the application of known algorithms (i.e., to transform tasks that are initially "heuristic" into tasks that are "algorithmic").

Clearly this account provides an engineering interpretation of a number of the findings indicating that rewards may have detrimental effects on task performance. Whether it provides a complete account, however, is not at all clear. One might well argue, for example, that there are some sorts of tasks, notably those that appear to require "insight" for task solution, for which it may not be possible to design appropriately algorithmic contingency systems. Perhaps the McGraw and McCullers (1979) data on tasks involving "breaking set" would provide one example; at present the issue remains open.

Effects on Subsequent Intrinsic Interest

A similar set of issues, of course, may be raised concerning the import of findings illustrating the potential deleterious effects of extrinsic rewards on subsequent intrinsic interest. Here, I believe a consideration of these results in terms of an engineering analysis is considerably more complex. There is, for example, a very simple, but theoretically irrelevant, engineering solution to these difficulties that parallels exactly our preceding suggestions. It involves the simple extension of the contingency system to any other setting in which we may care about the child's behavior. If a contingency system instituted to decrease inappropriate behavior during subjects' afternoon classes should prove to have opposite, detrimental effects on those same children's behavior in their morning classes where the contingency system is not in effect, for example, one might simply extend the reward system to encompass the child's entire school day (Meichenbaum, Bowers, & Ross, 1968). In this way, we may disregard whatever effects the program may have on intrinsic interest and need only make certain that our reward system is sufficiently powerful to control behavior in both settings. For many practical purposes, depending upon one's goals in instituting a reward program, this may prove to be the "right" answer; and the "programming" of environments in which "generalization" is to be assessed can be quite effective in producing continued functional control (Kazdin, 1974, 1977; O'Leary, 1978). At the same time, such efforts simply do not speak to issues concerning the effects of the program on later intrinsic interest: the potential problem is concealed, and escalated, but not resolved, by such solutions.

For theoretical purposes, then, let us restrict our consideration to methods for overcoming and reversing the negative effects of extrinsic rewards on intrinsic interest in subsequent situations in which there are no further extrinsic constraints or incentives contingent upon task performance or engagement. In this sense, there are three major classes of engineering solutions that have been suggested. Two of these, the use of performance-contingent and multiple-trial reward systems, are implicit in our earlier review. The third, involving the gradual withdrawal of rewards over time, has not yet received explicit study.

Given our earlier review, for example, it might be suggested that many of the adverse effects of rewards on subsequent intrinsic interest could be eliminated through the use of performance-contingent, rather than merely task-contingent, rewards. The idea has intuitive appeal and some research support. It also has some inherent limitations. First, it seems clear that this strategy is more applicable to some sorts of activities and responses than others. It seems, for example, particularly applicable to cases in which the target response involves performance on tasks that involve clear criteria of accuracy or excellence. Here it is easy to set relevant performance standards by which children's performances can be evaluated in either absolute or relative terms. It seems less applicable, by contrast, to cases in which the target behavior may involve the inhibition of particular responses, where criteria of excellence and perceptions of "competence'' may be considerably less relevant (Lepper, in press). Second, it is a strategy that appears to work best when the information that the rewards convey indicates to the child that his or her performance is superior to that of others. The obvious problem with this common use of rewards in normal classrooms is that the use of comparative systems necessarily involves exposure of equal numbers of children to evidence concerning their inferior, as well as superior, competence. Finally, the experimental results to date suggest that, even under ''optimal'' conditions, from these perspectives, this answer is only a partial one. In none of the relevant comparative studies, for instance, have performance-contingent rewards been shown to increase later intrinsic interest; nor have such procedures been universally successful (Deci, 1975; Harackiewicz, 1979; Sorenson & Maehr, 1976) even in making adverse effects less likely.

A second obvious possibility, also suggested by our earlier review, involves the use of demonstrably effective multiple-trial reinforcement procedures. Again, this strategy, as indicated earlier, appears at best a partial answer, since a number of studies have found later detrimental effects even when such multiple-trial procedures have been employed and there remain some important questions concerning the interpretation of previous studies showing positive effects on later ''intrinsic'' interest. Nonetheless, this is clearly an issue that deserves further investigation. My own bias—and let me label it clearly as such—is that such programs will be most likely to have long-term positive effects on subsequent intrinsic interest under two conditions. Most obviously, benefits should accrue from the use of demonstrably effective reinforcement programs when the target activity is one for which continued task engagement and performance will be likely to result in the acquisition of relevant skills and abilities that may themselves enhance the value of the activity or may prove relevant to the child's own interests in other contexts. To take a simple example, rewarding a child for progressing through a mathematics curriculum in which he or she may acquire skills that allow new insights into math problems, or even just permit him or her to compute that season's batting averages in Little League, seems inherently more likely to have long-term positive benefits than merely rewarding the child for not acting out in class during math periods (cf. Ayllon & Roberts, 1974; O'Leary, 1978). Perhaps more subtly, it may also prove to be important that such programs may serve to vividly inform and make salient to children the increases in their actual competence and proficiency that do occur over the course of time. In both cases, then, we may find the issues involving the use of multiple-trial rewards to overlap more than one might have expected with concerns of perceived competence and ability.

The third possible engineering solution to the negative effects of rewards on later intrinsic interest involves an issue that has not been investigated experimentally in this literature, although its possible importance has often been noted (Lepper & Greene, 1976, 1978b, 1978c; O'Leary, 1978; Vasta, in press). It involves the use of various ''fading'' procedures for gradually withdrawing extrinsic rewards previously provided for particular responses. From the standpoint of both an attributional model and traditional reinforcement models, such techniques might be predicted to decrease the probability of subsequent detrimental effects, though it is not clear, once again, that such effects would be reversed. Within the applied literature, for example, there is a small amount of evidence from comparisons across studies to suggest that this procedure may make some difference (cf. Kazdin, 1977; O'Leary, 1978), but most of these comparisons are confounded by other differences in procedure. Once again, the need for additional data seems apparent.

To summarize my speculations on the engineering question briefly, it seems to me that this proposal has both some merit and some limitations. With respect to the design of reward programs to reverse the adverse effects rewards may have on task performance measures, the analysis seems appropriate for many—though perhaps not all—of the major findings. With respect to the design of reward systems to reverse the adverse effects rewards may have on subsequent intrinsic interest, the picture is more complex. With the obvious exception of attempts to systematically program subsequent environments (which simply finesses questions of intrinsic interest), the engineering approaches considered have not yet proved effective in reversing, or even eliminating, adverse effects consistently.

Indeed, it is probably worth noting that I have addressed in this discussion only the weak form of the engineering argument, in that I have focused throughout on the question of the absolute effects of different sorts of reward programs—whether children are, colloquially, "better off," "worse off," or about the same as if they had not been exposed to the reward program. The stronger, and ultimately more significant, form of the question would, of course, go one step further—to ask whether children exposed to a particular program of one sort of another are better off than they would have been had other social control techniques, not involving the use of tangible rewards, been applied. In this stronger sense, then, we would want to know whether children exposed to performance-contingent rewards are "better" or "worse" off than children simply given equivalent information concerning their competence at the task in the absence of additional palpable rewards; and we would want to know whether children induced to engage in an activity through the use of tangible rewards would fare differently from others induced to engage in the activity for an equivalent period through other less powerfully coercive means (if, in the particular case, such alternative means can be found).[4]

---

[4]Whether, in a particular case, less obviously coercive techniques can be found that would prove equally effective in producing the desired response is an empirical reflection of the extent to which more powerful techniques would be, in fact, superfluous. The possible alternatives that might be considered, moreover, might take many forms, ranging from changes in the manner or format in which materials are presented to the use of less obvious, but still systematic, use of contingent social approval. The evident, but sometimes overlooked, point of this discussion is that it is possible to separate the use of tangible, material rewards per se from those other procedures and social control techniques that often accompany the introduction of a systematic reward program.

Training in Self-Reinforcement: A Brief Digression.   Before turning to the other two questions I wish to pose, let me digress for a moment to point to a fourth alternative means for potentially overcoming or reversing the negative effects of extrinsic rewards on later interest: the use of techniques designed explicitly to train children to evaluate and reinforce themselves contingent upon task engagement or performance. This approach is not, as I have defined the issue, a simple question of engineering and design. It involves fundamental changes in procedures and assumptions and not merely technical ones. The increasing attention that such techniques are currently receiving, however, and their potential significance prompts me to illustrate their use briefly.

In essence, the idea behind these approaches is to supplant initially externally-imposed contingency systems with comparable self-imposed contingencies through the gradual withdrawal of extrinsic rewards and explicit training procedures designed to induce children to evaluate their behavior systematically according to the same standards. Because self-imposed contingency systems are not inherently tied to particular situations in which others are present to evaluate and reinforce one's actions, they carry the potential for producing changes in behavior that may generalize to new settings in the absence of continued surveillance or constraints. Although good comparative studies are lacking, the results of initial clinical applications of such techniques in classrooms suggest that these techniques may be relatively more likely to produce changes in behavior that will be maintained once extrinsic rewards have been withdrawn and may be more likely to produce generalization of those changes in behavior to other settings (Bandura, 1976; Drabman, Spitalnik & O'Leary, 1973; Mahoney, 1977; O'Leary, 1978; Turkewitz, et al., 1975). Furthermore, recent experimental studies indicating that self-imposed contingency systems are less likely than equivalent externally-imposed contingency systems to produce decrements in later interest in the activity in the absence of further constraints (Brownell et al., 1977; Enzle & Look, 1980; Lepper et al., 1981a; Weiner & Dubanoski, 1975) suggest the theoretical relevance of these techniques to issues involving the reduction of perceptions of constraint and control.[5] Again, the outlook for additional research is promising.

The Ecological Relevance Question

Even if one were to accept completely the engineering argument and its underlying premise that the potential detrimental effects of extrinsic rewards can be reversed simply through the use of more sophisticated contingency systems, the

---

[5]Even self-determined contingency systems may sometimes prove inimical to subsequent intrinsic interest however (Dollinger & Thelen, 1978). To understand more concerning the conditions under which such programs will be effective, we will need further information on the way in which such programs may affect perceptions of both competence and constraint (cf. Lepper et al., 1981a).

question of the relevance of this literature to classroom practice would still remain open. That is, even if optimal methods of employing rewards to enhance performance and subsequent interest were known, one might still be appropriately concerned with what I will term the ecological relevance question—the extent to which there are non-optimal methods of using rewards that are common in classroom practice which may be illuminated by the research under consideration. It is important to distinguish, in short, between what is known about the most effective ways in which rewards may be employed (or even the applications of this knowledge embodied in professionally-designed research on the use of systematic reward programs in classrooms) and what typically goes on in a mundane, day-to-day sense in most classrooms.

Unfortunately, there are extraordinarily few data, and virtually none in sufficient detail, to help us answer this second question. Our own informal observations of classrooms and the largely anecdotal accounts of other observers (e.g., Holt, 1964; Jackson, 1968; Silberman, 1970; Sternberg, 1978), however, clearly suggest that rewards are often employed in non-optimal ways that may have, for some students, unintended negative consequences. That this is likely the case should come as no surprise, moreover, since the very prevalence and dramatic effectiveness of token economies in the classroom already stand as implicit testimony to the difficulties teachers have in using the conventional rewards at their disposal to achieve even immediate functional control over students' behavior.

Nor should this fact be viewed as an indictment or criticism of teachers. The fundamental premise of our educational system—that a single adult is charged with the simultaneous control and education of up to forty children representing a diversity of abilities and interests—seems virtually to insure that teachers are faced with an almost impossible task (Dreeben, 1968; Jackson, 1968). And it is the necessity for dealing with large groups of children in some consistent fashion that may make the inappropriate use of contingency systems more likely (Lepper & Dafoe, 1979). Indeed, my own interest in the educational relevance of this work stemmed initially from informal observations of Head Start programs, in which demonstrably effective, though amateurish, systematic reward programs were being used to induce children to engage, for short periods each day, in activities deemed of particular educational relevance—through the offer of candies and snacks contingent upon task engagement. An informal comparison of these programs with other comparable Head Start centers in which these same materials were made available to children without explicit contingencies suggested that the imposition of this contingency system may have had quite different effects on different children in these classes. Certainly, there were many children in the less ''structured'' programs who seemed never to engage in these activities; there were also, however, other children who seemed to find these very activities highly interesting and who would spend a considerable amount of time with these materials. The imposition of an explicit contingency system seemed to result in all children engaging in these activities during the reward period, but there was a complete lack of interest in these same activities during the remainder of the day. Inferentially, for those children with little or no initial intrinsic interest, task engagement had been enhanced; but for those children high in initial interest, the reward system appeared to have defined the activities as things to be done only when the rewards were available.

What is clearly needed, then, is more systematic observational data concerning the ways in which tangible rewards and extrinsic constraints are applied in normal classrooms—high quality research of the sort exemplified in the work of Brophy, Dweck, deCharms, and others on the complex contingencies that prevail in the average classroom (Brophy, 1981; Brophy & Evertson, 1976; Brophy & Good, 1974; deCharms, 1976; Dweck, Davidson, Nelson, & Enna, 1978). In addition to learning more about the sorts of contingency systems that are employed in classrooms, however, there is a second variety of evidence we would also need to be able to judge the relevance of the research I have described to current classroom practice—evidence concerning the activities, if any, that children are asked to undertake at school that are of potential or initial intrinsic interest to them.

Obviously, if all the activities that children were asked to undertake in school were inherently dull and boring and likely to remain so independent of one's proficiency at them, we should have no concern over the possibility that classroom practices might inadvertently decrease children's intrinsic interest. Not only is it literally impossible to undermine interest that does not exist; a number of recent studies suggest that the same sorts of extrinsic reward procedures that may decrease interest in activities of high intrinsic interest may also have a positive effect on later interest in activities that are not initially attractive to the subject (Calder & Staw, 1975; Loveland & Olley, 1979; McLoyd, 1979; Upton, 1974).

Although it may represent an overly romantic or naive view of school, I do not accept the premise that all academically profitable activities children confront in school are, or need be, intrinsically uninteresting. Let me share with you, however, what I think is an important observation that I have made over the past several years as a result of describing my own work on the possible negative effects of extrinsic rewards to teachers' groups of various sorts. The observation concerns teachers' perceptions of the relevance of these findings for classroom practice, as a function of the age of the children they teach. When I describe my research to teachers who work with young children, at the preschool or kindergarten level especially, their response is animated and enthusiastic. Not only are they interested in the work, however, they really seem to understand the concepts involved and appear to find them relevant to their own observations of children in school. They ask sensible questions, point to important qualifications, and frequently provide examples of cases that illustrate our basic phenomenon from their own classroom experiences. By contrast, when I deliver essentially the same talk to an audience of teachers who themselves work with older children, for example at the junior high level, the response seems quite different. The teachers are typically interested and often complimentary; but their first comment, almost invariably, is that the findings I have described simply don't have much application to their own classrooms *because* most of the work we ask children to do in school is not intrinsically motivating and one must apply contingencies if one is to get them to learn the material presented.

In fact, recent data reported by Harter (1981) suggest that there may be some truth to these teachers' perceptions that students' intrinsic interest in school subjects decreases as children progress through school, or at least that the children themselves share this perception. Using a collection of self-report measures designed to assess children's intrinsic versus extrinsic motivational orientation toward school with samples of third- through ninth-grade subjects, Harter found consistent monotonic decreases in reported intrinsic interest in school with increasing grade level. Across several different measures, children in the higher grades reported that they were more likely to undertake school work in order to win teacher approval or to satisfy the minimal performance requirements for good grades than to satisfy their own curiosity, learn for their own satisfaction, or master a challenging task.

Whether these differences in teachers' and students' perceptions at different levels in the schooling process are simply an objective reflection of differences in the curricula to which children are exposed at different ages, a function of biases in perception that result from the larger system of social controls in which both students and teachers are enmeshed (cf. Lepper & Greene, 1975), or a long-term consequence of precisely the sorts of processes we have discussed in this chapter seems to me a critical question for further investigation.

The Evaluation Question

In an important sense, both the engineering and ecological relevance questions are complex, but fundamentally empirical, questions. The third question I believe we may have to face, the issue of how different contingency systems may be evaluated, seems inherently less dependent upon questions of data than questions of values. Let me conclude with a couple of observations on this issue.

Most generally, it seems to me that the evaluation of particular reward programs will necessarily depend upon our goals and the relative values we may place on the multiple, and often conflicting, results that complex contingency systems may produce. These potential "trade-offs" involved in any particular program are likely, moreover, to appear on several different levels. For a given child and a given subject matter, for example, an analysis of the optimal conditions for enhancing motivation will depend upon the skills and knowledge the child initially possesses and those he or she is likely to acquire through additional engagement in the topic, the child's feelings of personal competence and ability, and the child's feelings of self-determination versus external constraint. If a single contingency system is to be imposed upon an entire classroom of children, it may be necessary to weigh the potential benefits of the use of that system for those children with little initial interest and few initial skills against the possible detrimental effects of the same system for other children who would approach the task with enthusiasm and a higher level of proficiency—to distinguish, in short, between individual students for whom a program may be necessary and sufficient to produce task engagement and learning, and those for whom it is superfluous and potentially inimical to later interest in the activity itself. Finally, there may be even broader issues involved: We may need to consider, for instance, not only the effects that a reward program may have on performance and intrinsic interest, but also the simultaneous effects it may have on children's later performance attributions and ability to persist in their efforts in the face of initial failures (Dweck et al., 1978).

Such complex and value-based decisions are, of course, not unique to the study of the uses of material rewards in the classroom. Comparable issues arise daily on the level of classrooms, schools, and entire districts concerning the optimal allocation of teachers' time and other scarce educational resources. Indeed, many of the same issues—concerning the interaction of treatment programs with individual differences in abilities or interests, for example, and the evaluation of programs in terms of their effects on both mean performance and individual variability within the classroom—may arise in both contexts (cf. Atkinson, 1972).

The question of the appropriate role of tangible rewards in the classroom has been a subject of considerable debate for a number of years (e.g., Brophy, 1972; Good, 1972; Hodges, 1972). Doubtless, it will remain a source of controversy for some years to come. The issues that underlie differences in approach are, as Bruner (1962) has noted, truly fundamental:

> The distinction between cognitive control and control by coercion and seduction is a deep one. The one operates by intrinsic "self-administered" rewards and punishments; the other is regulated by gains and losses that are extrinsically administered. . . . It is no exaggeration to say that the role given to each of these forms of control is a hallmark of any political theory of the state, and, by the same token, it is the single most telling feature of any psychological theory about the nature of man—whether one envisions man as ultimately captive of the shaping forces of his environment or as competent to shape a world of his own. (p. 133)

Our hope, in the research program I have outlined in this chapter, is that bringing the "hidden costs" of reward out into the open may both help to alert us to situations in which the programs we institute may have unintended adverse effects and aid us in examining the question of how to design future programs in ways that may alleviate or reverse the potential deleterious effects that inappropriate uses of tangible rewards may produce.

ACKNOWLEDGMENTS

Preparation of this report was supported, in part, by Research Grants from the National Institute of Child Health and Human Development (HD-MH-09814) and the National Science Foundation (BNS-79-14118). The chapter was written during the author's term as a Fellow at the Center for Advanced Study in the Behavioral Sciences, Stanford, California, and financial support for this fellowship from the Spencer Foundation and the National Science Foundation (BNS-78-24671) is gratefully acknowledged.

REFERENCES

Ayllon, T., & Roberts, M. D. Eliminating discipline problems by strengthening academic performance. *Journal of Applied Behavior Analysis,* 1974, *7,* 71-76.

Amabile, T. M. Effects of external evaluation on artistic creativity. *Journal of Personality and Social Psychology,* 1979, *37,* 221-233.

Amabile, T. M., DeJong, W., & Lepper, M. R. Effects of externally-imposed deadlines on subsequent intrinsic motivation. *Journal of Personality and Social Psychology,* 1976, *34,* 92-98.

Anderson, R., Manoogian, S. T., & Reznick, J. S. The undermining and enhancing of intrinsic motivation in preschool children. *Journal of Personality and Social Psychology,* 1976, *34,* 915-922.

Aronson, E. The psychology of insufficient justification: An analysis of some conflicting data. In S. Feldman (Ed.), *Cognitive consistency.* New York: Academic Press, 1966.

Atkinson, R. C. Ingredients for a theory of instruction. *American Psychologist,* 1972, *27,* 921-931.

Bandura, A. Self-reinforcement: Theoretical and methodological considerations. *Behaviorism,* 1976, *4,* 135-155.

Bandura, A. The self-system in reciprocal determinism. *American Psychologist,* 1978, *33,* 344-358.

Bem, D. J. Self-perception: An alternative interpretation of congitive dissonance phenomena. *Psychological Review,* 1967, *74,* 183-200.

Bem, D. J. Self-perception theory. In L. Berkowitz (Ed.), *Advances in experimental social psychology,* (Vol. 6). New York: Academic Press, 1972.

Blackwell, L. *Student choice in curriculum, feelings of control and causality, and academic motivation and performance.* Unpublished doctoral dissertation, Stanford University, 1974.

Blanck, P. D., Reis, H. T., & Jackson, L. *The effects of verbal reinforcement on intrinsic motivation.* Unpublished manuscript, University of Rochester, 1980.

Boggiano, A. K., & Ruble, D. N. Perception of competence and the overjustification effect: A developmental study. *Journal of Personality and Social Psychology,* 1979, *37,* 1462-1468.

Brophy, J. E. The role of rewards and reinforcements in early education programs: II. Fostering intrinsic motivation to learn. *Journal of School Psychology,* 1972, *10,* 243-251.

Brophy, J. E. Teacher praise: A functional analysis. *Review of Educational Research,* 1981, *51,* 5-32.

Brophy, J. E., & Evertson, C. M. *Learning from teaching: A developmental perspective.* Boston: Allyn & Bacon, 1976.

Brophy, J. E., & Good, T. L. *Teacher-student relationships: Causes and consequences.* New York: Holt, Rinehart, & Winston, 1974.

Brownell, K., Colletti, G., Ernser-Hershfield, R., Hershfield, S. M., & Wilson, G. T. Self-control in school children: Stringency and leniency in self-determined and externally-imposed performance standards. *Behavior Therapy,* 1977, *8,* 442-455.

Bruner, J. S. *On knowing: Essays for the left hand.* Cambridge, Mass.: Harvard University Press, 1962.

Calder, B. J., & Staw, B. M. Self-perception of intrinsic and extrinsic motivation. *Journal of Personality and Social Psychology*, 1975, *31*, 599-605.

Colvin, R. H. Imposed extrinsic reward in an elementary school setting: Effects on free-operant rates and choices. (Doctoral dissertation, Southern Illinois University, 1971.) *Dissertation Abstracts International*, 1972, *32*, 5034-A.

Condry, J. C. Enemies of exploration: Self-initiated versus other-initiated learning. *Journal of Personality and Social Psychology*, 1977, *35*, 459-477.

Condry, J., & Chambers, J. Intrinsic motivation and the process of learning. In M. R. Lepper & D. Greene (Eds.), *The hidden costs of reward*. Hillsdale, N.J.: Lawrence Erlbaum Associates, 1978.

Davidson, P., & Bucher, B. Intrinsic interest and extrinsic reward: The effects of a continuing token program on continuing nonconstrained preference. *Behavior Therapy*, 1978, *9*, 222-234.

deCharms, R. *Personal causation*. New York: Academic Press, 1968.

deCharms, R. *Enhancing motivation in the classroom*. New York: Wiley, 1976.

Deci, E. L. Effects of externally mediated rewards on intrinsic motivation. *Journal of Personality and Social Psychology*, 1971, *18*, 105-155.

Deci, E. L. Intrinsic motivation, extrinsic reinforcement, and inequity. *Journal of Personality and Social Psychology*, 1972, *22*, 113-120.

Deci, E. L. *Intrinsic motivation*. New York: Plenum Press, 1975.

Deci, E. L., & Porac, J. Cognitive evaluation theory and the study of human motivation. In M. R. Lepper & D. Greene (Eds.), *The hidden costs of reward*. Hillsdale, N.J.: Lawrence Erlbaum Associates, 1978.

Dollinger, S. J., & Thelen, M. H. Overjustification and children's intrinsic motivation: Comparative effects of four rewards. *Journal of Personality and Social Psychology*, 1978, *36*, 1259-1269.

Drabman, R. S., Spitalnik, R., & O'Leary, K. D. Teaching self-control to disruptive children. *Journal of Abnormal Psychology*, 1973, *82*, 10-16.

Dreeben, R. *On what is learned in school*. Reading, Mass.: Addison-Wesley, 1968.

Dweck, C. S., Davidson, W., Nelson, S., & Enna, B. Sex differences in learned helplessness: II. The contingencies of evaluative feedback in the classroom and III. An experimental analysis. *Developmental Psychology*, 1978, *14*, 268-276.

Easterbrook, J. A. The effect of emotion on cue utilization and organization of behavior. *Psychological Review*, 1959, *66*, 183-201.

Enzle, M. E., & Look, S. C. *Self versus other reward administration and the overjustification effect*. Unpublished manuscript, University of Alberta, 1980.

Enzle, M. E., & Ross, J. M. Increasing and decreasing intrinsic interest with contingent rewards: A test of cognitive evaluation theory. *Journal of Experimental Social Psychology*, 1978, *14*, 588-597.

Feingold, B. D., & Mahoney, M. J. Reinforcement effects on intrinsic interest: Undermining the overjustification hypothesis. *Behavior Therapy*, 1975, *6*, 367-377.

Folger, R., Rosenfield, D., & Hays, R. P. Equity and intrinsic motivation: The role of choice. *Journal of Personality and Social Psychology*, 1978, *36*, 557-564.

Garbarino, J. The impact of anticipated rewards on cross-age tutoring. *Journal of Personality and Social Psychology*, 1975, *32*, 421-428.

Glaser, R. (Ed.). *The nature of reinforcement*. New York: Academic Press, 1971.

Good, T. L. The role of rewards and reinforcements in early education programs: III. The use of concrete rewards. *Journal of School Psychology*, 1972, *10*, 252-261.

Greene, D., & Lepper, M. R. Effects of extrinsic rewards on children's subsequent intrinsic interest. *Child Development*, 1974, *45*, 1141-1145.

Greene, D., Sternberg, B., & Lepper, M. R. Overjustification in a token economy. *Journal of Personality and Social Psychology*, 1976, *34*, 1219-1234.

Harackiewicz, J. M. The effects of reward contingency and performance feedback on intrinsic motivation. *Journal of Personality and Social Psychology*, 1979, *37*, 1352-1361.

Harter, S. Pleasure derived from challenge and the effects of receiving grades on children's difficulty level choices. *Child Development,* 1978, *49,* 788-799. (a)

Harter, S. Effectance motivation reconsidered: Toward a developmental model. *Human Development,* 1978, *21,* 34-64. (b)

Harter, S. A new self-report scale of intrinsic versus extrinsic orientation in the classroom: Motivational and informational components. *Developmental Psychology,* 1981, *17,* 300-312.

Hodges, W. L. The role of rewards and reinforcements in early education programs: I. External reinforcement in early education. *Journal of School Psychology,* 1972, *10,* 233-241.

Holt, J. *How children fail.* New York: Dell, 1964.

Hunt, J. McV. *Intelligence and experience.* New York: Ronald Press, 1961.

Hunt, J. McV. Intrinsic motivation and its role in psychological development. In D. Levine (Ed.), *Nebraska symposium on motivation,* (Vol. 13). Lincoln, Neb.: University of Nebraska Press, 1965.

Jackson, P. W. *Life in classrooms.* New York: Holt, Rinehart, & Winston, 1968.

Johnson, E. J., Greene, D., & Carroll, J. S. *Overjustification and reasons: A test of the means-ends analysis.* Unpublished manuscript, Carnegie-Mellon University, 1980.

Karniol, R., & Ross, M. The effect of performance-relevant and performance-irrelevant rewards on children's intrinsic motivation. *Child Development,* 1977, *48,* 482-487.

Kazdin, A. E. Recent advances in token economy research. In M. Hersen, R. M. Eisler, & P. M. Miller (Eds.), *Progress in behavior modification,* (Vol. 1). New York: Academic Press, 1975.

Kazdin, A. E. *Behavior modification in applied settings.* Homewood, Ill.: The Dorsey Press, 1975.

Kazdin, A. E. *The token economy.* New York: Plenum Press, 1977.

Kazdin, A. E., & Bootzin, R. R. The token economy: An evaluative review. *Journal of Applied Behavior Analysis,* 1972, *5,* 343-372.

Kazdin, A. E., & Bootzin, R. R. The token economy: An examination of issues. In R. D. Rubin, J. P. Brady, & J. D. Henderson (Eds.), *Advances in behavior therapy,* (Vol. 4). New York: Academic Press, 1973.

Kelley, H. H. Attribution theory in social psychology. In D. Levine (Ed.), *Nebraska symposium on motivation,* (Vol. 15). Lincoln, Neb.: University of Nebraska Press, 1967.

Kelley, H. H. The processes of causal attribution. *American Psychologist,* 1973, *28,* 107-128.

Krantz, D. L. The separate worlds of operant and non-operant psychology. *Journal of Applied Behavior Analysis,* 1971, *4,* 61-70.

Kruglanski, A. W. Endogenous attribution and intrinsic motivation. In M. R. Lepper & D. Greene (Eds.), *The hidden costs of reward.* Hillsdale, N.J.: Lawrence Erlbaum Associates, 1978.

Kruglanski, A. W., Alon, S., & Lewis, T. Retrospective misattribution and task enjoyment. *Journal of Experimental Social Psychology,* 1972, *8,* 493-501.

Kruglanski, A. W., Friedman, I., & Zeevi, G. The effects of extrinsic incentives on some qualitative aspects of task performance. *Journal of Personality,* 1971, *39,* 606-617.

Kruglanski, A. W., Riter, A., Amatai, A., Margolin, B., Shabtai, L., & Zaksh, D. Can money enhance intrinsic motivation: A test of the content-consequences hypothesis. *Journal of Personality and Social Psychology,* 1975, *31,* 744-750.

Kruglanski, A. W., Stein, C., & Riter, A. Contingencies of exogenous reward and task performance: On the "minimax" principle in instrumental behavior. *Journal of Applied Social Psychology,* 1977, *7,* 141-148.

Kuhn, T. S. *The structure of scientific revolutions.* Chicago: University of Chicago Press, 1970.

Lepper, M. R. Dissonance, self-perception, and honesty in children. *Journal of Personality and Social Psychology,* 1973, *25,* 65-74.

Lepper, M. R. Intrinsic and extrinsic motivation in children: Detrimental effects of superfluous social controls. In W. A. Collins (Ed.), *Minnesota symposium on child psychology,* (Vol. 14). Hillsdale, N.J.: Lawrence Erlbaum Associates, 1981.

Lepper, M. R. Social control processes and the internalization of social values: An attributional perspective. In T. E. Higgins, D. N. Ruble, & W. W. Hartup (Eds.), *Developmental social cognition: A sociocultural perspective*. New York: Cambridge University Press, in press.

Lepper, M. R., & Dafoe, J. Incentives, constraints, and motivation in the classroom: An attributional analysis. In I. Frieze, D. Bar-Tal, & J. Carroll (Eds.), *New approaches to social problems: Applications of attribution theory*. San Francisco: Jossey-Bass, 1979.

Lepper, M. R., & Gilovich, T. T. The multiple functions of reward: A social-developmental perspective. In S. S. Brehm, S. M. Kassin, & F. X. Gibbons (Eds.), *Developmental social psychology*. New York: Oxford University Press, 1981.

Lepper, M. R., & Greene, D. Turning play into work: Effects of adult surveillance and extrinsic rewards on children's intrinsic motivation. *Journal of Personality and Social Psychology*, 1975, *31*, 479-486.

Lepper, M. R., & Greene, D. On understanding "overjustification": A reply to Reiss and Sushinsky. *Journal of Personality and Social Psychology*, 1976, *33*, 25-35.

Lepper, M. R., & Greene, D. (Eds.). *The hidden costs of reward*. Hillsdale, N.J.: Lawrence Erlbaum Associates, 1978. (a)

Lepper, M. R., & Greene, D. Overjustification research and beyond: Toward a means-end analysis of intrinsic and extrinsic motivation. In M. R. Lepper & D. Greene (Eds.), *The hidden costs of reward*. Hillsdale, N.J.: Lawrence Erlbaum Associates, 1978. (b)

Lepper, M. R., & Greene, D. Divergent approaches to the study of rewards. In M. R. Lepper & D. Greene (Eds.), *The hidden costs of reward*. Hillsdale, N.J.: Lawrence Erlbaum Associates, 1978. (c)

Lepper, M. R., Greene, D., & Nisbett, R. E. Undermining children's intrinsic interest with extrinsic rewards: A test of the "overjustification" hypothesis. *Journal of Personality and Social Psychology*, 1973, *28*, 129-137.

Lepper, M. R., Sagotsky, G., Dafoe, J., & Greene, D. Consequences of superfluous social constraints: Effects of nominal contingencies on children's subsequent intrinsic interest. *Journal of Personality and Social Psychology*, in press.

Lepper, M. R., Sagotsky, G., & Greene, D. *Self-determination, extrinsic rewards, and intrinsic interest in preschool children*. Unpublished manuscript, Stanford University, 1981. (a)

Lepper, M. R., Sagotsky, G., & Greene, D. *Overjustification effects following multiple-trial reinforcement procedures: Experimental evidence concerning the assessment of intrinsic interest*. Unpublished manuscript, Stanford University, 1981. (b)

Lepper, M. R., Zanna, M. P., & Abelson, R. P. Cognitive irreversibility in a dissonance-reduction situation. *Journal of Personality and Social Psychology*, 1970, *16*, 191-198.

Loveland, K. K., & Olley, J. G. The effect of external reward on interest and quality of task performance in children of high and low intrinsic motivation. *Child Development*, 1979, *50*, 1207-1210.

Maehr, M. L. Continuing motivation: An analysis of a seldom considered educational outcome. *Review of Educational Research*, 1976, *46*, 443-462.

Mahoney, M. J. Reflections on the cognitive-learning trend in psychotherapy. *American Psychologist*, 1977, *32*, 5-13.

McCullers, J. C. Issues in learning and motivation. In M. R. Lepper & D. Greene (Eds.), *The hidden costs of reward*. Hillsdale, N.J.: Lawrence Erlbaum Associates, 1978.

McGraw, K. O. The detrimental effects of reward on performance: A literature review and a prediction model. In M. R. Lepper & D. Greene (Eds.), *The hidden costs of reward*. Hillsdale, N.J.: Lawrence Erlbaum Associates, 1978.

McGraw, K. O., & McCullers, J. C. Evidence of a detrimental effect of extrinsic incentives on breaking a mental set. *Journal of Experimental Social Psychology*, 1979, *15*, 285-294.

McLoyd, V. C. The effects of extrinsic rewards of differential value on high and low intrinsic interest. *Child Development*, 1979, *50*, 1010–1019.

Meichenbaum, D. H., Bowers, K. S., & Ross, R. R. Modification of classroom behavior of institutionalized female adolescent offenders. *Behavior Research and Therapy*, 1968, *6*, 343–353.

O'Leary, K. D. The operant and social pscyhology of token systems. In A. C. Catanià & T. A. Brigham (Eds.), *Handbook of applied behavior analyses*. New York: Irvington, 1978.

O'Leary, K. D., & Drabman, R. Token reinforcement programs in the classroom: A review. *Psychological Bulletin*, 1971, *75*, 379–398.

Perry, D. G., Bussey, K., & Redman, J. Reward-induced decreased play effects: Reattribution of motivation, competing responses, or avoiding frustration. *Child Development*, 1977, *48*, 1369–1374.

Pinder, C. C. Additivity versus nonadditivity of intrinsic and extrinsic incentives: Implications for work motivation, performance, and attitudes. *Journal of Applied Psychology*, 1976, *61*, 693–700.

Pittman, T. S., Cooper, E. E., & Smith, T. W. Attribution of causality and the overjustification effect. *Personality and Social Psychology Bulletin*, 1977, *3*, 280–283.

Pittman, T. S., Davey, M. E., Alafat, K. A., Wetherill, K. V., & Kramer, N. A. Informational vs. controlling verbal rewards. *Personality and Social Psychology Bulletin*, 1980, *6*, 228–233.

Pritchard, R. D., Campbell, K. M., & Campbell, D. J. Effects of extrinsic financial rewards on intrinsic motivation. *Journal of Applied Psychology*, 1977, *62*, 9–15.

Reiss, S., & Sushinsky, L. W. Overjustification, competing responses, and the acquisition of intrinsic interest. *Journal of Personality and Social Psychology*, 1975, *31*, 1116–1125.

Rosenhan, D. Some origins of concern for others. In P. A. Mussen, J. Langer, & M. Covington (Eds.), *Trends and issues in developmental psychology*. New York: Holt, Rinehart & Winston, 1969.

Ross, M. Salience of reward and intrinsic motivation. *Journal of Personality and Social Psychology*, 1975, *32*, 245–254.

Ross, M. The self-perception of intrinsic motivation. In J. H. Harvey, W. J. Ickes, & R. F. Kidd (Eds.), *New directions in attribution research*, (Vol. 1). Hillsdale, N.J.: Lawrence Erlbaum Associates, 1976.

Ross, M., Karniol, R., & Rothstein, M. Reward contingency and intrinsic motivation in children: A test of the delay of gratification hypothesis. *Journal of Personality and Social Psychology*, 1976, *33*, 442–447.

Scott, C. A., & Yalch, R. F. A test of the self-perception explanation of the effects of rewards on intrinsic interest. *Journal of Experimental Social Psychology*, 1978, *14*, 180–192.

Shapira, Z. Expectancy determinants of intrinsically motivated behavior. *Journal of Personality and Social Psychology*, 1976, *34*, 1235–1244.

Silberman, C. *Crisis in the classroom*. New York: Random House, 1970.

Simon, H. A. Motivational and emotional controls of cognition. *Psychological Review*, 1967, *74*, 29–39.

Smith, T. W., & Pittman, T. S. Reward, distraction, and the overjustification effect. *Journal of Personality and Social Psychology*, 1978, *36*, 565–572.

Smith, W. F. *The effects of social and monetary rewards on intrinsic motivation*. Unpublished doctoral dissertation, Cornell University, 1976.

Sorenson, R. L., & Maehr, M. L. Toward the experimental analysis of "continuing motivation". *Journal of Educational Research*, 1976, *69*, 319–322.

Spence, K. W. *Behavior theory and conditioning*. New Haven, Conn.: Yale University, 1956.

Sternberg, B. J. *What do tokens and trophies teach?* Unpublished doctoral dissertation, Stanford University, 1978.

Swann, W. B., Jr., & Pittman, T. S. Initiating play activity of children: The moderating influence of verbal cues on intrinsic motivation. *Child Development*, 1977, *48*, 1125–1132.

Turkewitz, H., O'Leary, K. D., & Ironsmith, M. Producing generalization of appropriate behavior through self-control. *Journal of Consulting and Clinical Psychology,* 1975, *43,* 577–583.

Upton, W. Altruism, attribution, and intrinsic motivation in the recruitment of blood donors. (Doctoral dissertation, Cornell University, 1973.) *Dissertation Abstracts International,* 1974, *34,* 6260–B.

Vasta, R. On token rewards and real dangers—A look at the data. *Behavior Modification,* 1981, *5,* 129–140.

Vasta, R., Andrews, D. E., McLaughlin, A. M., Stirpe, L. A., & Comfort, C. Reinforcement effects on intrinsic interest: A classroom analog. *Journal of School Psychology,* 1978, *16,* 161–166.

Vasta, R., & Stirpe, L.A. Reinforcement effects on three measures of children's interest in math. *Behavior Modification,* 1979, *3,* 223–244.

Weiner, B. (Eds.). *Achievement motivation and attribution theory.* Morristown, N.J.: General Learning Press, 1974.

Weiner, H. R., & Dubanoski, R. A. Resistance to extinction as a function of self- or externally determined schedules of reinforcement. *Journal of Personality and Social Psychology,* 1975, *31,* 905–910.

Weiner, M. J., & Mander, A. M. The effects of reward and perception of competency upon intrinsic motivation. *Motivation and Emotion,* 1978, *2,* 67–73.

Wells, D., & Shultz, T. R. Developmental distinctions between behavior and judgment in the operation of the discounting principle. *Child Development,* 1980, *51,* 1307–1310.

Wilson, T. D., Hull, J. G., & Johnson, J. H. Awareness and self-perception: Verbal reports on internal states. *Journal of Personality and Social Psychology,* 1981, *40,* 53–70.

Winett, R. A., & Winkler, R. C. Current behavior modification in the classroom: Be still, be quiet, be docile. *Journal of Applied Behavior Analysis,* 1972, *5,* 499–504.

Zajonc, R. B. Attitudinal effects of mere exposure. *Journal of Personality and Social Psychology,* Monograph Supplements, 1968, *9,* No. 2, 1–17.

Zajonc, R. B. Feeling and thinking: Preferences need no inferences. *American Psychologist,* 1980, *35,* 151–175.

Zanna, M. P., Lepper, M. R., & Abelson, R. P. Attentional mechanisms in children's devaluation of a forbidden activity in a forced-compliance situation. *Journal of Personality and Social Psychology,* 1973, *28,* 355–359.

13
Intrinsic and Extrinsic Motivational Orientations: Limiting Conditions on the Undermining and Enhancing Effects of Reward on Intrinsic Motivation

Thane S. Pittman
Gettysburg College

Ann K. Boggiano
Fordham University

Diane N. Ruble
University of Toronto

One of the most fundamental principles of psychology is the Law of Effect; if we know anything, we know that rewards work. In countless demonstrations with animals and humans, in laboratories, classrooms, and clinical settings, we have found that behaviors can be made more or less likely through the judicious application of positive and negative reinforcement. Against this background, recent documentations of the detrimental effects of rewards on intrinsic interest are striking. This research indicates that for activities that are initially of high interest, the addition of a variety of unnecessary rewards (e.g., money, toys, awards, candy) leads to a reduction in interest in those activities after the rewards are withdrawn (see Lepper & Greene, 1978, and Lepper, this volume, for reviews of much of this research).

These reward-produced changes in interest appear to be the result of a change in motivational orientation. We approach some activities with an intrinsic motivation orientation; the rewards we anticipate are inherent in, or intrinsic to, engaging in the activity or, put another way, the activity is an end in itself (Kruglanski, 1975). Most of us have such an orientation toward the activities we choose in our free or leisure time. On the other hand, many activities are approached from an orientation that is extrinsically motivated; in these cases, we have our eyes on rewards which are mediated by but are not part of the activity in question—we approach the activity as a means to a desirable end. We frequently have such an orientation toward jobs and duties. What the ground-breaking studies reported by Deci (1971; 1972) and Lepper, Greene, and Nisbett (1973) showed was that the addition of tangible rewards (such as money and "Good Player Awards") to initially intrinsically interesting activities seemed to cause a change in motivational orientation from intrinsic to extrinsic. After experience with working on the activities in order to obtain rewards, subjects were less likely to choose those activities in subsequent free choice periods than were subjects who had engaged in the activities without such rewards.

Subsequent studies have confirmed the hypothesis that the detrimental effects of the introduction and withdrawal of rewards on intrinsic interest are due to a change in motivational orientation. Although other explanations have been offered, such as Reiss and Sushinsky's (1975) hypothesis that rewards are distractors and not motivational orientation changers, the recent research indicates that these alternatives do not explain the effects of reward on interest (Greene, Sternberg, & Lepper, 1976; Ross, 1975; Smith & Pittman, 1978) and that direct manipulations of self-attributed motivation do modulate the effects of reward on subsequent free choice interest, as would be expected from the intrinsic-extrinsic orientation analysis (Kruglanski, Alon, & Lewis, 1972; Pittman, Cooper, & Smith, 1977). One of the major purposes of this chapter is to pursue further implications of this analysis.

The basic undermining effect has been demonstrated with an impressive variety of settings and populations. For example, decreases in interest have been obtained with a variety of rewards (e.g., money—Deci, 1971; good player awards—Lepper, Greene, & Nisbett, 1973; candy—Boggiano & Ruble, 1979); with populations varying widely in age (e.g., nursery school children—Lepper, Greene, & Nisbett, 1973; second graders—Swann & Pittman, 1977; fourth graders—Boggiano & Ruble, 1979; high school students—Harackiewicz, 1979; college students—Deci, 1971; psychiatric outpatients—Bogart, Loeb, & Rutman, 1969), and with a variety of activities (e.g., drawing pictures—Lepper, Greene, & Nisbett, 1973; finding hidden figures—Boggiano & Ruble, 1979; writing headlines—Deci, 1971; adult motor skill games—Pittman, Cooper, & Smith, 1977; mathematical problems—Greene, Sternberg, & Lepper, 1976). However, rewards do not always have a detrimental impact on subsequent interest. Delineating the nature of the boundary conditions on this undermining effect is the other major purpose of this chapter.

In the first section of this chapter we focus on when rewards do not decrease subsequent intrinsic motivation and when rewards may be expected to cause an actual increase in intrinsic motivation. In the second section, some further implications of the intrinsic-extrinsic motivational orientation concepts are developed and then applied to an analysis of the interactions between motivational orientations and tasks of varying levels of difficulty and complexity.

EXCEPTIONS TO THE UNDERMINING EFFECTS OF REWARDS

Verbal Rewards

In the process of establishing the external validity of the intrinsic-extrinsic shift in motivational orientation, several exceptions to the usual finding of detrimental effects of rewards on intrinsic interest have been discovered. One exception, first noted by Deci (1971), is that verbal rewards seem to have the opposite effect of tangible rewards: they enhance intrinsic interest. This effect has been obtained with adults (Deci, 1971; 1972) and children (Anderson, Manoogian, & Reznick, 1976; Swann & Pittman, 1977). Verbal rewards by themselves tend to increase intrinsic interest above the levels shown by baseline comparison groups (Anderson et al., 1976); in combination with tangible rewards, verbal rewards can also cancel the detrimental effects of tangible rewards on intrinsic interest (Swann & Pittman, 1977).

The positive effects of verbal reward are intriguing for two reasons. Theoretically, the opposing effects of tangible and verbal rewards complicate explanations of the way in which rewards affect intrinsic and extrinsic motivational orientations. From a practical point of view, verbal rewards seem to offer a simple and feasible method of counteracting the potentially detrimental effects of tangible rewards on intrinsic interest.

Deci (1975) has argued that the effects of verbal and tangible rewards can be explained by assuming that rewards in general can have two functions. One function of rewards is that they control; they exert control over the behavior on which they are contingent. The second function of rewards is that they provide information; they tell us how well we are doing, indicate whether or not we understand the task in question, and signal competence or mastery. When the controlling function of a reward is salient, we would expect the kind of shift in motivational orientation described earlier (i.e., a person who thinks of a reward as controlling his or her behavior will tend to adopt an extrinsic motivational orientation to the activity). On the other hand, if the informational function of a reward is salient, we would not expect such a shift in motivational orientation. Instead, the informational aspects of reward should augment the very things that make an activity intrinsically interesting; in Deci's terms, they should enhance feelings of competence and self-determination. We will have more to say about the nature of intrinsic motivation later on, but for now the important point is that rewards may increase or decrease intrinsic motivation depending upon the relative salience of their informational or controlling functions.

Using this distinction, the different effects of verbal and tangible rewards can be explained by assuming that the informational aspect of verbal rewards is likely to be more prominent. In contrast, the controlling aspect of tangible rewards is typically most salient. Such an assumption has the ring of intuitive plausibility. We quickly learn to think of tangible rewards, such as money, as things that are often given in exchange for the performance of services. We are probably less likely to think of praise from another person in such a way, and in fact we may be motivated to avoid thinking of ourselves as the kind of person who would work solely for the praise of others, because such behavior is often associated with negative labels (e.g., conformist, sycophant). In addition, the relative permanence of tangible rewards may continue to remind us of how they were acquired; more fleeting verbal rewards may leave us with a warm glow that is not so explicitly tied to its source.

This explanation of the positive effects of verbal reward on intrinsic interest was given an explicit test by Pittman, Davey, Alafat, Wetherill, and Kramer (1980). In one set of conditions, verbal rewards were given in a fashion which was likely to be seen as informational rather than controlling. In a second set of conditions, the same verbal rewards were given, but a controlling emphasis was added. Intrinsic interest was expected to be enhanced only in the former conditions.

The informational-controlling variable was employed to allow a test of the theoretical interpretation of the effects of rewards suggested by Deci (1975). A second variable, degree of surveillance, was included to assess one possible limitation on the practical usefulness of verbal rewards for enhancing intrinsic interest. In a previous study, Lepper and Greene (1975) found that children's intrinsic interest declined when they engaged in an interesting activity under close surveillance. This effect of surveillance is consistent with the intrinsic-extrinsic motivational orientation analysis: working on an activity under conditions of surveillance may have led the children to think of the activity as something that they were doing because they were being observed, rather than something that was simply an end in itself. Since verbal rewards may often be delivered in the context of close surveillance (e.g., in the classroom, in a token economy), their otherwise beneficial effects on intrinsic interest may often be counteracted by the effects of being under scrutiny.

In the Pittman et al. experiment, undergraduate college students worked with the same Soma puzzles that were employed in the original investigations reported by Deci (1971; 1972). The basic procedures, physical layout of the room, and free choice methodology in this study had been used in previous demonstrations of the undermining effects of tangible reward (e.g., Smith & Pittman, 1978). In the low surveillance conditions, the experimenter left the room and was not present during the 15 minute initial task session; in the medium surveillance conditions, the experimenter remained in the room during the initial session, but sat reading a magazine in the corner farthest from the subject; in the high surveillance conditions, the experimenter sat next to the subject and observed his or her performance throughout the initial session.

In the informational verbal reward conditions, the experimenter praised the subjects' performance after they had been working with the puzzles for 6 minutes ("Compared to most of my subjects, you're doing really well") and again at the end of the initial 15 minute session ("You did really well"). Consistent with previous findings and the informational-controlling hypothesis, we expected this reward to be seen as informational and to augment intrinsic interest in the activity in the subsequent free choice session. In the controlling verbal reward conditions, a controlling context was added to the verbal rewards at both the 6 minute point ("I haven't been able to use most of the data I've gotten so far, but you're doing really well, and if you keep it up I'll be able to use yours") and at the end of the initial session ("You did really well, I'll be able to use your data"). In this controlling context the interest-enhancing effects of verbal reward were not expected to be evidenced. In all conditions, after the initial session the subjects were left alone in the room for a 10 minute free choice period, and the proportion of time spent with the puzzles was determined by using a concealed closed-circuit television system. The use of an unobtrusive measure of subsequent interest was considered to be of crucial importance in our research. As Lepper has noted, one critical factor which has been shown to alter the effect of extrinsic constraints on later interest, either in a positive or negative direction, is the presence of an observer (e.g., Lepper, Sagotsky, & Greene, 1979). Thus, in order to eliminate demand characteristics as an alternative explanation of the results of the present experiment, care was taken to make subjects unaware that their behavior in the final session was being monitored.

The results of the Pittman et al. experiment were quite consistent with the informational-controlling analysis (see Table 13.1). In the low surveillance conditions, the informational verbal reward enhanced intrinsic interest compared to both the no reward baseline and the controlling verbal reward. The controlling reward had no effect when compared to no reward. Moreover, this differential effect of the informational and controlling verbal rewards on intrinsic interest was maintained across all levels of surveillance; the overall main effect for

TABLE 13.1
Mean Proportion of Time Spent with the Target Activity
During the Free Choice Period

	Surveillance		
Verbal Reward	High	Medium	Low
Controlling	.28	.54	.68
Informational	.54	.73	.91
None	—	—	.56

(from Pittman, Davey, Alafat, Wetherill, and Kramer, 1980)

reward was highly significant, and the nonsignificant interaction indicated that this relationship did not change across levels of surveillance.

The overall analysis also indicated that, as expected, when surveillance increased intrinsic interest declined. This finding suggests two important limitations on the usefulness of verbal rewards for increasing intrinsic interest: verbal rewards will not increase intrinsic interest when they are delivered in a controlling context or when they are delivered under close surveillance of performance. The combination of controlling verbal rewards and close surveillance in fact produced a decrease in intrinsic interest compared to the no reward condition—a finding with obvious practical implications.

In summary, this study demonstrates that the informational and controlling components of verbal reward are separable. When the informational component is emphasized intrinsic motivation is enhanced, but when the controlling component is emphasized it is not. When these results are combined with those from other studies that have manipulated control directly by giving or removing choice in the initial session (Swann & Pittman, 1977; Zuckerman, Porac, Lathin, Smith, & Deci, 1978), and with Ransen's (1980) finding that one of the effects of tangible reward is a reduction in perceived control, there is considerable evidence that the informational-controlling distinction is an important one.

Performance-Contingent Reward

A second empirical exception to the general finding that rewards decrease intrinsic motivation is that tangible rewards that are made contingent on the quality of performance do not always decrease intrinsic interest. For example, in two recent studies it was found that although rewards that were contingent only on engaging in an activity decreased interest, when the same rewards were made contingent on actual level of performance on the activity they did not decrease interest (Karniol & Ross, 1977) or actually increased interest (Enzle & Ross, 1978). These findings can also be understood using the informational-controlling analysis. When rewards are contingent on the quality or level of performance, then the receipt of reward can indicate a relatively high level of competence or mastery on the activity. When this informational aspect of performance-contingent rewards outweighs their controlling aspect, intrinsic interest should not decrease.

Although the informational-controlling distinction can explain the results of studies which find that performance-contingent rewards do not decrease intrinsic motivation, the literature on the effects of performance-contingent reward is by no means unequivocal. There are a number of studies in which performance-contingent rewards have *decreased* intrinsic motivation (e.g., Deci, 1971, 1972; Greene & Lepper, 1974; Harackiewicz, 1979; Pittman, Cooper, & Smith, 1977; Smith & Pittman, 1978). In at least some of these studies, it is probable that these performance-contingent rewards actually carried little information about competence or mastery. For example, in two studies (Pittman, Cooper, & Smith, 1977; Smith & Pittman, 1978), subjects had no way of knowing how their performance compared with that of others, since the rewards were contingent on the absolute scores obtained on a novel game, and the experimenter did not provide direct information about competence, such as social comparison information. In addition, the average performance scores were nowhere near the maximum scores possible, so that the reward could not signal mastery in an absolute sense. Thus, the controlling aspect of reward may have actually been more salient in those studies, thereby making the reductions in intrinsic motivation that were obtained explicable. This interpretation is, however, admittedly post hoc and may not be sufficient to explain all of the contradictory data (e.g., Harackiewicz, 1979). That the issue of competence feedback is vital to an understanding of the effects of tangible reward on intrinsic-extrinsic motivational orientation is, nevertheless, unquestionable, as a recent study by Boggiano and Ruble (1979) makes clear.

In this study, competence information was manipulated in two ways. In one set of conditions, a tangible reward was made contingent on attainment of an absolute performance standard. Because of the mastery information contained in the reward, no decrease in intrinsic motivation was expected in these conditions. In the other set of conditions, the reward was contingent on task engagement but not on level of performance. This procedure was expected to cause a shift in motivational orientation from intrinsic to extrinsic. Crossed with the task-contingent—performance-contingent manipulation was a *direct* manipulation of competence information. This was accomplished by providing social comparison information about how others had done on the activity. In one set of conditions, the subjects learned that their performance was better than that of similar others; in a second set of conditions, subjects instead learned that they had not done as well as similar others; in a final set of baseline conditions, no social comparison information was provided. If an intrinsic motivational orientation toward an activity includes the desire to exercise mastery and competence, then this direct social comparison information about relative superiority or inferiority at an activity should enhance or deflate intrinsic motivation, respectively.

In addition to these two methods of manipulating competence information, a third perspective on the operation of this variable was examined by including a developmental analysis of the use of social comparison information. According to Veroff's (1969) developmental theory of achievement motivation, children learn to judge their performance against absolute standards at a very young age, but do not begin to use comparative standards until they are 7 or 8 years old. Since this developmental hypothesis regarding children's interest in and use of social comparison for ability assessment has been confirmed in several recent studies (Ruble, Boggiano, Feldman, & Loebl, 1980; Ruble, Feldman, & Boggiano, 1976; Ruble, Parsons, & Ross, 1976), an additional perspective on the relationship between competence feedback and intrinsic motivation was gained by using both preschool and middle elementary school children. The preschool

TABLE 13.2
Mean Proportion of Time Spent Playing with Target Task

Contingency of Reward to Performance	Social Comparison Condition		
	Others Better (Indicating Incompetence)	Others Worse (Indicating Competence)	No Information
Younger Children			
Performance Contingent	.44	.41	.62
Task Contingent	.23	.27	.27
Control (No Reward-No Standard)			.73
Older Children			
Performance Contingent	.28	.67	.55
Task Contingent	.32	.68	.29
Control (No Reward-No Standard)			.68

(from Boggiano and Ruble, 1979)

children were expected to be sensitive to absolute but not comparative information, whereas the older children were expected to be affected by both sources of competence information.

To examine the competency hypothesis, the proportion of time the children spent with the target task (embedded figures) during a 6 minute free play interval, the critical measure of intrinsic motivation, was subjected to a 2 (nursery/ elementary school children) × 2 (performance-contingent reward/task-contingent reward) × 3 (relative competence/relative incompetence/no information regarding competence) analysis of variance. The results of the analysis and comparisons with the no-reward/no information control provided strong support for the major hypothesis regarding the effect of different types of competence information on intrinsic motivation in children (Table 13.2).

First a significant grade X relative competence interaction demonstrated that the social comparison information had the predicted effect on the subsequent interest of the older but not younger children. Within-grade analyses indicated that, for the older children, information about comparatively excellent performance produced more interest in the target task than information regarding relatively inferior performance or no information regarding performance level relative to peers. In contrast, comparative information had virtually no effect on intrinsic motivation in the nursery school children, as predicted. Thus, direct information about superior relative competence sustained interest in spite of reward but only for older children.

The second major prediction concerned contingency of reward. As expected, reward made contingent on meeting an absolute standard of success produced more interest than reward contingent on merely performing the task. In addition, for the younger age group, only task contingent reward undermined interest. For the older children, on the other hand, contingency of reward did not independently affect interest level or interact with the comparative information. Information about relative performance appeared to supersede the reward contingency in its effect on intrinsic motivation for the older age group. That is, task-contingent reward decreased interest relative to control and performance-contingent reward only when *no* information regarding relative competence was available to this age group.

Both of the exceptions to the otherwise deleterious effects of reward on intrinsic motivation we have reviewed implicate the manner in which reward is given and the setting in which the rewarded activity takes place as crucial determinants of subsequent motivational orientations toward the activity in question. Verbal rewards may enhance intrinsic motivation, but not if the way they are delivered or the context in which they are delivered emphasizes their controlling aspects. Tangible rewards may reduce intrinsic motivation, but not if the way in which they are delivered or the context in which they are delivered emphasizes their informational aspects as symbols of mastery and achievement. Both context and reward combine to determine how an activity is categorized and what kind of motivational orientation is fostered. In the next section we develop further the nature of intrinsic and extrinsic motivational orientations and explore some of the implications of those developments.

THE NATURE OF INTRINSIC AND EXTRINSIC MOTIVATIONAL ORIENTATIONS

We have proceeded thus far as though there were such things as intrinsic and extrinsic motivational orientations. This is partly because such a distinction is intuitively appealing, and partly because the distinction has proven to be very useful in developing an understanding of the phenomena we have reviewed. But assessing the ultimate usefulness of the intrinsic-extrinsic motivational dichotomy requires further consideration of the nature of each motivational orientation.

The notion of a set of motives that is characteristic of humans but is not associated with some form of deprivation (e.g., hunger) has been advanced in various forms. Such concepts as optimal levels of stimulation (Hunt, 1965), curiosity (Berlyne, 1960), effectance (White, 1959), and personal causation (deCharms, 1968) are broadly consistent with our assumptions about intrinsic motivation. We assume that an intrinsic motivational orientation has two general aspects. First, it means that the selection of behaviors will be guided by motives such as curiosity and effectance. Second, it includes our learned ability to classify behaviors, activities, and sources of stimulation as relevant or irrelevant to the satisfaction of intrinsic motivation.

Similarly, we learn that behaviors and activities, perhaps uninteresting in themselves, can serve as means toward the satisfaction of needs—an extrinsic motivational orientation. In the process of satisfying various needs, we are bound to learn that some activities are particularly useful or instrumental in helping us to achieve desired external goals and we learn to select behaviors or activities that are most useful for reaching such goals. In addition, as with intrinsic orientations, we also learn to classify behaviors, activities, and sources of stimulation according to their relevance for meeting these extrinsic needs.

We thus learn to approach and label approaches as either intrinsically or extrinsically interesting. A particular activity can, of course, be approached from either an intrinsic or an extrinsic orientation. For example, a student may approach a learning task (playing the piano) as an opportunity to have fun, to exercise skills, and to acquire new forms of mastery; the same task can also be approached as a means to induce his or her parents to come through with that long-coveted bicycle. But taking either approach is also likely to lead us to think of that activity as being related to the approach taken, rather than to the approach foregone. In other words, while we may think of activities as relevant to both intrinsic and extrinsic motivational orientations, in practice we probably tend to categorize them with one or the other orientation. This is how a previously intrinsically motivated activity can, by serving as a mediator to some other goal, come to be approached as an extrinsically motivated one. This general idea has some similarity to the phenomenon of functional fixedness (Duncker, 1945). If a hammer is labeled as a nail-pounder, we may not think to use it as a weight; if drawing is labeled as an award-getter, we may not think to use it as a form of entertainment.

Thus, adopting an intrinsic or an extrinsic orientation toward an activity for whatever reason may lead to labeling or categorizing that activity in a simple way. Such categorizing may then *carry over* to subsequent interactions with the activity, such that future interactions may be characterized by that orientation. But what are the characteristics of intrinsic and extrinsic orientations? What are we looking for when we adopt one or the other orientation? Without trying to make an exhaustive or exclusive list, we suggest that some of the salient features of an *intrinsic* orientation include desires for challenge, for the exercise of mastery, for the experience of competent and effective interaction with the environment, and for novel stimulation. When an *extrinsic* orientation is adopted, the primary concern is to obtain the goal or reward in question; concomitant concerns then include the desire to avoid frustration, to successfully complete tasks as expediently as possible, and perhaps to make calculations of the equity of outcomes.

These different orientations imply that when operating from an intrinsic orientation, we should prefer tasks that are difficult and challenging (but not impossible), that are likely to show a gain in competence over time, and that are somewhat unpredictable and fun. In contrast, when operating from an extrinsic orientation, we should prefer tasks that are relatively simple and predictable. Since, with extrinsic orientations, the key desire is to get the reward, we would prefer an easy, uncomplicated way to achieve this desired goal.

Evidence for this kind of difference in preferences among various forms of an activity has been reported by Harter (1978). She found that children who approached a set of anagrams as a game chose more difficult forms of the task than did children who were working on the anagrams for a grade. This sort of finding is not surprising. Given that important rewards are contingent on successful performance of an activity, it is to be expected that simple, easily controlled forms of the activity will be preferred if they are available. What may be less obvious is that such form preferences may also carry over to new settings where external contingencies are no longer present. It has been shown repeatedly that experience with working on an activity from an extrinsic motivational orientation (i.e., for reward) reduces the likelihood that the activity will be chosen in a subsequent free choice period. The point stressed here is that even if the activity is chosen in a context in which rewards are no longer present, it is still likely to be approached with the preferences for form that are characteristic of an extrinsic orientation. More specifically, we are arguing that when an activity is approached from an extrinsic motivational orientation, and when forms of the task varying in complexity and/or difficulty are available, the less complex, simple forms will be preferred, even when rewards are no longer available.

Carry-Over Effects on Preference for Complexity

To test this "carryover" hypothesis, Pittman, Emery, and Boggiano (in press) conducted a study in which, following an initial experience with an activity under one of several reward conditions, children were given a choice among several forms of the target activity which varied in complexity and challenge. Second-grade children were shown a Good Player Award and were asked if they would like to win one. In one reward condition, the children were told that they would win the award simply if they played the target game two times (task-contingent reward). This kind of procedure has been shown to produce the overjustification effect. In the second reward condition, which served as a control for any effects of simply getting a reward, the children were told that they could win the award simply by waiting 5 minutes (task-noncontingent reward). They then played the target game twice. In a no reward condition, the children were simply asked if they would like to play with the game, and nothing about awards was mentioned.

The target activity was a game which consisted of a large plexiglass board with different shapes. The object of the game was to see how many of the shapes could be covered with other colored shapes of the same design before a one-minute timer rang. After playing the game (which was of moderate complexity level) twice, children in the two reward conditions were given their Good Player Awards, along with a reiteration of their respective contingencies, and were allowed to place their awards on an "Honor Roll Board." All children were then introduced to the rating session.

After being asked if they would like to play another game with the shapes, all children were shown a seven-point "happy face" rating scale, which ranged from −3 (big frown) to a +3 (big smile). The experimenter used several sample shapes to teach the children how to use the scale and then had them rate each of the 12 shapes that had been used in the target game for likeability.

Following the ratings, all children were told that there was still some time left before they had to go back to their classrooms. The experimenter then produced the original target game, two new forms of the game, and a slinky, a set of tinker toys, and a toy piano. The two new forms of the game included one which had only relatively simple shapes (3 to 10 sides) and one which had only relatively complex shapes (13 to 40 sides). The experimenter then surreptitiously recorded the amount of time spent with each form of the target activity during the 5 minute free choice period.

An analysis of the number of shapes covered during the initial training trials indicated that there were no significant differences in initial performance. Analysis of the happy face ratings of the random shapes also indicated that the reward manipulations did not systematically affect the relationship between stimulus complexity and ratings of liking. These ratings were quite variable, but in general they showed a small decline in liking as complexity increased.

The amount of free play time spent with each of the target activities was subjected to a 3 (no reward, task-contingent reward, task-noncontingent reward) × 3 (simple, same, complex games) analysis of variance. Neither main effect was significant, but there was a significant interaction between the reward and complexity variables (see Figure 13.1). Subsequent analyses revealed that this interaction was the result of changes in complexity preferences, as a function of reward, that were in line with the initial hypothesis. Task-contingent reward subjects preferred the simple game more than did the no reward and task-noncontingent reward subjects. The no reward subjects tended to prefer the intermediate complexity game more than did the other two groups, but these differences were not significant. The task-noncontingent reward subjects preferred the complex game more than did the no reward subjects or the task-contingent reward subjects. In short, while no reward subjects preferred the game that was intermediate in complexity, the task contingent reward subjects came to prefer the simple game, while the task-noncontingent subjects preferred the most complex game.

The results of this study were consistent with the hypothesized carryover effects associated with the adoption of an extrinsic motivational orientation. Specifically, it appears that the particular reward contingency provided led to a shift in preferences for the form or difficulty level of the task. This shift is presumed to be mediated by classifying the task as appropriate for an extrinsic or an intrinsic motivational orientation. Interestingly, there was no undermining effect of rewards in the traditional sense. Instead, the different motivational orientations induced by the reward contingencies were manifested in the *form* of

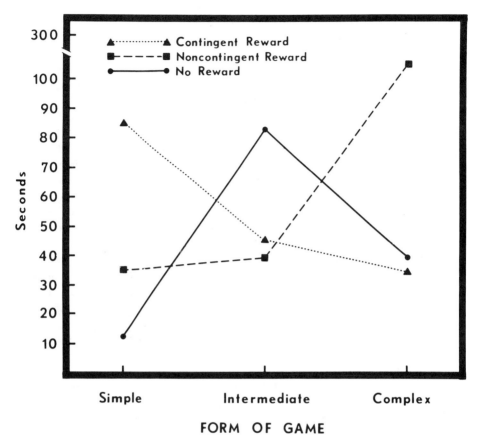

FIG. 13.1.   Mean number of seconds with the target activity during the free choice period as a function of task complexity and reward contingency (from Pittman, Emery, & Boggiano, in press).

the target task preferred—in this case, task difficulty—and did not lead subjects to ignore the task altogether.

Reward and Task Difficulty

The Pittman, Emery, and Boggiano findings implicate task difficulty as an important variable in understanding intrinsic versus extrinsic motivational orientations. For example, an activity of intermediate difficulty is ideal when one is operating from an intrinsic motivational orientation. Such activities, as numerous studies of achievement motivation have shown (e.g. Atkinson, 1964), offer an attractive combination of challenge and likelihood of eventual mastery. Such a preference was again illustrated in the free choice behavior of the no reward subjects in the Pittman et al. study. Given that intermediate difficulty tasks are attractive to individuals who have an intrinsic motivational orientation, the decreases in free choice interest caused by experience with working from an extrinsic motivational orientation ought to be clearly observed on activities of intermediate difficulty. On the other hand, it may also be possible to enhance an intrinsic motivational orientation toward such tasks; for example, positive information about relative competence should enhance the attractiveness of these activities in intrinsic motivational orientation settings.

However, we would expect a quite different state of affairs for tasks that are simple and unchallenging, which by their nature are ill-suited for the preferences associated with an intrinsic motivational orientation. Experience with working on such tasks for reward should also foster an extrinsic motivational orientation, but we would not expect this to produce decreases in free choice involvement. Instead, as Calder and Staw (1975) have found, experience with an extrinsic orientation toward these tasks should produce an increase in interest, for two reasons. First, given the relatively low level of attractiveness, conditioning of reward-produced positive affect should increase the tendency to choose simple tasks. Second, and more pertinent to our general line of reasoning, simple tasks are quite desirable when one is adopting an extrinsic motivational orientation. As was seen in the Pittman, Emery, and Boggiano study, previous experience with an extrinsic orientation enhanced the attractiveness of a simple activity during the free choice period. Therefore, to the extent that an extrinsic motivational orientation toward a simple activity persists, free choice interest should be enhanced. We would not, however, expect competence feedback to enhance interest in a simple task. With such a task, challenge and mastery considerations are largely irrelevant; information about competence would at best simply confirm these notions, still leaving the task relatively uninteresting from an intrinsic motivational orientation.

With very difficult tasks, yet a third set of effects should obtain. When an extrinsic orientation is fostered by working for reward, very difficult tasks should be unappealing since they have characteristics that are incompatible with that kind of motivation (e.g., they are difficult to complete and relatively unpredictable). At the same time, however, such tasks are not as intrinsically appealing as tasks of intermediate complexity level because of the low probability of mastery. Therefore, reward-produced decreases in free choice interest should be found, but the magnitude of such effects should be less than would be found with a task of intermediate difficulty. Competence feedback, however, should be very effective in enhancing free choice interest in these tasks since tasks of very high difficulty have many features that should match the pattern of task preferences associated with an intrinsic motivational orientation: they are challenging, unpredictable, and stimulating. Their major drawback is that they may appear to be unmasterable. But since information indicating task competence should reduce this appearance, we would expect competence information both to foster an intrinsic motivational orientation and to enhance or at least maintain task interest for those who adopt such an orientation.

To summarize our analysis of the effects of task difficulty, rewards, and competence information on free choice interest, we predict (1) that tasks of intermediate difficulty level will be preferred to relatively complex or easy tasks under conditions fostering an intrinsic motivational orientation, (2) that experience with working on an activity in order to obtain task contingent reward will enhance subsequent free choice interest in simple tasks, but will reduce interest in tasks of intermediate and high difficulty, and (3) that information indicating task competence will have little or no effect on interest in simple tasks, but will enhance or maintain interest in tasks of intermediate and high difficulty.

Boggiano, Ruble, and Pittman (1981) conducted a study to test these hypotheses concerning the differential effect of reward and competence information on challenging versus nonchallenging tasks. Fourth-grade children were randomly assigned to either a no reward condition or were offered a tangible reward (i.e., a rubber ball) simply for performing an embedded figures task. Crossed with the reward manipulation was a task difficulty manipulation. All of the children performed the *same* embedded figures task; however, difficulty level was manipulated by making the figures easy to find (the unchallenging task), or by making the figures moderately difficult *or* very difficult to find (challenging tasks). In the easy task condition, the task was designed so that subjects would obtain a score of 10 out of a maximum score of 12; whereas subjects in the moderate and difficult task conditions received scores of 7 and 4, respectively, out of a possible score of 12.

Competence information was manipulated by means of social comparison information. Children in the competence condition were shown a scoreboard before the free play period, indicating that they had performed *better* than same age others. Children in the no competence information condition were also shown a scoreboard upon which they were told they would put their scores upon completion of the task; however, no mention was made of performance level of peers.

An analysis of the percent of free play time the children spent with the embedded figures as opposed to alternative attractive games was subjected to a 2 (reward/no reward) $\times$ 2 (competence/no competence information) $\times$ 3 (easy/moderate/difficult task) analysis of variance. The resulting significant three-way interaction was further analyzed in terms of planned contrasts. (See Table 13.3.)

First, given no reward or information regarding competence, the predicted curvilinear relationship between task difficulty and intrinsic interest was demonstrated by means of a significant quadratic component. The moderately challenging task was preferred more than the very challenging task which, in turn, was preferred to the easy task.

The second major prediction concerned the effect of reward on easy versus challenging tasks (moderately and very challenging tasks). A 2 (reward/no re-

TABLE 13.3
Mean Proportion of Time Spent Playing with Target Task

Reward and Competence Conditions	Task Difficulty		
	Simple	Intermediate	Difficult
No Competence Information			
No Reward	.28	.62	.38
Reward	.57	.37	.22
Competence Information			
No Reward	.34	.18	.49
Reward	.62	.67	.53

(from Boggiano, Ruble, & Pittman, 1981)

ward) $\times$ 2 (challenging versus unchallenging task) analysis of variance of free play time in the no competence conditions indicated that reward decreased interest in challenging tasks, but increased interest in an easy task, as predicted.

Finally, comparisons were performed within tasks of varying complexity level to test predictions regarding the differential effect of competence information versus reward on unchallenging and challenging tasks. Reward but not competence information was predicted to have a positive effect on later interest in an easy task, because of the extrinsic motivational orientation. As expected, reward produced more interest than no reward given an easy task, and competence information had virtually no effect given this type of task. In contrast, competence information sustained interest in very challenging tasks; and reward undermined interest in this type of task only when competence information was not provided. The predicted positive effect of competence information on moderately challenging tasks was not demonstrated. Competence information sustained interest in this type of task only when provided in the context of reward attainment. Surprisingly, competence information by itself reduced free choice interest in the moderate difficulty version of the task, a result that needs further study to be understood. Except for this single unexpected finding, however, the results were generally quite consistent with the predictions derived from our analysis.

This study illustrates some of the complexities involved in matching activities and motivational orientations. For challenging tasks, reward can decrease subsequent task engagement by inducing an extrinsic motivational orientation. Emphasis on competence tends to have the opposite effect and can eliminate the otherwise detrimental impact of reward on intrinsic interest. Simple tasks, however, are well-suited to the preferences associated with an extrinsic motivational orientation; the use of reward on these tasks therefore leads to increased task interest or favorability which carries over to subsequent interactions. Attempts to enhance interest with competence information appear to be ineffective with simple activities because such attempts emphasize an aspect of intrinsic interest that is irrelevant to performance on these tasks.

SUMMARY AND IMPLICATIONS

In summary, we have tried to explore and elaborate on the concepts of intrinsic and extrinsic motivational orientation in a way that would allow us to begin to understand some inconsistencies in previous findings and to be able to predict the various effects that reward might have on intrinsic interest. Our findings emphasize once again that the use of rewards does not bear a simple relationship to subsequent motivation. Most importantly, the general concepts of intrinsic and extrinsic motivational orientations allow us to organize our findings concerning exceptions to the undermining effects of rewards on subsequent intrinsic interest. Rewards that either by their nature (e.g., verbal rewards) or their context (i.e., contingency based on quality of performance, or a context emphasizing competence) emphasize the qualities associated with an intrinsic motivational orientation do not decrease and may enhance the attractiveness of an activity during subsequent free choice periods. However, the nature of the activity in question is also important. By considering the extent to which an activity matches the preferences associated with a particular motivational orientation, it becomes possible to understand some of the complex relationships between task difficulty, reward, and subsequent interest.

Nature or Context of the Reward

Verbal Reward.   Verbal rewards, unlike their tangible counterparts, have been shown to cause an increase in subsequent intrinsic motivation in a number of studies. That is apparently because verbal rewards are seen as signals of competence or success, and not as controllers of behavior. As signals of competent performance, verbal rewards serve to encourage the continuation of an intrinsic motivational orientation. However, if the controlling aspects of verbal rewards are made salient, as they were in the Pittman et al. (1980) study, then increases in intrinsic motivation are unlikely. But even if verbal rewards are given in a way that emphasizes information about mastery, their otherwise positive effects can be negated by their inclusion in a broader context that emphasizes an extrinsic motivational orientation, as was seen in the close surveillance condition of the Pittman et al. study. Verbal rewards, then, can enhance intrinsic motivation, but only if care is taken to avoid methods and contexts of delivery that might work against such enhancement.

Competence: Reward Contingency and Social Comparison Information.   The analysis we have developed implies that it should be possible to deliver tangible rewards in a way that emphasizes mastery and competence and that tangible rewards so delivered should not decrease subsequent interest. The Boggiano and Ruble (1979) study demonstrates several aspects of this prediction. When rewards were made contingent on the *quality* of performance, so that receipt of reward indicated competence or mastery, no decrease in subsequent free choice interest was found. Similarly, when middle elementary school children were given feedback indicating that they had done very well compared with the performance of other children, subsequent interest was maintained. However, while preschool age children were sensitive to absolute indications of competence (i.e., performance-contingent reward), they were unaffected by social comparison information. This finding suggests surprisingly that a teacher giving a nursery school child a gold star for being the best in the class at painting may inadvertently undermine the child's subsequent interest in painting, because of the child's failure to make an inference about competence on the basis of information conveyed in relative terms. In contrast, offering a gold star for doing well in an absolute sense would be expected to maintain that child's interest.

Similar considerations may apply to the use of verbal rewards. The Boggiano and Ruble findings imply that praise couched in comparative language may be ineffective with young children. The contingency of verbal reward is also relevant. The kinds of verbal rewards used in the literature thus far can be considered to be performance-contingent (e.g., "You drew a really nice picture"; "You did really well on that task"). The notion of verbal reward not contingent on quality of performance is not as unlikely as it might seem. For example, if a teacher praises everyone's work all the time, the value of praise as a signal of competence for the students will dissipate. Although the appropriate studies have not yet been done, we expect that verbal rewards contingent on task engagement but not on quality of performance may well produce decreases rather than increases in subsequent interest, just as task-contingent tangible rewards have been shown to do.

If the indiscriminate use of verbal reward leads to weakened or reversed effects on intrinsic motivation, then judicious use of such rewards is indicated. In other words, if verbal rewards are to be effective in sustaining an intrinsic motivational orientation, then they should be given for good performance but withheld for poor performance. This line of reasoning leads to another issue raised by the Boggiano and Ruble data. Negative social comparison information, indicating relative incompetence, decreased subsequent interest for older children in that study. To the extent that the withholding of reward indicates failure to a student, the institution of a performance-contingent reward system based on comparative performance may enhance or maintain interest for some but will probably decrease it for others. One solution to this dilemma is to use absolute standards, tailored to the individual, that set challenging but obtainable goals. Once again, however, we point out that such standards need to be introduced in a noncontrolling way if maintenance of subsequent interest is a goal of the teacher.

Nature of the Task

Complexity Preferences Following Reward.   When a person adopts an extrinsic motivational orientation, a set of preferences corresponding to that orientation is activated. Tasks that are simple, predictable, and easily mastered will be preferred. If the activity in question allows selection from a variety of forms, the simplest, most expedient forms will be preferred. These preferences carry over into post-reward interactions with the activity, as Pittman, Emery, and Boggiano (in press) demonstrated. Extrapolating from this finding we would expect that, for example, students who have adopted an extrinsic motivational orientation (a) would be less likely to engage in optional homework related to the activity or activities in question and (b) would choose simple, expedient methods when they did choose to try such assignments. Required assignments would also be approached in this way (see Lepper, this volume, for a discussion of how this kind of approach can be suppressed by careful specifications of reward contingencies).

Initial Task Difficulty, Competence Feedback, and Reward.   In the first three studies reviewed in this chapter, and in studies of the effects of reward on subsequent interest in general, care was taken to select activities that were relatively fun, interesting, and challenging—activities compatible with the preferences associated with an intrinsic motivational orientation. For these activities, reward tends to foster an extrinsic motivational orientation that leads to reduced interest in subsequent free choice periods. Competence information, on the other hand, tends to maintain an intrinsic motivational orientation. In the Boggiano, Ruble, and Pittman (1981) study, we found a different state of affairs for simple, unchallenging activities. The unchallenging nature of these activities does not match well the preferences associated with an intrinsic motivational orientation. Attempts to enhance interest through competence signals will not be effective since competence is not an issue with these activities. Tangible, task-contingent reward, however, was found to increase subsequent interest, probably for two reasons: (a) association with reward made the task more attractive via conditioning and (b) reward induced an extrinsic motivational orientation that matched well the properties of the simple task.

These task difficulty findings raise some interesting and important educational issues. There may be some learning tasks that are necessary but that are simply by their nature not inherently interesting. Furthermore, there may be some school activities that we do not expect or wish students to choose in their free time; it is, for example, not essential that students construct multiplication tables or diagram sentences in their free time. Tangible rewards may be most appropriate for these kinds of activities. Those that are amenable to rather simple approaches, such as rote memorization, fit well with the preferences associated with an extrinsic motivational orientation, and their interest value may actually be enhanced by encouraging an extrinsic approach. Tangible rewards might also be used on more complex activities if subsequent interest is judged to be of little or no importance, but such judgments should obviously be made consicously and with care, and potential effects of reward on performance during the reward period need to be considered (see Lepper, this volume).

One can take the point of view that learning a skill is often not fun—is it hard work. The fun comes *after* proficiency is acquired. Graduate training programs sometimes embrace this philosophy: Being a graduate student is not fun and was never meant to be. It is what you can do *after* you have been a graduate student that is fun. (The same story can be told to untenured faculty, with minor modifications.) Learning to play the piano provides another example. Countless parents have tried to convince their sullen children that although practicing the piano might seem like drudgery now, they will be glad they did it in 10 or 20 years. Many of those parents speak from experience; they refused to do the drudgery, but now they wish they had the abilities that would have come from practice. The source of this wisdom reveals the weakness of the argument. There are many enjoyable skills that require the prior acquisition of more fundamental abilities. If care is not taken with these fundamental skills, and future interest is not carefully considered, then the joys of exercising more complex abilities may never be realized. We need to know more about how the shift from an extrinsic to an intrinsic motivational orientation can be made; we cannot simply assume that such transitions are automatic or easy.

In summary, rewards can have detrimental effects on subsequent interest, but this is not inevitable. Verbal rewards can enhance interest if they signal competence rather than control. Similarly, tangible rewards may not decrease interest if they serve an informational function or if they are combined with competence feedback, but a sensitivity to developmental changes in the ability to use such information is needed. Finally, analysis of the nature of intrinsic and extrinsic motivational orientations points to the complexities associated with the difficulty of the activity in question, both during and after sessions with reward. But we are not yet to the point at which a list of "do's" and "don'ts" can be made. The teacher who wishes to make use of these findings needs to adopt an intrinsic motivational orientation toward the activity of working with student interest and needs to take pleasure in the challenges and opportunities for creative mastery therein.

ACKNOWLEDGMENT

The preparation of this manuscript and portions of the research reported herein were supported by a grant from the Andrew Mellon Foundation to the first author. Ann Boggiano is now at the University of Colorado; Diane Ruble is at New York University.

REFERENCES

Anderson, R., Manoogian, S., & Reznick, J. The undermining and enhancing of intrinsic motivation in preschool children. *Journal of Personality and Social Psychology*, 1976, *34*, 915-922.
Atkinson, J. W. *An introduction to motivation.* Princeton, N.J.: Van Nostrand, 1964.

Berlyne, D. D. *Conflict, arousal, and curiosity.* New York: McGraw-Hill, 1960.

Bogart, K., Loeb, A., & Rutman, I. D. *A dissonance approach to behavior modification.* Paper presented at the meeting of the Eastern Psychological Association, Philadelphia, 1969.

Boggiano, A. K., & Ruble, D. N. Competence and the overjustification effect: A developmental study. *Journal of Personality and Social Psychology,* 1979, *37,* 1462-1468.

Boggiano, A. K., Ruble, D. N., & Pittman, T. S. The mastery hypothesis and the overjustification effect. *Social Cognition,* in press.

Calder, B. J., & Staw, B. M. Self-perception of intrinsic and extrinsic motivation. *Journal of Personality and Social Psychology,* 1975, *31,* 599-605.

deCharms, R. *Personal causation.* New York: Academic Press, 1968.

Deci, E. L. Effects of externally mediated rewards on intrinsic motivation. *Journal of Personality and Social Psychology,* 1971, *18,* 105-115.

Deci, E. L. Intrinsic motivation, extrinsic reinforcement and inequity. *Journal of Personality and Social Psychology,* 1972, *22,* 113-120.

Deci, E. L. *Intrinsic motivation.* New York: Plenum, 1975.

Duncker, K. On problem-solving. *Psychological Monographs,* 1945, *58,* (No. 270).

Enzle, M. E., & Ross, J. M. Increasing and decreasing intrinsic interest with contingent rewards: A test of cognitive evaluation theory. *Journal of Experimental Social Psychology,* 1978, *14,* 588-597.

Greene, D., Sternberg, B., & Lepper, M. R. Overjustification in a token economy. *Journal of Personality and Social Psychology,* 1976, *34,* 1219-1234.

Harackiewicz, J. M. The effects of reward contingency and performance feedback on intrinsic motivation. *Journal of Personality and Social Psychology,* 1979, *37,* 1352-1363.

Harter, S. Pleasure derived from challenge and the effects of receiving grades on children's difficulty level choices. *Child Development,* 1978, *49,* 788-799.

Hunt, J. McV. Intrinsic motivation and its role in psychological development. In D. Levin (Ed.), *Nebraska symposium on motivation* (vol. 13). Lincoln: University of Nebraska Press, 1965.

Karniol, R., & Ross, M. The effect of performance-relevant and performance-irrelevant rewards on children's intrinsic motivation. *Child Development,* 1977, 48, 482-487.

Kruglanski, A. W. The endogenous-exogenous partition in attribution theory. *Psychological Review,* 1975, *83,* 387-406.

Kruglanski, A. W., Alon, S., & Lewis, T. Retrospective misattribution and task enjoyment. *Journal of Experimental Social Psychology,* 1972, *8,* 493-501.

Lepper, M. R., & Greene, D. Turning play into work: Effects of adult surveillance and extrinsic rewards on children's intrinsic motivation. *Journal of Personality and Social Psychology,* 1975, *31,* 479-486.

Lepper, M. R., & Greene, D. *The hidden costs of rewards.* Hillsdale, N.J.: Lawrence Erlbaum Associates, 1978.

Lepper, M. R., Greene, D., & Nisbett, R. E. Undermining children's intrinsic interest with extrinsic reward: A test of the overjustification hypothesis. *Journal of Personality and Social Psychology,* 1973, *28,* 129-137.

Lepper, M. R., Sagotsky, G., & Greene, D. *Overjustification effects following multiple-trial reinforcement procedures: Experimental evidence concerning the assessment of intrinsic interest.* Unpublished manuscript, Stanford University, 1979.

Pittman, T. S., Cooper, E. E., & Smith, T. W. Attribution of causality and the overjustification effect. *Personality and Social Psychology Bulletin,* 1977, *3,* 280-283.

Pittman, T. S., Davey, M. E., Alafat, K. A., Wetherill, K. V., & Kramer, N. A. Informational versus controlling verbal rewards. *Personality and Social Psychology Bulletin,* 1980, *6,* 228-233.

Pittman, T. S., Emery, J., & Boggiano, A. K. Intrinsic and extrinsic motivational orientations: Reward induced changes in preference for complexity. *Journal of Personality and Social Psychology,* in press.

Ransen, D. L. The mediation of reward induced motivation decrements in early and middle childhood: A template matching approach. *Journal of Personality and Social Psychology,* 1980, *39,* 1088–1100.

Reiss, S., & Sushinsky, L. W. Overjustification, competing responses, and the acquisition of intrinsic interest. *Journal of Personality and Social Psychology,* 1975, *31,* 1116–1125.

Ross, M. Salience of reward and intrinsic motivation. *Journal of Personality and Social Psychology,* 1975, *32,* 245–254.

Ruble, D. N., Boggiano, A. K., Feldman, N. S., & Loebl, J. H. The concept of competence: A developmental analysis of self-evaluation through social comparison. *Developmental Psychology,* 1980, *16,* 105–115.

Ruble, D. N., Feldman, N. S., & Boggiano, A. K. Social comparison between young children in achievement situations. *Developmental Psychology,* 1976, *12,* 192–197.

Ruble, D. N., Parsons, J. E., & Ross, J. Self-evaluative responses of children in an achievement setting. *Child Development,* 1976, *47,* 990–997.

Smith, T. W., & Pittman, T. S. Reward, distraction, and the overjustification effect. *Journal of Personality and Social Psychology,* 1978, *36,* 565–572.

Swann, W. B., & Pittman, T. S. Initiating play activity of children: The moderating influence of verbal cues on intrinsic motivation. *Child Development,* 1977, *48,* 1128–1132.

Veroff, J. Social comparision and the development of achievement motivation. In C. P. Smith (Ed.), *Achievement related motives in children.* New York: Russell Sage, 1969.

White, R. W. Motivation reconsidered: The concept of competence. *Psychological Review,* 1959, *66,* 297–333.

Zuckerman, M., Porac, J., Lathin, D., Smith, R., & Deci, E. L. On the importance of self-determination for intrinsically motivated behavior. *Personality and Social Psychology Bulletin,* 1978, *4,* 443–446.

14 Non-Cognitive Outcomes of Cooperative Learning

Robert E. Slavin
Johns Hopkins University

People are at their best when they are working together. Everyone admires the selfless "team player" who puts the interests of the group ahead of his own, the coworker who works long hours to help the entire company prosper, the soldier who risks his own life to save his buddies. Everyone has experienced the thrill of working shoulder to shoulder with others to accomplish a great task and the closeness and camaraderie that result from striving together. Working together is fun, it is stimulating, and it makes people feel that others care what they do and care about them. People who have put their shoulders to the same wheel are unlikely to be prejudiced toward one another or to reject one another. Many, if not most, of our most lasting friendships arise in cooperative groups, such as sports teams, clubs, political groups, military squads, and work groups.

The majority of roles we take on as adults are primarily or exclusively cooperative ones. When we act as coworkers, family members, neighbors, members of social or political groups, and so on, we are most often in cooperation with others to accomplish some purpose, and there is nothing we value in adults quite as much as the ability to take leadership in directing a group to a superordinate goal.

It would seem logical that, because we expect adults to get along with others in cooperative situations, we might value and reward children's cooperative behaviors in school. However, the traditional classroom is one of the least cooperative institutions in society. In the classroom, and almost nowhere else, peers are often actually forbidden to help one another, and they are rarely encouraged to offer help. Our schools often promote the idea that the purpose of life is to be first and that the many who are unlikely to be first are to be scorned or ignored. Further, schools often teach that students have responsibility only for themselves and that working together is cheating.

341

Is this the best way to prepare children to take on cooperative adult roles? It hardly seems so, yet the competitive-individualistic classroom system is centuries old and nearly universal in the Western world.

What would happen if we set up the classroom to encourage and reward students for cooperating? That is the question addressed by the studies reviewed in this chapter. The studies included in this review are all true field experiments, in which a technique that could be used as a primary instructional methodology was evaluated for at least two weeks, usually much longer. This approach differs from laboratory studies, which typically tell us much about theory but little about classrooms and alternative ways of organizing them.

Cooperative Learning

Cooperative Learning is a term that refers to a set of instructional programs in which students work in small groups to learn academic materials. The methods vary widely, but most reward students for doing well as a group with recognition, grades, or other rewards. To win the rewards, students must help their group-mates learn.

Much of the interest in cooperative learning methods has focused on their effects on student achievement. The positive effects on achievement of such cooperative learning methods as Student Teams-Achievement Divisions (Slavin, 1978a), Teams-Games-Tournament (DeVries & Slavin, 1978), and Jigsaw Teaching (Lucker, Rosenfield, Sikes, & Aronson, 1976), as well as other methods, have been well documented. These effects are highlighted in a recent review of cooperative learning research (Slavin, 1980a). However, in many ways it is the noncognitive outcomes of cooperative learning that have generated the greatest interest in these methods. This is probably true because, while there are many instructional programs that can document positive effects on student achievement, cooperative learning methods are relatively unique in explicitly seeking to increase such major noncognitive outcomes as positive intergroup relations, student self-esteem, and positive peer norms concerning achievement, as well as achievement itself. For this reason, the growing cooperative learning movement has attracted many researchers and practitioners who value humanistic educational methods and prosocial student outcomes, but recognize the importance of achieving both cognitive and affective gains instead of sacrificing one for the other.

Basic Features of Cooperative Learning

There are many cooperative learning strategies now in use or in the literature. They vary enormously in their details, philosophies, and applications, but almost all share these characteristics:

1. Students work in small (4–6 member) learning teams that remain stable in composition for many weeks.
2. Students are encouraged to help other group members to learn academic material or to perform a group task.
3. In most techniques, students are given rewards based on their group performance. These rewards may range from recognition to tokens to grades.

In essence, get students to cooperate in teams on learning tasks and you have a cooperative learning technique. In their important particulars, however, cooperative learning methods vary widely. In most, students are assigned by the teacher to teams that are heterogeneous in sex, race, academic performance, and other dimensions, whereas in others students choose their own teams. In some, the group reward is explicit; in others, students are simply asked to do their best as a group. In some techniques students are clearly individually accountable for their contributions to their teams, but in others there is a group product in which individual contributions are hard to quantify. Some techniques allow students considerable autonomy within their teams, leaving to the teams such decisions as what they will study, how they will study it, and what they will produce at the end. Most, however, provide at least a well-structured set of learning objectives and activities, within which the team may still organize its efforts. These differences between the various cooperative learning methods may be important determinants of the effectiveness of the strategies, but we are far from a science of classroom structure for optimizing cooperative learning.

Classroom Cooperative Learning Techniques

The bulk of the research on practical cooperative learning techniques has focused on four major models: Teams-Games-Tournament (DeVries & Slavin, 1978), Student Teams-Achievement Divisions (Slavin, 1978a), Jigsaw (Aronson, 1978), and Group-Investigation (Sharan & Sharan, 1976). These techniques will be emphasized both because they have been well researched in field settings and because they are well-defined teaching strategies that are in use in many classrooms. All four have books or manuals written about them so that teachers can easily implement them. Other classroom research involving less widely used cooperative techniques will also be reviewed.

Teams-Games-Tournament. Teams-Games-Tournament (TGT) is built around two major components: 4–5 member student teams, and instructional tournaments. The teams are the cooperative element of TGT. Students are assigned to teams according to a procedure that maximizes heterogeneity of ability levels, sex, and race. The primary function of the team is to prepare its members to do well in the tournament. Following an initial class presentation by the teacher, the teams are given worksheets covering academic material similar to that to be included in the tournament. Teammates study together and quiz each other to be sure that all team members are prepared.

After the team practice session, team members must demonstrate their learning in the tournament, which is usually held once each week. For the tournament, students are assigned to three-person "tournament tables." The assignment is done so that competition at each table will be fair—the highest three students in past performance are assigned to Table 1, the next three to Table 2, and so on. At the tables, the students compete on simple academic games covering content that has been presented in class by the teacher and on the worksheets. The games consist of a set of items and a deck of numbered cards. Students take turns picking cards and answering the corresponding items; other students may challenge their answers. Students at the tournament tables are competing as representatives of their teams, and the score each student earns at his or her tournament table is added into an overall team score. Because students are assigned to ability-homogeneous tournament tables, each student has an equal chance of contributing a maximum score to his or her team, as the first place scorer at every table brings the same number of points to the team. Following the tournament, the teacher prepares a newsletter which recognizes successful teams and first-place scorers. While team assignments always remain the same, tournament table assignments are changed for every tournament according to a system that maintains equality of past performance at each table. For a complete description of Teams-Games-Tournament, see Slavin (1978b).

Student Teams-Achievement Divisions.   Student Teams-Achievement Divisions (STAD) uses the same 4–5 member heterogenous teams used in TGT, but replaces the games and tournaments with 15-minute quizzes, which students take after studying in their teams. In the first studies of STAD (Slavin, 1977a; Slavin, 1978c; Slavin, 1979; Slavin, 1980b; Slavin & Karweit, in press), quiz scores were translated into team scores using a system called "achievement divisions." The quiz scores of the highest six students in past performance were compared, and the top scorer in this group (the achievement division) earned eight points for his or her team, the second scorer earned six points, etc. Then the quiz scores of the next highest six students in past performance were compared, and so on. In this way, students' scores were compared only with those of an ability-homogeneous reference group instead of the entire class. In the more recent STAD studies (Madden & Slavin, 1980; Oickle, 1980; Slavin & Oickle, 1981) an "improvement score" system was used, in which the scores students contributed to their teams were based on the degree to which their weekly quiz scores exceeded their own past performance. Both the improvement scores and the achievement division system give students equal opportunities to contribute maximum points to their team scores, as in TGT. A complete description of STAD appears in Slavin (1978b).

Jigsaw.   In Jigsaw, students are assigned to small heterogeneous teams, as in TGT and STAD. Academic material is broken into as many sections as there are team members. For example, a biography might be broken into "early years," "schooling," "first accomplishments," etc. The students study their sections with members of other teams who have the same sections. Then they return to their teams and teach their sections to the other team members. Finally, all team members are quizzed on the entire unit. The quiz scores contribute to individual grades, not to a team score as in TGT and STAD. In this sense, the Jigsaw technique may be seen as high in task interdependence but low in reward interdependence, as individual performances do not contribute directly to a group goal. In the Jigsaw technique, individual performances contribute to others' individual goals only; since the group is not rewarded as a group, there is no formal group goal. However, because the positive behavior of each team member (learning his or her section) helps the other group members to be rewarded (because they need each other's information), the essential dynamics of the cooperative reward structure are present.

Slavin (1978b) constructed a modification of Jigsaw called Jigsaw II. In Jigsaw II, students all read the same material but focus on separate topics. The students from different teams who have the same topics meet to discuss their topics and then return to teach them to their teammates. The team members then take a quiz, and the quiz scores are used to form team scores as in STAD. Thus, Jigsaw II involves less task interdependence and more reward interdependence than Jigsaw.

Group-Investigation.   Group-Investigation is a general classroom organizational plan in which students work in small groups using cooperative inquiry, discussion, and cooperative planning and projects. In Group-Investigation, students form their own 2–6 member teams. The teams choose subtopics from a unit being studied by the entire class, further break their subtopics into individual tasks, and carry out the activities needed to achieve their group goal. The group then makes a presentation or display to communicate its findings to the class. In Group-Investigation, cooperative rewards are not well specified; students are simply asked to work together to achieve group goals. For a complete description of Group-Investigation, see Sharan and Sharan (1976).

Other Classroom Studies.   In addition to the four major techniques, there are several other cooperative learning methods that differ from the four techniques described above primarily in that they have been used almost exclusively in research and are not in wide classroom use. Studies of these methods are nevertheless useful in helping us to understand the effects of cooperative learning on students.

Three of these studies (Cooper, Johnson, Johnson, & Wilderson, in press; Johnson, Johnson, Johnson, & Anderson, 1976; Johnson, Johnson, & Scott, 1978) used a simple cooperative technique in which students were assigned to small groups and instructed to work together on academic tasks and hand in a single assignment as a group. The teachers praised the group as a whole, but no formal group rewards were given. This cooperative technique resembles practical techniques presented in Johnson and Johnson's book, *Learning Together and Alone* (1975), but according to the authors the studies and practical techniques are not similar enough to allow the studies to constitute an evaluation of the strategies outlined in the book.

Three additional studies (Ryan & Wheeler, 1977; Wheeler, 1977; Wheeler & Ryan, 1973) used a cooperative technique similar to that used by the Johnsons, but considerably more structured. Students were assigned specific roles within cooperative groups and worked on social studies inquiry activities to produce a single workbook. The group making the best workbook received a prize.

Weigel, Wiser, and Cook (1975) used a combination of cooperative techniques over a long period of time (in their junior high school sample, an entire school year). These techniques involved various small-group activities, with information-gathering, discussion, and interpretation conducted by the student group. Prizes were given to winning groups based on the quality of the group product.

Non-Cognitive Outcomes

At least in theory, cooperative learning represents a major change in the basic organization or the classroom and in what students experience in school. For example, regardless of their particulars, cooperative learning methods always involve much more contact during class time on school tasks than would be likely to occur in a traditional classroom. This contact by itself is likely to change the social system of the classroom and the students' friendship networks. Theories of cooperation and competition would predict that students in cooperative learning would care about one another's school performance and express proacademic norms in their peer groups more than would students in traditional, competitively structured classrooms. Common sense would predict that, because students (and others) like to interact with others and tend to choose social over solitary activities, they would like learning cooperatively more than they would traditional instruction.

Much of the research on cooperative learning methods has focused on assessing their effects on such variables as students' ability or predisposition to cooperate; students' mutual concern or liking, especially between individuals of different races and between mainstreamed students and their normal-progress classmates; and students' liking of school, self-esteem, norms concerning academic achievement, and locus of control. Almost all of the studies reviewed in this chapter measured student achievement as well as the noncognitive variables reported, and almost all measured multiple noncognitive variables.

The following section summarizes the research on the various cooperative learning methods by categories of noncognitive outcomes. Because of the multiple measurement strategies used in most of the research, each technique appears under several different dependent variables.

The Research

The research on the various cooperative learning techniques has been conducted in field experiments, in which the cooperative methods were compared to control classes. The studies vary widely in terms of designs, measures, populations, and other features, which makes it difficult to compare results from study to study or, more importantly, from technique to technique. A research review has to ignore these methodological differences to some extent and assume that positive and negative findings mean what they appear to mean on the average, but the reader should bear in mind that differences in findings between studies and between methods can be caused by many factors. However, the studies have been screened for adequate methodological rigor. Whenever an "effect" is reported, this means that the experimental group was significantly different from the control group ($p < .05$) unless otherwise noted, and that some procedure, either random assignment or analysis of covariance or both, was used to insure that the differences were due to the treatments and not to preexisting differences. There were a few cases in which effects claimed by authors were discounted because of obvious methodological or statistical problems, but in general findings are reported as the authors reported them. This review is limited to studies of cooperative learning methods that could be used as practical alternatives to traditional instruction and that were evaluated for at least 2 weeks in elementary or secondary classrooms. This excludes literally hundreds of laboratory and laboratory-like studies of cooperation and a few instructional studies at the college level. Within these restrictions, this chapter attempts to review all published and available unpublished studies of cooperative learning that involve non-cognitive measures.

Table 14.1 provides a summary of the characteristics and noncognitive outcomes of cooperative learning studies. A "+" in the table indicates a statistically significant difference between the experimental and control groups ($p < .05$) in favor of the experimental group; a "0" indicates no difference; a "(+)" indicates a marginally significant effect ($p < .10$) in favor of the experimental group. A blank indicates either that the particular measure was not used or that if used a methodological problem precludes interpretation of the finding. In no instance has a significant difference in favor of the control group been reported for any of the major noncognitive variables reviewed in this chapter. The table is a simplification of what are often complex issues, and therefore the text

TABLE 14.1

Characteristics and Non-Cognitive Outcomes of Cooperative Learning Studies

	Characteristics					Outcomes							
Major Reports	Number of Students	Ethnicity	Grade Level	Duration Weeks	Subject Area	Cooperation	Mutual Concern	Race Relations	Main-streaming	Liking of School	Self-Esteem	Pro Academic Norms	Locus of Control
TGT													
1. DeVries, Edwards, & Slavin, 1978	96	W-70% B-30%	7	9	Math			+					
2. DeVries & Edwards, 1973; DeVries & Edwards, 1974	110	W-57% B-43%	7	4	Math		+						
3. Edwards & DeVries, 1974	128	W-49% B-51%	7	12	Math Social Studies		+	0		0			
4. Hulten & DeVries, 1976; Slavin, DeVries, & Hulten, 1975	299	W-100%	7	10	Math		+	+		+		+	
5. DeVries. Edwards, & Wells, 1974	191	B-90% W-10%	10-12	12	Social Studies		+	+		+			
6. DeVries & Mescon, 1975	60	W-100%	3	6	Language Arts		0	0		0			

Study	N	Race	Grade	Weeks	Subject						
7. DeVries, Mescon, & Shackman, 1975	53	W-100%	3	6			0		0		
8. DeVries, Lucasse, & Shackman, 1979	1742	W-100%	7-8	10	Language Arts		0	+	0		
9. Slavin, 1975; Slavin, 1977b	57	W-100%	7-9	10	Social Studies	+	0		+	+	

STAD

Study	N	Race	Grade	Weeks	Subject						
10. Slavin, 1978c	205	W-99%	7	10	Language Arts	+	0		+	+	+
11. Slavin, 1977a	62	W-39% B-61%	7	10	Language Arts	0	0	+	0		
12. Slavin, 1980b	424	W-100%	4	12	Language Arts	+	+				
13. Slavin, 1979	420	W-61% B-39%	7-8	12	Language Arts	+	0	+	0		
14. Slavin & Oickle, 1981	175	W-66% B-34%	6-8	12	Language Arts	+		+			
15. Madden & Slavin, 1980	175	W-100%	3-6	6	Math	0	+		+	+	
16. Oickle, 1980	1029	W-93% B-7%	6-8	12	Language Arts	+	0		+	+	

(continued)

TABLE 14.1 (Continued)

	Characteristics					Outcomes							
Major Reports	Number of Students	Ethnicity	Grade Level	Duration Weeks	Subject Area	Cooperation	Mutual Concern	Race Relations	Main-Streaming	Liking of School	Self-Esteem	Pro Academic Norms	Locus of Control
JIGSAW													
17. Blaney et al., 1977	304	W-59% B-23% H-16%	5	6	Social Studies	+	0			0	+		
18. Gonzales, 1979	326	W-48% H-44% A-6%	9-12	10	Social Studies			+		0	0		+
19. Geffner, 1978	218	W-46% H-44% B-5% A-5%	5	8	Social Studies						+		
TGT + STAD + JIGSAW II													
20. Slavin & Karweit, 1981	456	W-99%	4-5	16	Math Lang. Arts Soc. St.		+			+	+	0	(+)
Group-Investigation													
21. Hertz-Lazarowitz, Sharan, & Steinberg, 1980	393	W-100%	3-7	54	All	+	+						
Other Studies													
22. Johnson, Johnson, Johnson, & Anderson, 1976	30	W-100%	5	4	Language Arts	+	+			0			

No.	Study	N	Composition	Grade	Weeks	Subject						
23.	Johnson, Johnson, & Scott, 1978	30	W-100%	5-6	10	Math	+		+			
24.	Cooper, Johnson, Johnson, & Wilderson, 1980	60	W-67% B-33%	5-6	3	Science Geog. English						
25.	Armstrong, Balow, & Johnson, 1977	40	W-98%	5-6	4	Language Arts		0	+			
26.	Wheeler & Ryan, 1973	58	W-100%	5-6	4	Social Studies			+			
27.	Wheeler, 1977	40	W-83% B-17%	5-6	2	Social Studies		+	+			
28.	Ryan & Wheeler, 1977	48	W-100%	5-6	4	Social Studies		+	+		+	
29.	Weigel, Wiser, & Cook, 1975	324	W-71% B-17% H-12%	7-10	20-30	English		+		+		
30.	Ballard, Corman, Gottlieb, & Kaufman, 1977	37 (EMR)	H-57% B-41% W-2%	3-5	8	Various			+	+		+

1. + - Effect in favor of cooperative group at p < .05; 0 = no difference; (+) = marginally significant effect (p < .10); Blank - not measured, or if measured not interpretable due to methodological shortcomings of study.

2. W = Non-Hispanic whites; B = Blacks; H = Hispanic-Americans; A = Asian-Americans

should be read to explain each finding. Note that if two measures of the same outcome were used, and one showed a significant difference and the other did not, a "+" was entered in the table. This is explained in the text.

Cooperation. One obvious noncognitive outcome that would be anticipated as a consequence of a cooperative experience in schools is that students would become more cooperative or altruistic. Perhaps because this outcome is widely assumed, it has not been studied as much as many others.

One frequently-used measure of a preference for altruism or cooperation, as opposed to individual gain or competition, is a choice board devised by Kagan and Madsen (1971) in which students allocate rewards to actual or imagined peers. The choices with which students are confronted are to give the "peer" more rewards (altruism), the same number of rewards (equality), or fewer rewards (competition) than the students receive themselves. Using measures based on this paradigm, Hertz-Lazarowitz, Sharan, and Steinberg (1980) showed that students who had experienced Group-Investigation made more altruistic choices than did control students. Johnson, Johnson, Johnson, and Anderson (1976) also found that when students engaged in cooperative activities in class, they made more altruistic choices on a task similar to the choice board than did students who had worked competitively or individualistically. Ryan and Wheeler (1977) found that students who had studied cooperatively made more cooperative and helpful decisions in a subsequent simulation game than did students who had studied competitively.

Another outcome related to cooperation is preference for cooperation or competition. Blaney, Stephan, Rosenfield, Aronson, and Sikes (1977) found that, following an experience with Jigsaw, students expressed less agreement with the statement "I would rather beat a classmate at schoolwork than help him" than did control students. Wheeler and Ryan (1973) also documented a positive effect of cooperative classroom experience on student attitudes toward cooperation.

Finally, an important component of the ability to cooperate with others is the ability to understand the perspective of someone else. Bridgeman (1977; not listed in Table 14.1) found that students who had worked cooperatively using Jigsaw were better able to take the perspective of another person than were control students, and Johnson et al. (1976) found that students who had worked cooperatively were better able to identify feelings in taped conversations than were students who had worked individually.

Thus, it is clear that cooperative experiences do increase components of cooperative and altruistic behaviors more than do competitive or individualistic experiences. These findings are very important, because they suggest that cooperative learning may produce positive changes in the kinds of pro-social behaviors that are increasingly needed in a society in which the ability to get along with others is more and more crucial. However, it is possible that these effects are due in part to a social desirability bias on the part of students who have just gone through a cooperative experience. It must be apparent to such students that if they have just gone through several weeks of cooperative work, in which the importance of cooperation and caring about groupmates has been repeatedly expressed, they are expected to give altruistic or procooperative responses on a posttest. The research described above would be strengthened by followup assessments by independent testers long enough after the conclusion of the study to allow any social desirability bias to wear off. It would also be strengthened by a demonstration that cooperative learning leads not only to an improvement in cooperative *predisposition,* but also to an improvement in the ability to cooperate with others to get things done. Such a measure would be less subject to social desirability bias and would greatly strengthen the argument that cooperative learning prepares students for cooperative activity.

Mutual Concern.   When individuals work together as equals toward a common goal, they come to like one another. This has been perhaps the most studied and most consistently found outcome in the long tradition of research on cooperation and competition (see Johnson & Johnson, 1974, and Slavin 1977c for reviews), and most cooperative learning studies have included such measures as student liking of others, feelings of being liked by others, and number of friends named on an open-ended sociometric instrument.

The evidence for positive effects of cooperative learning on mutual concern is strong, but not entirely consistent. Mutual concern was measured in six studies of TGT (see Table 14.1 and DeVries & Slavin, 1978). Significantly positive effects were documented in four, but no differences were found in two. Both of these latter studies involved third graders, for whom reliable paper-and-pencil measures of attitudes are difficult to obtain and whose generally positive attitudes make ceiling effects a problem (e.g., *no* experimental or control students disagreed with the statement, "Students in this class are friendly toward me"). Mutual concern was measured in six STAD studies, and while significantly positive effects were found in four, no differences were found in the other two. In a study in which TGT, STAD, and Jigsaw were used together with the same sample (Slavin & Karweit, in press), positive effects on mutual concern were also found.

The effects of Jigsaw on mutual concern are unclear. Blaney et al. (1977) found no difference between the experimental and control groups in overall ratings of classmates, but they found an effect favoring the *control* group in students' feelings of being liked, a most unusual finding in research on cooperative groups. On the other hand, liking among groupmates increased in the Jigsaw classes.

Johnson et al. (1976) found that their form of cooperative learning made students feel more accepted by their peers than did individualized instruction, but this was not replicated by Cooper, Johnson, Johnson, and Wilderson (1980), who found no difference. Cooper et al. did, however, find a positive effect of cooperation on rating of all classmates. Wheeler (1977) found that students who worked cooperatively reported more favorable attitudes toward their peers than did students who worked competitively, and he additionally found a substantial interaction between cooperative-competitive treatment and predisposition to cooperate or compete, such that cooperatively predisposed students in the cooperative condition gained far more in attitudes toward their classmates than did competitively predisposed students in either group and cooperatively predisposed students in the competitive group.

One interesting study was conducted by Slavin (1977b), who used TGT with emotionally disturbed adolescents. He found that the TGT students named significantly more of their peers as friends than did control students. Behavioral observations revealed that experimental students interacted appropriately with one another more than did control students. Further, a 5-month observational followup of the students, who were by then in completely different classes, showed that the students who had been in the TGT classes still interacted appropriately with other students more than did students who had been in the control group.

Race Relations.   In terms of psychological theory, relationships between students of different races or ethnicities is merely a special case of mutual liking among students in general. Yet, in practice, race relations are of critical importance in American schools, and much of the interest in cooperative learning both in the research community and in the schools has been focused on this outcome. The need for some way to break down racial and ethnic barriers to friendship is obvious to anyone who works in a desegregated secondary school. Students of different races or ethnicities may be in the same schools and the same classrooms, but in the lunchroom, at the bus stop, at recess, and everywhere else where students have free choice over who they associate with, there are almost always ethnically identifiable peer groups and very frequently little or no racial or ethnic mixing at all. Sociometric studies have documented this problem and have shown that, far from improving over time, this situation tends to remain stable or deteriorate in the months or years after desegregation (see Gerard and Miller, 1975).

Even before *Brown vs. Board of Education,* Allport (1954) recognized that for improving race relations desegregation alone might not be enough. He emphasized equal-status, cooperative interaction as the prime condition for positive relations between individuals of different races. This proposition has been successfully demonstrated in the laboratory many times (see Cook, 1978), and a major correlational study of desegregated high schools has suggested that cooperative interracial interaction in the classroom or in sports teams is the *only* widely used school program that consistently improves student race relations (Slavin & Madden, 1979). Yet it took more than twenty years after Allport's book for practical programs that incorporate equal status, cooperative interaction into the ongoing instructional procedure of the classroom to be developed, researched, and made available to teachers.

The results of the studies of cooperative learning and race relations show that cooperative learning can improve this outcome, but as with other variables, there are some inconsistencies. The strongest and most consistent effects on race relations, as measured by the number of cross-race choices made on a sociometric instrument, have been found in the three STAD studies that took place in integrated schools (Slavin, 1977a; Slavin, 1979; Slavin & Oickle, 1981), although in one of these (Slavin & Oickle, 1981) the effects were entirely due to increases in black friends chosen by whites; there were no differences in whites chosen by blacks in this study. In another of these studies, Slavin (1979) conducted a nine-month followup of the race relations measure and found that even in the next school year, when students were assigned to different classes and different teachers, students who had been in the experimental group still named more friends of the other race than did students who had been in the control group.

Research on TGT, which is very similar to STAD, also found effects on cross-racial friendships that were relatively consistent. Three of the four studies in desegregated schools found positive effects of TGT on this variable, and one showed no difference (see DeVries, Edwards, & Slavin, 1978).

One of the largest and longest studies of cooperative learning was conducted by Weigel, Wiser, and Cook (1975) in tri-ethnic (Chicano, Anglo, black) classrooms. These investigators found positive effects of cooperative learning on whites' attitudes toward Mexican-Americans, but not on white-black, black-white, black-Chicano, Chicano-black, or Chicano-white attitudes. They also found positive effects of cooperative learning on teachers' reports of less interethnic conflict.

One well-known study evaluated the effects of Jigsaw on race relations (Blaney et al., 1977). Unfortunately, the authors used an odd measure of race relations. The Jigsaw treatment involves assignment of students to six-member teams that are heterogeneous in sex, ethnicity, and academic ability. Blaney et al. compared students' ratings of their teammates to their ratings of their non-teammate classmates and interpreted the higher ratings of teammates as an indication of interethnic attraction, even though the non-teammate classmates were of about the same ethnic composition as the teammates. This is an indirect measure at best, and thus the effects of Jigsaw on interethnic attraction in this case are uncertain. However, in a recent study in mixed Mexican-American—Anglo—Asian classrooms, Gonzales (1979) found more positive attitudes toward Mexican-Americans in Jigsaw than in control classes, although no effects were found on attitudes toward whites or Asians.

Finally, Cooper, Johnson, Johnson, and Wilderson (1980) found greater friendship across race lines in a cooperative treatment than in an individualistic treatment.

One of the STAD studies (Slavin, 1979) was recently reanalyzed by Hansell and Slavin (1981) to determine why STAD affects race relations. The results were quite interesting. In that study, the effects of the treatment on cross-racial friendship choices made and received did not differ by race, by sex, or by academic ability of the chooser or receiver. That is, the treatment effects were essentially across-the-board increases for all students in the number of cross-racial choices made and received. An examination of the order of choices made showed that the treatment effects were strongest for choices high in each student's list of friends, and examination of reciprocated versus unreciprocated choices showed that the treatment worked because it increased mutual, reciprocated choices, which tend to be the stronger, more long-lasting choices. In other words, the Hansell and Slavin findings confirm that the effects of STAD on race relations are not artifactual or limited to one or another segment of the student population, but that they are strong, meaningful, and general.

In summary, cooperative learning methods taken together appear to have relatively consistent positive effects on student race relations. However, the indication that the effects were strongest and most consistent for the STAD and TGT methods is interesting. These methods are the only cooperative learning techniques in which scoring is used that gives each student an equal chance to contribute maximum points to the team if the student does his or her best work. This is accomplished in STAD by the use of improvement scores and in TGT by the use of competition between equals. These scoring systems make it unlikely that any team member will automatically be seen by his or her teammates as a drag on the team. In classrooms in which different ethnic groups have different levels of achievement, Allport's "equal status" criterion for positive race relations may be difficult to achieve without the use of "equal opportunity" scoring systems, such as those used in TGT and STAD. There is no direct evidence of this, but it is possible that it is these scoring systems that account for the particularly positive effects of TGT and STAD on race relations.

Although the overall effects are encouraging, there is still much to be known about cooperative learning and race relations. One unresolved issue is the degree to which the cross-racial friendships generated in the classroom extend to other settings, such as the lunchroom and out-of-school situations. Another is the effect of cooperative learning on prejudice, as contrasted with cross-racial friendships. A third is the effect of cooperative learning in preventing interracial or interethnic conflict. Also, the most successful research has taken place in black–white settings; it is not clear that the methods would work equally well in improving relations between other groups, such as Hispanics, Native Americans, Asian Americans, and so on. The effects of cooperative learning on race relations are certainly among the most exciting and important of the noncognitive outcomes, and for this reason these effects warrant much more study.

Mainstreaming.   The positive effects of cooperative learning on mutual concern among students in general and on relationships between students of different ethnic backgrounds in particular suggest that these methods may be useful in improving relationships between students in any situation in which there are significant barriers to friendships. Besides the race barrier, perhaps the most important impediment to positive relations between students is that between mainstreamed, low-achieving students and their normal-progress classmates. Several studies (e.g., Scranton & Ryckman, 1979; Siperstein, Bopp, & Bak, 1978) have shown that when low achieving students are mainstreamed in regular classrooms, they are less well accepted and more frequently rejected than their normal-progress peers.

Because it has been successful in breaking down racial barriers to friendships, cooperative learning is an obvious means of attempting to improve relations between mainstreamed and normal-progress students. Ballard, Corman, Gottlieb, and Kaufman (1977) demonstrated that when normal-progress and mainstreamed students interacted cooperatively on group projects, the normal-progress students came to accept their learning-disabled peers more than did normal-progress students in control classes. Armstrong, Johnson, & Balow (1981) found that normal-progress students who had worked cooperatively in language class rated their learning-disabled peers as smarter and more valuable than did students who had worked individualistically. Cooper et al. (1980) found that normal-progress students named significantly more of their learning-disabled classmates as students they would like to party with than did individualistically taught students and named marginally more learning-disabled students as friends and as students they would like to do schoolwork with. Finally, Madden and Slavin (1980) evaluated STAD in mainstreamed classrooms and found that this method decreased the number of learning-disabled students rejected by their normal-progress peers, but did not increase the number of learning-disabled students chosen as friends or as desired workmates. This study also showed that the STAD method significantly increased achievement and self-esteem for all students, making this technique attractive as a means of simultaneously improving the educational experience for learning-disabled and normal-progress students.

Much more needs to be done in the area of cooperative learning as a means of facilitating mainstreaming, both because of the critical importance of mainstreaming to education today and because of the potential of cooperative learning as a way to improve the outcomes of mainstreaming for mainstreamed and normal-progress students alike. Among the issues that need to be studied are the effects of cooperative learning on mainstreaming of physically handicapped and emotionally disturbed students. Current research has dealt almost exclusively with academically handicapped students. Secondly, there is a need for development and evaluation of more comprehensive mainstreaming strategies involving cooperative learning, in which the instructional activities of the resource teacher or special education teacher are coordinated with the activities of the regular classroom teacher, so that what the mainstreamed student learns outside of the regular class helps him or her to be more successful in a cooperative activity in the regular class. There are many other issues that need to be resolved in this area, and much more attention to them is clearly warranted.

Liking of School.   Anyone walking into a class using any cooperative learning strategy can see that the great majority of students enjoy working in groups. When students who worked in groups are asked whether they would prefer to go back to traditional methods, the students overwhelmingly prefer to stay in groups. In general the data on measures of satisfaction or liking of school support this impression, but there are many exceptions.

For TGT, satisfaction was measured in eight studies, and positive effects were found in three. No differences were found in the other five (see Table 14.1 and DeVries & Slavin, 1978). These instances of no differences were surprising given that, of all the techniques, TGT seems most exciting to students, as it uses frequent active academic games. In many cases, especially in the elementary school studies, the failure to find enhanced satisfaction was due to ceiling effects, in which students expressed highly positive attitudes toward school on the pretest. Ceiling effects were also a problem in the STAD research, in which positive effects on satisfaction were found in two of six studies (Slavin, 1978a; Madden & Slavin, 1980). In the study in which TGT, STAD, and Jigsaw were combined (Slavin & Karweit, in press), positive effects on student liking of school were found.

The effects of Jigsaw on student liking of school are also mixed. Blaney et al. (1977) found a positive effect of Jigsaw on this variable for Anglos, no effect for blacks, and effects in favor of the control group for Mexican-Americans. Gonzales (1979) found no differences for any group. Johnson et al. (1976) found no significant differences in liking of instructional method between a cooperative technique and an individualistic one, but, using somewhat similar methods, Wheeler and Ryan (1973) found that cooperative learning improved attitudes toward social studies.

The inconsistency of the effects of cooperative learning on liking of school are surprising and perhaps say more about instrumentation than about substantive aspects of the cooperative learning technique. One clue to a possible instrumentation problem is provided by Madden and Slavin (1980). They found no differences between STAD and control conditions on the kind of satisfaction measure used in the TGT and STAD studies, consisting of such statements as "I like this class" and "This class is a lot of fun," to which students indicated agreement or disagreement. However, they did find strong differences on a questionnaire specifically asking about the STAD and control methods; students in the STAD condition more consistently agreed with the statement, "I like this way of learning," than did control students, when the questionnaire made it clear that they were responding to their respective treatment. In other words, it may be that, because of ceiling effects in younger students' attitudes and because attitudes toward class and toward school may be influenced by many factors not changed by the treatments, measures of general satisfaction may be hard to change, but when the students are asked specifically about the method they experienced, they give realistic appraisals.

Self-Esteem.   Several of the cooperative learning studies have included measures of student self-esteem. Self-esteem has been anticipated as an outcome of cooperative learning both because students in cooperative groups feel more liked by their classmates (which they usually are) and because they are likely to feel more successful academically (which they also usually are).

The technique most directly targeted to improving student self-esteem is Jigsaw, in which students are each given special information that makes them indispensable to their groups. Positive effects on self-esteem have been found in two studies (Blaney et al., 1977; Geffner, 1978), but not in a third (Gonzales, 1979).

TGT and STAD have each been shown to affect student self-esteem (DeVries, Lucasse, & Shackman, 1979; Madden & Slavin, 1980; Oickle, 1980). Also, the combined TGT-STAD-Jigsaw II program (Slavin & Karweit, in press) showed positive effects on this variable. The DeVries et al. and Slavin and Karweit studies used the general, social, and academic subscales of the Coopersmith Self-Esteem Inventory. In the DeVries et al. study, significant effects were found for the social self-esteem subscale only, with no differences appearing on the general or academic self-esteem subscales. On the other hand, Slavin and Karweit's findings showed that cooperative learning students were significantly higher than control students in general self-esteem and marginally (p < .10) higher in academic self-esteem; no difference was found in social self-esteem. The Slavin and Karweit study also showed that the cooperative learning students were marginally less anxious than the control students.

The effects of the Johnson method on self-esteem related variables are also inconsistent. Cooperatively taught students more consistently agreed that they were "doing a good job of learning" in the Johnson, Johnson, and Scott (1978) study, but no differences were found in self-acceptance by Cooper, Johnson, Johnson, and Wilderson (1980).

Thus, as with most of the noncognitive outcomes reviewed in this chapter, the effect of cooperative learning on student self-esteem is generally positive but somewhat inconsistent. What is remarkable with a variable thought to be such an integral part of a person's personality is that any changes at all have been documented. Positive effects of cooperative learning on self-esteem have been found as frequently, relative to the number of times they have been assessed, as positive effects on liking of school, a variable that on the surface would seem to be much easier to influence.

Pro-Academic Norms.   Slavin (1977c) has argued that, all other things being equal, when cooperative learning strategies have effects on student academic performance, it is primarily because they create a situation in which students express norms in favor of their peers doing their best academically. That is, unless students can be influenced to care how much their classmates are learning, they are unlikely to try very hard to help them learn and to encourage them to come to class and do their work. Cooperative learning is hypothesized to create peer norms favoring achievement by making students interdependent for success; because students must get their groupmates to learn if they want their groups to be successful, they are likely to express norms in favor of learning.

The research on cooperative learning and peer norms generally supports this link, although again not always. Hulten and DeVries (1976) and Slavin (1977b) found that students who had experienced TGT felt that their classmates' achievement was important to them. Slavin (1978c) and Madden and Slavin (1980) found the same effect for STAD. Slavin, DeVries, and Hulten (1975) and Slavin (1975) demonstrated that although students who performed better than usual in TGT gained friends, the students in control conditions lost friends, suggesting that achievement was positively related to peer status in the team condition and negatively related in the control group. On the other hand, De-Vries, Mescon, and Shackman (1975), Slavin (1977a), Slavin (1979), and Slavin and Karweit (in press) found no differences between cooperative learning and control on this measure.

Locus of Control.   One particularly interesting set of findings concerns the effects of cooperative learning on students' locus of control, the degree to which students feel that their outcomes depend on their own efforts (as opposed to luck). Gonzales (1979), Johnson, Johnson, and Scott (1978), Slavin (1978c), and Wheeler and Ryan (1973) have all found significantly positive effects of different cooperative learning strategies on this variable, and Slavin and Karweit (in press) found marginally positive effects (p < .10). These effects are probably due to the fact that cooperative learning is usually accompanied by very clear tasks for students to accomplish to achieve success, which give students a feeling that they control their destinies. Also, cooperative learning usually gives students experiences of success that they may not have had before. Because individuals tend to attribute success to their own efforts but failure to other factors (Weiner & Kukla, 1970), it is likely that the experience of success will lead to an increase in feelings of internal locus of control.

Conclusion

The breadth of the outcomes affected by cooperative learning strategies is staggering. There exist special programs focused solely on improving students' self-esteem, internal locus of control, race relations, mainstreaming experiences, or achievement, but cooperative learning strategies have been shown to positively influence all of these outcomes and several others. What is more remarkable is that each of several quite different cooperative learning methods have been shown to have positive effects on a wide variety of outcomes. The differences in patterns of outcomes between methods are not as interesting as their similarities. TGT and STAD appear to be somewhat more effective for race relations and achievement; Jigsaw for self-esteem; the Johnson methods for mainstreaming; and Group-Investigation for cooperation. Yet, one or two more studies in each of these areas could change these impressions. In general, take any desired outcome of schooling, administer a cooperative learning statement, and about two-thirds of the time there will be a significant difference between the experimental and control groups in favor of the experimental groups.

It is possible that the effects of cooperative learning techniques on non-cognitive outcomes are due less to any linkage between the methods and particular outcomes than to an overall "halo" effect that produces generally positive responses to any question. This is unlikely, because one would think that the first variable to show a "halo" effect would be liking of school, the non-cognitive variable that has been influenced least consistently by the cooperative learning methods.

It is relatively unlikely that the effects summarized in this chapter are due to any systematic methodological bias, because the methodologies of the various studies are so different from one another. For example, "Hawthorne" effects could be a problem in some studies, but in most of the TGT and STAD studies and in most of the Johnson studies the control groups were given a special treatment with its own training procedures and materials identical to those used in the experimental group, so that control teachers used a "new" method. Teachers were randomly assigned to treatments in the TGT and STAD studies, so at least for these studies teacher differences due to different levels of interest in a new method are not a factor. Random assignment of students or matching plus analysis of covariance or equivalent statistical methods insured that pre-existing differences did not account for the effects obtained in any of the studies. The robustness of the findings is supported by the wide range of subject areas, student ages, geographical locations, and research methodologies and staffs used in the various studies.

While the effects of cooperative learning on the non-cognitive outcomes reviewed in this chapter appear to be real and relatively robust, there is much work yet to be done in this area. Research conducted to date has dealt primarily with validation of the various cooperative learning models of the "Brand X versus Brand Y" variety, where Brand X is some form of cooperative learning and Brand Y is a competitive, individualistic, or untreated control treatment. There have been some factorial treatments in the TGT-STAD tradition (e.g., Hulten & DeVries, 1976; Slavin, 1978c; Slavin, 1980b), but these have focused on achievement outcomes. There is a need both for careful analysis of what goes on in a cooperative classroom and for more attention to just how the various outcomes come about. A great deal is changed when a teacher adopts cooperative learning: the classroom tasks, reward-evaluation-feedback systems, authority systems, and even the teacher's role all change substantially. Which of these changes accounts for the effects on cognitive and non-cognitive outcomes? There are hypotheses, but little solid evidence. Long term field experimentation is probably the only way firm answers can be obtained about instructional programs, but anyone who conducts or reviews such studies knows that they are a powerful but blunt instrument, especially for detecting subtle differences.

The other direction in which research and development must go is to work on expanding and refining existing methods to make them capable of being used as true alternatives to traditional instruction. Thousands of teachers throughout the United States and other countries are currently using TGT, STAD, and Jigsaw II through the Johns Hopkins Student Team Learning Project (see Slavin and Hollifield, 1979); others use Group-Investigation, the Johnsons' methods, and original Jigsaw. However, relatively few of these teachers, perhaps one in ten, uses what could be called a true cooperative classroom, in which cooperation between students in small groups is the primary way in which instruction is organized. The Slavin and Karweit (in press) study showed that such an intensive use of cooperative learning is both possible and effective, but much remains to be done in this area.

In summary, cooperative learning has been shown in a large number and wide variety of studies to positively influence a host of important cognitive and non-cognitive variables. This chapter focuses on the latter and concludes that, while there are nonsystematic failures to find differences in some studies for each variable, the overall effects of cooperative learning on student cooperation, mutual concern, race relations and relations with mainstreamed students, liking of school, self-esteem, and internal locus of control are positive and robust.

REFERENCES

Allport, G. *The Nature of Prejudice*. Cambridge, Mass.: Addison-Wesley 1954.

Armstrong, B., Johnson, D. W., & Balow, B. Effects of cooperative vs. individualistic learning experiences on interpersonal attraction between learning-disabled and normal-progress elementary school students. *Contemporary Educational Psychology*, 1981, 6, 102–109.

Aronson, E. *The Jigsaw Classroom*. Beverly Hills, Calif.: Sage Publications, 1978.

Ballard, M., Corman, L., Gottlieb, J., & Kaufman, M. Improving the social status of mainstreamed retarded children. *Journal of Educational Psychology*, 1977, 69, 605–611.

Blaney, N. T., Stephan, S., Rosenfield, D., Aronson, E., & Sikes, J. Interdependence in the classroom: A field study. *Journal of Educational Psychology*, 1977, 69(2), 121–128.

Bridgeman, D. *The influence of cooperative, interdependent learning on role taking and moral reasoning: A theoretical and empirical field study with fifth-grade students*. Unpublished doctoral dissertation, University of California, Santa Cruz, 1977.

Cook, S. W. Interpersonal and attitudinal outcomes of cooperating inter-racial groups. *Journal of Research and Development in Education*, 1978, 12, 97–113.

Cooper, L., Johnson, D. W., Johnson, R., & Wilderson, F. The effects of cooperative, competitive, and individualistic experiences on interpersonal attraction among heterogeneous peers. *Journal of Social Psychology,* 1980, *111,* 243–252.

DeVries, D. L., & Edwards, K. J. Learning games and student teams: Their effects on classroom process. *American Educational Research Journal,* 1973, *10,* 307–318.

DeVries, D. L., & Edwards, K. J. Student teams and learning games: Their effects on cross-race and cross-sex interaction. *Journal of Educational Psychology,* 1974, *66,* 741–749.

DeVries, D. L., Edwards, K. J., & Slavin, R. E. Biracial learning teams and race relations in the classroom: Four field experiments on Teams-Games-Tournament. *Journal of Educational Psychology,* 1978, *70,* 356–362.

DeVries, D. L., Edwards, K. J., & Wells, E. H. *Teams-Games-Tournament in the social studies classroom: Effects on academic achievement, student attitudes, cognitive beliefs, and classroom climate.* Center Report No. 173. Center for Social Organization of Schools, The Johns Hopkins University, 1974.

DeVries, D., Lucasse, P., & Shackman, S. *Small group versus individualized instruction: A field test of their relative effectiveness.* Paper presented at the annual convention of the American Psychological Association, New York, 1979.

DeVries, D. L., & Mescon, I. T. *Teams-Games-Tournament: An effective task and reward structure in the elementary grades.* Center Report No. 189. Center for Social Organization of Schools, The Johns Hopkins University, 1975.

DeVries, D. L., Mescon, I. T., & Shackman, S. L. *Teams-Games-Tournament in the elementary classroom: A replication.* Center Report No. 190. Center for Social Organization of Schools, The Johns Hopkins University, 1975.

DeVries, D. L., & Slavin, R. E. Teams-Games-Tournament (TGT): Review of ten classroom experiments. *Journal of Research and Development in Education,* 1978, *12,* 28–38.

Edwards, K. J., & DeVries, D. L. *The effects of Teams-Games-Tournament and two structural variations on classroom process, student attitudes, and student achievement.* Center Report No. 172. Center for Social Organization of Schools, The Johns Hopkins University, 1974.

Geffner, R. *The effects of interdependent learning on self-esteem, interethnic relations, and intraethnic attitudes of elementary school children: A field experiment.* Unpublished doctoral dissertation, University of California, Santa Cruz, 1978.

Gerard, H. B., & Miller, N. *School Desegregation: A Long-Range Study.* New York, N.Y.: Plenum Press, 1975.

Gonzales, A. *Classroom cooperation and ethnic balance.* Paper presented at the annual convention of the American Psychological Association, New York, 1979.

Hansell, S., & Slavin, R. Cooperative learning and the structure of interracial friendships. *Sociology of Education,* 1981, *54,* 98–106.

Hertz-Lazarowitz, R., Sharan, S., & Steinberg, R. *Classroom learning style and cooperative behavior of elementary school children.* Unpublished manuscript, Haifa University (Israel), 1978.

Hulten, B. H., & DeVries, D. L. *Team competition and group practice: Effects on student achievement and attitudes.* Center Report No. 212. Center for Social Organization of Schools, The Johns Hopkins University, 1976.

Johnson, D. W., & Johnson, R. T. Instructional goal structure: Cooperative, competitive, or individualistic. *Review of Educational Research, 44,* 213–240, 1974.

Johnson, D. W., & Johnson, R. T. *Learning together and alone.* Englewood Cliffs, N.J.: Prentice-Hall, Inc., 1975.

Johnson, D. W., Johnson, R., Johnson, J., & Anderson, D. The effects of cooperative vs. individualized instruction on student prosocial behavior, attitudes toward learning, and achievement. *Journal of Educational Psychology,* 1976, *68,* 446–452.

Johnson, D. W., Johnson, R. T., & Scott, L. The effects of cooperative and individualized instruction on student attitudes and achievement. *Journal of Social Psychology,* 1978, *104.* 207–216.

Kagan, S., & Madsen, M. C. Cooperation and competition of Mexican, Mexican-American, and Anglo-American children of two ages under four instructional sets. *Developmental Psychology,* 1971, *5,* 32-39.

Lucker, G. W., Rosenfield, D., Sikes, J., & Aronson, E. Performance in the interdependent classroom: A field study. *American Educational Research Journal,* 1976, *13,* 115-123.

Madden, N. A., & Slavin, R. *Cooperative learning and social acceptance of mainstreamed academically handicapped students.* Paper presented at the annual convention of the American Psychological Association, Montreal, Canada, 1980.

Oickle, E. *A Comparison of Individual and Team Learning.* Unpublished doctoral dissertation, University of Maryland, 1980.

Ryan, F., & Wheeler, R. The effects of cooperative and competitive background experiences of students on the play of a simulation game. *Journal of Educational Research,* 1977, *70,* 295-299.

Scranton, T., & Ryckman, D. Sociometric status of learning disabled children in an integrative program. *Journal of Learning Disabilities,* 1979, *12,* 402-407.

Sharan, S., & Sharan, Y. *Small-group teaching.* Englewood Cliffs, N.J.: Educational Technology Publications, 1976.

Siperstein, G., Bopp, M., & Bak, J. Social status of learning disabled children. *Journal of Learning Disabilities,* 1978, *11,* 98-102.

Slavin, R. E. *Classroom reward structure: Effects on academic performance, social connectedness, and peer norms.* Unpublished doctoral dissertation, The Johns Hopkins University, 1975.

Slavin, R. E. How student learning teams can integrate the desegregated classroom. *Integrated Education,* 1977, *15*(6), 56-58. (a)

Slavin, R. E. A student team approach to teaching adolescents with special emotional and behavioral needs. *Psychology in the Schools,* 1977, *14*(1), 77-84. (b)

Slavin, R. E. Classroom reward structure: An analytic and practical review. *Review of Educational Research,* 1977, *47*(4), 633-640. (c)

Slavin, R. E. Student teams and achievement divisions. *Journal of Research and Development in Education,* 1978, *12,* 39-49. (a)

Slavin, R. E. *Using student team learning.* Baltimore, Md.: Center for Social Organization of Schools, The Johns Hopkins University, 1978. (b)

Slavin, R. E. Student teams and comparison among equals: Effects on academic performance and student attitudes. *Journal of Educational Psychology,* 1978, *70,* 532-538. (c)

Slavin, R. E. Effects of biracial learning teams on cross-racial friendships. *Journal of Educational Psychology,* 1979, *71,* 381-387.

Slavin, R. E. Cooperative learning. *Review of Educational Research,* 1980, 50, 314-342. (a)

Slavin, R. E. Effects of student teams and peer tutoring on academic achievement and time on-task. *Journal of Experimental Education,* 1980, 48, 252-257. (b)

Slavin, R. E., DeVries, D. L., & Hulten, B. H. *Individual vs. team competition: The interpersonal consequences of academic performance.* Center Report No. 188. Center for Social Organization of Schools, The Johns Hopkins University, 1975.

Slavin, R. E., & Hollifield, J. H. *Anatomy of a successful dissemination.* Center for Social Organization of Schools, The Johns Hopkins University, 1979.

Slavin, R. E., & Karweit, N. Cognitive and affective outcomes of an intensive Student Team Learning experience. *Journal of Experimental Education,* in press.

Slavin, R. E., & Madden, N. A. School practices that improve race relations. *American Educational Research Journal,* 1979, *16*(2), 169-180.

Slavin, R. E., & Oickle, E. Effects of cooperative learning teams on student achievement and race relations: Treatment by race interactions. *Sociology of Education,* 1981, *54,* 174-180.

Weigel, R. H., Wiser, P. L., & Cook, S. W. Impact of cooperative learning experiences on cross-ethnic relations and attitudes. *Journal of Social Issues,* 1975, *31*(1), 219-245.

Weiner, B., & Kukla, A. An attributional analysis of achievement motivation. *Journal of Personality and Social Psychology*, 1970, *15*, 1-20.

Wheeler, R. *Predisposition toward cooperation and competition: Cooperative and competitive classroom effects.* Paper presented at the annual convention of the American Psychological Association, San Francisco, 1977.

Wheeler, R., & Ryan, F. L. Effects of cooperative and competitive classroom environments on the attitudes and achievement of elementary school students engaged in social studies inquiry activities. *Journal of Educational Psychology*, 1973, *65*, 402-407.

15

Impact of the Role of Tutor on Behavior and Self-Perceptions

Vernon L. Allen
University of Wisconsin

According to Ariès (1962), the fifteenth century first gave rise to the concept of childhood as a distinct stage of life characterized by innocence and, especially, incompetence. The legacy of this view of childhood is still with us; it is useful to remind outselves frequently that children are much more competent than usually acknowledged by adults. Much of the recent research in child psychology documents this point of view. It is particularly important to realize that children are capable of participating actively in the education of themselves and their fellow students—contrary to the traditional expectations of the role of passive student. Many teachers have recognized the potential contribution that students can make in supplementing, in informal ways, their own instructional effort (e.g., correcting papers, drilling slower classmates, or preparing simple curricular materials).

Within the past several years many schools have begun to involve students in the instructional system in a more formal way through the medium of peer tutoring programs. Several reasons can be given for the widespread popularity that tutoring has attained in the elementary and secondary schools (and even at the college level) in recent years. The use of children as tutors permits the individualization of instruction for a large number of young or less advanced students which would otherwise not be available. One of the central justifications offered for establishing a tutoring program is the claim that it produces important benefits for the tutor as well as for the learner. In fact, in some cases tutoring seems to have helped the tutor even more than the tutee.

The purpose of the present chapter is to discuss the impact of tutoring on the tutor. For this purpose, I must don the hat of the applied social psychologist and attempt to analyze "real-life" behavior by using conceptual language taken from psychology. In the case of tutoring, the practical situation is a very complex one.

Our task is to attempt to dissect the situation and look at its constituent components and processes with the aid of current theoretical knowledge in psychology. After a descent into a detailed analysis of tutoring I hope that our re-emergence to the reality of the everyday world will be accompanied by greater understanding than before. A theoretical analysis should be consistent with available empirical data, offer new insights and suggestions for further research, and be useful in designing programs that will enhance the impact of tutoring on the tutor.

The present chapter is divided into four sections: First, we discuss the potential impact of tutoring on the tutor by citing the claims made by advocates of the tutoring technique. (Negative outcomes are also a possibility and are mentioned.) A second section offers a general role theoretical framework for analyzing the procedures by which tutoring may exert its impact on the tutor. In the third section, available empirical literature is summarized. Finally, the fourth section offers some suggestions concerning role-specificity of behavior in the light of empirical data and theoretical analysis.

POTENTIAL BENEFITS OF TUTORING FOR THE TUTOR

Both practitioners and theoretically-oriented writers alike usually place considerable emphasis on the important benefits that tutoring can provide for the tutor, quite apart from any help derived by the tutee. In many instances it is clear that a tutoring program was designed (either explicitly or implicitly) with the primary goal of helping the tutor rather than the tutee. But by placing too much emphasis on benefits to the tutor, the goal of improving the learning of the tutee may be compromised (Allen & Feldman, 1974). Often it will simply not be possible to create conditions that will optimize outcomes simultaneously for both tutor and tutee. Leaving aside these broader (and critical) issues, I will summarize the benefits for the tutor that have been claimed for tutoring programs. A brief foray into social history may be appropriate at this point.

Tutoring is by no means a recent innovation in education; it has deep roots in earlier periods of history. Long before attention was paid to the systematic use of tutoring by children in the classroom, many sensitive observers had recognized that teaching is a very effective way to increase one's own understanding. In many primitive societies, older children are given a great deal of responsibility for helping the younger children to acquire essential skills needed to participate successfully in the culture (Hartup, 1976). There are, indeed, in Bruner's (1972) words, "uses of immaturity."

We can often trace an idea in Western thought back to the ancient Romans and Greeks; often we find that they had thought about it—or at least talked about it—long ago. Thus, in the first century, Quintilian, a Roman teacher, stated in his book *Institutio Oratorio* that younger children can learn a great deal from older children in the same class (cited in Wright, 1960). And since ancient times tutoring by children has been used in Hindu schools. Recommendations for using tutoring in a more formal way appeared at the end of the Renaissance. A teacher in Germany, Valentin Trotzendorf, used advanced students to teach others in his school in the 1530s. When the college of Lisbon was established by the Spanish Jesuits in 1553, they instituted a tutorial system that placed one student in charge of ten others. John Comenius, the famous Moravian teacher, articulated the benefits of learning by tutoring in the following comments made in the 1630s:

> The saying, "He who teaches others, teaches himself," is very true, not only because constant repetition impresses a fact indelibly on the mind, but because the process of teaching in itself gives a deeper insight into the subject taught. The gifted Joachim Fortius used to say that, if he had heard or read anything once, it slipped out of his memory within a month; but that if he taught it to others it became as much a part of himself as his fingers, and that he did not believe that anything short of death could deprive him of it. His advice, therefore, was that, if a student wished to make progress, he should arrange to give lessons daily in the subjects which he was studying, even if he had to hire his pupils. "It is worth your while," he says, "to sacrifice your bodily comfort to a certain extent for the sake of having someone who will listen while you teach, or, in other words, while you make intellectual progress." (cited in Wright, 1960)

In the late 18th century Andrew Bell, an Anglican cleric from Scotland who was in charge of a school for orphans in Madras, India, rediscovered the mutual teaching procedure (Bell, 1797). The orphanage school in Madras had been established for the care of "indigent and destitute" children of the British Army (mainly offspring of British soldiers and Indian women). The school had been a source of great frustration to previous headmasters and teachers. As Bell said, the students were "... in general, stubborn, perverse, and obstinate." Bell had a "Eureka" experience while observing a class of children from a native Indian school who were being taught on the seashore. Bell thereupon proceeded to reorganize his school thoroughly, so that in every class all the children were paired off into tutor and learner. Soon the entire school was being taught by the students themselves, under the direction of a single adult teacher. (In part, this state of affairs transpired because all the adult teachers resigned in protest against Bell's seemingly foolish experiment of using mere children as teachers.) Bell claimed in his 1797 book, which reported his experiences with the Madras system of education, that "... any boy who can read, can teach... ALTHOUGH HE KNOWS NOTHING ABOUT IT: and, in teaching, will imperceptibly acquire the knowledge he is destitute of, when he begins to teach, by reading" (capitals in original).

Joseph Lancaster, a professional educator in England, eagerly accepted Bell's ideas, embellished and added to them, and spent the remainder of his life proselytizing for his famous "monitorial system" of education (Lancaster, 1803). The first of several publications describing the success of his system of schooling appeared in 1803; by 1835 it was reported that 60 percent of the English working-class children attended monitorial schools (Bamford, 1967). In the Lancasterian school a monitor (i.e., tutor) received a great deal of reinforcement. In Lancaster's words, "To be a monitor is coveted by the whole school, it being an office at once honourable and productive of emolument: 'solid pudding, as well as empty praise.' " The direct reinforcement that Lancaster used is very similar to behavior modification techniques currently being used in some classrooms. Thus, the tutors were rewarded for the performance of their students: When a student was promoted to a more advanced class, the tutor as well as the learner received a prize. Successful monitors (those who had many of their students promoted to higher classes) were allowed to wear a sign that read "Commendable Monitor." In addition, team competitions were held, and prizes were given to monitors when their groups performed well.

Both Bell and Lancaster were clearly aware of the beneficial social as well as cognitive consequences of tutoring for the tutor. To quote Lancaster (1803) once again: "I have ever found, the surest way to cure a *mischievous* boy was to *make him a monitor*. I never knew any thing to succeed much better, if as well" (underlining in original). And in Bell's 1797 report the following statement appears: "For months together it has not been found necessary to inflict a single punishment." In view of the extensive reliance on punishment by teachers at that time, Bell's statement is indeed a remarkable testament to the docility of students in his school.

Hence, we see that proponents of tutoring in the past were aware of the benefits that tutoring seemed to bring to the tutor and articulated these benefits very clearly; even so, greater emphasis was always placed on the value of tutoring as a way to provide inexpensive instruction for a large number of poor children. The tutorial system continued to be used widely throughout the 19th century, but with a gradual waning of the initial enthusiasm created by the writings of Bell and Lancaster.

Moving now to contemporary times, one of the best-known recent publications on the topic—and one that did a great deal to popularize the tutoring technique in schools—is the book by Gartner, Kohler, and Riessman (1971) entitled *Children Teach Children*. Significantly, it has the subtitle, "Learning by Teaching." The authors of this book stressed the usefulness of tutoring as a technique for improving the learning of tutors. They assert that students can learn more by teaching other children than by being students themselves—a claim that, as we have seen, evokes a familiar echo in the halls of history. On the basis of this conclusion they recommend that every child in school should be given the opportunity to be a teacher.

At this time let me simply present the variety of outcomes that have been claimed as consequences of tutoring, without any critical evaluation. The impact of tutoring on performance has been observed on several types of academic material such as reading, spelling, arithmetic, and language. In addition to the tutor's learning the specific material used in teaching, transfer may possibly occur to other related material as well. Further, the tutor may claim a new understanding or a deeper insight into material that has already been well learned. A still more general and indirect effect on learning may occur by virtue of gaining a better understanding of the processes involved in studying and learning. That is, "learning how to learn" has been suggested as a potential consequence of being a tutor. An even broader impact of tutoring has been claimed by some authors who assert that tutoring results in a "self-conscious, analytic orientation in dealing with all kinds of problems, not just academic work" (Gartner et al., p. 4).

Several tutoring programs place more emphasis on the social-emotional effects of tutoring than on academic achievement. Thus, Lippitt and Lohman (1965) strongly advocate cross-age tutoring because of the positive impact it supposedly has on socialization of children (e.g., increased maturity, sense of responsibility, ability to work cooperatively with others, prosocial behavior, and concern for others). Thelen (1969) has advocated tutoring as a way of reducing prejudice in children.

Changes in various aspects of school-related behavior have been examined in conjunction with being a tutor. One study by Newmark and Malarago (cited in Gartner et al., 1971) investigated the effect of tutoring on absenteeism and tardiness in school. More participation in class, better attitudes toward school, and more interest in learning have also been mentioned as outcomes in several reports. It has also been asserted that tutoring increases level of aspiration and may help clarify career goals (e.g., whether to become a teacher).

Many teachers claim that tutoring is an effective way to improve the behavior of disruptive children who create disciplinary problems in their own classroom. (In this regard recall Lancaster's comment about the effect of tutoring on the "mischievous child.") In one report a teacher noted that a "difficult" child in the class showed his best behavior when teaching a younger child.

Several writers have mentioned that children who have been tutors tend to show an increase in sympathy and empathy with the classroom teacher. Other purported outcomes of tutoring that are frequently mentioned include: improved ability to communicate with other children, better understanding of other people, development of new friendships, and better social skills.

Among the most important and widely cited positive consequences of tutoring is an enhancement in the tutor's self-image (self-concept or self-esteem) and an improvement in the related areas of personal efficacy and confidence. It should be noted, finally, that tutoring seems almost always to be a very enjoyable experience for the children who are doing the tutoring.

It can be seen that a plethora of positive consequences has been attributed to the experience of tutoring. In spite of a considerable degree of overlap, it is possible to simplify these consequences by organizing the purported positive benefits into the time-honored categories of cognitiion, behavior, and affect (thought, action, and feeling). The first category of outcomes, which can be classified as cognitive, includes the learning of new material, rehearsal of familiar material, reorganization or restructuring of old material, and better understanding of the process of learning. In the second category (behavior) can be placed school attendance, disruptive behavior in the classroom, participation in the classroom, empathy with the classroom teacher, prosocial and cooperative behavior, and social skills such as improved communication and better social interaction with others. And in the third category (affective) can be classified positive attitudes toward school (or toward learning and authority figures), enjoyment of tutoring, and the important set of self-referent attitudes known by terms such as self-concept, self-esteem, sense of competence, self-confidence, and the like. It should be noted that the use of these categories does not imply independence among them in the real world; but it may still be worthwhile to assume conceptual independence.

Although not alluded to by proponents of the tutoring technique, I should mention in passing that tutoring may sometimes produce negative as well as positive consequences for the tutor. Thus, tutoring may not always improve learning; it may even lead to the tutor's becoming more confused about the material. And lack of success as a tutor may result in a negative self-concept and lower sense of competence. If the tutor dislikes the tutee or vice-versa, tutoring will be an unpleasant social experience. Holding a great deal of responsibility and power over another person can be an unpleasant experience for anyone—and especially so for a child. If the teaching task is routine or too simple, the tutor will simply become bored and dissatisfied. If it is obvious that teachers have chosen lower-achieving children as tutors (in order to improve their academic performance), the self-labeling resulting from the stigma of being singled out will further reinforce a negative self-image. Finally, being in control of another child (and especially a younger one) provides an opportunity for the tutor to engage in authoritarian or abusive behavior which is certainly not conducive to positive personality development of the tutor.

A ROLE THEORETICAL ANALYSIS

It is not easy to provide a referent case for tutoring because such a wide range of differences exist among programs, particularly at the level of the actual interaction between tutor and tutee. We could probably agree, though, that in spite of the tremendous variability among tutoring programs most of them have at least the following common elements: One child is given responsibility for helping another child (usually younger) with schoolwork over an extended period of time in a personal (face-to-face) setting.

I should like to suggest that the conceptual system of role theory provides a useful framework for understanding the processes and outcomes of tutoring. A number of specific causal mechanisms can be subsumed by this analysis. It is a basic tenet of role theory that enactment of a role produces changes in behavior, cognition, and affect in a direction consistent with the expectations associated with the role. And there is a substantial amount of empirical data demonstrating that role enactment does indeed produce such changes in individuals (Sarbin & Allen, 1968).

Role Relationship

In discussing the role of tutor, the critical unit of analysis should be (as in any role) the role relationship itself—the role in question and its complementary or reciprocal role. When discussing the minutiae of cognitive processes in tutoring and in learning, it is easy to lose sight of the centrality of the larger and perhaps more important processes involved in the interpersonal relationship itself. What are the critical factors of the role relationship that exists between the tutor and tutee in a tutoring program?

Insight into the nature of the role relationship in tutoring may be gained by an examination of the etymology of the term. Originally, the word "tutor," from the Latin, had the special meaning, "to protect, to guard, to care for."[1] And these connotations still persist in contemporary tutor-tutee dyads, insofar as academic assistance is provided within the social context of a personal, affective, and caring relationship. The tutor role involves being a friend as well as a teacher (Sarbin, 1976). The affective component of the role relationship is likely to be especially salient when the tutee is considerably younger than the tutor. In communicating affect, nonverbal responses carry a great deal of weight. We designed a study to investigate nonverbal (paralinguistic) responses as a function of age similarity between tutor and tutee (Plazewski & Allen, 1978). It was predicted that a tutor will attempt to convey stronger positive affect when communicating with a younger child than with a peer. We asked undergraduates to role-play teaching a lesson in mathematics to a same-age peer and to a 4th-grade child. The subject was required to read a standard lesson aloud. Results showed a significant difference in paralinguistic responses as a function of age of target: The teacher's tone of voice was rated as displaying more friendliness and warmth when the teacher interacted with a younger as compared to a same-age target. Also, teachers read more slowly and directed more gazes toward the younger

---

[1] According to Moore (1968), the word "tutor" is not found before the 15th century (although there were synonyms), when four citizens of Padua were permitted to be "reformatores or tutores studii." These early "tutors" were not teachers primarily, but personal guardians (similar to God-parents) who had the responsibility of supervising the conduct and financial affairs of their charges.

learner than to a same-age learner. Consistent with our results are the findings of an experiment by Ludeke (1978) in which the age between children was varied in a teaching situation. Results showed that the child who served as teacher made a greater effort at role-taking and was more helpful when the learner was a younger as opposed to a same-age child.

The affective nature of the role relationship between the tutor and tutee is a reciprocal one, of course, since respect and liking is also conveyed by the tutee. This affective relationship may help constrain the tutor's behavior along socially desirable paths. A tutor who believes that he or she is being emulated by a younger child may be less likely to engage in undesirable behavior. Since a strong relationship should produce benefits for the tutor, a great deal of care should be devoted to composing the tutor-tutee dyad in order to create optimum compatibility on affective and cognitive dimensions.

I have argued that we should use the role relationship, rather than simply the individual characteristics of the tutor or tutee, as the unit of analysis. Since the role of tutee is integrally connected with the role of tutor, more attention should be paid to preparing the tutee for the role. Typically, students do receive some minimal amount of training for the role of tutor, but the tutee should receive some preparation as well. Enacting the tutee role well—being a "good" tutee—would increase the likelihood of effective role enactment (and, hence, of positive consequences) for the tutor. Thus, the tutee should provide verbal and nonverbal feedback, ask questions, give reinforcement, and so on; such behavior would facilitate interaction since it is complementary to the role behavior exhibited by the tutor. Evidence consistent with this analysis is available in a recent experiment reported by Patterson and Massad (1980). In a two-person communication situation, listeners (children) were trained to engage in behavior appropriate to the "good student" role (e.g., to ask questions when the task was ambiguous, etc.). In this condition there was an improvement in the adequacy of the messages and in the communication accuracy.

Another (and related) point which should be made about the tutoring relationship from the perspective of role theory is that enacting the role of tutor (teacher) provides a child with the experience of role reversal in relation to the usual role of student in the classroom. Role reversal—having the experience of enacting a role that is the reciprocal of one's usual role—should increase understanding and ability to take-the-role-of-the-other when reverting back to the original role.

Characteristics of the Tutor Role

As I have noted, the central characteristic of the tutor-tutee role relationship is the combination of positive affect and helping (teaching). A few comments are in order concerning the helping feature of the role relationship. It has often been observed that a helping relationship is beneficial to the helper as well as to the help-recipient.[2] Research has shown that young persons engaged in volunteer service (e.g., Peace Corps) obtain a variety of personal benefits from the experience. And in programs that have used college students to interact with patients in mental hospitals it has been found that the experience clarified self-identity and increased feelings of personal competence (Holtzberg, Knapp, & Turner, 1966). In our society children have few opportunities to help other persons; they are usually the recipients of help. Hence, tutoring can contribute to children's feelings of being useful and needed by others. A study by Garbarino (1975) found that the nature of the interaction between tutor and tutee varied according to whether or not the tutor anticipated a reward for his teaching. Tutors who did not expect an external reward (i.e., money) exhibited more positive emotionally toned behaviors and were more effective teachers than tutors who expected to be paid. Results of the study suggest that tutors' intrinsic motivation in the form of altruism toward others may be an important factor in determining the success of tutoring.

The role of teacher in our society carries with it many positive features such as high status, prestige, authority, and competence; these aspects of the role are also applicable to tutoring—which is a teacher role in miniature. There is a wide range and variety of rewards connected with being a tutor; it is easy to see why this role would be attractive to children.

Tutoring often involves receiving material rewards directly—in some tutoring programs students are paid an hourly wage. To provide social rewards, an attempt is often made to heighten the prestige and status of tutoring. In some schools it is made clear that only the best students are selected as tutors. Course credit is sometimes given for tutoring, and in other cases it is recorded on the school record as an extracurricular activity. Being excused from class and traveling to another school for tutoring have been mentioned by tutors as mundane reasons for their enjoying tutoring. Being a tutor also means receiving a great deal of attention from and contact with adults (in a quasi-colleagueal way). An important source of social reinforcement is the respect and prestige accorded to tutors by their tutees. Finally, there is the excitement and uncertainty that comes from engaging in any new activity ("Hawthorne effect"). Finally, when the tutee is successful in the lesson or shows an improvement in classwork, the tutor may experience self-reinforcement for having contributed to the tutee's outcomes. (And perhaps direct social reinforcement is received from the tutee, also.) All these sources of positive affect to the tutor may contribute to an increased sense of subjective competence (Bowerman, 1978).

---

[2]Stated in the rhetoric of economics, many people who begin with the intention of doing *good* end up by doing *well*. For example, in England the Quakers started manufacturing chocolate in an attempt to change the habits of lower-class persons from gin-drinking to candy-eating. Perhaps the most important outcome of this charitable impulse was the success of the Cadbury Chocolate Company, which made capitalists from altruists in the best tradition of the Protestant Ethic.

Effectiveness of Role Enactment

It is posited by role theory that the impact of role enactment on behavior, cognition, and affect is a direct function of the effectiveness (i.e., convincingness, appropriateness, and propriety) of the role performance. According to Sarbin and Allen (1968) the effectiveness of role enactment is determined by six major variables: (1) accuracy of location of self in the social system; (2) clarity of role expectations; (3) congruence between characteristics of self and the role requirements; (4) role skills (cognitive, social, and motoric); (5) role demands; and (6) reinforcement and discriminative cues from the audience. Particularly appropriate to an analysis of the effectiveness of enactment of the role of tutor are three of these variables: role expectations, role skills, and reactions from the audience. The applications of these three variables to the tutor role will be illustrated briefly.

Clarity of role expectations will influence the effectiveness of the behavior that a person displays when enacting a role. From experience as a student (and from other sources) children are well aware of the expectations (the rights and duties) associated with the role of teacher and the complementary role of student. The role-appropriate behavior that one engages in while tutoring (and any improvement in achievement by the tutee) will lead the tutor to perceive self in a way that is consistent with the role expectations. As a general principle, it can be said that anything that helps validate one's occupancy of a social position should create changes in self-perception in a direction consistent with the relevant role expectations.

Following implications from role theory, in tutoring studies we have conducted in schools the tutors were provided with appropriate symbolic cues in an attempt to increase the clarity of role expectations for the tutor and to increase the visibility of the role for other persons. Several distinctive appurtenances (symbols and tokens of position or office) were provided; these included a certificate designating the tutor as a "student teacher," a portfolio for keeping a daily log and lesson plans, and other equipment typically possessed by a "real" teacher. Also, tutors were given considerable responsibility for developing curricular materials.

Expectations of the tutor role involve cognitive as well as social and affective features. To enact the tutoring role successfully requires that an individual organize and rehearse the material to be taught and then present it in an effective manner to the tutee. Some of the improvement in learning by the tutor as a result of tutoring is no doubt due to spending the time on the material necessary to understand and explain it clearly to the tutee. In addition, research indicates that the nature of learning differs when one has the expectation of teaching material to someone else as opposed to the expectation of learning it from a teacher. Stated in a more general way, the psychological set to send or receive information influences the way it is structured and organized (Zajonc, 1960). Hence, tutoring not only influences the amount of learning, but also produces a qualitative effect on the nature of the learning as well.

Role skills contribute in a significant way to the outcome of role enactment, since enacting the role of tutor is more effective if one possesses the requisite role skills. Conforming to the expectations of the teacher role requires the tutor to engage in a complex set of verbal and nonverbal behaviors. One common problem faced by tutors is that a tutee often prefers to spend a great deal of time talking casually instead of working on the lesson. The tutor must tactfully bring the focus of the session back to the lesson; but at the same time the tutor must not be too task-oriented. Thus, the amount of socializing to be allowed is a problem that the tutor has to deal with. The tutor must also overcome any shyness and try to communicate effectively with the tutee. Moreover, an appropriate response by the tutor is called for when the student makes an error or fails to understand a point. The tutor's task is to keep the tutee interested and motivated in the lesson by providing reinforcement, but this reinforcement must not conflict with the tutee's actual task performance.

It is obvious that verbal behavior is extensively used in tutoring; less obvious, perhaps, is the importance of nonverbal behavior. As in any other social interaction, the tutor and tutee continuously monitor each other's nonverbal responses. The tutor should be adept in presenting his or her own nonverbal behavior in an appropriate way and, in addition, be able to decode nonverbal responses which indicate the cognitive and affective states of the learner (such as understanding or boredom). For example, in a face-to-face teaching situation it is often necessary for the teacher to rely heavily on nonverbal cues to determine as accurately as possible how well the student really understands the material being taught. Little is known, however, about the determinants of the accuracy of an observer's estimate of another person's cognitive state on the basis of nonverbal cues alone (Allen & Feldman, 1976). Further, there will be times when the tutor is bored with the lesson, frustrated, impatient, or angry with the tutee. To avoid conveying these emotional reactions to the tutee requires very careful self-monitoring and control of nonverbal responses on the part of the tutor (Feldman, Devin-Sheehan, & Allen, 1978). These examples will give some indication of the kinds of social skills that are necessary in tutoring. The effectiveness of role enactment will depend upon the tutor's being able to utilize the relevant role skills. Tutoring provides a useful setting for a tutor to obtain practice in using a wide range of social skills.

The reaction of other persons (the audience) is a variable which influences the effectiveness of enacting the role of tutor. Appropriate behavior will be elicited from other persons when a role is enacted convincingly. Thus, persons who are enacting complementary roles will respond to the role performer in a way consistent with the characteristics of the role (assuming that the performer's occupancy of a social position is known by other persons). It is interesting to note that some children take the trouble to dress more formally when tutoring, which makes the role more visible. Thus, reactions from other persons—tutee, other students, teachers, and other adults—convey to the tutor that he or she is viewed as possessing the characteristics associated with the teacher role (a tutor is competent, knowledgeable, mature, responsible, etc.). And, of course, it is a truism in social science that to a very large extent one's self-perception rests upon the responses received from others.

"Playing-at" a Role

Finally, a more speculative point may be mentioned concerning the role of tutor. As I said earlier, the role of tutor is perceived as being the teacher role in miniature, but with the important qualification that the tutor is not really a teacher in the sense of legitimately occupying this position in the macrosocial structure. Though it is indeed a serious role, in the sense that important consequences occur to both the tutee and tutor, nevertheless tutoring by children still is not entirely authentic, not really a part of adult reality. The activity partakes of a certain degree of pretense, of play, of having a game-like quality. Although somewhat different from pretending to be cowboys and Indians or even the game of teacher and student when "playing school" at home, enacting the tutor role still retains a certain "let's pretend" quality; it is "playing-at" a role, to use Coutu's (1951) term. This quasi-realistic nature of the tutor role may contribute to the impact of enacting the role. For often in such pretend, game, or play-type situations, a person feels freer to take risks, make mistakes, and explore his or her capabilities. The tutor's enjoyment of tutoring may derive in part from its being construed as "play." Learning that occurs when one is enacting a pretend role is *play,* and hence enjoyable; learning that occurs when one is enacting a serious role is, by contrast, simply "*work.*"

EMPIRICAL LITERATURE

It should be pointed out immediately that the quality of a great deal of research on the effects of tutoring on the tutor is woefully inadequate, even by the most lenient interpretation of standards of scientific rigor. Much of the evidence in the area consists of anecdotal reports and testimonials. It is all too easy to detect what appears to be a change of behavior in a single child and to leap to a conclusion about the overall impact of a program which simply cannot be justified by objective criteria.

In addition to the prevalent practice of failing to collect rigorous data in many programs, a flaw in many research designs is the absence of pertinent control groups. Although it is sometimes difficult to use control groups in an ongoing school program, the necessity is obvious. One factor not controlled is the special attention and extensive personal contact that participants (and especially tutors) receive from adults and teachers during the program. An area of concern related to control groups is the method of selecting tutors and tutees. An experimental group of volunteers should not be compared to a control group of nonvolunteers. Unfortunately, for practical reasons this is not an uncommon practice in tutoring research. Many of the factors for which control groups are needed seem to be integral components of tutoring programs. Nevertheless, it is important to attempt to disentangle the critical variables from among the many nonessential ones. In the absence of appropriate control groups, one cannot say with confidence whether outcomes can be attributed to tutoring, per se, or to other factors merely associated with but not essential to the program. With these caveats, a brief overview follows of research on the effect of tutoring on the tutor.

Several long-term programs have systematically evaluated the effects of tutoring on participants. The cross-age tutoring program developed by Lippitt and Lippitt (1968) attempts to stimulate older tutors, provide academic and motivational help for younger children, and develop friendships among students of different ages. Data are not available from the Lippitts' project, but the Ontario-Montclair School District in California followed several of their guidelines in developing a cross-age tutoring program (Ontario-Montclair School District, 1968–71). Six schools in two school districts were involved in a 3-year program. Students from seventh and eighth grades tutored 120 low-achieving students from fourth, fifth, and sixth grades in reading, arithmetic, and language. Tutoring occurred three times a week in 35–45 minute sessions. Results from systematic evaluations showed that both tutors and tutees made academic gains compared to control groups in some of the areas tutored, although results varied from year to year. Data on attendance were inconsistent, but in the third year of the program tutors had lower absenteeism than controls. Data also showed that tutors improved in terms of disciplinary problems during the third year. The project was successful in increasing the teachers' opinions of the self-concept of tutors, but results from a self-concept scale did not reveal any improvement for tutors. Overall, then, the results were somewhat inconsistent and ambiguous; the strongest positive findings were in the area of academic gains for both tutors and tutees.

An extensive tutoring program, the "High School Homework Helpers Program," was developed in New York City in 1962–63. By 1973 approximately 1,000 tutors (mainly high school juniors and seniors) were working with 6,000 high school students (mostly 9th- and 10th-graders). The program attempted to improve the tutees' academic achievement and attitude toward school, and also to increase the confidence and academic motivation of the tutors. Tutoring usually lasted 2 hours a day for 2 days a week. Tutors were paid on an hourly basis. Evaluation reports have been prepared annually (Neckritz, 1971, 1972; Teaching and Learning Research Corporation, 1969–70). Responses to questionnaires indicated that tutors consistently experienced a high level of satisfaction with the program. However, the tutors' attitude toward school, school-related activities, and their self-concept did not appear to change.

Cloward (1967) conducted a carefully designed experimental study of the Homework Helpers Program. Student volunteers (11th graders) were paid to tutor fourth- and fifth-grade pupils who were reading below grade level. Tutoring continued for 26 weeks. Tutoring was academically beneficial for both tutors and tutees, compared to control groups. The tutors showed even greater gains in reading than did the tutees. But the tutors did not differ from the control group on school marks, attitude toward school and school-related activities, educational aspirations, and social values. Negative results on these measures were attributed to the positive attitudes and high aspirations held by students from the beginning of the program.

Another set of tutoring programs designed to benefit underachieving, disadvantaged teen-agers and their counterparts in the elementary school is the "Youth Tutoring Youth" model (National Commission on Resources for Youth, Inc., 1972). A systematic and well-controlled evaluation was conducted on sites in Washington, D.C., and Chicago. Results revealed that tutors showed an improvement in language skills, a more positive self-image, and an increased interest in going to school.

Several experimental studies have evaluated more short-term tutoring programs; a few of these are mentioned briefly. A study by Morgan and Toy (1970) is an example of a carefully implemented and well-controlled field experiment. The study evaluated a 4-month tutoring program in a rural school system. Pupils in grades two through five who needed tutoring (according to teachers) were randomly assigned either to an experimental or control group. Students in grades 8 through 12 volunteered to be tutors and were randomly assigned to a tutoring or control group. Analysis of the data indicated that only the tutors showed significantly higher gains than controls, and only on the reading subtest.

The effect of tutoring on underachieving high school children was investigated by Haggerty (1971). (These tutors manifested behavior problems as well.) Results revealed an improvement in the self-concept of the tutors relative to the control group, but tutors did not improve their attitude toward school. By contrast, other studies have reported that children who engaged in tutoring did improve their attitude toward school and toward teachers (Hassinger & Via, 1969; Mohan, 1972; Strodtbeck & Granick, 1972).

Strodtbeck and Granick (1972) investigated two aspects of change in self-perception as a consequence of tutoring: self-esteem and personal efficacy. Results of this study did not reveal a general improvement in self-esteem for all tutors, but only for those who had attended school more regularly after tutoring and had improved their writing ability. A similar interaction effect was found for personal efficacy. That is, tutoring did not have an overall effect on sense of personal efficacy; an improvement was obtained, however, for the subgroup of children who scored high on the "ego-development" scale.

Studies investigating the academic effects of tutoring typically compare children who have engaged in tutoring with those who did not receive any special treatment. Hence, it is difficult to determine whether any academic improvement is due to the tutoring itself or simply to having spent additional time studying the lesson. A few studies have addressed this problem. Allen and Feldman (1974) designed an experiment in which low-achieving fifth graders either taught reading to a third grader or studied alone during the series of daily sessions. At the end of the 2-week period, the tutors were performing significantly better on the material than the children who had simply studied alone. It is important to point out that initially the tutors did not perform as well as the children assigned to the group that studied alone. Thus, the tutoring itself—and not just the extra time spent studying the lessons—contributed to the improvement in academic performance.

In a study by Fitz-Gibbon (1977) one group of ninth-grade children tutored fourth-grade children in math, while other ninth graders practiced the same material in the classroom for the 3-week tutoring period. Results disclosed that the children who tutored scored higher than the controls on the material (fractions) they had taught to the younger children; furthermore, this superiority persisted when the tutors were retested 3 months later. In a similar study fifth and sixth graders either taught mathematics to younger children or received regular classroom instruction in the same subject (Mohan, 1972). Analysis of the data indicated that tutors performed better than controls on the material they had taught. It should be noted, however, that some tutoring programs have failed to obtain positive results for tutors (Bremmer, 1972; Edler, 1967; Foster, 1972).

Before commenting on the overall results of the findings from the large-scale programs and other studies reported above, it will be helpful to examine certain aspects of the tutoring situation, namely, characteristics of tutors and the composition of the tutoring dyad.

Personal characteristics of tutors have been examined in several studies. In one study low-achieving students in reading (sixth graders) made significant gains in reading following their 2 months of tutoring second-grade children (Klentschy, 1971). Marascuilo, Levin, and James (1969) showed that ninth-grade remedial readers gained significantly in reading comprehension following their (paid) tutoring of seventh-grade low-achievers (in reading). Likewise, Erickson and Cromack (1972) found that seventh-grade underachievers improved significantly in reading after tutoring third graders. In another study, fifth graders who were poor readers did not improve in reading achievement as a result of tutoring, but did show more positive attitudes toward teachers, reading, and an improvement in self-concept (Robertson, 1972). Underachieving sophomore and junior boys who had discipline problems tutored elementary school children twice a week in a study reported by Haggerty (1971). Results revealed a significant improvement in self-concept, self-acceptance, and grade-point average; attitude toward school did not improve, however.

Rust (1970) examined the effect of acting as a tutor in arithmetic on low-achieving, misbehaving, and unpopular sixth graders. To help determine the locus of causality for any positive effects on the tutors, this study employed a special control group of subjects who acted as a friend or buddy to a third grader but did not engage in any tutoring. From this condition it is possible to determine whether changes in the behavior of tutors is due simply to their interaction with a younger child or whether the role of tutor is crucial. Despite the promise of this design, no differences in social behavior were found among conditions, although there was an increase in the mathematics achievement of tutors.

A study by Yamamoto and Klentschy (1972) investigated the effect of tutoring on attitudes of inner-city children in Los Angeles. Low-achieving fifth- and sixth-grade boys and girls were assigned to one of three groups: (a) an experimental group received training and then tutored first graders; (b) a control group was trained but did not tutor; and (c) a control group was not trained and did not tutor. The three groups were matched on sex and pretest scores on measures of attitude toward school and self. Tutoring took place 3 days a week. An analysis of posttest scores (semantic differential) showed that subjects who tutored had significantly more positive attitudes towards both school and self than did subjects in either of the control conditions. Mohan (1972) found that poorly motivated students were positively affected when they tutored unmotivated younger children. On both objective attitude scales and subjective teacher ratings, the tutors showed an increase in motivation level, self-concept, attitudes toward school, and mathematics achievement (the subject they had taught). In sum, the literature on characteristics of tutors suggests quite convincingly that a wide range of students may benefit from acting as a tutor.[3]

Most tutoring programs use same-sex pairs, but there are little empirical data available to support this practice. In one relevant tutoring program, sixth-grade low-achievers tutored second and third graders in reading or mathematics for a 4-month period (Klentschy, 1971). Males seemed to benefit more than females from acting as a tutor, but there were no differences due to working with same-sex or cross-sex tutees. Another question regarding sex factors in tutoring is whether males or females benefit more from tutoring, regardless of the sex of the person with whom they are paired. Two studies revealed that male tutors (as well

---

[3]It is conceivable that the type of student who seems to benefit most from being a tutor (the low-achiever, the child with behavior problems, the unmotivated child) may in fact be the least beneficial type of teacher for the tutee. The empirical evidence on this point yields conflicting results. Some studies have shown that low-achieving tutors can be effective teachers for younger children (e.g., Robertson, 1972); other studies report a lack of improvement by tutees (e.g., Erickson & Cromack, 1972; Kelly, 1972).

as tutees) benefited academically significantly more from tutoring than female tutors and tutees (Klentschy, 1971, 1972). It appears, then, that same-sex pairing of tutors and tutees is not superior to opposite-sex dyads; sex composition does not appear to exert any significant effect on outcome.

Only a small amount of systematic research has been conducted on racial and socioeconomic factors associated with tutoring. Hypothesizing that cross-race tutoring promotes the development of more positive racial attitudes, Witte (1972) conducted two tutoring programs using interracial dyads. Results indicated an increase in interracial interaction and acceptance by tutors and tutees, but no significant gains occurred in academic performance. On the other hand, McMonagel (1972) found no effect on white tutors' attitudes toward black children as a function of tutoring.

As can be seen, a review of the literature indicates mixed results at best for the outcomes of tutoring on the tutor. (More complete reviews can be found in Devin-Sheehan, Feldman, and Allen, 1976 and Goodlad, 1979.) In the domain of academic achievement, the data indicate quite clearly in many studies that tutors learn the material that they are charged with teaching to the tutees. As has been pointed out by Olds (1976), however, the evidence is not strong for an improvement in learning by tutors on related material which was not taught directly during the tutoring sessions. Of even more interest for the present purpose is the impact of tutoring on social behavior and self-perceptions. In this area the data are very inconsistent across studies, and results are often ambiguous. The initial enthusiasm of proponents of tutoring concerning a strong positive impact on the tutor's self-concept and attitudes has not received strong and unequivocal support from the data. For example, results for self-esteem (and similar self-perceptions) do not agree across studies. There is some evidence to suggest that an increase in positive self-perceptions may depend upon the tutor's having improved in academic performance.

The conclusion drawn from the literature review stands in sharp contrast to the glowing reports from practitioners and participants about the strong impact of tutoring on the tutor. As Goodlad (1979) states in his recent book: "Nearly everyone who has observed tutoring in action is astonished by the responsible way in which even troublesome teenagers can settle into the role of tutor and apparently derive satisfaction from it" (p.76). How can we account for the often-observed negative findings from research in the face of contrary evidence based on the personal experience of many sensitive and observant persons who have worked extensively in tutoring programs? First, in many studies the instruments, procedures, and designs have been faulty, as pointed out earlier. Moreover, since a wide variety of specific components are used to constitute tutoring programs, it is very difficult to know whether or not those factors that are essential for successful outcomes are included in a particular program. A very plausible explanation for negative findings in many instances is that the "experimental treatment" (that is, the tutoring experience) was simply too weak to produce a measurable impact on the tutor. Sufficient time must be devoted to the tutoring (in terms of number of sessions each week and length of the program) to produce a significant impact.

Another interpretation of the mixed-bag of empirical results can be suggested, however, which goes beyond mere methodological considerations and contains some interesting implications. Concerning improvement in social behavior, in particular, the results of some well-controlled studies indicate that a high degree of situational specificity exists in the tutor's behavior. For example, in Olds' (1976) experiment, the children seemed to behave in a remarkably mature and responsible way while they were tutoring. But systematic assessment of the tutors' prosocial behavior in the classroom failed to show any significant effect due to the experience of tutoring. In other words, the prosocial behavior manifested in the tutor role did not appear to generalize to the student role. Another example vividly illustrates this type of finding. In one study children who had a record of poor school attendance were assigned to be tutors (Fitz-Gibbon, 1977). The tutors' school attendance showed a dramatic improvement—but only for that portion of the school day which they devoted to tutoring. That is, the tutors attended school during the tutoring session and then left for the rest of the day! Similar role-specific effects can be found when one looks closely at other reports dealing with various kinds of social-emotional and behavioral outcomes of tutoring. Thus, it can be suggested that the influence of tutoring on behavior and self-evaluation tends to be rather specific to the role. This conclusion is in accord with other findings which demonstrate a remarkable degree of situational specificity for a wide range of behaviors (Magnusson, 1980). Therefore, rigorous studies that attempt to measure the *general* impact of tutoring, rather than its role-specific effects, are likely to fail to detect change in the tutors' responses.

OVERCOMING ROLE-SPECIFICITY IN TUTORING

Before offering suggestions from the perspective of role theory for increasing the generality of the impact of tutoring on the tutor, two caveats should be mentioned. First, we must recognize that the problem of the apparent nongeneralizability of the effects of tutoring may be due to some extent to the insensitivity of available measuring instruments, as was mentioned earlier. Secondly, we must realize that tutoring may be differentially effective for children. General effects of tutoring may occur, but only for certain types of children or certain kinds of tutor-tutee relationships. Precisely this kind of finding was reported in a study of tutoring by Strodtbeck and associates (Strodtbeck & Granick, 1972; Strodtbeck, Ronchi, and Hansell, 1976); results of the data analysis showed that personal efficacy increased only for that subsample of tutors who were high on an ego-development scale. Keeping in mind these qualifications, it is still worthwhile to ask why the impact of tutoring seems to be relatively role-specific. Is it possible to increase the likelihood that consequences of tutoring for the tutor will generalize to other situations?

Organismic Involvement

Role theory provides some straightforward suggestions. First, a general or permanent change in self-perception or behavior is more likely to occur with high than with low levels of organismic involvement of self in the role (Janis & Mann, 1965; Sarbin & Allen, 1968). At high degrees of involvement (when self and role are minimally differentiated) permanent changes in self-perception—and even dramatic changes in social identity—tend to occur. The degree of involvement in the tutoring role could be increased by using several appropriate techniques (e.g., rituals and ceremonies consistent with being a tutor, such as initiation into a club; increasing the salience and importance of the consequences; etc.). But extremely high levels of involvement probably cannot be created under the conditions of the typical tutoring program.

Preemptiveness

A second suggestion from role theory is that the greater the preemptiveness of the role, the more likely that changes in self-perception or behavior will be permanent and, hence, generalizable across situations. Preemptiveness can be defined as the amount of time an individual spends enacting the role. It is a well-documented finding that persons who spend a large proportion of their time enacting a role tend to reveal characteristics of self consistent with the role in many other situations as well (Sarbin & Allen, 1968). (Two roles that have been investigated with regard to this phenomenon are bureaucrat and teacher.) But it is simply not feasible for a child to spend as much time enacting the tutor role as most of us spend in an occupational role; the role of tutor cannot be enacted for 40 hours a week. Practical exigencies of being a student make it impractical for tutors to spend even a moderate proportion of their time engaged in tutoring another child. Nevertheless, a great deal more time could be devoted to the tutoring role than the typical schedule of one or two brief sessions a week.

Role Penetration

I will suggest one other concept that might be useful in increasing cross-situational generality of outcomes due to role enactment—a concept that I shall call ''role penetration.'' By this term I refer to the extent to which a role is connected with or impinges upon (''penetrates'') other roles. Any experience of success and positive evaluation about the tutor's competence must be seen by him or her as the result of being connected in a direct way to the student role—to those occasions when the child (tutor) is a learner in the classroom, for example.

This concept holds several implications that can be applied to the present problem. The tutoring role can be made to penetrate other roles by using techniques such as the following: The tutor should teach several different students who have a variety of academic needs rather than staying with one student. The tutor should teach several different types of academic curricula rather than only a single subject. Tutoring should take place across several different physical settings rather than always in one place. An effort should be made to ensure that the tutor is perceived by others (and by self) as occupying the position of tutor in several situations other than just in the tutoring session. The wearing of badges, insignia, uniforms, and the like outside the tutoring session (and in the playground, in particular) would help ensure that the role of tutor is perceived as penetrating other roles that are encountered during the course of the day's activities. Verbal labels or special titles should be applied to tutors by the teachers. The same effect could be accomplished by composing a class entirely of tutors and by the teacher frequently reminding them of their tutor status.

Approaching the problem from another perspective, role penetration could be accomplished by increasing the degree of permeability among different roles. If the distinctiveness and rigidity of the boundaries of different roles could be attenuated, the consequences of enacting a particular role might be less likely to be role-specific. Fuzzy role boundaries (to borrow a term from the "fuzzy logic" area) should enhance the flow of psychological phenomena across the boundary of the role which generated them. One way of creating greater role permeability is to reduce the distinctiveness among roles either initially or after the identity of separate roles has been clearly established. Another practical method of increasing role permeability is by switching frequently across roles or reversing roles within a given temporal and spatial context. For example, the child could switch within a tutoring session or across sessions from being a tutor to being a learner (Rosen, Powell, & Schubot, 1977); or while in the classroom a child could often switch back and forth for brief periods of time from being a tutor in the classroom to being a regular student. Similar suggestions could be made that would involve several of the roles that are enacted by the child during (and outside) the school day.

Without belaboring the point further by extending these examples, suffice it to say that it is indeed possible to devise a variety of practical techniques which are based on the idea that the tutor role should impinge upon other roles. According to theory, greater role penetration would increase the generalization of the sense of competence and social responsibility experienced in the tutoring role because the role would be associated with a variety of other roles that the child enacts in the course of the school day and beyond.

A Quixotic Solution

Finally, a rather extreme suggestion can be made. As noted earlier, the role of tutor appears to provide many benefits for the tutor, but the effects seem to be relatively role-specific. Recall the report of the children who attended school during the time they were scheduled to be tutors, but who were truant for the remainder of the school day. Perhaps we should take very seriously the lesson that can be learned from this dramatic example. The children's strongly divergent reactions to these two situations—being a tutor for another child and being a student in the classroom—may be a valid assessment of the relative interestingness and usefulness of the two situations to the child. Therefore, rather than attempting to design techniques to increase the cross-situational generalization of the effects of tutoring, perhaps we should try to change the school situation so that it would possess more of the psychological characteristics that are intrinsic to the role of tutor. But an exploration of this possibility goes far beyond the scope of the present chapter and will be left for other visionaries to pursue.

ACKNOWLEDGMENTS

This chapter was written while the author was a Fellow at the Netherlands Institute for Advanced Study in the Humanities and Social Sciences, Wassenaar, The Netherlands. I am grateful to William R. Bowerman for many helpful suggestions.

REFERENCES

Allen, V. L., & Feldman, R. S. Learning through tutoring: Low-achieving children as tutors. *The Journal of Experimental Education*, 1974, *42*, 1-5.

Allen, V. L., & Feldman, R. S. Studies on the role of the tutor. Chapter in V. L. Allen (Ed.), *Children as teachers: Theory and research on tutoring*. New York: Academic Press, 1976.

Ariès, P. *Centuries of childhood*. New York: Knopf, 1962. (Trans. from the French by R. Balkick.) Originally published under the title, *L'enfant et la vie familiale sous l'ancien regime*. Paris: Libraire Plon, 1960.

Bamford, T. W. *Rise of the public schools*. London: Thomas Nelson, 1967.

Bell, A. *An experiment in education made at the male asylum of Madras: Suggesting a system by which a school or family may teach itself under the superintendence of the master or parent*. London: Cadell & Davis, 1797.

Bowerman, W. R. Subjective competence: The structure, process, and function of self-referent causal attributions. *Journal for the Theory of Social Behavior*, 1978, *8*, 45-75.

Bremmer, B. L. *Students helping students program*. Seattle Public School, Planning and Evaluation Department, August, 1972.

Bruner, J. Immaturity-Its uses, nature and management. *The Times Educational Supplement*. London, October 27, 1972.

Cloward, R. D. Studies in tutoring. *Journal of Experimental Education*, 1967, *36*, 14-25.

Coutu, W. Role-playing vs. role-taking: An appeal for clarification. *American Sociological Review*, 1951, *16*, 180-187.

Devin-Sheehan, L., Feldman, R. S., & Allen, V. L. Research on children tutoring children: A critical review. *Review of Educational Research*, 1976, *46*, 355-385.

Edler, L. A. The use of students as tutors in after-school study centers. *Dissertation Abstracts International*, 1967, *28*(1-A), 74.

Erickson, M. R., & Cromack, T. Evaluating a tutoring program. *Journal of Experimental Education*, 1972, *41*, 27-31.

Feldman, R. S., Devin-Sheehan, L., & Allen, V. L. Nonverbal cues as indicators of verbal dissembling. *American Educational Research Journal*, 1978, *15*, 217-231.

Fitz-Gibbon, C. T. *CSE Report on Tutoring no. 5: An analysis of the literature on cross-age tutoring*. Center for the Study of Evaluation, UCLA Graduate School of Education, Los Angeles, Calif., November, 1977.

Foster, P. B. Attitudinal effects on 5th graders of tutoring younger children. *Dissertation Abstracts International*, 1972, *33*(5-A), 2235.

Garbarino, J. The impact of anticipated reward upon cross-age tutoring. *Journal of Personality and Social Psychology*, 1975, *32*, 421-428.

Gartner, A., Kohler, M., & Riessman, F. *Children teach children*. New York: Harper, 1971.

Goodlad, S. *Learning by teaching*. London: Community Service Volunteers, 1979.

Haggerty, M. The effects of being a tutor and being a counselee in a group on self-concept and achievement level of underachieving adolescent males. *Dissertation Abstracts International*, 1971, *31*(9-A), 4460.

Hartup, W. W. Cross-age versus same-age peer interaction: Ethological and cross-cultural perspectives. In V. L. Allen (Ed.), *Children as teachers: Theory and research on tutoring*. New York: Academic Press, 1976.

Hassinger, J., & Via, M. How much does a tutor learn through reading. *Journal of Secondary Education*, 1969, *44*, 42-44.

Holzberg, J. D., Knapp, R. H., & Turner, J. L. Companionship with the mentally ill: Effects on the personalities of college student volunteers. *Psychiatry*, 1966, *29*, 395-405.

Janis, I. L., & Mann, L. Effectiveness of emotional role-playing in modifying smoking habits and attitudes. *Journal of Experimental Research on Personality*, 1965, *1*, 84-90.

Kelly, M. R. Pupil tutoring in reading of low-achieving second-grade pupils by low-achieving fourth-grade pupils. *Dissertation Abstracts International*, 1972, *32*(9-A), 4881.

Klentschy, M. *An examination of sex-pairing effectiveness for reading tutoring*. Paper presented at the meeting of the California Educational Research Association, San Diego, November, 1971.

Klentschy, M. P. *The effect of sixth-grade tutors on the word attack attainment of second graders*. Paper presented at the meeting of the California Educational Research Association, San Jose, Calif., November, 1972.

Lancaster, J. *Improvements in education as it respects the industrious classes of the community*. London: Darton & Harvey, 1803.

Lippitt, R., & Lippitt, P. Cross-age helpers. *Today's Education*, 1968, *57*, 24-26.

Lippitt, P., & Lohman, J. E. Cross-age relationships—An educational resource. *Children*, 1965, *12*, 113-117.

Ludeke, R. J. *Teaching behaviors of 11-year-old and 9-year-old girls in same-age and mixed-age dyads*. Doctoral dissertation, University of Minnesota, 1978.

Magnusson, D. (Ed). *Toward a psychology of situations: An interactional perspective*. Hillsdale, N.J.: Lawrence Erlbaum Associates, 1980.

Marascuilo, L., Levin, J., & James, H. Evaluation report for the Berkeley Unified School District's remedial reading program sponsored under SB28. September 15, 1969.

McMonagle, L. An investigation of attitude change in college tutors toward black children as a function of required tutoring. *Dissertation Abstracts International*, 1972, *33*(4-A), 1521.

Mohan, M. *Peer tutoring as a technique for teaching the unmotivated, a research report*. Teacher Education Research Center, State University College, Fredonia, New York, March, 1972.

Moore, W. G. *The tutorial system and its future*. Oxford: Pergamon Press, 1968.

Morgan, R. F., & Toy, T. B. Learning by teaching: A student-to-student compensatory tutoring program in a rural school system and its relevance to the educational cooperative. *Psychological Record*, 1970, *20*, 159-169.

National Commission on Resources for Youth, Inc. *An evaluation of the Youth Tutoring Youth model for In-School Neighborhood Youth Corps*. New York, December, 1972.

Neckritz, B. *Evaluation report high school homework-helper program: 1970-1971.* Function No. 17-04467. New York: Bureau of Education Research, Board of Education of the City of New York, September, 1971.

Neckritz, B. *Evaluation report high school homework-helper program: 1971-1972.* Function No. 17-C5467. New York: Bureau of Education Research, Board of Education of the City of New York, November, 1972.

Teaching and Learning Research Corporation. *Final report on the evaluation of the 1969-1970 homework-helper program.* Function No. 923631. New York: Board of Education of the City of New York.

Olds, D. *Cross-age tutoring and parent involvement.* Doctoral dissertation, Cornell University, 1976.

Ontario-Montclair School District. Final report on cross-age teaching. No. 68-06138-0. Ontario, Calif., 1968-1971.

Patterson, C. J., & Massad, C. M. Facilitating referential communication among children: The listener as teacher. *Journal of Experimental Child Psychology,* 1980, *29,* 357-370.

Plazewski, J. G., & Allen, V. L. Differential use of paralanguage and nonverbal behavior by tutors as a function of relative age of the student. *Technical Report No. 491,* Wisconsin Research and Development Center for Individualized schooling, December 1978.

Robertson, D. J. Intergrade teaching: Children learn from children. In S. L. Sebesta & C. J. Wallen (Eds.), *The first R: Readings on teaching reading.* Chicago: Scientific Research Association, 1972.

Rosen, S., Powell, E. R., & Schubot, D. B. Peer-tutoring outcomes as influenced by the equity and type of role assignment. *Journal of Educational Psychology,* 1977, *69,* 244-252.

Rust, S. P., Jr. The effect of tutoring on the tutor's behavior, academic achievement, and social status. *Dissertation Abstracts International,* 1970, *30*(11-A), 4862.

Sarbin, T. R. Social identity and tutoring. In V. L. Allen (Eds.), *Children teaching children: Theory and research on tutoring.* New York: Academic Press, 1976.

Sarbin, T. R., & Allen, V. L. Role theory. In G. Lindzey and E. Aronson (Eds.), *Handbook of social psychology* (Vol. I). Reading, Mass.: Addison-Wesley, 1968.

Strodtbeck, F., & Granick, L. *An evaluation of the youth tutoring youth model for in-school neighborhood youth corps.* The National Commission on Resources for Youth, Inc., December, 1972.

Strodtbeck, R., Ronchi, D., & Hansell, S. Tutoring and growth. In V. L. Allen (Ed.), *Children as tutors: Theory and research on tutoring.* New York: Academic Press, 1976.

Teaching and Learning Research Corporation. *Final report on the evaluation of the 1969-1970 homework-helper program.* Function No. 923631. New York: Board of Education of the City of New York.

Thelen, H. A. Tutoring by students: What makes it so exciting? *The School Review,* 1969, *77,* 229-244.

Witte, P. H. The effects of group reward structure on interracial acceptance, peer tutoring and academic performance. *Dissertation Abstracts International,* 1972, *32*(9-A), 5367.

Wright, B. Should children teach? *Elementary School Journal,* 1960, *60,* 353-369.

Yamamoto, J. Y., & Klentschy, M. *An examination of intergrade tutoring experience on attitudinal development of inner-city children.* Paper presented at the meeting of the California Educational Research Association, San Jose, Calif., November, 1972.

Zajonc, R. B. The process of cognitive tuning in communication. *Journal of Abnormal and Social Psychology,* 1960, *61,* 159-167.

16

Intrinsic Motivation, Peer Tutoring, and Cooperative Learning: Practical Maxims

Richard deCharms
Washington University

The four preceding chapters are difficult to bring together into a whole cloth. Mark Lepper presents an impressively comprehensive overview of recent research demonstrating the detrimental effects of offering concrete rewards for a behavior that is intrinsically motivated. Pittman, Boggiano, and Ruble note limiting conditions on the detrimental effects of rewards and state the case for enhancing effects. Robert Slavin presents an overview of research on cooperative learning with emphasis on noncognitive outcomes. Vernon Allen brings us a review of peer tutoring research and its effects on self-perception.

Obviously, the first two chapters share a common theme (the effects of rewards). The other two may be sewn together with the common thread of group phenomena in the classroom. But to connect these two couplets is like sewing together two independent flags. At the risk of being an arbitrary Betsy Ross, I shall try to produce a flag where practical maxims from the chapters stand out as stars in a constellation. The stars produce a figure and the invisible connections between the stars are theoretical implications. The theoretical figure that emerges has a common motivational theme.

"Efficient practice precedes the theory of it; ... It was because Aristotle found himself and others reasoning now intelligently and now stupidly and it was because Izaak Walton found himself and others angling sometimes effectively and sometimes ineffectively that both were able to give to their pupils maxims and prescriptions of their arts'' (Ryle, 1949, p. 30).

THE USE OF REWARDS IN THE CLASSROOM

Researchers typically ask the epistemic question—How do we know what we know? Yet a more basic practical question is—What do we know how to do as a result of research? For a while it appeared that all we had learned was how to undermine intrinsic interest in the classroom. This is not a very useful outcome from a teacher's point of view. Worse, it appeared that one of the most practical tools for teachers, namely, behavior modification, was seriously questioned by this research. The very great merit of Mark Lepper's chapter is that it goes beyond these apparently negative implications. Lepper argues that teachers need not give up rewards entirely. Research can show us how to use rewards more effectively.

How questions often reduce to when—*when* should teachers use rewards? The two extreme positions mentioned early in Lepper's chapter seem to imply either "always" or "never." Yet, neither answer is practical or empirically defensible. Perhaps we should ask—when should a teacher *not* use rewards? Lepper implies that rewards are useful if applied appropriately, yet he takes the conservative stance and shows when rewards will not undermine intrinsic interest. Pittman and his colleagues take the more positive stance and try to show enhancement of intrinsic interest by use of rewards.

Both chapters suggest that when rewards are contingent on quality of performance (i.e., when they give information about competence), they do not undermine subsequent interest. When rewards are experienced as controlling, they do have undermining effects. The negative maxim is clear.

Maxim I.   Do not use rewards when they are experienced by the student as controlling or constraining.

Pittman et al. make the positive claim that noncontrolling verbal rewards enhance subsequent intrinsic interest. This would be a very useful finding, yet I have two concerns about their data. First, they report no baseline data obtained before verbal rewards were introduced from which a positive enhancing change could be assessed. Second, Lepper has shown that the most adequate measure of intrinsic interest is unobtrusive, where Ss in no way associate the activity with the experimenter. Such a condition was not obtained by Pittman and his colleagues. In their experiment when the subsequent free choice period was monitored by the concealed closed-circuit television system, the Ss may have been trying to please the experimenter. To quote Lepper (this volume), "The question . . . is whether children in these studies—when confronted with the same set of activities, . . . in a setting identical . . . to that in which they had received prior differential rewards . . . —believed that the experimenter expected them to . . . engage in the previously rewarded activity. If children continue to engage in the activity in order to please the experimenter . . . we would not wish to infer that their behavior reflected 'intrinsic' interest in the activity. Hence, the relevant experimental test would involve an examination of children's choice of the target activity in a dissociated setting."

Pittman's second point is based on the assumption that children learn "to approach and label activities from both intrinsic and extrinsic motivational orientations.'' Given that, they hypothesize: if a person labels a task as extrinsic then he or she will tend to choose easy forms of that task; and if a person labels a task as intrinsic then he or she will tend to choose intermediate or difficult forms of that task. These are intriguing hypotheses and would lead to a practical maxim.

Maxim II.   Do not use rewards if you want children to try difficult tasks.

Comparing one-shot reward with multiple-trial reward procedures, Lepper has cited evidence that undermining occurs when the student does not expect the task-reward connection to hold in the future.

Maxim III.   Do not use rewards when transfer to later non-reward situations is the goal.

Apparently there are certain types of tasks where rewards are, to use Lepper's term, superfluous. Performance on some types of tasks are not even enhanced while *being* reinforced, to say nothing of subsequent interest. There is a maxim here.

Maxim IV.   Do not use rewards when they are superfluous.

The question remains—when are rewards superfluous? In order to answer that question we must turn our attention to the tasks themselves and away from the rewards. For the teacher, the most practical information would be tasks x and y (reading and writing, for instance) should not be rewarded while task z (arithmetic) should be rewarded. Obviously, we cannot say that because the problem is not that simple.

Lepper suggests a distinction between algorithmic and heuristic tasks. Simple repetitive tasks, like solving numerical problems with an algorithm, are enhanced by immediate rewards. Heuristic activities, like problem solving or creative endeavors, are interfered with even during immediate reward procedures. Clearly, most subjects taught by teachers contain both algorithmic and heuristic aspects. Mathematics is a good example.

Maxim V.   Do reward habitual, algorithmic and/or memorization tasks; do not reward problem solving or creativity.

PEER TUTORING IN THE CLASSROOM

Allen discusses positive effects of peer tutoring on the tutor and traces a history from the Greeks and Romans through the Lancastrian schools, even Hindu schools, since ancient times.

> *Maxim VI.   Make students tutors to enhance their own learning and self-perception.*

Deriving his position from role-theory (Sarbin & Allen, 1968), Allen suggests three ways to enhance the positive effects of tutoring—increased "organismic involvement, role preemptiveness, and role-penetration." All three are expected to enhance self-perception of the tutor. Self-perception is equated with self-image, self-concept, self-esteem, personal efficacy, and confidence.

> *Maxim VII.   To enhance self-perception, enhance involvement in the tutorial role.*

Allen suggests that some negative effects of tutoring may be the result of the tutor's misuse of power that produces authoritarian behavior.

> *Maxim VIII.   Do not make students tutors when they will misuse power.*

The problem is to know when the situation will lead to these negative results. Here a motivation concept may be helpful. Perhaps too much of Maxim VII (*over*-involvement) leads to the negative consequences of Maxim VIII (misuse of power). Perhaps there is a curvilinear effect (reminiscent of the Yerkes–Dodson Law, Yerkes & Dodson, 1908) or perhaps external inducements (rewards) change intrinsic involvement in tutoring to preoccupation with the inducements.

Garbarino (1975) studied the effects of rewards given to tutors on cross-age tutoring. Tutors in the reward condition more often made negative evaluations of the tutees, and children taught by rewarded tutors showed less learning and more errors. Here we have a link between the effects of rewards and peer tutoring that suggests the following maxim.

> *Maxim IX.   Do not use concrete or excessively salient rewards for tutors.*

COOPERATIVE LEARNING

Slavin reviews 30 studies using diverse cooperative learning techniques in real classrooms and concludes "take any desired outcome of schooling, administer a cooperative learning treatment, and about two-thirds of the time there will be a significant difference between experimental and control groups in favor of the experimental groups."

Operationally Slavin has defined cooperative techniques as any of the four documented methods—Student Teams-Achievement Divisions, Teams-Games-Tournament, Jigsaw teaching, or Group-Investigation. The evidence is "robust" when these methods are compared explicitly with more competitive methods or with the "traditional classroom" which "is one of the least cooperative institutions in society."

Maxim X.   To produce desired schooling outcomes teachers should use cooperative learning techniques.

Certainly compared to "traditional classrooms" the methods described are more cooperative. But what is the implicit conceptual definition of cooperation? It seems to derive from Deutsch's (1949) classic definition. Cooperative group structure is obtained when members are "promotively interdependent" in pursuing goals. Competitive group structure is obtained when members are "contriently interdependent." In the Teams-Games-Tournament, to take one example, the first element (Teams) is the cooperative element. "Teammates study together and quiz each other to be sure that all team members are prepared." The goal is to learn, and the team members are promotively interdependent. In the tournament, however, the goal shifts to gaining points, a scarce commodity. Within teams the members are still promotively interdependent; each member wins points for the team. In the tournament the teams are contriently interdependent. Competition is the major element of the tournament.

Compare this with another experiment with two groups of normal 12-year-old boys at a summer camp. The counselor-experimenters set up a series of activities in the form of tournaments between the two groups—games such as football, baseball, etc. The outcome of the tournaments was emphasized by awarding special prizes to the winning team. This is, of course, the Robber's Cave study (Sherif, Harvey, White, Hood, & Sherif, 1961). But this method, so similar to that described by Slavin in the Teams-Games-Tournament, was used to promote competition not cooperation and, in fact, led to hostility and ill-will between teams that took considerable time and ingenuity to reduce. Using a series of superordinate goals that promoted cooperation between the tournament rivals— solving equipment failures that blocked all campers alike from normal activities—the Sherif group finally reduced the hostility and began to produce harmony. "An important revelation coming out of this research is the fact that, in the final analysis, interdependence, cooperation and harmony among children was not achieved as a result of one team or one individual being rewarded for another's defeat, but rather through common goals which were shared by all. To introduce conflicts between groups in order to create harmony within groups is neither necessary nor justified, and in terms of cooperation and harmony among mankind is counterproductive" (Orlick, 1978a, p. 34).

Orlick's book, *Winning Through Cooperation,* represents the cooperative end of the continuum and gives another perspective on Slavin's work. Orlick describes a continuum from "competitive rivalry" to "cooperative helpfulness." The first element of cooperation appears in the category "cooperative competition'' in the middle of the continuum. The motivation for cooperative competition is "to achieve a personal goal which is not mutually exclusive nor an attempt to devalue or destroy others" (p. 137). This description applies to the teams part of Teams-Games-Tournament but not to the tournament. Although Orlick has concentrated on sports in developing cooperative exercises (Orlick, 1978b), it would be possible to devise analogous learning exercises that do not depend ultimately on a competitive tournament for their motivational punch.

THE COMMON ELEMENT

By now the figure formed by the stars on the flag that I started out to manufacture should be emerging. The motivational concept that ties together the maxims is an intrinsic rather than an extrinsic connection between means and ends as experienced by the student. Yet the means-ends analysis so adequate for conceptualizing experimenter-controlled, extrinsic rewards (scarce commodities) always trails off into vagueness when applied to intrinsic aspects of behavior.

In ordinary language we speak of a person's reason or intention for acting. If a child's reason for drawing a picture is to win a good player award, that is quite different from when the reason is that he or she enjoys drawing. This cannot be directly inferred from Maxims I through V but it is the kernel contained within them. A tutor who is intent on gaining rewards or prestige is quite different from one who is teaching to help others to learn (Maxims VII-IX). Cooperative learning with the ultimate goal of winning points in a tournament is quite different from cooperative helpfulness (Maxim X).

All of the maxims entail reward at least indirectly. Even in peer tutoring and cooperative learning, rewards are prominent. Typically we divide activities into interesting tasks (drawing, teaching, learning, games) followed by rewards (awards, prestige, points). This is an arbitrary division made by an observer. What is experienced by the participant in the task is not a series of discrete events like draw-picture-get-reward or draw-picture-not-get-reward. The two situations are totally different. Just because children are using felt pens, for instance, does not make the two situations motivationally similar for the children. Adding a good player award changes the whole event; it does not just add a reward. Posing the problem as I did originally (deCharms, 1968, p.328ff) as one of additivity now seems a mistake.

If we take the point of view of the actor experiencing the activity rather than the experimenter observing, we can divide human activities into three somewhat overlapping types. Type A is "in-order-to" behavior; type B is problem solving or epistemic behavior (Berlyne, 1960); type C is simply "fun." To operationalize these distinctions we ask the actor why he engages in the activity. The answer in the case of type A is, "I do it in order to get money, prestige, approval, etc.," i.e., some kind of extrinsic other-provided reward. The answer in the case of type B is, "I do it to find an answer, to create something new," i.e., some kind of actor-produced outcome. The answer to type C is often vague, "I don't know, I just do it for fun." We all have personal knowledge of the three types of activities. Why do you take an unpleasant job when you need money? Why do you play chess or program a computer or undertake intellectual tasks? Why do you chew gum, whistle, sail a boat? We all know these are clusters of distinctly different experiences.

Scientifically we know quite a bit about type A experiences, far too little about type B, and almost nothing about type C. Recently, we have learned how to turn Type C (fun) into type A (in-order-to behavior). Can we now learn how to reverse the process—change an in-order-to sequence into a for-its-own-sake sequence, change peer tutoring for rewards into a purer learning experience, reduce the competitive aspects of cooperative learning?

Ultimately, to get entirely away from rewards, we need to ask a final "how to" question, namely, how to enhance intrinsic motivation without the use of rewards. Very little has been said to answer that question. Perhaps we should drop our fascination with rewards and self-perception and investigate experiences of complete involvement in a task (as suggested by role-theory)—experiences called "flow" experiences by Csikszentmihalyi (1975). In the flow experience, self and self-perception appear to be minimal. The task and the person are one. Allen would say "self and role are minimally differentiated." "Perhaps the clearest sign of flow is the merging of action and awareness. A person in flow has no dualistic perspective: he [or she] is aware of his actions but not of the awareness itself ... When awareness becomes split, so that one perceives the activity from 'outside', flow is interrupted" (Csikszentmihalyi, 1975, p.38). If this description is adequate, then self-perception theory can never explain flow experiences and rewards will always interfere with them.

To summarize, if we look at the total experience of intrinsically motivated actions, we may learn much more about how to enhance them in the classroom. We should try whenever possible *not* to cut them up analytically into cognition *or* affect (as role-theory does) and *not* to separate action sequences into observable elements like task plus reward as the means-ends analysis does. Rather we should try to understand the experience of the students.

REFERENCES

Berlyne, D. E. *Conflict, Arousal and Curiosity*. New York: McGraw-Hill, 1960.

Csikszentmihalyi, M. *Beyond boredom and anxiety*. San Francisco: Jossey-Bass, 1975.

DeCharms, R. *Personal causation*. New York: Academic Press, 1968.

Deutsch, M. Experimental study of the effects of cooperation and competition upon group processes. *Human Relations*, 1949, *2*, 199–232.

Garbarino, J. The impact of anticipated reward upon cross-age tutoring. *Journal of Personality and Social Psychology*, 1975, *32*, 421–28.

Orlick, T. *Winning through cooperation*. Washington, D.C.: Acropolis Books, 1978. (a)

Orlick, T. *The cooperative sports & games book*. New York: Pantheon, 1978. (b)

Ryle, G. *The concept of mind*. New York: Barnes & Noble, 1949.

Sarbin, T. R. & Allen, V. L. Role theory. In G. Lindzey & E. Aronson (eds.), *Handbook of social psychology* (Vol. I). Reading, Mass.: Addison-Wesley, 1968,

Sherif, M., Harvey, O. J., White, B. J., Hood, W. R., & Sherif, C. W. *Intergroup conflict and cooperation: the robbers cave experiment*. Norman, Okla.: University Book Exchange, 1961.

Yerkes, R. M., & Dodson, J. D. The relation of strength of stimulus to rapidity of habit-formation. *Journal of Comparative and Neurological Psychology,* 1908, *18,* 459–82.

Author Index

Numbers in *italics* indicate pages with bibliographic information.

A

Abramson, L. Y., 5, *24*, 84, *103*
Adler, A., 12, *24*
Agard, J. A., 30, *51*
Alafat, K. A., 288, *316*, 322, 323, 335, *339*
Albert, S., 17, *24*, 31, 38, *49*
Allen, V. L., 41, 49, 368, 373, 377, 381, 383, *387, 388*, 394, *398*
Allport, G., 354, *362*
Alon, S., 288, 289, *314*, 320, *339*
Alwin, D. F., 252, *260*
Amabile, T. M., 288, 289, 292, 298, 303, *312*
Amatai, A., 288, *314*
Ames, C., 42, 43, 44, 45, *49*, 122, *123*
Ames, R., 42, 43, 44, *49*, 105, 106, 107, 108, 111, 122, *123*
Anderson, D., 346, 350, 352, 353, 358, *363*
Anderson, H. H., 40, 41, *49*
Anderson, L., 187, *189*
Anderson, R., 288, 290, *312*, 321, *338*
Anderson, T., 193, *211*
Andrews, D. E., 293, *317*
Andrews, G. R., 57, *73*
Ariès, P., 367, *387*
Arlin, M., 219, 220, *243*
Armstrong, B., 351, 357, *362*

Armstrong, S., 33, *54*
Aronfreed, J., *189, 190*
Aronson, E., 31, 42, 44, 45, *49, 54*, 342, 343, 350, 352, 353, 355, 358, 359, *362, 364*
Aronson, R., 285, *312*
Arrowood, A. J., 34, *54*
Atkinson, J. W., 9, *24, 26, 61, 73*, 331, *338*
Atkinson, R. C., 311, *312*
Ayllon, T., 305, *312*

B

Bachman, J. G., 46, 47, *49*
Bakan, D., 23, *24*
Bak, J., 357, *364*
Ballard, M., 351, 357, *362*
Balow, B., 351, 357, *362*
Bamford, T. W., 370, *387*
Bandura, A., 15, *24, 190*, 220, *244*, 293, 307, *312*
Barnes, J., 216, *245*
Baron, R., 196, 198, 208, *210, 211*
Bar-Tal, D., 7, 8, *24, 26*, 81, *103*, 143, *190*
Beady, C. H., 252, *270*
Beckman, L. J., 105, 106, *123*
Beckerman, T., 129, *138*
Beery, R., 107, *123, 190*, 220, *244*

399

Subject Index

Teaching behaviors
  under Adaptive Learning Environments
    Model, 236–239
  and expectations for student performance,
    195–196
  as interpreted by students, 136–138
  and problem-solving strategies, 94–100, 102
Teacher expectations and performance assess-
    ments, 17
Teacher role, 148–150, 186–189
  and grade differences, 168
  and sex of student, 169
  and social class of student, 170
Teams-Games-Tournament (TGT), 343–344,
    353–356, 358–362
Temporal comparison theory, 38
"Token economy" programs in schools,
    282

Tutoring, 367–387, 393–394
  in classroom, 393–394
  overcoming role-specificity, 384–386
  potential benefits, 368–372
  research, 378–384
  role theoretical analysis, 372–378

V

Value-belief model for teacher attributions,
    108–122, 132–133
  description, 108–113
  research, 113–119
  theory, 119–122
Values
  and influence on success affect, 20–23
  and teacher attributions, 107–122, 132–133
Verbal rewards, 321–324, 335–336